DATE DUE

MY 23 00			
SE 29 05			

DEMCO 38-296

Competing in the Information Age

R

Competing
in the
Information Age

Strategic Alignment in Practice

EDITED BY

JERRY N. LUFTMAN

New York   Oxford
OXFORD UNIVERSITY PRESS
1996

Oxford University Press

Oxford   New York
Athens   Auckland   Bangkok   Bogotá   Bombay
Buenos Aires   Calcutta   Cape Town   Dar es Salaam
Delhi   Florence   Hong Kong   Istanbul   Karachi
Kuala Lumpur   Madras   Madrid   Melbourne
Mexico City   Nairobi   Paris   Singapore
Taipei   Tokyo   Toronto

and associated companies in
Berlin   Ibadan

Copyright © 1996 by Oxford University Press, Inc.

198 Madison Avenue, New York, New York 10016

Oxford is a registered trademark of Oxford University Press

Library of Congress Cataloging-in-Publication Data
Competing in the information age : strategic alignment in practice /
edited by Jerry N. Luftman.
p. cm. Includes bibliographical references and index.
ISBN 0-19-509016-0
1. Organizational change.   2. Strategic planning.   3. Information
techology—Management.   4. Competition.   I. Luftman, Jerry N.
HD58.8.C646   1996
658.4'038—dc20   95-9343

3 5 7 9 8 6 4 2

Printed in the United States of America
on acid-free paper

Foreword

In today's information age, senior executives are faced with the challenge of harnessing information technology to help their business:

- execute its strategy
- improve its operations
- and enhance the perceived value of its own products and services

This book provides a powerful tool, the Strategic Alignment Model, to help executives realize the full value of information technology available to them.

A key premise of this book is that to capture the full value of information technology it is essential to closely align strategic and operational planning. The Strategic Alignment Model does just that. The model identifies four key elements—business strategy, information technology strategy, business infrastructure and information technology infrastructure—that need to be managed in tandem to derive full value from the investment in information technology. It provides a systematic way of planning a successful business strategy with the necessary information systems to support it.

The model also helps bridge the communications gap between the business unit executive and the information systems executive by requiring a disciplined discussion of key business strategies. Thus, each executive has a major role to play.

The business unit executive must clearly be able to describe the strategy, key decision points, and the degree of flexibility required for the business plan. The information systems executive must be able to explain the advantages and disadvantages of different information architectures and technologies, their relative costs, and their implementation times.

Both executives need to know the questions to ask each other, not only to have an informed conversation, but to make informed decisions. The Strategic Alignment Model provides the forum for this dialogue.

The book is the result of our experience at the IBM Consulting Group. Our approach has been to combine a number of intensive research programs with leading academics with on-site consulting. The work with academics has provided the conceptual underpinnings of the Strategic Alignment Model. We have then applied the model with clients who were seeking to maximize the value of their information systems in their strategic planning. Thus, the book has been tested in the crucible of the real world.

This experience has taught us that information technology needs to be discussed early on in the strategy formulation process. For most firms, addressing alignment at this point is the beginning of an important new dialogue between business and information systems executives on the critical role technology will play in the future of their company. Our conclusion: Information technology decisions must naturally flow from the business review. Information technology enables and supports the agenda.

It is axiomatic today that understanding how information technology delivers value is the critical new skill for the twenty-first century executive. Thoughtful managers and executives will find the concepts explained in this book to be a significant contribution to their understanding of value delivery through investment in information systems.

General Manager, IBM Consulting Group   Joseph F. Movizzo

Preface

The purpose of this book is to provide a practical—and powerful—way to ensure that businesses get the full benefit from their investments in information technology. The essential tool is what we call the Strategic Alignment Model. While it may sound forbidding, it is actually a means of giving clarity and order to the process of bringing an organization's business plan into harmony with the information technology that is necessary to make that plan work. Only when the business strategy and the information systems have been "aligned" can the business move ahead successfully.

The methods described in this book will provide valuable guidance to managers. They have been successfully applied to hundreds of organizations already. Much of the practical value of this book derives from the work of the IBM Consulting Group, which has supported important research by outstanding academics in the field of applying information technologies to business problems. In turn, the group has worked with clients to put the results of the research into practice. This support gives the book a solid basis in the real world of today's business.

The information age is well under way. The rapid evolution and increasing complexity of information technology continue to challenge managers on how to leverage it for maximum value. To suggest that information technology is transforming industries is easy. The challenging task is to define what will be demanded of managers and firms to survive and succeed in this new age. This book will prepare organizations to accomplish that task.

November 1995   *J. L.*

Acknowledgments

This book has its origins in research that began in the mid 1980s. Much of the original work has been published and presented around the world. The demand to align business and information technology strategies remains a top issue facing management today.

The chapters portray an evolution of the original research, with an emphasis on its practical application. An international team of authoritative practitioners, researchers, consultants, and teachers in the components that comprise strategic alignment make up the authors of this important book. Vitae of the contributing authors immediately follows.

While researching, writing, and editing this book, I have become indebted to a large group of individuals, only a few of whom can be mentioned here. I am greatly appreciative to the IBM Consulting Group, Advanced Business Institute, and *Systems Journal* for the opportunity to pursue and publish this important research. Recognition is due to Stevens Institute of Technology for giving me the time to research and teach these important ideas to the future leaders of industry and executives participating in its graduate information management programs.

Of course a large degree of thanks is due to the hundreds of companies that have been used in creating, developing, and maturing the application of the strategic alignment model. This includes the hundreds of students attending seminars and courses at IBM's Advanced Business Institute and Stevens, where thought-provoking discussions have led to many new insights.

I am also indebted to Herb Addison from Oxford University Press for his literary direction and support. The original manuscripts were reviewed and improved tremendously by Carolyn White.

This book is dedicated to the families of all of its contributors. I especially want to dedicate it to my father, Jack, who probably would have read and appreciated the ideas presented.

Contents

Contributors

Andrew C. Boynton
Dr. Boynton received his B.S. from Boston College and his M.B.A. and Ph.D. from the University of North Carolina at Chapel Hill. He is Associate Professor of business administration at the Kenan-Flagler Business School at Chapel Hill, teaching strategic management, leadership, and information technology. Dr. Boynton has published several books on topics related to managing IT and many articles on IT planning, critical success factors, and strategic organizational change in several professional journals. He is currently a visiting professor at the International Institute for Management Development in Switzerland.

Marianne Broadbent
Dr. Broadbent is Director of the Key Centre for Technology Management at the Melbourne Business School, University of Melbourne. She has taught information systems management for the M.B.A. and executive education programs and has developed field-based research and consulting programs for masters students. Dr. Broadbent's research and consulting activities focus on the alignment of business and information strategies, deriving business value from IT investments, strategic management processes, and business process redesign. She has published and edited for several professional journals. Before joining Melbourne Business School, she was head of the Department of Information Services at the Royal Melbourne Institute of Technology.

Janet C. Caldow
Janet C. Caldow is the Director of IBM's Institute for Electronic Government. She is one of the authors of the consulting method in use worldwide for reshaping

corporate culture to leverage business consulting. She has worldwide clients in a variety of industries including finance, public sector, utilities, retailing, and IBM's internal projects. Prior to IBM, Ms. Caldow was the Director of Strategic Management for the County of Fairfax outside Washington, DC. She holds an M.B.A. with a concentration in management from Virginia Polytechnic Institute. Her bachelor's degree is in sociology from George Mason University.

John L. Daniels

John Daniels joined IBM in the fall of 1991 as Vice President of IBM Consulting responsible for all IBM management consulting activities in Europe, The Middle East, and Africa. He was one of the leaders of the team that developed IBM's reengineering methods. Mr. Daniels specializes in improving business performance in large, international corporations through the more effective combination of people, processes, and information technology. Before joining IBM, Mr. Daniels was a managing principal of Nolan, Norton & Co. for twelve years. He has a bachelor's degree from Harvard University.

N. Caroline Daniels

Dr. Daniels is a researcher at Templeton College, Oxford University, and a member of the Economist Intelligence Unit

Editorial Board. She has twenty years' experience in strategic business and consulting, a Ph.D. in information management from the London Business School, a master's in the science of management from the Sloan School of MIT, and an honors degree in literature from Boston University. Dr. Daniels is often quoted in the *Financial Times, The Economist,* and other newspapers and periodicals. She has authored several books on business strategy and IT.

William H. Davidson

Dr. Davidson is Associate Professor of Management and Organization at the School of Business, University of Southern California. The coauthor of *2020 Vision* (Simon and Schuster, 1991) and *Managing the Global Corporation* (McGraw-Hill, 1990), he has written seven books and many journal articles. Dr. Davidson holds A.B., M.B.A., and doctoral degrees from Harvard University and has been a visiting professor in France, China, and Japan. He has served as Vice President of the Academy of International Business and is the founder of Management Education Services Associates (MESA), an organization dedicated to research and education in contemporary and future management issues.

Rocki-Lee DeWitt

Dr. DeWitt is Assistant Professor

of Strategic Management. Her research interests focus on how organizations plan for and implement downsizing and restructuring. Dr. DeWitt's research papers have appeared in several professional journals. At Penn State she teaches graduate students in the School of Management. Dr. DeWitt received her Ph.D. in strategic management from Columbia University, her M.S. from Ohio State, and her B.S. from New York University.

Steve H. Haeckel

Steve Haeckel is Director of Strategic Studies at IBM's Advanced Business Institute. He does research, teaches, and advises executives on the use of information and technology to create and manage adaptive organizations in information-rich environments. His IBM career includes executive responsibilities in Europe and on the corporate staff. Mr. Haeckel is Chairman of the Research Policy Committee of the Marketing Science Institute and Vice Chairman of its Executive Committee. He represents IBM on the Marketing Council of the American Management Association. From 1985 to 1986, he served a two-year term on the Advisory Council of the Federal National Mortgage Association. Mr. Haeckel has engineering and M.B.A. degrees from Washington University in St. Louis.

John C. Henderson

Dr. Henderson is Professor of Management Information Systems and Director of the Systems Research Center at the Boston University School of Management. He earned his Ph.D., M.S., and B.S. degrees from the University of Texas at Austin. His current research is focused in three areas. They are the alignment of business and IT strategies, the role of IT in building and managing strategic partnerships, and the use of IT to support software development teams. Before coming to Boston University, Professor Henderson was on the faculty of the Sloan School of Management at MIT. His articles have appeared in many professional journals.

Peter G. W. Keen

Dr. Keen is chairman of the International Center for Information Technologies. He has been on the faculties of Harvard University, The Sloan School of Management, MIT, Stanford University, with visiting positions at Oxford University, The London Business School, The Wharton School, and Fordham University. He is the author of many books and articles related to managing IT. He is known internationally as a leader in the field. In 1986 he founded the International Center for Information Technologies, whose aim is to provide senior managers with reliable research, education, and advice on the planning, development, and use of IT.

John Kirby

John Kirby is Vice President of IBM Consulting, responsible for the transformation of IBM. He was instrumental in the start-up of IBM Consulting Group's worldwide business transformation practice. Mr. Kirby specializes in helping clients from a variety of industries transform their companies in response to customer requirements, business needs, and competitive pressure. Mr. Kirby has held a variety of management and technical positions, including management positions for IBM's popular mid-range systems, where they were a Malcolm Baldridge winner. He holds a master of science degree from Purdue University and a bachelor of science degree from Villanova.

Benn Konsynski

Dr. Konsynski is the George S. Craft Distinguished Professor of Business Administration and Area Coordinator for Decision and Information Analysis at Goizueta Business School at Emory University in Atlanta. He is also a fellow at the Carter Presidential Center. Dr. Konsynski spent six years on the faculty at the Harvard Business School, where he taught in the M.B.A. and executive programs. He holds a Ph.D. in computer science from Purdue University. Professor Konsynski

specializes in issues of IT in relationships across organizations. His research papers have appeared in several professional journals.

Jerry N. Luftman

Dr. Luftman is the Execuive Director of the Stevens Institute of Technology's information management research center and a Distinguished Services Professor for the school's graduate management degrees. His twenty-two-year career with IBM includes strategic positions in management (IT and consulting), management consulting, information systems, marketing, and executive education. Dr. Luftman played a leading role in defining and introducing IBM's Consulting Group. As a practitioner he held several positions in IT, including a CIO. Dr. Luftman's research papers have appeared in several professional journals. His doctoral degree in information management was received at Stevens Institute of Technology. His undergraduate work was conducted at New York University.

Joseph F. Movizzo

Joseph F. Movizzo is General Manager of IBM Consulting responsible for IBM's worldwide business consulting. His expertise is in business process reengineering, quality, change management, management systems, and the framework that must exist to ensure the successful transformation of a business. Mr.

Movizzo's client base includes companies in the insurance, financial services, petroleum, utilities, transportation, and communications industries, including IBM's internal projects. Mr. Movizzo graduated from the University of Wisconsin with B.S. and M.S. degrees.

Richard L. Nolan

Dr. Nolan earned his B.A. from the University of Washington in production and operations research in 1962 and his M.B.A. and Ph.D. in 1963 and 1966, respectively. From 1969 to 1977, he was an associate professor at the Harvard Business School and returned to the faculty of Harvard Business School in 1991. Besides teaching there, he was an assistant professor at the University of Illinois. Professor Nolan's business experience includes 14 years as Chairman of Nolan, Norton & Co., a firm he cofounded with David Norton. He has also worked in the Office of the Secretary of Defense (systems analysis) and at Boeing Aerospace Company.

Scott Oldach

Scott Oldach is Vice President of IBM Consulting. In this role he fosters the growth of global organizations. He consults with businesses transforming themselves due to competitive realities, strategic changes, and/or increasing customer expectations. During his twenty years of consulting, Mr. Oldach has assisted clients in industries including finance, insurance, manufacturing, petroleum, travel, telecommunications, and retail/distribution. Before joining IBM Mr. Oldach held positions with several other consulting firms. He is a graduate of MIT with a B.S. in management science and operations research.

B. Joseph Pine II

B. Joseph Pine II is the founder and president of Ridgefield, Connecticut-based Strategic Horizons, Inc., a management consulting firm specializing in helping companies envision and realize the future. Mr. Pine is the author of the highly acclaimed book *Mass Customization: The New Frontier in Business Competition* (Boston: Harvard Business School Press, 1993). In it he details the historic shift from mass production to mass customization—the low-cost, high-quality creation of individually customized goods and services. He has also written articles for several magazines and journals, including the *Harvard Business Review, The Wall Street Journal, Planning Review*, the *IBM Systems Journal, Chief Executive*, and *CIO*.

Patti L. Prairie

Patti L. Prairie is Vice President of IBM's Financial Services Industries consulting practice. She is responsible for the development of

IBM's strategy in the sector, leading to the creation of new finance-specific services and offerings and integrating IBM's resources and capabilities in serving financial institutions. Some issues that Ms. Prairie has addressed with clients include revenue generation while implementing staff decreases from corporate downsizing, improving customer relations, distinguishing services from the competition, and identifying the technology solutions that best implement the client's overall corporate goals.

Donald R. St.Clair

Donald R. St.Clair joined IBM in 1992 and serves as Vice President of IBM Consulting in Singapore. He is responsible for building business transformation management consulting operations throughout the Asia Pacific region. This draws upon his twenty-five years' experience in consulting and line management in Asian and North American companies. Mr. St.Clair specializes in improving business performance by maximizing the strategic business leverage obtained from investments. Before joining IBM, Mr. St.Clair held several line positions in the telecommunications, financial services, and consulting industries. He is a graduate of Bradley University, Stanford University, and the University of Chicago.

James B. Thomas

Dr. Thomas is Associate Professor of Management, Smeal College of Business Administration at the Pennsylvania State University. He has a B.A. from Penn State, an M.S. from Florida State, and a Ph.D. from the University of Texas at Austin. His research interests focus on the decision processes and prescriptive decision methodologies associated with the strategic management of organizations. Dr. Thomas has published research papers in several professional journals and has served as a consultant in many industry settings, including health care, computer technology, and government. Professor Thomas teaches courses in competitive strategy and organizational decision making at the graduate level and is actively involved in executive development programs throughout the United States and abroad.

N. Venkatraman

Dr. Venkatraman is Associate Professor of Management at Boston University School of Management. Before his arrival at Boston University, he was Associate Professor of Management in the Sloan School of Management at MIT. He has written an influential chapter on the role of IT in *The Corporation of the 1990s* (Oxford University Press, 1991). His doctoral thesis was awarded the 1986 AT Kearney

Award for Outstanding Research in General Management by the Academy of Management. Dr. Venkatraman's research papers have appeared in several professional journals. He holds a Ph.D. in business administration from the University of Pittsburgh.

Bart Victor
Dr. Victor is Associate Professor of Management in the Kenan-Flagler Graduate School of Business Administration at the University of North Carolina at Chapel Hill. He received his B.A. from the University of California at Berkeley. After college he founded and operated several businesses in California, Illinois, and New York. Dr. Victor received his Ph.D. in management from the University of North Carolina. Dr. Victor teaches graduate and undergraduate courses in organization design and business ethics. His interests have focused on organizational culture and business ethics. Dr. Victor's

work has been published in many professional journals. He consults with firms nationally and in Japan on issues of management, organizational design, and business culture.

Peter Weill
Dr. Weill is the Foundation Chair of Management and a member of the Board of Directors of Melbourne Business School at the University of Melbourne. He has developed and taught IS management programs for the M.B.A., the Master of Management, and executive education. His research and advising activities center on the role and value of IT organizations. Dr. Weill has published and edited widely, including books, journal articles, and case studies. He regularly advises corporations and governments on issues of IT investment and payoff and aligning the IT portfolio to business strategy.

Competing in the Information Age

1

Introduction

JERRY N. LUFTMAN and SCOTT H. OLDACH

Businesses are still striving to achieve competitive advantage using information systems, despite nearly two decades and billions of dollars worth of investment. Frustratingly, organizations seem to find it difficult or impossible to harness the power of information technology (IT) for their own long-term benefit, even though there is worldwide evidence that IT has the power to transform whole industries and markets.

Too often, the problem was that too much attention was placed on the technology itself, rather than its links with other business operations, customer value, and management decision-making. Companies raced to have state-of-the-art systems without considering their impact on the rest of the business. For example, retail banks invested heavily in automatic teller machines (ATMs) in the 1980s, believing them an essential aspect of customer service and critical to maintaining market share. As a result, ATMs rapidly ceased to be a competitive advantage and instead became an added cost of doing business.

Instead of reducing business costs and increasing market share as they hoped, the bankers were left with the expense of maintenance and continuing enhancements to the ATM systems in an environment of decreasing margins and profit pressures. These costs have been passed on to ATM users. While technology was not the only cause, perhaps not even the primary cause, of this fallout, there has been a reduction in the number of U.S. banks. The question remains: Did each competitor need to invest individually, or was there a less disruptive way of achieving the same value? The answer is not clear, but it may be that in the end the rush to ATMs was justified because they were the banks' first step in offering a range of electronic banking services for consumers. Today, the rush is on to create

3

the "virtual bank." Remote banking using personal computer networks, kiosks located throughout the community, and the Internet are providing services that go beyond the traditional bank. Nevertheless, industry commentators believe that the declining number of banks is only the beginning of a major shakeout process, as it becomes increasingly absurd for dozens of banks to offer the same services to the same customer segments.

It is a story which has parallels in many other industries (e.g., airlines, petroleum, retail), and through learning the hard way about IT potential, senior executives are now much more aware of the importance of building organizational structures and sets of business processes and offerings that reflect the interdependence of enterprise strategy and IT capabilities. Conceived and developed in the 1960s and 1970s by the U.S. Department of Defense, the Internet today links more than 48,000 different networks that connect 35 million users throughout over 60 countries. Estimates suggest that there will be over 100 million users before the turn of the century. As the Internet evolves to replace existing Electronic Data Interchange (EDI) value added networks and private networks as competitive weapons, will these lessons be applied?

The strategic alignment framework that is the subject of this book is a powerful conceptual tool that has transformed managers' understanding of these issues since it was first developed by John Henderson and N. Venkatraman in the mid-1980s. In essence, the model is very simple. It recognizes that different sets of business decisions are often taken at different times and by different people in an organization. However, it emphasizes that the decisions need to be coordinated to achieve value. Decisions of business strategy set the direction of the enterprise based on an understanding of the enterprise's resources, competitors' positioning, and market needs. These strategic decisions structure the available resources to best compete. Decisions about business infrastructure (including organization, people, and processes) are often designed in considerable detail and after business strategy decisions have been made. It is clear from our experience that this design must be linked to both the business strategy and the IT capabilities of the firm.

Decisions of IT strategy, intended to translate business strategy into an IT infrastructure that allows the enterprise to compete effectively, are often made after the decisions on business strategy. These decisions must also influence the initial decisions on business strategy since not all things are possible in either the IT strategy or infrastructure. It is clear, therefore, that these four sets of decisions—on business strategy, IT strategy, business infrastructure, and IT infrastructure—need to be coordinated, or, as we term it "aligned." The relationship of these elements will be explained in Chapter 2 and expanded in Chapter 3.

The Business Challenge

The model helps executives evaluate the business implications of IT decisions. Too often, the language and presentation of IT propositions obscure an objective evaluation of their merits or demerits. The model provides a systematic way of describing a business strategy or business choice with IT options. IT can certainly change the rules of competition very fast (almost overnight when Federal Express used a new combination of systems and business operations for overnight delivery of small packages, for example); however, it is rarely capable of delivering lasting value by itself.

Eventually, a competitor will always find a way of copying or improving upon any new IT system. At the end of the day, lasting advantage is derived only from using IT in conjunction with business operational change to add value to a company. In most situations lasting value comes only from a commitment to continuous change using IT.

By working through the interactions of the four quadrants of the alignment model, the impact of IT decisions can be evaluated on a par with other, more familiar business investment decisions. It is worth remembering that, although IT investments are often huge—perhaps $10–50 million, with lasting operational cost implications as well—executives routinely live with the risk of business decisions worth far more—perhaps $100 million–$1 billion for a new factory or acquisition. The challenge is to put IT on an equal footing with other business investments. To achieve this understanding—how IT delivers value in this broader context—is a critical new skill for twenty-first-century executives. Although IT is now all-pervasive, it is also true that it is more mission-critical in some firms than others.

It is often necessary for executives to evaluate the importance of an IT initiative alongside perhaps half a dozen other strategic programs which may be in progress. All programs have an equivalent multiyear history of prior investments, successes, and failures. The strategic alignment model provides a route to link them appropriately and create a cohesive strategic framework.

Dealing with Uncertainty

Uncertainty has become a way of life; companies are finding it ever more difficult to predict changes in their competitive environments. Customers are becoming competitors, competitors are becoming partners, and unconventional competition is emerging. Businesses must go on despite potentially dramatically new business environments that are currently not well understood. IT investments, like others, need to continue in this uncertain environment: How do you make IT investments in this climate?

For example, in early 1994 a merger was contemplated between four European airlines: SAS, Swissair, Air Austria, and KLM. This merger would have had far-reaching implications on the disparate systems and operations of the four partners. The partners understood the potential problems that would have to be solved and created fifteen to twenty task forces to study all aspects of the merger. For a variety of reasons, at the end of the day the merger did not take place, but nevertheless, the individual companies had to continue to trade—and compete—while they conducted their negotiations. In addition, while IT was included in the task forces, each potential partner needed to continue investing in IT during the study since any postponement would have wasted valuable time.

Investing in flexibility is not always the way to cope with uncertainty. Typically, systems flexibility is obtained at a high ongoing cost. The time taken to build such systems might even mean that the delivered flexibility will not match a changed competitive situation months or years after the investment was decided. The alignment model helps executives understand how to translate flexibility into operational value.

Understanding Customers

Central to creating value is an intimate understanding of a firm's customer base. The goal is to deeply understand customer/client needs and to translate these into a unique value-added statement. It is not easy to balance the level of service and quality to customers with the associated cost. The problem is compounded a hundredfold for companies operating in different cultural environments.

For example, banks offer a broad range of products ranging from ATMs to mortgages, but delivering instantaneous cash is very different from delivering loans. Customers are far more interested in making careful, informed choices when taking out a mortgage than when receiving policies and documents quickly. While a fifteen-minute mortgage may occasionally be required in some special situations, most customers desire only rapid commitment. Paperwork can follow the commitment by days or months. Spending a great deal of money in reengineering a company to deliver a fifteen-minute mortgage service to every customer is likely to be inappropriate in some instances.

It has been suggested[1] that by the year 2020 some 80% of business profits and market values will come from the part of the enterprise that is built around the business of information. Companies capturing and applying information at each point of contact with customers will be better off than those that do not. Lester Thurow contends that companies will have to be able to apply and integrate ITs (e.g., CAD/CAM) into the entire product process (including research, design, manufacturing, distribution, marketing, and service).[2]

As an indicator of the new ways of interfacing with customers, traffic on Internet is doubling every year. Three of ten U.S. homes have a personal computer. Two of five computers in the United States are part of a network. The traffic over these networks is growing 30% every year. Every firm needs to analyze both the impact this might have on its range of products and services and its strategies for distribution and marketing.

Since the customer must eventually pay, it is vital to check that the customer values the systems and services provided and understands clearly how they interface with perceived needs. Bank ATMs or airline reservation systems are obviously useful applications of technology to which some customers can relate. However, in each case there are other stakeholders (internal or external) who may not value this system directly and must be convinced to participate. This may require special action to ensure participation or value capture.

Understanding Globalization

As telecommunications break down barriers of time and location in doing business, distinctions are also breaking down between large and small companies. Small, agile firms are now effectively competing with industry giants because IT can make a consortium of small firms look, feel, and act big, reaching for customers once beyond their grasp. Their success is provoking large companies to adopt two alternative strategies: either using IT themselves to give the impression to customers that they are small and close or divesting (outsourcing) areas which are not core competencies of their business.

Such divestments are restructuring whole industries, not necessarily acrimoniously: strategic alliances of all kinds abound—for example, joint ventures, partnerships, minority holdings, franchises, syndicates, and knowledge exchanges. Systems can deepen individual competence for a partner, coordinate partners to make distinct organizations look as one, or build a shared competency. Obviously, as the number of stakeholders with diverse objectives increases, the complexity of managing and operating IT grows, but so does the benefit from integrating IT with those business objectives.

The cost of IT is now so low that it is easy for small companies to acquire global systems that perform as well as, or better than, larger systems in use at much bigger competitors. As more members of competitive markets automate and information becomes standard, it is natural to develop communal sharing and a higher level of benefits for a market. Increasingly, IT-based regulatory standards—for example, in the use of electronic data interchange (EDI)—are becoming basic requirements for entering some areas of business. In addition, the boundaries of customers, competitors, and suppliers have blurred and diffused geographically.

The Reality Behind Transformation

Executives should bear in mind that even the most carefully worked through alignment plans can founder because the existing culture of an organization has not been taken into account.

Take the example of a group of suppliers of fresh produce in the United States. Their products are very perishable, and customer demand varies seasonally. Buyers have to make thousands of decisions about sources of supply, preparation of the product, pricing, and distribution in difficult, almost commodity, conditions. The culture, or mindset, of such businesses is not naturally disposed to advanced technology. In practice, the market leader invested heavily, and successfully, in IT decision-support systems. They aligned operational decision-making with the availability of new information to achieve small improvements in thousands of decisions daily. The net result was a significant improvement overall.

Other players invested in the same systems without understanding how they were being used to create value. One is partially automated, having bought the systems to emulate the market leader, but has so far failed to integrate them with its existing culture. The decision-making processes have not been aligned with the new technology, resulting in confusion, resentment, and poor financial performance. The other competitor rejected technology and continues to operate successfully on manual systems, judgment, and intuition. In fact, the manual company outperforms many of its partially automated competitors.

Another problem that companies may have in tackling transformation is simply battle fatigue. Take a telecommunications manufacturing company as a typical example. As a company it has embraced over a dozen new management programs over the last fifteen years, such as total quality, empowerment, time-based competition, process management, and team-building. Perhaps half a dozen of these programs are still ongoing in the organization. Why should they embrace strategic alignment as well? The presentation and introduction of the concept needs to be handled with considerable care and forethought if it is not to be rejected outright by tired and disillusioned employees.

The Key IT Challenges

As indicated above, the issues concerning investment in IT are often fatally obscured by lack of communication between business and IT decision-makers. It is a fertile area for myths concerning what can and cannot be changed and what those changes might mean for future investments and business strategies.

Flexibility

Most companies, once they begin to realize the true potential of IT, would like to opt for maximal flexibility and keep their options open. However, for this to be a successful strategy, there has to be a pragmatic understanding of the business implications of the flexibility needed. For example, a Swiss bank was persuaded by its chief information officer (CIO) to spend $50–100 million on a new systems architecture, positioned as a "flexible" infrastructure. Unfortunately, neither the CIO nor the board really understood the demands of migrating from a product-centered to a customer-centered business strategy. In addition, management never understood the additional operating cost of the "flexible" solution. The product envisioned by the systems organization did not suit the banking environment of the late 1980s; in addition, the operational cost structure meant that they were paying a 30–50% penalty to buy the migratory system. The business executives had been insufficiently imaginative about how they would respond in the future, had not properly understood the potential of technology to support them in these endeavors, and were, therefore, unable to properly evaluate the proposals from the CIO. He, for his part, was insufficiently informed about future changes in the banking environment or possible competitive responses to these situations: he could not, therefore, suggest appropriate IT investments.

In every business someone needs to know the business drivers and to communicate them to key decision-makers within the business and IT organization. Both sets of executives need to know the questions to ask each other and to understand each others' decision-making processes to agree on informed strategies about future IT flexibility.

Managing Change and Integrating Systems

The pace of technological change and innovation is truly formidable. The rate at which new technology is being introduced is increasing by 20–30% annually.[3] The technological pace will continue to increase and be magnified by new network communications, object-oriented programming, and open systems opportunities. Integrating these new technologies with each other and existing technologies is one of the biggest challenges facing organizations.

The problem for companies striving for alignment is far greater than just overcoming technical system incompatibility. As several chapters in this book show, the challenge of creating a modular, snap-together architecture that can be reconfigured at will to support new business strategies is becoming an article of faith for many forward-looking CIOs.

However, in their rush to address IT infrastructural issues, IT executives are perhaps underestimating what they can do with their existing capabilities. It is an alignment issue that goes deeper than the IT organization and reflects the business strategy perspective at the center of the company. Some organizations define themselves as market-driven, frequently changing their internal resources and capabilities to respond to changing customer demands. This may require importing new skills to support the company in a new strategy. Others take a different perspective, based on an in-depth understanding of their own internal core competencies and resources. These companies become market leaders by suggesting products and services to customers, rather than simply fulfilling existing demand. IT infrastructures are a key resource that many companies ought to consider.

When reviewing technological infrastructures, it is worth considering the business strategies it could support, either now or in the future, before embarking on the long, expensive, and difficult process of replacement.

Take the example of a major U.S. consumer finance organization which had some years ago decided to use airline control programs (ACP) to deal with transactions because their business requirements were similar to an airline in terms of volume, speed, and so on. The ACP platform proved expensive to modify and became limiting to the firm's business strategy. The company decided to change to a simpler, more open system, forcing a major transformation of the IT department.

Because of their difficulties in getting staff, the company eventually developed its own pool of highly trained programmers, staff who were in great demand by the airline industry. Why not sell them back to them? They did this through creating an ACP-based information business to sell. Simultaneous with this, they worked with IBM to build a new, greenfield data center. As they developed their own capability to run that, they gradually became less reliant on the consultants' staff and had an additional supply of income from the sale of the ACP capability. Managing infrastructure is often a matter of making careful decisions on what and when you really need to own capability to support business strategy.

Structure of the Book

The twelve chapters and appendices in the book have been compiled by a team of experts to provide a set of models, frameworks, and methods to ease the changes and support the transformations that organizations are experiencing. Each expert has sought to minimize the technical aspect of his or her topic and to stress the practical application of the theory in a way that will be valuable to both IT and business professionals. The description of the application of the strategic alignment model represents the continued evolution of the theory into practice and the depth of the insights available through its use.

Chapter 2, by Henderson, Venkatraman, and Oldach, introduces and updates the original research conducted in the mid-1980s on strategic alignment. The authors outline the four key components of their strategic alignment model—business strategy, IT strategy, organizational infrastructure, and IT infrastructure—and explain how these components interact with each other to form four different perspectives on alignment, depending on what drives the business.

At the beginning of the chapter they pose the question: How much IT do executives need to understand to effectively determine the role of IT in their firm? The level of business executive understanding of IT will form a repeated motif throughout the book. The authors of the model have frequently been asked which of the four original perspectives (strategy execution, technology potential, competitive potential, or service level) are "correct." They answer cautiously that any business should be looked at in turn from all of the different perspectives to decide what is right for that particular company at a given point in time.

To help in this process, they introduce four management tools for envisaging how any particular alignment strategy might translate into operational reality and suggest how these four processes can maintain alignment in a changing environment. First, a company should assess what value or business benefits might accrue (*value alignment*). Second, it should look at who will actually make decisions in the new structure and discuss the implications of this; it may be an outside partner, for instance (*partnership alignment*). Third, it should recognize what the new rules will be for ensuring that the required technological capabilities will be developed and decide if such projects will always take precedence over others (*technology alignment*). Finally, the firm's team needs to look at the organizational implications of what they are planning and if they have the skills or the structures to implement the plan (*governance alignment*).

Luftman's Chapter 3 takes the strategic alignment model a stage further and describes what has been learned by putting it into practice in companies. The chapter describes in more detail the roles that business and IT executives adopt under each alignment perspective, what measures of success are appropriate, and what strategic planning method is relevant to each perspective.

To answer the question so often posed to the authors of Chapter 2— Which perspective is best—a process of "cycling" through the model is described and illustrated by detailed examples from companies. Effectively, no perspective is "best"; each needs to be addressed in turn, and, in fact, one often acts as a catalyst for the next.

Chapters 2 and 3 provide a basic grounding to the concepts and topics discussed in the rest of the book. Subsequent chapters have been arranged in four sections, corresponding to the four essential components of the alignment model: business strategy, IT strategy, organizational infrastructure, and IT infrastructure. Although some of these chapters specifically address the Henderson and Venkatraman model of Chapter 2, others do not. Instead, they form a diverse and often provocative view on the essential terms and assumptions being used. As such, they provide a thoughtful and useful commentary on the very real problems of aligning business and IT strategies.

Business Strategy

Victor, Pine, and Boynton in Chapter 4 put the strategic alignment model of Chapter 2 into a larger frame. Their "product–process–change" matrix looks at the effect of change on product and process innovation and identifies four possible modes: mass production, continuous improvement, invention, and mass customization. Of the four, mass customization and/or continuous improvement are identified as the most prevalent corporate responses to today's business environment, though the others are still relevant in some industry sectors.

The role of IT in each of these modes differs markedly, and to distinguish them the authors draw a useful distinction between IT systems which automate human skills and tasks and those which augment them—i.e., help people and organizations to learn. Mass production is a classic case of automation; both invention and continuous improvement are largely dependent on augmenting knowledge, particularly between teams. Mass customization requires a bit of both. Each will obviously require a very different approach to creating a viable IT architecture for the firm.

Identifying which of these dimensions the firm is choosing to compete in, therefore, has profound implications for all of the elements of the strategic alignment model.

Chapter 5, by Daniels and Daniels, adds another layer to the concept of the firm so far discussed. Although the previous models show the firm responding to various changes in the business environment, they do not consider the specific problems of large firms, operating in multiple environments with possibly multiple challenges of strategic alignment to coordinate and control.

The authors believe that globalization is an inevitable fact of life for firms which want to compete in the twenty-first century and identify three common structures which give clues to where any particular organization might be on its way to becoming global: global exporter, multinational, and multilocal. Each of these structures has very different attitudes to the way it wants to communicate within the firm and with its customers. Global exporters have strong internal communications but, if possible, try to adopt a mass production approach to getting their goods and services into markets; they differentiate as little as possible. Multinationals are more flexible with their customers, tailoring their products to a certain extent in different national markets, but score less well on internal communication and agreement about common goals. Multilocals are even more extreme; they tend to practice mass customization in their local markets and are virtually autonomous in their relations with their corporate centers. Devising an IT strategy and architecture for each is quite a different task, made doubly difficult by the path of evolution that the firm is on toward becoming a truly global company.

The authors advocate getting to global as fast as possible and envisage worldwide, flexible, bolt-together IT structures which seamlessly connect individuals, products and processes. Globalization, therefore, becomes an extra dimension to the business frame proposed by Chapter 4.

IT Strategy

Keen opens the IT strategy section with Chapter 6 by re-addressing the initial question of Chapter 2: How much IT do executives need to know to steer their business? Unlike many commentators, he is a proponent of greater computer illiteracy. In effect, he is an advocate of frequently going beyond aligning business strategies with the appropriate IT strategic response.

Keen does not underplay the role of IT in the firm; in fact, he regards it as the only route to achieving competitive quality and service standards at a price customers are prepared to pay. However, he sees the complexity of the language in which IT strategy is usually discussed as a smoke screen for the real issues. Using the analogy of electricity supply, which nobody needs to understand to plug in an appliance, he asserts that the major issue business executives need to understand about IT is its potential for inter-connectivity, or business networking.

He asserts that developments in telecommunications have already fun-damentally changed companies' assumptions about the way they can do business. Executives should be concentrating on the extent to which their companies require an IT platform for distributed computing to enable busi-ness networking. They should communicate this requirement to their IT professionals in the form of business policy guidelines, what Keen refers to as "the big rules," and then "get out of the way."

He believes that IT should be such a fundamental part of business strategy and that if a rapprochement is seen to be required, it is probably too late to be of use.

Chapter 7, by Haeckel and Nolan, draws on a number of themes raised in earlier chapters. Essentially, like Keen, the authors are advocates of busi-ness networking: "separate networks reinforce tribal mentalities. . . . [This] lobotomization of the corporate intellect remains perhaps the single biggest impediment to realizing the potential of technology to help manage larger companies."

Using the analogy of "managing by wire," which refers to the complex systems used by pilots to fly planes (not to be confused with autopilot systems), Haeckel and Nolan describe some ambitious attempts to use what are known as enterprise modeling methodologies to construct models of corporate behavior. The idea is to reduce "how we do things around here" to an IT system which supports employee actions and continually records internal and external information.

They argue that we now operate in a "sense-and-respond" environment, rather than a "make-and-sell" situation. They believe that the only way large organizations can "learn" and survive in this world of carefully tailored cus-tomer requirements is to capture each piece of information in a form that can be reused by others in similar, but different, situations.

Object-oriented programming and connected computer networks thus become the basis of IT strategy, but they stress that the definition of the data to be captured and linked must always remain the responsibility of the business managers.

Chapter 8, by Konsynski, provides additional case study evidence to show how emerging information technology not only enable business networking but in the process transform the traditional organizational and legal boundaries of the enterprise. He shows that IT capabilities can play a large part in determining business strategy.

Chapter 8 describes the very wide range of inter- and intraorganizational systems which are already in use in companies and how they are creating a whole new raft of management challenges for executives. Suddenly, firms are finding they have to spend time and money making sure their systems are compatible with those of customers, suppliers, trading partners, and sometimes even competitors. In particular, government-backed EDI initiatives are changing the rules for both large and small firms.

Konsynski believes that the challenge of making these systems talk to each other will provide jobs for IT professionals for years to come but wonders whether in many instances this increased networking leads to measurable bottom-line impact. Too often, he fears, it "speeds up the mess" because firms do not adjust their other organizational processes to take account of the new way of doing business. The strategic alignment model is very useful for pointing to where such deficiencies might occur.

Chapter 9, by Prairie, concludes Section II on IT strategy by, appropriately, picking up on the concerns expressed in Chapter 8 that, however exciting telecommunications-led opportunities might be in the future, so far IT investments have failed to deliver measurable business results in many firms.

The work on benchmarking strategic IT processes goes beyond the usual cost- and efficiency-based comparisons of most IT benchmarking exercises and looks instead at ways of measuring the alignment of IT expenditure with business strategy as a means of extracting maximal value from IT.

Using the results of an IBM Consulting Group benchmarking project, Prairie derives eight key processes to benchmarking, using the Baldrige Quality Award scheme to suggest appropriate metrics for the eight processes. A case study from American Express shows how benchmarking strategic alignment can be carried out in practice. The results of this research suggest that if firms intend to start "cycling" around the strategic alignment model described in Chapter 3, they should, at the very least, proceed with appropriate benchmarking knowledge.

Organizational Infrastructure

Chapter 10, by Caldow and Kirby, takes the four business modes outlined in Chapter 4—invention, mass production, continuous improvement, and mass customization—and looks at their associated business cultures. Essentially, the theme is that even the best thought-out strategies can fail if the business culture of a firm is not properly understood and managed as part of the alignment process.

Corporate culture is notoriously difficult to define; Caldow and Kirby's concept of culture is all-embracing, starting with vision, values, and cultural symbols but also including organization design, human resource policies, and the core competencies of individuals and the firm. Using these elements, they show that invention strategies typically thrive in entrepreneurial cultures, that mass production strategies depend on hierarchical cultures, that continuous improvement strategies demand partnership cultures, and that mass customization demands a new formulation: modular cultures.

Each of these cultures has different attitudes to using IT; some depend on extensive intra- and interfirm networking (as described in Chapters 6 and 7), others definitely discourage it. Firms wishing to move from one strategic mode to another should take cultural style, or "how we do things around here," very seriously, as it can fatally impede even getting critical alignment issues discussed, let alone resolved.

Davidson and Movizzo in Chapter 11 address some of the cultural issues described above but in a different way. Their chapter focuses on how to manage a transformation process: who should initiate it, who should be involved at each stage, and what the outcomes might be. They describe a six-stage process, which really only begins to address IT strategy issues at stage 3, which may well be a year or so into the project.

Stages 1 and 2 are all about getting buy-in, first from the CEO and second from the top team. As such, it addresses the sort of hidden cultural agendas described in Chapter 10 as business transformation can work only when the senior management team is in agreement about the future direction of the company and the sacrifices they will have to make to achieve their objectives.

The authors are clear that the CIO should be part of this team—indeed, they present several cases of what can go wrong if they are not included—but they believe that decisions on IT infrastructure fall out of the business review and do not set its agenda. However, the process they describe is close to Keen's vision in Chapter 6, where the IT opportunities are discussed so early in the process that subsequent misalignment—alignment should not occur.

In describing the final three stages of a transformation process, the authors give an interesting perspective on how much time these initiatives take, which is of relevance to the "cycling" process described in Luftman's Chapter 3. On average, companies take about five years to go through the first iteration of business transformation, and while in the process they certainly learn about new opportunities, these authors seriously question whether the same management team should lead a second or subsequent cycle.

IT Infrastructure

In Chapter 12 Weill, Broadbent, and St. Clair contend that nonalignment is the natural state of most firms. From this point of view they believe the most useful strategy and role for the IT department is to concentrate on providing a flexible IT infrastructure that can be adapted to changing business needs.

A firm's IT infrastructure is the underlying base on which all transactional, informational, and strategic applications are built. A useful analogy is a country's road, rail, and air links, which make communications and travel possible. A flexible IT infrastructure enables a company to reform itself as and when it likes to meet changing business needs.

Using the concepts of "reach" and "range" introduced in Chapter 6, the authors describe three possible stages a firm may be in vis-à-vis the development of its infrastructure: utility, dependent, and enabling. A utility approach is not very flexible and is driven by cost savings; a dependent attitude is very focused on the current business strategies, providing services to make them work; an enabling approach looks to future business needs.

Interestingly, the authors assert that none of the approaches needs to be more expensive than the other and that a good IT infrastructure is one corporate asset that competitors will find very difficult to copy.

There are two appendices. Appendix A, by Thomas and DeWitt, is a literature review, describing the current state of research on strategic alignment and recommending future research directions. The book concludes with Appendix B, a glossary of strategic alignment terms.

Whether an organization has applied IT to transform the enterprise, is experiencing difficulties in making strategic use of IT, or is somewhere between the two, the description of the methods for transformation covered in this book should prove valuable.

The executive team must ensure that it has chosen the proper approach, however. The application of strategic alignment provides a vehicle for tough thinking about strategy. It is a technique for continuously testing organizational direction. The essential issue is how IT can achieve enough competitive and strategic advantage to exploit the rapid, significant changes that organizations are experiencing.

Notes

1. S. Davis, B. Davidson, *2020 Vision Transforms Your Business Today to Succeed in Tomorrow's Economy* (New York: Simon & Schuster, 1991).
2. L. C. Thurow, *Head To Head: The Coming Economic Battle Among Japan, Europe, and America* (New York: William Morrow and Company, 1992).
3. M. S. Scott Morton, *The Corporation of the 1990's, Information Technology and Organizational Transformation* (New York: Oxford University Press, 1991).

I

The Strategic Alignment Model

2

Aligning Business and IT Strategies

❖

JOHN C. HENDERSON, N. VENKATRAMAN

and SCOTT OLDACH

❖

Chapter Summary

1. IT is often highly complex, and difficult for non-specialists to understand, yet it is critical that business executives do understand enough in order to take significant, and far-reaching strategic decisions.

2. Historically, IT was easier to comprehend, in that its main role was seen as automating well-understood functional activities. Now that it is clear that a major new source of competitive advantage lies in breaking down such boundaries, and that IT can play a key role in doing this, executives need to understand far more about technological developments, and what they might mean for their company.

3. The strategic alignment model essentially adds this critical IT dimension to the external and internal issues that are the usual focus of business strategy. Just as a firm considers how its products and organization are positioned in the marketplace, it should also consider how its IT strategy and infrastructure compares. The model therefore has four quadrants: (a) business strategy; (b) IT strategy; (c) organizational infrastructure and processes and (d) IT infrastructure and processes.

4. Few firms are in a position to make strategic decisions on either IT or business strategy without considering the impact on their internal structures. Similarly, most of the messages arising from process reengineering focus on the impact of internal structures on external strategy.

5. Through isolating the four areas which need to be aligned, the model allows the impact of each quadrant on the others to be assessed more accurately. The authors, in fact, identify four main patterns of linkage between the quadrants which they name: (a) strategy execution; (b) technology potential; (c) competitive potential and (d) service level.

6. Each of these patterns has very different implications for the role that business and IT managers should play in determining strategy, and the performance indicators they should adopt.

7. It is tempting to use this model to make extensive evaluations of strategic options, yet overlook the practical implementation problems. Four 'reality checks' are suggested: (a) calculating the financial returns; (b) checking where the power to make decisions ends up; (c) assessing the company's present technological capability and (d) its organizational (or skills) capability.

8. Seeing the real issues lying behind alignment in this way allows a better assessment on the value of IT investments. No one alignment perspective is best, and the firm should continually consider them all as possible responses to changes in the business environment.

Too often, the IT planning process appears to executives to be stuck in a bygone era. The outputs seem to be an interminable list of projects, pleas for more money, and an additional, complicated need to enforce apparently conflicting (and difficult to understand) sets of priorities and rigid standards. The strategic alignment model developed by Henderson and Venkatraman during the 1980s[1] sets out to provide an effective and flexible solution to this problem. This chapter summarizes the most recent evolution of the model and explains its practical application to real-life management dilemmas.

Essentially, this chapter sets out to answer two fundamental questions:

1. How much technology do executives need to understand to effectively determine the role of IT in their firm—i.e., produce a strategic IT plan that is appropriately aligned with the strategic business plan?

2. What are the structured management processes that are critical to effectively aligning business and IT strategies over time?

The Role of Interpretation

Understanding the role of IT in business is a strategic decision-making activity that involves a complex "sense-making" process in which judgment and interpretation by executives play critical roles.[2] It is important to stress interpretation because a particular technology-related event can, in fact, be understood quite differently by different executives. For example, executives have responded in many different ways to the impact in the United States of the electronic filing of taxes on the market of tax preparers (e.g., CPAs or H & R Block).[3] Some executives saw this development as an opportunity—e.g., "I will be able to attract new customers"—while others saw it as a threat—e.g., "If I do not have this capability, I might as well say good-bye to my business".[4] Still other executives saw electronic filing as an expensive nuisance—e.g., "We are quite efficient without using these computers, and I think that we will spend more time and incur more costs with this new technology".[5] The strategic alignment framework helps to clarify the kinds of knowledge which executives need to produce an effective strategic IT plan.

Developing a Continuous Strategic Process

Strategic IT choices made by the executive team are both the beginning of a process and the end of an event; aligning business and technology strategies is an ongoing executive responsibility. This chapter describes four key management mechanisms which, when taken together, assist both short-term decision-taking and long-term strategic planning:

- strategy execution
- technology potential
- competitive potential
- service level

The Evolving Role of Strategic Planning

To understand the contribution made by the strategic alignment model, it is important to understand the historical context in which it evolved. Strategic planning for information systems (IS) can be characterized in terms of stages or eras.[6] While these stages vary somewhat, in general they reflect

TABLE 2.1.   Evolution of Strategic IS Planning

	Era I (Resource Control)	Era II (IS Architecture)	Era III (Strategic Alignment)
Administrative perspective	Functional	Enterprise	Business network
Key planning product	Product portfolio	Defined architectures	External/internal strategic fit
Benefit	Efficiencies through automation	Product flexibility through architectures	Market-driven through dynamic alignment
Value management	Project management	Policy deployment	Strategy enabling

an evolution from an internal, functional perspective to an external, competitive perspective (Table 2.1).[7]

Era 1: Resource Control

IS planning was focused on the automation of processes. The administrative role of the IS planning process was to provide for control of functional resources. Hence, the planning products (decisions, recommendations, and policies) focused primarily on product development—i.e., applications and the required resources and timing to deliver these products. Importantly, the planning process employed a functional model of the business as the frame of reference to bind these decisions. Thus, the IS planning product from Era I typically identified and detailed a set of functional applications— e.g., marketing systems; financial systems; and the associated resources, priorities, and timetables for their development.

Era II: IS Architecture

The IS planning process extended its scope. Now, the context of the plan was the enterprise and the primary focus was on cross-functional integration. The planning process was used to create architectures to support a wide range of system applications, many of them cross-functional in nature. Planning decisions were extended beyond the project level to architectural design and the development of technological principles. The IS strategy provided the means to establish an organizational view of technology. An additional benefit from this perspective was a means of defining and deploying policies for the overall management of IS. Given this expanded role, the key concept used to describe the IS planning process was linkage—i.e., linkage of the IS strategy to a business strategy.

Era III: Strategic Alignment

ITs are viewed as not only a means of functional integration but as an opportunity to enhance the competitive capability of the firm. The value-added models of the enterprise that begin with the acquisition of materials and end in the sale of a product do not allow for a planning context that reflects the opportunities to compete in turbulent markets.[8] This type of planning context encompasses the interactions among a wide range of suppliers, customers, and competitors.

In Era III, the context of the IS strategy is expanded to an interorganizational business network.[9] The administrative role of the IT plan is to define and enable new organizational capabilities. Concepts like business process engineering or radical restructuring are seen as the driving concepts behind the planning process. By its very nature, the IT plan must demonstrate a much more dynamic state, reflecting both internal and external issues. Executives must now understand not only the product markets in which they compete but the IT market from which they acquire key resources. The IT market is often unfamiliar to them and is increasingly turbulent. Thus, the IT planning process must aid the executive in understanding how to position the firm in the dynamic market of technology as well as how to organize the delivery of IT products and services to meet business goals.

The Strategic Alignment Model

The concept of strategic alignment is based on two building blocks: strategic fit and functional integration (shown as the vertical and horizontal axes of Fig. 2.1). The glossary in Appendix B defines strategic alignment terms.

Strategic Fit

The strategic fit axis recognizes the need for any strategy to address both external and internal domains. The external domain is the arena in which the firm competes and is concerned with (1) business scope decisions such as product-market offerings, (2) distinctive competency decisions—the choice that determines the distinctive attributes of the strategy that differ-

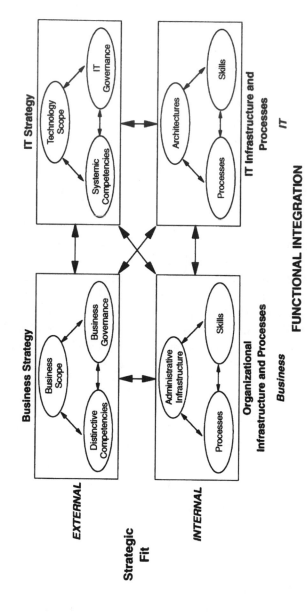

Figure 2.1. Strategic Alignment Model

entiate the firm from its competitors—and (3) governance decisions—i.e., choices that focus on partnerships and alliances.

In contrast, the internal domain is concerned with choices that define (1) the administrative structure (functional or divisional or matrix organization), (2) the design or redesign of critical business processes (product delivery, product development, customer service), and (3) the acquisition and development of human resource skills.

Within the business strategy field, the fit between external positioning and internal arrangement has long been argued as critical to economic performance. The strategic alignment model proposes that an IT strategy should also be defined in terms of an external domain—how the firm is positioned in the IT marketplace—and an internal domain—how the IT infrastructure should be configured and managed.

The two right-hand boxes in Figure 2.1 compare the external and internal choices facing IT strategy with those relating to business strategy. In the external dimension, IT strategy is driven by:

1. *Technology scope*—those critical information technologies that support business strategy initiatives or shape new business strategy initiatives for the firm. This is analogous to business scope, which deals with choices pertaining to product–market offerings in the output market.

2. *Systemic competencies*—those attributes of IT strategy (e.g., system reliability, interconnectivity, flexibility) that contribute positively to the creation of new business strategies or better support of existing business strategy. This is analogous to the concept of distinctive competencies that contribute to a unique, comparative advantage for the firm over its competitors.

3. *IT governance*—selection and use of relationships such as strategic alliances or joint ventures to obtain key IT competencies. This is analogous to business governance, which involves make-vs.-buy choices in business strategy. Such choices cover a complex array of interfirm relationships, such as strategic alliances, joint ventures, marketing exchange, and technology licensing.

The internal IS domain is dominated by three major issues:

1. *IT architecture*—choices that define the portfolio of applications; the configuration of hardware, software, and communication; and the data architectures that collectively define the technical infra-

structure. Given the view that the architectures define key principles, policies, standards, and rules, these choices are analogous to the business infrastructure choice of administrative structure.

2. *IT processes*—choices that define the work processes central to operations of the IS infrastructure, such as systems development or operations. This is analogous to the need for designing the business processes that support and shape the ability of the firm to execute business strategies.

3. *IT skills*—choices pertaining to the acquisition, training, and development of the knowledge and capabilities of the individuals required to effectively manage and operate the IT infrastructure within the organization. This is analogous to the skills required within the business domain to execute a given strategy.

Functional Integration

As described above, the need to integrate IT and business strategies has long been advocated by both researchers and practitioners. The functional dimension specifically considers how choices made in the IT domain impact (enhance or threaten) those made in the business domain and vice versa.

The strategic alignment model identifies the need to specify two types of integration between business and IT domains. The first is at the strategic level (top two boxes in Fig. 2.1), looking at the potential for IT to both shape and support business strategy. The second is at the operational level (bottom two boxes in Fig. 2.1), looking at the link between organizational infrastructure and processes and IS infrastructure and processes.

Using the Model

Research has shown that effective management of IT means achieving a balance among the choices made across all four domains. The question, then, is how to conceptualize and achieve this type of alignment.

The simplest approach calls for considering all combinations of any two domains. If, for instance, the organizational and IT infrastructures can be reconfigured easily, then a perspective that reflected only a strategic view of integration—i.e., the fit between business and IT strategies—could suffice. That is, if the firm could easily adapt its internal processes (both business and IT) to support any possible market positioning strategy, the executives could delegate this issue and spend their time understanding the dynamics of markets.

Unfortunately, there exists a significant possibility that internal inconsistencies will occur. For instance, a simple two-way perspective that considered only external issues (business and IT strategies without any regard for the internal, organizational domains) could seriously underestimate the difficulty (risks) of redesigning key business processes. We argue that, at a minimum, any given planning process must consider the interaction between both dimensions of strategic fit and functional integration.[10]

Four Dominant Alignment Perspectives

To understand the interactions between choices that create fit and those that create integration, an alignment perspective must be taken. Figure 2.2 summarizes four dominant alignment perspectives, each representing a "triangle" of issues for both business and IT domains as well as internal and external domains. Each perspective is unique in terms of the driver—i.e., the specific domain that establishes the distinct management orientation— and the relaxation conditions—i.e., those choices that are not incorporated into the planning process.

PERSPECTIVE ONE: STRATEGY EXECUTION

This perspective reflects a notion that the business strategy is the driver for both organizational design and IT infrastructure choices. In this perspective, strategic goals are evaluated in terms of how critical processes affect them and the subsequent requirements for IS products and services. This is a widely understood alignment perspective, reflecting the classic hierarchical view of strategic management. Several different methodologies are available to operationalize this perspective, including critical success factors.[11]

More recently, this perspective has been expanded to emphasize how possible radical changes in business processes (process redesign) could better support the business strategy.[12] The role for top management in this perspective is strategy formulator—i.e., to articulate the logic and choices pertaining to business strategy. The role for IS management is strategy implementor—i.e., to efficiently and effectively design and implement the required IS products and services to support the business strategy. Performance criteria in this perspective are based on financial gains and/or increased efficiency of business processes.

a) Perspective One: Strategy Execution

Business Strategy → Organizational Infrastructure → IS Infrastructure

Driver:	Business Strategy
Role of Top Management:	Strategy Formulator
Role of IS Management:	Strategy Implementor
Performance Criteria:	Cost/Service Center

b) Perspective Two: Technology Potential

Business Strategy → IT Strategy → IS Infrastructure

Driver:	Business Strategy
Role of Top Management:	Technology Visionary
Role of IS Management:	Technology Architect
Performance Criteria:	Technology Leadership

c) Perspective Three: Competitive Potential

IT Strategy → Business Strategy → Organizational Infrastructure

Driver:	IT Strategy
Role of Top Management:	Business Visionary
Role of IS Management:	Catalyst
Performance Criteria:	Business Leadership

d) Perspective Four: Service Level

IT Strategy → IS Infrastructure → Organizational Infrastructure

Driver:	IT Strategy
Role of Top Management:	Prioritizer
Role of IS Management:	Executive Leadership
Performance Criteria:	Customer Satisfaction

Figure 2.2. Four Dominant Alignment Perspectives

PERSPECTIVE TWO: TECHNOLOGY POTENTIAL

This alignment perspective involves developing an IT strategy in response to a business strategy and using the corresponding choices to define the required IS infrastructure and processes. In contrast to the strategy execution logic, this perspective does not use the business strategy to explore and define the organizational structure. Rather, it seeks to identify the best possible IT competencies through appropriate positioning in the IT marketplace. Further, the choices for positioning the firm with respect to key technologies and alliances must be adequately reflected in the design of the internal IS infrastructure.

Alignment for this perspective requires that executives understand the impact of business strategy on IT strategy and the corresponding implications for IS infrastructure and processes. The executive management team provides the technological vision to articulate the IT logic and choices that would best support the chosen business strategy. The IS manager should be a technology architect, who efficiently and effectively designs and implements the required IS infrastructure that is consistent with the external component of IT strategy (scope, competencies, and governance). Performance criteria in this perspective are based on technological leadership, with qualitative but insightful benchmarking along a set of critical measures pertaining to positioning in the IT marketplace.

PERSPECTIVE THREE: COMPETITIVE POTENTIAL

This alignment perspective is concerned with the exploitation of emerging IT capabilities to impact new products and services (i.e., business scope), influence the key attributes of strategy (distinctive competencies), as well as develop new forms of relationships (i.e., business governance). Unlike the two previous perspectives, which consider business strategy as given, this perspective allows the modification of business strategy via emerging IT capabilities. Beginning with the three dimensions of IT strategy, this perspective seeks to identify the most strategic set of options for business and the corresponding set of decisions pertaining to organizational infrastructure and processes.

The specific role for top management to make this perspective succeed is the business visionary, who articulates how the emerging IT competencies and functionality, as well as the changing governance patterns in the IT marketplace, would impact the business strategy. The role of the IS manager, in contrast, is the catalyst, who helps to identify and interpret the trends in the IT environment to assist the business manager's understanding of the potential opportunities and threats from IT. Performance criteria in this perspective are based on leadership, with qualitative and quantitative measurements pertaining to product market leadership (market share, growth, new product introduction, etc.).

PERSPECTIVE FOUR: SERVICE LEVEL

This alignment perspective focuses on the need to build a world-class IS service organization. This service level is anchored by choices that define the external dimensions of IT strategy. As with the other perspectives, the implications of the "strategic fit" dimensions are reflected in terms of the products and services provided to the organization—i.e., in support of the business process. This perspective is often viewed as necessary but not sufficient to ensure the effective use of IT resources in a growing and fast-changing world. Methodologies reflecting this perspective require a systematic analysis of the IT markets as well as approaches that focus on internal customer service. The use of total quality management approaches by IS executives reflects one way to implement this perspective.

The specific role for top management to make this perspective succeed is the prioritizer, who articulates how best to allocate the scarce resources both within the organization and in the IT marketplace. The role of the IS manager, in contrast, is leadership, with the specific tasks of making the internal IS organization succeed within the operating guidelines from top management. Performance criteria in this perspective are based on customer satisfaction, with qualitative and quantitative measurements with internal and external benchmarking.

The strategic alignment model described here provides one framework to understand the substantive knowledge required to align business and technology strategies. By itself, however, it does not reflect the dynamic aspect of alignment. In the next section we describe four key executive processes required to achieve this alignment over time.

Achieving Strategic Alignment

The management challenge of translating strategic choices into operational behaviors or achieving strategic alignment is considerable. Many companies, while devoting extensive attention to the evaluation of alternative choices within the four domains of the strategic alignment model, have not devoted sufficient thinking to the challenge of ensuring that these four domains are dynamically adjusted and consistently implemented. This is

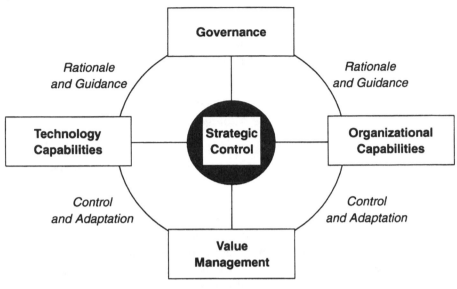

Figure 2.3.

akin to excellent strategy formulation efforts without corresponding attention to strategy implementation issues.

To help this process, four alignment mechanisms have been identified
(see Fig. 2.3).

1. *Value management* is the mechanism for ensuring that the maximal
   benefits are realized from IT investments.

2. *Governance* specifies the allocation of decision rights to the key
   executives or partners.

3. *Technological capability* is the mechanism for specifying and modifying the various IT capabilities required to support and shape business strategy.

4. *Organizational capability* is the mechanism for specifying, modifying, and perhaps reinventing the various skills and processes required to support and shape business strategy.

Finally, strategic control, the central area of Figure 2.3, represents the
essential need for an ongoing planning process task, which assesses and
adapts the above processes in a manner that achieves internal consistency.

These four mechanisms address the interrelationships indicated by the two two-way arrows in the center of Figure 2.1. Each mechanism is defined below in terms of three key management processes: definition, development, and adaptation. Table 2.2 summarizes the alignment mechanisms and key processes.

Value Management

Value management is the organizational mechanism for ensuring that IT resources invested throughout the organization deliver anticipated or greater returns.

Defining value means articulating the investment principles. These principles reflect high-level priorities (e.g., low-cost operation, flexible infrastructure), which guide specific decisions concerning the funding and priorities of individual IT projects. This enables the individual business unit and area managers to prioritize their many investment opportunities and to concentrate their efforts on a coordinated set of goals.

Developing value consists of defining and instituting performance criteria or value measures in the firm. These value measures provide a means to insure a consistent, on-going value delivery process associated with any IT investment. The measures should both follow from and support the investment principles.

For example, if one of the investment principles is "creating a flexible IT infrastructure," executives could use an approach such as a real options[13] or business scenario modeling methodology to establish both a range of organizational impacts achievable through IT investments and an understanding of what key processes need to be redesigned to achieve these impacts. From this foundation, a performance measurement system could be developed, perhaps considering the cause–effect relationships of IT as a resource enabler, the ability to achieve desired process performance using IT, and the ultimate impact measured in terms of economic or market-based performance.[14]

This would lead to a consistent, integrated view of performance across the individual, work unit, and business unit levels of the organization. The resulting performance measurement system would provide a coherent framework for managing the change process over time, and this increases the likelihood that value will be achieved from IT investments.

Adapting value involves two aspects. First, value management helps to monitor the status and effectiveness of specific IT investments. Second, and perhaps more importantly, adapting values provides a systematic way

TABLE 2.2. Alignment Mechanisms and Key Processes

			Alignment Mechanisms	
Key Processes	Value Management	Governance	Technological Capability	Organizational Capability
Design	Investment strategy	Roles and relationships	Technological capability	Organizational and human capabilities
Development	Measures/criteria	Decision rights allocation	Technological principles, policies, and rules	Skills and operating structure
Adaptation	Monitor investments and learn about performance	Monitor decision rights exercised and efficacy	Monitor systems and adapt continuously	Monitor deployment and transform organizational learning

for executives to learn how and why an IT initiative did or did not realize its anticipated value.

Monitoring project performance is an area where most companies have focused significant attention. Field research suggests, however, that it is critical for this monitoring process to consider all of the factors addressed by the strategic alignment model. For instance, executives should not focus solely on issues of efficiency, such as the productivity of programming, but also, perhaps, on the extent to which the projects lead to the desired change in key business processes and, subsequently, to the ultimate economic performance goal.

With respect to the learning process, the key issue is to design into the change process the means to adapt and learn as the initiative unfolds. It is not sufficient to know that a project has met or has failed to meet a goal. It is necessary to discover the underlying causes of the success or failure. A classic example of this is found in the effective use of postimplementation audits. Using a monitoring perspective, a postimplementation audit determines the extent to which projected benefits are realized. A learning perspective, in contrast, would be equally focused on discovering unanticipated consequences, both positive and negative, and documenting lessons learned.

Governance

The governance mechanism specifies the allocation of decision rights for IT activities to the various decision-makers within the organization as well as to outside vendors and partners. It is not concerned with the day-to-day operational decisions but with the distribution of decision rights that is consistent with the logic and perspective of strategic alignment. For example, to achieve its strategy of superior customer service, a large insurance company may partner with a computer vendor to operate and maintain its data center. Governance is concerned with the structure and effectiveness of that relationship.

Defining governance focuses on the design of decision rights, or simply the roles and responsibilities utilized to implement the strategy. Roles may be distributed internally to business areas, individual managers, teams, or departments at the corporate or business unit level. This is the traditional component. Recent research[15] has shown that roles may also be distributed to external parties, such as technology vendors or systems integrators. Together, these two dimensions of governance are called the *locus of control*.

Locus of control issues range between, on the one hand, decentralization and centralization decisions and, on the other hand, levels of competency. For example, a large, multi-national insurance company might give each business unit (e.g., individual, pensions, group) its own IT group, which would be responsible for systems development, but also have a corporate IT group responsible for maintenance, operations, and corporate-wide applications such as infrastructure. Who should make what decisions? Competence to make decisions might include not only internal resources but also the skills and abilities of external partners—e.g., outsourcing vendors.

Effective governance involves balancing both sets of options: centralization/decentralization and inside/outside. Some decisions, like infrastructural standards, may be more appropriately vested with a central body, while other decisions, such as leveraging IS applications for business purposes, may be more suitably decentralized to the business units. Similarly, in the wake of managing the IT function using interorganizational alliances and partnerships (including outsourcing), some decisions, such as operations and maintenance, may be more appropriately shifted outside, while other decisions, such as infrastructure or migration plans, may be kept inside the organization.

Developing governance means, in practice, empowering the various decision-making units. For example, they may have different levels of management involvement, such as responsibility or monitoring or providing input. Hence, a governance profile can be designed which is consistent with the roles and responsibilities and clearly delineates the decision rights. For example, corporate IS may be responsible for IT planning, whereas the business unit IS is responsible for systems development. Additionally, line managers may monitor training and external organizations may have input for architecture and infrastructure.

Adapting governance may be done through formal contracts—e.g., specifically delineating roles and responsibilities for external vendors—but the internal allocation of decision rights is usually far less formal. However, even if specified, the allocation scheme may not be put into effect exactly as planned. It is important to track these changes and to understand why the decision rights allocated varied from those exercised. This process would also signal when decision rights are not being exercised at all.

Technological Capability

This alignment mechanism deals with the administrative process for creating the required IT capability for supporting and shaping the business strategy.

Defining technological capacity means scanning the technological environment to identify those existing and potential IT-related capabilities that could support and shape business strategy. It is important to recognize that the focus is not simply to identify a set of technologies but rather to define the totality of the capabilities offered by the chosen set of technologies. For example, in the case of a financial services organization, an important technological capability is global, seamless information access and analysis across different data sources and distinct media. The specific set of technologies selected to achieve this capability may involve trade-offs along several criteria, which ultimately must be consistent with specific standards set by the firm.

Developing technological capacity deals with the principles, policies, and rules that will govern the development and implementation of these capabilities. For instance, what should the relationships be between the required technological capability for the future and the current standards? What if they are inconsistent? Similar to the analysis of the impact of a new product on the profitability of existing products, this mechanism must assess the trade-off between current standards and new functionality.

Adapting technological capacity focuses on migration issues. The importance of this can easily be appreciated, given the dynamic evolution in the price–performance ratio of new IT products and the proliferation of multiple, competing standards. This issue is most commonly linked with the problems of "legacy systems," which have been in existence for some time and cannot be easily changed without incurring a significant commitment of financial resources and time. Thus, while such systems may be efficient (low-cost, given that the initial capital may be amortized), they restrict the development of new technological capabilities for the organization. Addressing technological capacity ensures that this issue cannot be swept under the carpet.

Organizational Capability

This alignment mechanism deals with the administrative processes for creating the required human skills and the capability for supporting and shaping the business strategy.

Defining human skills is more than the specification of traditional job descriptions for hiring or promotion; it also involves the articulation of how human skills support and complement the available or potential IT capabilities. Neither technology nor human skills alone would be effective as they fail to leverage important complementary sources of capabilities. For instance, the definition of the skills of a customer service manager will vary greatly, depending on how the customer support process is defined.

Developing and *adapting* organizations focus on the need to assess and adapt the processes and skills of the organization as technology changes. Companies often spend a great deal of resources developing human skills independent of their investments in IT capabilities. Investment in training to leverage IT functionality is minimal compared to the investment in technological systems and applications. If done well, development and adaptation enable organizational capability to be continually updated, thus minimizing the need for large-scale layoffs that are invariably due to the mismatch between existing human skills and the emerging technology. In essence, organizational capability defines and redesigns the basic operating structure of the business.

Putting the Alignment Model, Perspectives, and Mechanisms Together

A major reason for the current dissatisfaction with the level of integration between the business and IT domains, and possibly the absence of value derived from IT investments, lies in the lack of understanding of the enabling strategic choices that bind a business strategy to the IS infrastructure. Viewed from within the strategic alignment model, the direct link between business strategy (top left of Fig. 2.1) and IS infrastructure (bottom right of Fig. 2.1) can derive its logic only within the context of the two alignment perspectives that have business strategy as the driver: *strategy execution* and *technology potential* refered to as IT Intrastructure Fusion by Luftman in Chapter 3. In the former case, the link derives its meaning from translating the implications of business strategy for the organizational infrastructure into subsequent demands for IS products and services. In the latter case, the link is achieved through the effective positioning of the firm in the IT marketplace—namely, specification of the three components of IT strategy and the consequent implications for the three internal components of the IT infrastructure and processes.

Similarly, the direct link between IT strategy (top right of Fig. 2.1) and organizational infrastructure (bottom left of Fig. 2.1) has no direct meaning. One cannot and should not seek simply to identify and adopt the best available technologies to restructure the organization or streamline the business processes without due consideration to the two relevant alignment perspectives that have IT strategy as the driver: *competitive potential* and *service level* refered to as Organization Infrastructure Fusion by Luftman. The former identifies the potential impact of IT strategy on business strategy, with consequent implications for organizational infrastructure. The latter provides the best possible service to the internal client by developing the appropriate basis for the redesign of the IS infrastructure. It is expected that in the absence of such understanding, there would be a significant probability that investments made to transfer business processes may well fail due to an inability to provide the information necessary to execute the processes.

The specification of individual dimensions of the four domains of the strategic alignment model, as well as the selection of one or more alignment perspectives, is only part of the overall management challenge to realize benefits from IT investments. The alignment mechanisms suggested in Figure 2.3 help ensure that the appropriate logic for allocating decision rights has been put in place and that the required technological and human capabilities are being harnessed on a continuous basis within the overall scheme of value management. These alignment mechanisms over time create the dynamic capabilities to transform the corporation effectively.

Dynamic capability is also created through the key processes. Field work demonstrates that organizations are both adaptive and innovative in their implementations of the key processes. Initial work in North American companies substantiates the existence of the three processes—design, development, and adaptation. However, work is continuing and may suggest additional processes. For example, the adaptation process may be an aggregation of two related processes, such as monitoring and learning. Similarly, organizations have described communication as an integral component of each process.

Use of this approach and the underlying models requires an understanding of its intrinsic dynamic nature. Much of the strategic planning techniques popularized in the 1970s and 1980s have gone out of favor, not because of the weakness in their logic but because of their failure to recognize the dynamic nature of strategy. Managers are painfully aware that the real business challenge is not static alignment among the four domains at any one point in time (when the strategic planning exercise is carried out!) but ensuring continual assessment of the trends across these four domains to allow repositioning of the firm in the external environment and the rearrangement of the internal infrastructure, as described by Luftman in the next chapter.

Managers are seriously urged to recognize the need to evolve from one perspective to another based on the shifts in the business environment, both internal and external. This is consistent with the current emphasis on the centrality of learning and adaptation for achieving successful organizational transformation. As one senior manager in the midst of adopting the strategic alignment model said: "The most important lesson to keep in mind is that strategic alignment is a journey and not an event."

Many executives have asked: Which alignment perspective is the best? Researchers and observers of strategic management phenomena do not believe that there is one universally superior mode to formulate and implement strategy. If there were, it would not be strategic because all firms would adopt it. The four dominant alignment perspectives that use the two strategies as the driver are equally useful and powerful in determining the role of IT in organizational transformation. Indeed, managers are urged not to consider IT as a panacea and consequently focus only on those two perspectives, with IT strategy as the starting point (namely, competitive potential and service level), nor is it argued that business strategy should always be the starting point and adopt only the other two perspectives on strategic alignment. The potential for IT impact is so varied and complex that the executive team must consider all of these perspectives as alternative conceptual lenses and only then institutionalize the appropriate set of alignment mechanisms.

Notes

Portions of this chapter originally appeared in IBM Systems Journal Vol. 32, No. 1, 1993.

1. John C. Henderson, N. Venkatraman, "Understanding Strategic Alignment," *Business Quarterly*, 55:3 (Winter, 1991):8–14; John C. Henderson, N. Venkatraman, "Strategic Alignment: Leveraging Information Technology for Transforming Organizations," *IBM Systems Journal*, 32:1 (1993): 4–16; J. C. Henderson, N. Venkatraman, "Strategic Alignment: A Model for Organizational Transformation via Information Technology," in *Information Technology and the Corporation of the 1990s*, Thomas J. Allen and Michael Scott Morton, eds. (New York: Oxford University Press, 1993) chapt. 9.
2. I. Ansoff, "Strategic Issue Management," *Strategic Management Journal*, 1 (1980): 131–148; R. L. Daft, K. E. Weick, "Toward a Model of Organizations as Interpretive Systems," *Academy of Management Review* (1984): 234–295; James B. Thomas, Reuben R. McDaniel, Jr., "Interpreting Strategic Issues: Effects of Strategy and the Information-Processing Structure of Top Management Teams," *Academy of Management Review*, 33:2 (1990): 286–306.
3. Ari Ginsberg, N. Venkatraman, "Investing in New Information Technology: The Role of Competitive Posture and Issue Diagnosis," *Strategic Management Journal*, Special Issue on Strategy Process Research, 1992; N. Venkatraman, A. Kambil, "The Check's Not in the Mail: Strategies for Electronic Integration in Tax Return Filing," *Sloan Management Review*, 32:2 (Winter, 1991): 33–43.

4. Venkatraman and Kambil, "The Check's Not in the Mail," 39.
5. Ibid.
6. John F. Rockart, M. S. Scott Morton, "Implications of Changes in Information Technology for Corporate Strategy," *Interfaces*, 14:1 (1984): 84–95.
7. Ibid. See also C. Wiseman, *Strategy and Computers: Information Systems as Competitive Weapons*, (Homewood, IL: Dow Jones-Irwin, 1985).
8. John K. Shank, V. Govindarajan, "Strategic Cost Management and the Value Chain," *Journal of Cost Management* (Winter, 1992): 5–21.
9. James I. Cash, Benn R. Konsynski, "IS Redraws Competitive Boundaries," *Harvard Business Review* (1985): 134–142; N. Venkatraman, "Information Technology-Induced Business Reconfiguration: The New Strategic Management Challenge," in *The Corporation of the 1990s*, Michael S. Scott Morton, ed. (New York: Oxford University Press, 1991).
10. Henderson and Venkatraman, "Understanding Strategic Alignment," 1991; "Strategic Alignment: Leveraging," 1993; "Strategic Alignment: A Model," 1993.
11. John F. Rockart, "Chief Executives Define Their Own Data Needs," *Harvard Business Review*, 57:2 (1979): 81–93.
12. Thomas H. Davenport, *Process Innovation: Reengineering Work Through Information Technology*, (Boston: Harvard Business School Press, 1993).
13. John C. Henderson, A. Kambil, H. Mohsenzadeh, "Strategic Management of Information Technology Investments: An Options Perspective," in *Strategic Information Technology Management: Perspectives on Organizational Growth and Competitive Advantage*, Rajiv D. Banker, Robert J. Kauffman, Mo Adam Mahmood, eds. (City: Idea Group Publishing, 1993), 161–178.
14. Kathleen Foley Curley, J. C. Henderson, "Evaluating Investments in Information Technology: A Review of Key Models with Proposed Framework for Future Research," in *The ACM/OIS Proceedings on Value, Impact and Benefits of Information Technology* (Minneapolis: May 1989, revised October 1989).
15. N. Venkatraman, L. Loh, "Strategic Issues in Information Technology Sourcing: Patterns, Perspectives and Prescriptions," (Boston: MIT Center for Information Systems Research, Working Paper 251 February 1993).

3

Applying the Strategic Alignment Model

❖

JERRY N. LUFTMAN

❖

Chapter Summary

1. A central question of Chapter 2 was 'how much IT do executives need to know?'. This chapter pursues the roles of both IT and business executives in more detail, and describes the measures and strategic planning approaches appropriate to the strategy execution, technology potential, competitive potential and service level perspectives of the strategic alignment model. Important enablers and inhibitors of strategic alignment are also described.

2. This chapter conveys new insights on the four original perspectives described in Chapter 2, and defines eight additional perspectives.

3. The authors of Chapter 2 commented that no alignment perspective was better than another, and that a business should use them all as a lens for viewing the business. This chapter describes how organizations 'cycle' around each in turn, finding the place to start by identifying which quadrant of the model offers the largest opportunity for improvement (named the 'domain pivot').

4. Next, the quadrant representing the change forces that will drive the domain pivot is identified, and last the quadrant that will be impacted by the improvements. This establishes the direction for 'cycling' around the model.

5. Cycling around a model such as this will only be effective if the strategy team is clear about the company's current and future objectives, and are experienced in working together as an effective team.

The model forces confrontation of many assumptions about the business, and can only be useful if the team is prepared to address these with an open mind. The described approach for applying the strategic alignment model has effectively been used by over 300 organizations.

Understanding Domains

Chapter 2 explained in detail the strategic alignment model's components and original four alignment perspectives (strategy execution, technology potential, competitive potential, and service level) and indicated that each was "driven" by a particular management orientation. Figure 3.1 illustrates another way of understanding each of these relationships.

Domain Anchor

In each case, the first of the three boxes is called the domain anchor (indicated by an anchor icon), which is the catalyst or the enabler of the perspective. At times it is the driver of change. The domain anchor is the starting point. It is the box that is typically the most stable. Usually, it is the area that has most recently been addressed. It is in a strong position to drive the planning process.

Domain Pivot

The second box, the *domain pivot*, is typically the area that has the problem or opportunity that is being addressed. The domain anchor is the catalyst to help address the domain pivot.

Impact Domain

The third and last box, the *impact domain*, is the area that is being affected by the change to the domain pivot. Therefore, there is a need to ensure an understanding of the implications of those changes to the impact domain.

The fourth box in each case is by no means irrelevant but acts as a symbol for the dynamic nature of what is occurring. It is the area most likely to be affected by the next iteration of this cycle.

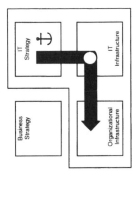

b) The Technology Potential Perspective
- Business Strategy--the anchor domain
- IT Strategy--the pivot domain
- IT Infrastructure--the impact domain

d) The Service Level Perspective
- IT Strategy--the anchor domain
- IT Infrastructure--the pivot domain
- Organizational Infrastructure--the impact domain

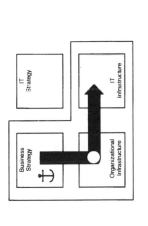

a) The Strategy Execution Perspective
- Business Strategy--the anchor domain
- Organizational Infrastructure--the pivot domain
- IT Infrastructure--the impact domain

c) The Competitive Potential Perspective
- IT Strategy--the anchor domain
- Business Strategy--the pivot domain
- Organizational Infrastructure--the impact domain

Figure 3.1.

Using Domains to Make Decisions

Chapter 2 introduced four management methods for evaluating and tracking different aspects of strategic alignment: value management, governance, technological capability, and organizational capability. Figure 3.2 shows another way of looking at the situation. The matrix describes the role of top management, the role of IT management, the focus of IT, the value of IT, and the appropriate strategic planning method for each of the four original strategic perspectives.

The framework and its application resulted from research begun by Henderson and Thomas[1]. As of this writing, Figure 3.2 is based on evaluating over sixty case studies and conducting over three hundred company assessments over 18 months ending December 1994. Research is under way in IBM's Advanced Business Institute (Luftman, Papp, Brier) to provide additional insights in this area. Besides enhancing the framework, the research is focused on identifying trends and establishing benchmarks against exemplary organizations. The matrix provides valuable insight into just how much knowledge executives need to manage IT effectively.

Enablers & Inhibitors to Alignment

A computer-based assessment model developed by Luftman and Brier is used to assesses the alignment of business and IT. The first question asked of executives participating in the strategic alignment assessment was to rate the strength of the alignment within their companies. Only fifty percent indicated that their firms business and IT strategies were properly aligned. Over forty-two percent indicated that the strategies were not. Seven percent were unsure or had no opinion. The executives were then asked to rank the top enablers to achieving alignment. The results are illustrated in Figure 3.3. Identifying these enablers is significant because they show the importance of executive support and backing, the ability to achieve the strategic goals set by IT, and the need to identify with the business plan.

The most common inhibitors to achieving alignment, asked next, are illustrated in Figure 3.4. These inhibitors shed light on the problems firms face as they strive for alignment. The primary problem was one of affiliation. Business and IT are going in different directions with poor communication and interaction between them. Close behind was the need for IT to improve how it sets it priorities. The problem associated with the traditional IT backlog is addressed by the inhibitor failure of IT to meet its

	Strategic Execution	Technology Potential	Competitive Potential	Service Level
Nature of Domain Relationships		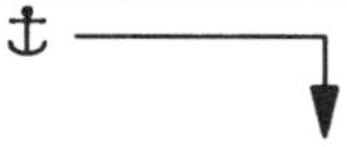		
Role of Top Management	Leader	Technological Visionary	Business Visionary	Prioritizor
Role of IT Management	Functional Manager	Technological Architect	Business Architect	Service Manager
IT Focus	Reactive / Responsive	Enable Value–Add to Business	Drive Value–-Add to Business	Business within a Business
IT Performance Criteria	Financial	IT Value to Product / Service	Product / Service Value from IT	Customer Satisfaction
Strategic Planning Method	Business Process Reengineering or IT Planning	IT Strategy	Business Strategy	IT Planning, IT Reengineering, or Execution

Figure 3.2. Four Strategic Perspectives

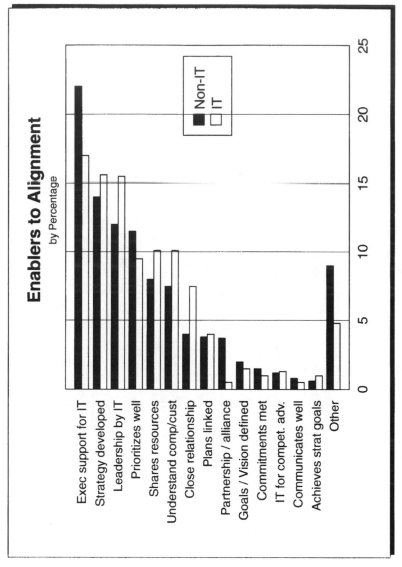

Figure 3.3.

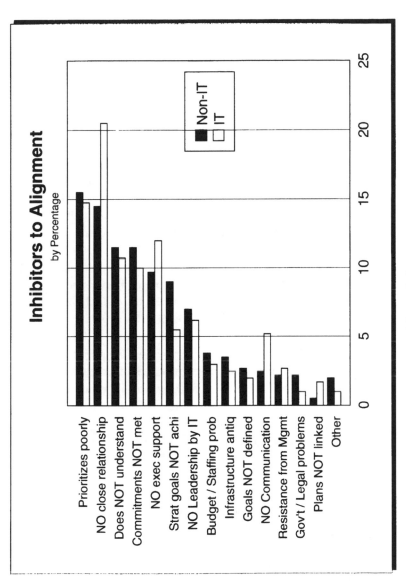

Figure 3.4.

commitments. The problems described here are not unique or new to IT. Such constraints have plagued IT almost since its inception as a functional area. As the importance and role of technology increases, these problems are compounded.

When evaluating the top enablers to alignment by title/function both IT executives and business (non-IT) executives agreed on the relative positioning of these enablers to alignment. However, for non-IT executives, the need for "executive support for IT" out paced the others by a significant margin (21.8%). This suggests that business executives are aware of the need to support IT and contend that it is the most significant means to achieve alignment. IT executives also ranked this enabler first (16.7%), but it was followed very closely by their partnership role in the development of the firms strategy (16.2%). This suggests that IT believes that not only is executive support needed, but IT should have a larger role in the formulation of the overall business strategy. Leadership was the third enabler identified by both IT (15.2%) and non-IT executives (11.5%). This supports the need to increase ITs role in the business strategy formulation. Implicit is IT's ability to determine business opportunities/problems and propose technology solutions in business terms.

When evaluating the top inhibitors to alignment by title/function, the IT executives believed that the greatest problem in the achievement of alignment was the lack of a close relationship between IT and business (20.7%). Business ranked this second (14.3%). The top inhibitor among business (non-IT) executives was poor prioritization by IT (16%). This was also seen as a problem by IT. However, it was a distant second (14.6%). The next major inhibitor for IT executives was lack of executive support for IT (11.6%), which was ranked fifth (9.5%) by non-IT executives. Implicit is IT's ability to effectively manage its resources, understand the business, and communicate.

Application of the strategic alignment model begins by identifying and assigning a cross-functional team consisting of from six to twelve executives from the major business units and IT. The team would typically report to the senior executives, who would report to the highest level executive of the organization. Their knowledge of the business is key.

The process begins by analyzing the current ("as is") and future ("to be") states for each of the twelve components (ellipses introduced in Chapter 2, defined in the Appendix B) of the strategic alignment model. The individual team members' points of view and discussions provide the dynamism that creates a list of opportunities and problems. Naturally, a strong facilitator can prove invaluable. Evaluating the gaps between the current and future states will provide the:

- major content of the business and IT strategies
- identification of a prioritized list of new opportunities to leverage the business by applying IT
- team involved with a great learning experience regarding the business and its future
- rest of the organization with a vehicle to communicate and understand the role and value of IT

The process continues by having the team formally assess and identify the current strategic alignment perspective that fits the organization. Once a consensus is reached, the team will have a firm understanding of the roles required by the executive team, how to assess the value of IT, what the focus of IT should be, and what strategic planning method is appropriate, applying Figure 3.2.

Strategy Execution Perspective

Strategy execution uses business strategy as the anchor domain, organizational infrastructure as the pivot domain, and IT infrastructure as the impact domain (see Fig. 3.1a). This perspective represents where most organizations (approximately 60%) focus and remain, though it might not be the most appropriate perspective. After formal assessment, only 6% of the companies were actually in this perspective. This suggests that over 50% of the organizations were focused inappropriately when building their strategies and plans.

EXECUTIVE ROLE AS DEFINERS AND COMMUNICATORS OF STRATEGY

In this top-down approach the role of executive management is that of a leader. The leader must identify critical areas of the business to address, motivate the resources to carry them out, and formulate and communicate the complete business strategy. Communicating the strategy to everybody in the organization should be considered a critical success factor.

IT MANAGERS IMPLEMENT BUSINESS STRATEGY

The role of IT management is that of a functional manager. In essence, IT implements and supports the business priorities much like any of the other functional managers in the organization. IT Management's focus is reactive or responsive, depending on whether IT is prepared to support the technological and infrastructural demands. Changes to the IT infrastructure take years to carry out.

FINANCIAL OR PRODUCTIVITY MEASURES OF IT VALUE

In either event, IT takes the business strategy and replies to the requirements that are necessary to support it. The objective is to meet the demands of the business strategy as defined by top management. IT performance criteria are the same as those of a cost center. IT typically focuses on performance efficiency, using traditional financial measurements such as cost displacement, cost reduction, return on investment, return on equity, return on assets, net present value, break-even analysis, and, most recently, activity-based costing.

STRATEGIC PLANNING APPROACH

This perspective's strategic planning method (see Appendix B) will either be business process reengineering or IT planning. The decision will be based on the state of the business processes. If the business processes need to be reviewed, reengineering should be the strategic planning approach applied. However, if the business processes have been recently reviewed and transformed, then IT planning would be appropriate. IT planning is also appropriate if the technological and infrastructural demands are significant. This approach is attractive because it recognizes that systems must be developed with strong linkages to important business processes and that the IT strategy is based on future business needs.

If business process reengineering is appropriate, there is a tight linkage to IT planning methods. Traditional techniques, such as critical success factors[2] or business systems planning (BSP),[3] will be interwoven or follow the business transformation effort. Prototyping can be used to demonstrate that the concept is an effective approach. The prototype is frequently deployed to an operational environment. Creating systems architectures and deriving and carrying out technical plans for application development, end-user workstations, systems management, and/or network management typically follow.

CASE EXAMPLES

IBM Credit Corporation, which reduced the amount of time necessary to arrive at a quote for most requests, for computer financing from six days to ninety minutes, is a well-documented example of this perspective. Process improvements resulted from enabling one person to perform all of the necessary tasks, thus eliminating paper handoffs. The company issues more than ten times as many quotes as it did before the changes, using a computer for more than half the quotes.

The strategy of Harry Kavetas, the senior executive, to improve customer service led to the opportunity to reduce case time. This brought the opportunity to reduce paper and a redesign of the business process. The enhanced process and support systems have recently enabled IBM account executives to be more proactive in the loan process. By providing account executives access to the system, they have become representatives of IBM Credit. IBM Credit is currently exploring providing customers with access to the system, enabling them to become their own loan advisors.

A second example is Mutual Benefit Life Insurance (MBL). This is an early successful example (described in Chapter 6) of business process reengineering. Behind the leadership of its CEO, Hank Keates, MBL successfully reengineered its process for underwriting and issuing insurance policies. Costs were reduced by 40%. The time to process an application was reduced to two to five days from five to twenty-five days. The old process required forty steps, twelve functions, and eighty jobs. The enhanced process requires one person with two assistants.

A third example is McGraw-Hill's redesign of its processes for editing, marketing, and distributing college textbooks. Their Primis electronic publishing system, built to support the new processes, lets college instructors select from a database of educational and professional information to create a customized textbook tailored to the specific needs of a particular course and its students. These edited books are distributed online to university bookstores, where they are printed, bound, and sold to students. This improved service, which is revolutionizing the textbook industry, originated from the leadership of their textbook division executive Bob Lynch. Each of the above cases will be discussed further in this chapter.

The American Standard, Progressive Insurance, and Automated Data Processing initiatives described in Chapter 11 and Mrs. Fields described in Chapter 7 are other examples of strategy execution.

Technology Potential

The second perspective is technology potential. This is sometimes called technology transformation and is pictured in Figure 3.1b. Twenty percent of the companies formally assessing themselves were in this perspective. The change force again is top-down. It is driven by the business strategy, the anchor domain. In this perspective the direction is clockwise. The area being addressed (the domain pivot) is IT strategy. The third box, the impact domain, or the area being affected by the change to IT strategy, is IT infrastructure.

EXECUTIVE ROLE OF TECHNOLOGICAL VISIONARIES

In the technology potential perspective the role of top management is that of technological visionary. Here, business executives identify how the business can apply technology. Business executives must understand both the technological marketplace and the strengths and weaknesses of their own IT infrastructures. At issue is the need to manage technical risk effectively. The executive not only has to choose an effective position in the technological market but must ensure that the embedded technology, systems, and people can be changed in ways to support these technological choices.

IT MANAGERS ACT AS IT ARCHITECTS

The role of IT management is that of technological architect. The IT executive in this perspective must design and manage the technology that has been defined by the business executive. The focus of IT is that of adding value to the business, for example, by providing the technical leadership necessary to enable the executive vision.

ADDED VALUE PERFORMANCE MEASURES FOR IT

The value (how to measure the performance of IT) is in how or what IT adds to the firm's final product or service. Tangible measures could be competitive gain, risk reduction, new services to customers, or revenue increases. Other areas to consider include the relationship between the company and customer (e.g., reduced time to market, flexibility) and/or how well the company has met the competition in an offering that they have previously carried out. Here, IT is typically a profit center or an investment center.

STRATEGIC PLANNING APPROACH

In the technology potential perspective the strategic planning method is to devise an IT strategy. Some business process reengineering and IT planning techniques will be interwoven into the IT strategy effort and/or IT planning, and reengineering will follow the IT strategy. Rapid prototyping techniques are also effective here.

CASE EXAMPLES

The United Services Automobile Association (USAA) had a business strategy generated by their CEO, General McDermott[4] (see also Chapters 4, 6, and 11). His strategy was to reach a paperless office environment and improve the service to its clients using imaging technology. By placing most of its client information online, using imaging technology, the company found that it could gain more value than just reducing paper and the several thousand feet of storage space it required.

Having client information online and accessible to its staff provided a significant service improvement for its clients. A client calling USAA could speak with any agent. All agents now had access to all information about that specific client. Any agent could discuss recent transactions and potential opportunities with any client. In essence the company provided a one-stop shop capability by enabling their case managers. USAA has also documented tangible benefits of a 1% increase in revenue and a 1% reduction in direct mailing costs because of the imaging technology project.

A second illustration is Rosenbluth Travel.[5] Within Rosenbluth there are two examples of technology potential. The first is CEO Hal Rosenbluth's strategy to integrate the different airline reservation systems. The IT organization consolidated data from the different airline reservation systems, creating a single source of airline information. This enabled the Rosenbluth agents to provide the best solutions for their customers (e.g., lowest cost, time and seat selection). A second example was Hal Rosenbluth's strategy to expand his firm's services globally by providing its global partners with access to Rosenbluth IT.

The two preceding cases will be discussed further in this chapter. Other well-known and often referenced cases that fit the technology potential perspective include Otis Elevator[6] and Frito Lay.[7] Levi Strauss, described in Chapter 11, represents another example.

Competitive Potential Perspective

The third strategic perspective, the competitive potential perspective, is pictured in Figure 3.1c. Eight percent of the companies formally assessing themselves were in this perspective. This perspective reflects how technology (current and emerging) could influence or enable new business strategies (e.g., new market opportunities), thus creating competitive advantage. Here, IT strategy is the anchor domain. IT strategy will provide the change forces that are applied to the pivot domain, the business strategy. The impact domain in this perspective is organizational infrastructure.

Executive Role as Business Visionaries

In a competitive potential perspective the role of executive management is that of a business visionary. Business managers must understand how to leverage IT to transform the business. It is critical to ensure that senior executives are aware of the potential of IT, that their visioning processes are awakened to new business/service opportunities, and that they can assess the strategic importance that IT can have on their strategies.

IT Management Role as Business Catalyst

The role of IT management is that of a business architect and catalyst. IT managers must be part of the management team and must ensure that the business executives are aware of technologies and, what is most important, how the technologies can be applied to affect the business and business strategies. Business knowledge related to technical expertise and ability to communicate IT's value in business terms is key.

IT's focus is to add value to the business strategy. IT is going to enable new opportunities for the business. How the business applies technology to influence the business strategy and create competitive advantage becomes paramount. The approach centers on ways to enhance awareness, discover opportunities, and position the firm to use IT creatively.

IT Valued on Competitive Potential

The IT performance criteria in this competitive potential perspective are consistent with the performance criteria of the previously discussed technology potential perspective. Like technology potential, competitive potential assesses how the application of IT can have a direct influence on the company's clients and customers. IT is typically a profit center or investment center. Again, areas such as competitive advantage, revenue increases, improving customer relationships, and reducing risks are evaluated.

STRATEGIC PLANNING APPROACH

The strategic planning method for competitive potential is to leverage the IT strategy into a business strategy. Here, techniques such as Porter's value chain[8] and technology scans can play a major role in helping to identify how technologies can be applied to the business. There is a tight linkage to business process reengineering. Some techniques will be interwoven into the business strategy effort, and/or reengineering will follow the IT strategy effort. This is necessary to bring process issues into accord with changes in technology. Prototyping provides techniques to visualize how the technology will work in the business environment

CASE STUDIES

American Airlines' *SABRE* computerized reservation system,[9] as of 1990, manages over forty-five million fares and over four hundred million changes per month. *SABRE* supports over two thousand messages per second and over five hundred thousand passenger names every day. Clearly, CEO Bob Crandall's business vision of how to apply technology was critical. However, the relationship that CIO Max Hopper has had with Bob Crandall and the other business executives of American Airlines was key to recognizing and leveraging the technologies that have been available since the mid-1960s. Technologies driving the business in American Airlines began with fixed-head disk technology and have evolved through on-line terminal improvements, networks, and especially EDI technologies.

A second example is Baxter International.[10] Baxter's buyout of American Hospital Supply (discussed in Chapter 11) was motivated by their ASAP (Analytical Systems Automatic Purchasing) system. ASAP provides the capability for Baxter customers to order, track, and manage the status of purchases for the over one hundred thousand products that are available in the health care industry. The technology that improved service to American Hospital Supply customers started with prepunched IBM cards in 1963. It evolved from touch-tone telephone (1967), teletype (early 1970s), and bar codes (1981) to microcomputers in 1984. To respond to new competitor systems and hospital demands to consolidate different vendor systems, ASAP provided a multivendor system in 1988. Providing early direct access of ASAP to its customers gave Baxter a significant competitive advantage. The CEO of American Hospital Supply, Karl Bays, who led the effort, states: "The computer is at the heart of our success."

A third example is McGraw-Hill, described earlier as an example of strategy execution. McGraw-Hill has evolved to the competitive potential perspective. After reengineering the key textbook processes, it implemented the IT infrastructure and applications to support the changes. Currently, McGraw-Hill's business strategy for college textbooks is being driven by IT. The Primis electronic publishing system, consisting of the educational and professional material available in its data base and the technology/architecture to deliver it, enables the strategy for McGraw-Hill's textbook market.

LEADING EDGE OR TRAILING EDGE?

In thinking about the competitive potential or technology potential perspectives, one must consider those firms that were/are second (and subsequent) to apply new technologies to augment business strategies. Questions such as the time it will take for these subsequent companies to carry out these technologies, especially as they relate to having the IT architecture in place to support these technologies, become critical.

If these infrastructural components are not in place, it might take several years for them to catch up with leading competitors. It might take more time then is permissible for the company to stay in business. Think about the second and third and other subsequent companies that set up ATMs in your area. Think about the need for the banks to have the respective architectures in place to support ATMs. Johnson & Johnson's response to ASAP, described in Chapter 11, further exemplifies this point. These subsequent firms did not have to go through time-consuming business cases to justify the technologies to ensure that they were providing similar offerings as their more assertive competitors.

The same ideas hold true for the other airline reservation companies that lagged behind American Airlines and United Airlines. The value to these enterprises might have been survival. As described by Keen in Chapter 4, once new technology is applied to change the rules of competition in an industry, at least 50% of the companies in the industry will disappear within a decade. These leading firms are leveraging their IT investments while building their IT competencies.

Service Level Perspective

The fourth strategic perspective is service level potential, pictured in Figure 3.1d. Sixteen percent of the organizations surveyed believe their organizations fit this perspective. Only 4% of the companies formally assessing themselves were in this perspective. This suggests that an additional 12% of the organizations were not focusing appropriately when defining their strategies. In this case many organizations did not recognize the potential of their IT organization. Here again the IT strategy provides the change forces (the anchor domain). In this perspective the direction is clockwise. The pivot domain is the IT infrastructure. The domain being affected by the pivot domain, the impact domain, is the organizational infrastructure. In the service level perspective the focus is on how IT can better deliver products and services to support business processes. Assessing how IT can improve its own business processes is also considered in this perspective.

Executive Role to Prioritize IT Projects

The role of top management is setting priorities for IT projects. Note that the business strategy box is not included in this perspective. Projects that are selected do not directly impact the business strategy. IT supports areas such as office systems and relational databases. They might even be migrating to client servers. Since the business will not be impacted by IT, top management tends not to play an active role. This leads to IT becoming a business within a business.

The objective should be for IT to become part of the business.

Here, business executives balance short-term objectives with the needs of long-term investment in IT architecture. Many companies in this perspective rely on steering committees, which consist of representatives of the management team, who meet to identify and set priorities for IT projects that do not have a direct impact on business strategies. Steering committees should focus more of their attention on strategic business issues and opportunities.

IT Managers are Service Providers

The role of IT management is that of a service manager. The primary focus is to satisfy the users of IT services. "Users" typically refers to employees of the enterprise. IT is focused on being a business within a business. The IT manager is the "executive leader" of the business, which primarily delivers services to the internal organization. Strategic management is now a process for deciding how to respond to the wants and needs of an internal customer.

IT Evaluated on End-User Satisfaction

Performance criteria are typically used to focus on end-user satisfaction. Applications of vehicles like service level agreements (SLA) are frequently used here. SLAs define the type of support that IT will provide. Too often, value assessments are based on technical achievements rather than value to the business. IT focuses on technical areas such as systems availability, performance increases, defect reduction, applying end-user surveys, and, most often, those end-users who complain about IT services.

These are important issues to understand for managing IT but not the business. In this environment IT takes on responsibilities such as formulating policies and controlling interorganizational transactions. The scope of the technologies to be coordinated by the IT function has expanded significantly as processors, networks, personal computing, and office automation have merged. This approach centers on understanding the viability of the IT function to plan and reflect changing structures and trends.

Strategic Planning Approach

The strategic planning method used in this service level perspective could either be IT planning, IT process reengineering, or executing a previously defined project. Which of the three planning approaches to apply depends on whether IT needs to focus on its own organization and processes or to develop or carry out a complex plan. These plans are based on the IT strategies that have been previously built. If the strategies and IT plans have been in place, look at more detailed functional plans that will help carry out the respective IT strategies. Frequently, IT executives in this perspective recognize the need to develop plans to educate their business executives on the value IT can have on the business. Depending on the situation, the difficulty and approach to accomplishing this may differ.

In this service level perspective there is opportunity for outsourcing IT services. This is especially true when IT is not providing support to the key business strategies. Establishing partnerships such as outsourcing IT (all or some part) becomes a major consideration for organizations in the service level perspective over a "long" period of time.

Automatic Data Processing (ADP) is a well-known company that provides outsourcing capabilities. Its payroll service, which supports over 12% of the U.S. work force, pays or supports the payroll for 225 thousand people. Manufacturers Hanover Trust, Canadian Trust, and Investors Diversified Services, examples described in Chapter 11, illustrate changes in IT organization and infrastructure. Chapter 12's presentation of a utility being driven by a concern for cost savings through economies of scale is consistent with the service level perspective over a "long" period of time.

Cycling through the Strategic Alignment Model

This section describes a structured approach for cycling through the model. The application of the strategic alignment model does not rest with just assessing the components of the model, identifying the initial perspective and the planning approach, and then applying it. How the enterprise cycles through the strategic alignment model as it executes different planning approaches is key.

Identifying the Current Perspective

To begin the first cycle, the current perspective must be known. Start by identifying which of the four quadrants must be addressed first. The assessment should identify which of the four boxes has the largest opportunity for improvement. It is the area that the executive team believes needs to be focused on, the domain pivot.

Having identified the domain pivot, next identify the domain anchor. The domain anchor is going to be the area that will provide the change forces that will be applied to the domain pivot. It is the domain that will be the enabler, the catalyst, and sometimes even the driver of change in the enterprise. With both the domain anchor and domain pivot identified, the general direction (clockwise or counterclockwise) that should be pursued will be clear. The third box is the impact domain. Thus, the three boxes and the direction are selected. Therefore, the perspective is identified.

The following examples show how (what is thought to be) the most common perspective—strategy execution—emerges in practice. The three cases previously described (IBM Credit, MBL, and McGraw-Hill) followed a similar pattern. Each recognized the need to reengineer key business processes. IBM Credit wanted to reduce the time required to arrive at quotes for computer financing. MBL wanted to enhance the underwriting and issuing of insurance policies. McGraw-Hill wanted to distinguish its editing, marketing, and distribution of college textbooks.

Each case began by reengineering important business processes. The pivot domain for all of these organizations was organizational infrastructure. The impetus for these changes came from the senior management team. The business strategy was well defined and communicated. The anchor domain was business strategy. Following the counterclockwise direction, the IT infrastructure became the impact domain.

The Next Iteration

Having identified the initial perspective and initial direction for the first iteration, continue in the same clockwise or counterclockwise direction. For the second iteration, the box that was the pivot in the previous iteration becomes the anchor domain, the domain that was the impact domain in the previous iteration becomes the pivot domain, and the box that was ignored in the previous iteration becomes the impact domain. The previous anchor domain is not included in this cycle. Therefore, the domain that was most recently addressed has become the catalyst for the next cycle. This should be the most current, and it should be in good position to drive the next cycle. It now becomes the impetus for the subsequent iteration. Following this cycle ensures alignment.

Continuing with the strategy execution examples begun earlier, in this second iteration the organizational infrastructure became the anchor, the IT infrastructure became the pivot, and the IT strategy became the impact domain. Therefore, the cycle continues in the counterclockwise direction. McGraw-Hill was previously described as evolving from the strategy execution perspective to the competitive potential perspective. Subsequent iterations would typically cycle in a counterclockwise direction. This example is continued in the next section of this chapter.

Cycling in a clockwise direction would evolve in a similar fashion. Continue to move what was the previous pivot domain to the role of anchor domain. This will drive changes to the perspective. Changing the perspective alters the strategic planning approach applied, which requires a reassessment of the roles of stakeholders, focus areas, and values. Changing the perspective and the strategic planning approach fosters the ability of the organization to identify innovative opportunities and to achieve alignment.

Some important points to consider include the fact that the initial cycle is usually the most difficult. This is true because the enterprise is using new information, new techniques, and new teams. However, once experienced, the subsequent processes flow well. The second point is to continue cycling or iterating clockwise or counterclockwise based on the initial flow. This is done primarily to ensure that the domains are kept in balance. The description of the other perspectives, later in this section, illustrates this point. The number of times one cycles depends upon the effort involved to complete the cycles and when diminishing returns are experienced. Naturally, before proceeding with an iteration, one should assess each of the four domains. This ensures that something hasn't arisen that would or should change the perspective, the direction, or the flow of the process. Remember, strategic alignment is not a single event. Strategic alignment is a continuous journey of transformation.

Other Perspectives

Thus far only the four original perspectives have been described. However, experience has clearly shown the need to define other perspectives.

ORGANIZATIONAL IT INFRASTRUCTURE

This perspective, illustrated in Figure 3.5a, focuses on exploiting changing organizational infrastructure capabilities with IT. 9% of the companies formally assessing themselves were in this perspective. In this perspective, the organizational infrastructure is viewed as providing the direction for IT. Organizational infrastructure is the anchor domain, IT infrastructure is the pivot domain, and IT strategy is the impact domain.

For example, after completing a reengineering effort in the strategy execution perspective, a plan might call for applying IT to the enhanced business processes. This was illustrated by the McGraw-Hill Primis example. In this perspective the role of top management is to prioritize projects and the role of IT management is to enable business process reengineering.

IT INFRASTRUCTURE STRATEGY

This perspective, illustrated in Figure 3.5b, focuses on exploiting emerging IT infrastructure capabilities to support new strategic IT offerings. Two percent of the companies formally assessing themselves were in this perspective. In this perspective, the role of IT infrastructure is viewed as driving or enabling the IT strategy. For example, after defining changes to the application delivery process, there is a need to apply new technological tools (e.g., Computer Aided Software Engineering or Object Oriented Programming System). A second example is when there are plans to expand the network calling for new network management tools. McGraw-Hill's implementation of the new Primis application fits this perspective, which calls for top management to sponsor a project and IT to manage the project.

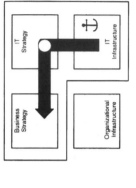

a) Organizational IT Infrastructure Perspective
- Organization Infrastructure--the anchor domain
- IT Infrastructure--the pivot domain
- IT Strategy--the impact domain

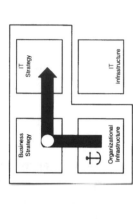

b) IT Infrastructure Strategy
- IT Infrastructure--the anchor domain
- IT Strategy--the pivot domain
- Business Strategy--the impact domain

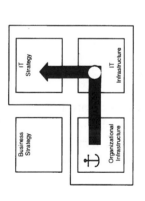

c) IT Organizational Infrastructure
- IT Infrastructure--the anchor domain
- Organizational Infrastructure--the pivot domain
- Business Strategy--the impact domain

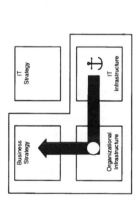

d) Organizational Infrastructure Strategy
- Organizational Infrastructure--the anchor domain
- Business Strategy--the pivot domain
- IT Strategy--the impact domain

Figure 3.5.

IT ORGANIZATIONAL INFRASTRUCTURE

This perspective, illustrated in Figure 3.5c, focuses on exploiting emerging IT infrastructure capabilities to enhance the organizational infrastructure. Eight percent of the companies formally assessing themselves were in this perspective. In this perspective, the IT infrastructure is viewed as enabling the organizational capability. IT infrastructure is the anchor domain, organizational infrastructure is the pivot domain, and business strategy is the impact domain.

For example, after completing a research and development prototype using imaging technology, the organization wants to enhance the processes that are candidates for applying the new technology. As USAA experienced, to exploit the potential process improvements from digitizing its customer records (described earlier in this chapter) they needed to reengineer their client service support process. The enabling view, driven primarily by the need for current and future flexibility of IT and described in Chapter 12, illustrates the application of IT-enabled changes to important business processes. This perspective calls for top management to play a leadership role and IT management to be a business process architect.

ORGANIZATIONAL INFRASTRUCTURE STRATEGY

This perspective, illustrated in Figure 3.5d, focuses on exploiting emerging organizational infrastructure capabilities to enhance new products and services, influence the critical aspects of strategy, and develop new forms of relationships. Over 3% of the companies formally assessing themselves were in this perspective. In this perspective, the role of organizational infrastructure is viewed as enabling enhancements to the business strategy. Organizational infrastructure is the domain anchor, business strategy is the domain pivot, and IT strategy is the impact domain.

After USAA carried out the technological vision of its CEO, it reengineered its agent process. The new process was used to enhance its business strategy. The strategy was to provide a "one-stop" interface for clients calling agents. In addition to enabling any agent to respond to any client, USAA decided to further empower its agents by providing them with online knowledge to suggest new service offerings at the time of the call. USAA is now offering its members the capability to do their banking and investing online. In this perspective the role of top management is business process visionary and IT management supports the transformation.

Fusion

There are occasions as described in Chapter 2 where the pivot domain is not directly next to the anchor domain. Forty percent of the companies formally assessing themselves were in one of the four fusion categories. For example, as pictured in Figure 3.6a, this is the situation if the IT infrastructure is identified as the box needing improvement (the pivot domain) and the business strategy is identified as the strongest box (the anchor domain). There is a solid business strategy that recognizes the need to enhance the IT infrastructure. None of the previously described perspectives fits. The diagonal is not followed because organizational infrastructure and IT strategy must play a strong role in these situations.

Apply the two perspectives that fuse toward IT infrastructure. It is recognized here that the business strategy is the anchor domain. The two perspectives that use business strategy as the anchor and IT infrastructure as the impact domain will be fused. This suggests carrying out both strategy execution (Fig. 3.1a) and technology potential (Fig. 3.1b) perspectives concurrently. Which of the two perspectives to begin with depends on the strength of the respective pivot domains.

Start with the perspective that has the weakest pivot. For example, if organizational infrastructure is considered weaker than IT strategy, the organization should start with the strategy execution perspective. Technology potential should follow close behind. The key in this example is to ensure that IT infrastructure is enhanced, thus the name "IT Infrastructure Fusion." This perspective is consistent with the Dependent View described in Chapter 12.

This is the most common fusion that occurs, by a significant margin. Twenty-six percent of the organizations formally assessing themselves were in this category. The other combinations are described here for completeness. The need to fuse IT strategy with business infrastructure is illustrated in Figure 3.6b. This example of organization infrastructure fusion suggests carrying out both competitive potential (Fig. 3.1a) and service level (Fig. 3.1d) perspectives concurrently. This fusion has been experienced in 6% of the assessments.

Business strategy fusion (Fig. 3.6c), which uses IT infrastructure as the anchor and business strategy as the pivot, has been seen in only 3% of the firms doing formal assessments.

IT strategy fusion (Fig. 3.6d), which uses organizational infrastructure as the anchor and IT strategy as the pivot, has been seen in 4% of the organizations formally assessing themselves.

Continuing to cycle through any of the fusion perspectives represents what is called a *double-loop process*. This approach goes beyond addressing

a) **IT Infrastructure Fusion**

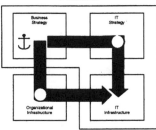

Combination of:
 • Strategy Execution Perspective
 • Technology Potential Perspective

b) **Organization Infrastructure Fusion**

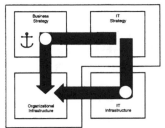

Combination of:
 • Competitive Potential Perspective
 • Service Level Perspective

c) **Business Strategy Fusion**

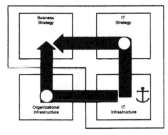

Combination of:
 • IT Infrastructure Strategy
 • IT Organizational Infrastructure

d) **IT Strategy Fusion**

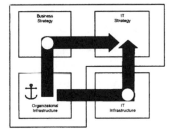

Combination of:
 • Organizational IT Infrastructure
 • Organizational Infrastructure Strategy

Figure 3.6. Fusion

all four domains like the previously described cycles. Cycling in both directions through fusion ensures that all of the domains are addressed from both clockwise and counterclockwise directions. Pursuing this approach demands additional time and expense. The recommended approach is to formally reassess the original perspective after completing each phase to ensure that the organization is cycling appropriately through the model.

Summary

There is no prescribed set of functions, organization, or methods appropriate for all situations and goals. Effective managers need to be familiar with the ideas presented to be able to choose the appropriate course of action. Assessing the current strategic alignment perspective with the associated roles and strategic planning methods provides a strong foundation to begin the journey. The strength of the strategic alignment model is that it addresses all of the factors that influence the potential of IT to provide business value in a systematic way.

The role of IT in transforming the enterprise is dependent on its perceived importance to the business as viewed by top management. The importance of IT is reflected in the way in which it participates in the strategy-formulation process. The IT function should become more influential during the creation of business strategies. The trend is to integrate IT into the formal strategic framework.

Following strategic alignment allows both IT- and business-oriented managers to communicate and become partners with each other. It ensures that new technologies will result in new commercial opportunities, leading to business growth, profits, and competitive and strategic advantage. The enterprise should recognize and exploit IT capabilities to positively influence business scope, governance, organization, and competitive forces. Strategic alignment provides a vehicle to reposition the IT function by ensuring the alignment of IT with the enterprise.

It is important to recognize that the selection of an approach to derive a strategy often imposes different perspectives. The executive team must ensure that it has chosen the right approach. The strategic management process should be viewed as dynamic and continuous. The derived strategy must be meaningful, understandable, and executable. Executives should regularly revise their planning process. Too often, the planning process reflects what an enterprise has done rather than what it should do. Shifting perspective requires carrying out new approaches, developing new ideas, and even defining new languages. In essence, it is this shift in perspective (cycle through the model) that is central to alignment. The planning processes must continuously adapt to ensure that, over time, an effective alignment of IT strategy, business strategy, infrastructure, and processes is achieved.

Establishing harmony between IT and business strategies should be included as a key part of management planning for the enterprise. Harmony will ensure that there is a focus on strategic achievement, not just organizational achievement. It should force the identification of specific business strategies and objectives and the role IT plays in achieving those strategies, using terms the business understands. This is strategic alignment.

Application of the strategic alignment model begins by analyzing the current and future states for each of the twelve model components. It continues by identifying the appropriate current perspective. After going through a strategic alignment assessment with a representative executive team, one of two results will occur: (1) There will be consensus regarding the current perspective of the organization. If this is the case, the framework provides the appropriate roadmap. (2) There will be disagreement among the management team regarding the current organizational perspective. If this occurs, further discussion will be required before proceeding. It is most important to ensure that the management team is in harmony before proceeding with its strategic planning process.

Having identified the perspective, evaluate the respective characteristics that are highlighted in the matrix in Figure 3.2. This will help identify and marshal the key stakeholders and the roles necessary to define the appropriate strategic planning method. Having defined the planning method, the next step is to carry it out. Good luck!

Notes

1. Henderson and Thomas, "Aligning Business and IT Domains: Strategic Planning in Hospitals," Hospital and Health Services Administration, 37: 1(1992): 71-87.
2. J. F. Rockart, "Chief Executives Define Their own Data Needs," *Harvard Business Review* 79209 (March 1979).
3. IBM Corporation, *Business Systems Planning Information. Systems Planning Guide* (1984).
4. Harvard Business School. United Services Automobile Association (USAA), 1/89.
5. IBM Advanced Business Institute, "Transforming Reservation Services," *Rosenbluth Travel Vignette* (December 1991).
6. Harvard Business School. Otisline Case Studies A, and B, 7/90; Otisline Revisited, University of Virginia, Darden, 6/90.
7. Harvard Business School. Frito Lay Inc Case Studies A, B, C, and D, 5/91.
8. M. E. Porter, V. E. Millar, "How Information Gives You Competitive Advantage," 85415 (August 1985).
9. M. D. Hopper, "Rattling SABRE—New Ways to Compete on Information," *Harvard Business Review* 90307 (June 1990).
10. Harvard Business School. Baxter Healthcare Corporation: ASAP Express, 9-186-005, 4/86, 9-188-080, 2/91.

II

Business Strategy

4

Aligning IT with New Competitive Strategies

❖

BART VICTOR, B. JOSEPH PINE II, and

ANDREW C. BOYNTON

❖

Chapter Summary

1. The way a firm views its business, customers and competition is critical to successfully aligning its business and IT strategy.

2. Firms in conditions of change have to evolve their products and processes in order to compete. There are four business models they can adopt: (a) invention—dynamic process and product change; (b) mass production—stable product and process change; (c) continuous improvement—stable product but dynamic process change and (d) mass customization—dynamic product but stable process change.

3. Of these models, continuous improvement or mass customization are the most needed today, although invention and mass production can still be successful under the right conditions.

4. Each of these models has significant implications for the style and structure of the organization, and its use of IT.

5. There are two useful ways of understanding how the use of IT will vary. Firstly, distinguishing between IT which automates (de-skills or eliminates people), and IT which augments (enhances skills). Secondly, to see how IT affects tasks vs relationships.

6. Essentially, (a) mass customization uses IT to enhance relationships, but de-skills tasks; (b) invention uses IT to enhance both relationships and skills; (c) mass production uses IT to de-skill tasks and focuses on processes rather than relationships; and (d) continu-

ous improvement uses IT to enhance skills, but again, focuses on processes rather than relationships.

7. Technologically speaking, mass production results in multiple IT infrastructures; invention relies on highly decentralized, and temporary application development; continuous improvement depends on highly-interactive and inter-connected databases; and mass customization focuses on modular systems that can be quickly and cheaply linked together, and then decoupled as the situation dictates.

8. The firm could benefit by deciding which of these modes, or combination of modes, it wants to be in, before trying to apply the strategic alignment model described in Chapters 2 and 3. Albeit, it relates most with the Strategy Execution Perspective.

Starting with the Right Business Model

Today, the importance of ensuring that a firm's IT supports and enhances its business cannot be overstated. However, we believe that the key issue is choosing what business model the firm should embrace. It is the firm's business model—its mind-set for viewing the nature of its business, its customers, and its competition—that governs both its business strategy and its use of IT.

For strategy and IT to be effectively aligned, they have to be suited to the same business model. That model, in turn, has to be appropriate for the business environment faced by the firm. Only limited success—and often disastrous consequences—can be expected unless all of these elements come together consciously, consistently, and cohesively.

This chapter describes a lens for viewing business, competition, and external and internal pressures, called the "product–process–change matrix," that gives rise to four distinct business models: invention, mass production, continuous improvement, and mass customization. Each of these models can be successful under the right conditions, though more and more companies are embracing the latter two to better deal with increasingly demanding customers, accelerating technological change, and intensifying competition.

Once the appropriate model is chosen, the strategic alignment framework can be used to determine how best to align IT with the right strategy and which are the most suitable infrastructures and processes to support the chosen approach.

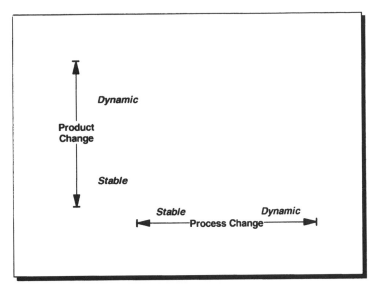

Figure 4.1. Product-Process Change Matrix

The Product–Process–Change Matrix

Most firms are now experiencing rapid and continuous change in their business environments. The product–process–change matrix shown in Figure 4.1 explains the impact on companies. On the vertical axis, product change reflects the demands for new goods or new services. Firms change products because of such needs as competitor moves, shifting customer preferences, or entering new geographical or national markets.

On the horizontal axis, process change means altering the procedures and technologies used to produce or deliver products or services. (*Process*, as it is used in this chapter, refers broadly to all of the organizational capabilities resulting from people, systems, technologies, and procedures that are used to develop, produce, market, and deliver products or services.)

These two types of change can be either stable or dynamic. Stable change is slow, evolutionary, and generally predictable, while dynamic change is rapid, often revolutionary, and generally unpredictable.[1] Taken together, these types of change provide four possible combinations of "change conditions" that can confront an organization. As illustrated in Figure 4.2, each combination defines a business model appropriate to the conditions:

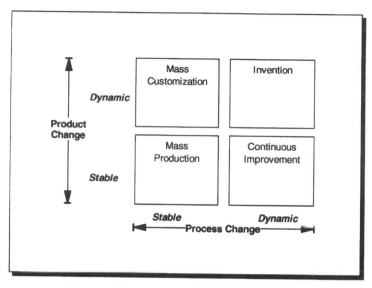

Figure 4.2.   Product-Process Change Matrix

- Invention: dynamic product and process change
- Mass Production: stable product and process change
- Continuous Improvement: stable product and dynamic process change
- Mass Customization: dynamic product and stable process change

The product–process–change matrix can serve as a valuable lens through which managers can (1) assess their competitive position by understanding where their firms have been in the past; (2) consciously choose a business model appropriate to today's (and tomorrow's anticipated) environment; and (3) clarify how to use the strategic alignment framework to craft the business and IT strategies, infrastructures, and processes appropriate to the model.

Old Competitive Strategies:
Mass Production and Invention

To understand how the matrix can be used to formulate strategy, each of the four quadrants is assessed in turn, beginning with invention and mass

TABLE 4.1. Old Competitive Business Models

Business Model	Invention	Mass Production
Focus	Creation through intellect and skill	Efficiency through stability and control
Strategic advantage	High differentiation	Low cost
Organizational form	Organic	Mechanistic
Structure	Fluid, ever-changing	Bureaucratic
Processes	Ill-defined, non-repeatable, always changing	Well-defined, rarely changed

production. Together, these quadrants represent what we call the *old competitive reality*. Table 4.1 summarizes the characteristics of each.

Invention: Dynamic Product and Process Change

This business model arose to take advantage of conditions involving both dynamic process and product change. The focus of invention organizations is on *creation through intellect and skill*. The people in these organizations—generally craftspeople, artisans, or professionals (such as scientists, engineers, and programmers)—use the knowledge and skills gained through education, apprenticeship, and experience to frequently create small volumes of new products, while constantly innovating the processes required to develop and produce them.[2]

To take advantage of the possibilities of change, workers in invention organizations are assumed to require a wide degree of latitude in the exploration of new ideas, highly skilled jobs, and little responsibility for the costs of production. These organizations are often separate research and development units within mass production organizations. Indeed, the prototypical invention design is a research organization like Bell Labs.

Of course, the strategic advantage of the invention model is high differentiation, or the ability to come up with new, distinct, and desired innovations. Within this generic advantage there is wide latitude for organizations to seek out their own competitive advantages through specific strategies that may emphasize innovativeness, quality, tailoring, frequency of introductions, and other such attributes. The invention organization is inherently designed for change since product specifications and work processes are unpredictable and constantly shifting. To compete under invention conditions, firms decentralize decision-making, broadly define jobs, develop few rules or procedures, and subjectively evaluate performance.

In keeping with the "organic" design of the organization (as it is often called because of its ever-changing nature), these firms themselves are generally smaller in size to ensure focus on product variety and process innovation. In such an environment, investment in product-specific process capabilities is a high risk since dynamic change rapidly renders structures, systems, and know-how obsolete. For example, National Starch, a maker of a variety of adhesive products, is a firm that competes through invention, creating new and revolutionary product breakthroughs with continual investments in changing process capabilities. The company is able to charge a premium for its products, and this premium offsets the cost of constant changes to process capabilities required to support unending product invention.

National Starch competes under conditions of both dynamic product and process change. Other firms that face similar conditions and choose the invention business model must understand that strategy must revolve around high differentiation, organizational structure must be organic and fluid, and processes are necessarily ill defined and constantly changing.

Mass Production: Stable Product and Process Change

Throughout this century most large companies have competed under conditions of stable product and stable process change. Under these conditions, product specifications and demand are relatively stable and predictable. This permits the firm to standardize products, centralize decision-making, routinize work and reward, develop and enforce standard rules and procedures, and allocate work to dedicated, specialized jobs—in other words, to mass-produce goods and services.[3]

The focus of firms choosing this business model is on *efficiency through stability and control*: if markets and products can be stabilized and inputs, processes, and outputs can be controlled, then the firm can gain the efficiency it needs to be successful. The strategy of such firms is always based on economies of scale and low costs, striving for the largest size and lowest cost structure in the industry.

The organizational form of mass production firms is mechanistic, resulting in a structure that is often large, hierarchical, bureaucratic, and vertically integrated. Strategy and command are isolated from the work itself in management control units.[4] Maximum efficiency is achieved by dedicating the capital and human assets of the firm to the production of standardized goods or services.[5] Competitive advantage and profitability are fundamentally founded on reduction of unit costs.

Change—even thinking about change—in either process or product is anathema to the mass production formula. Changes in product make machinery obsolete, force costly changeovers, and reduce managerial control. Changes in process complicate individual jobs, raise waste and error, and increase unit costs. Thus, by design the mass production or mechanistic organization is intended to respond to and initiate as little change as possible.[6]

This design for stability requires limiting product variety, as illustrated by Henry Ford's famous promise to deliver a car painted any color the customer desired, as long as it was black. The design also requires limiting process innovation: Du Pont managers used to classify production lines into those which had been standardized and those yet to be standardized.

The New Competitive Strategies: Continuous Improvement and Mass Customization

While mass production and invention have been the predominant forms of competition during the twentieth century, today that is changing. Many firms are facing neither simultaneous *dynamic–dynamic change* (where high costs of process innovation are supported because premium prices are available from the continuous product innovation) nor simultaneous *stable–stable change* (where the focus is on building stable, efficient processes in response to predictable product demands). Instead, these companies are facing a new and different set of conditions, marked by different characteristics and qualities of change: stable product and dynamic process change or dynamic product and stable process change.

Organizations competing under these new conditions of change are essentially operating in ways that contradict the old assumptions about competition.[7] For example, firms such as Westpac, Bally Engineered Structures, Asea Brown Boveri, Corning's Telecommunication Sector, and USAA are now competing on product or service customization or innovation without abandoning a cost advantage. Firms such as Citibank's U.S. Card Product Group (CPG) and IBM are frequently and significantly improving process quality, speed, and flexibility, while simultaneously lowering costs.

These firms, and others like them, are competing on new terms by embracing new business models suitable to these conditions. These models are summarized in Table 4.2.

TABLE 4.2. New Competitive Business Models

Business Model	Continuous Improvement	Mass Customization
Focus	Customer satisfaction through process improvement	Individual customer fulfillment through flexibility and responsiveness
Strategic advantage	Quality + low cost	Customization + low cost
Organizational form	Integrative	Dynamic network
Structure	Team-based	Modular
Processes	Always improving; undergoing microtransformations	Flexible, responsive, modular

Continuous Improvement: Stable Product and Dynamic Process Change

In some markets, the nature of product demand is still relatively mature, stable, large, and homogeneous. However, these markets are not necessarily havens for the traditional mass producer that achieves efficiencies through avoiding change. Rather, winning organizations are competing on dynamic process terms. That is, they are achieving constant advances in process quality, speed, and cost, advances that are providing them with real competitive advantage. The quality revolution and increasingly severe cost and time competition in such industries as automobiles, financial services, machine tools, and retailing are being led by a new kind of competitor, what we call the *continuous improvement model*.

The focus of this type of organization is on customer satisfaction through process improvement. As opposed to mass producers, these firms are very customer- or market-focused, striving to better satisfy the market as a whole through continuous process improvement. While still producing stable products and services, their strategic advantage is achieving lower costs and higher quality than those competing through the old model of mass production. Those embracing this new model thus compete under conditions of stable product change and dynamic process change.

This model is labeled "continuous improvement" because the organization manages rapid innovation and use of new process capabilities, continuously striving to better meet large, stable product requirements. In general, organizations facing a continuous improvement environment require systems and structures that facilitate long-term organizational learning about products but at the same time achieve rapid and radical changes in the processes employed to meet stable product demands.

THE IMPORTANCE OF TEAMS

Key to the continuous improvement model is an integrative organization, a team-based structure that creates an integrated and ongoing collaboration among process specialists.[8] Teams are intensive forums through which process change is pursued and implemented. The team structure permits the organization to make complex and truly value-adding transformations of its business processes. By integrating the specialized work of functional units and managing the rapid and effective refocusing of these functional units, the integrative organization can continually pursue process innovation while remaining cost-competitive with the mass producer.[9]

The importance of team-based structures for both product and process innovation has only recently been recognized in the management literature. The classic prescription in mass production has been to isolate process and product innovation from production to buffer production from the disruptions of the developers and to free the developers from the short-term concerns of production.[10] More recent research and practice have muddied this picture by demonstrating that the interdependence among functional units, production, product development, information systems, and marketing is, in reality, intensely reciprocal.

The IBM facility in Rochester, Minnesota, which won the Malcolm Baldrige National Quality Award in 1990, is a good example of this interdependence. One of the reasons cited by the Baldrige examiners for bestowing the award on the IBM development laboratory was its process for listening and reacting to business partners.

Through a program dubbed "early external involvement" hundreds of business partners and customers provided feedback directly to engineers and programmers on product functions still in development.[11] This activity resulted in a number of key incremental improvements to the product and the process.

First, the quality of the AS/400 system was greatly enhanced because hundreds of defects were found by the participants before the system's release, not after. Second, the product-development process was quickened by providing developers with a forum to air their problems and questions and gain immediate feedback; decisions were reached sooner with better consensus. Third, as a basic part of their involvement, the business partners readied thousands of applications that could be announced and shipped with the system. Key to this activity's success was the cross-functional team of development, manufacturing, and marketing personnel that made it happen.

Also crucial was that team's willingness to do whatever it took to achieve its goals, including breaking company rules or creating new ones. In contrast to the mass producer, which separates "doers" from "thinkers," the continuous improvement firm organizes labor not only to follow the rules and procedures but also to participate actively in the development of them.

While the mass producer achieves efficiency by isolating innovation from the concerns of the work force, the continuous improvement firm achieves efficiency by making innovation everyone's concern. For example, when asked how many process engineers he had, the plant manager at NUMMI, a Toyota-GM joint venture in Fremont, California, pointed to his production floor of twenty-one hundred workers and said, "twenty-one hundred."

To make process innovation efficient, continuous improvement organizations manage an ongoing sequence of what we call *microtransformations*. Innovation is pursued by cross-functional teams that collaborate to improve operating processes or plan for product enhancement. The members of these teams then turn to their function-specific work and execute the rules they just developed, accomplishing a microtransformation. In this sense the teams of continuous improvement firms are intended to be as process-innovative as invention organizations and as process-efficient as mass production firms.

The microtransformations that are created through the team-based structure have changed the role of supervision in these organizations. In the mass production design, the jobs of "doers" are designed for maximum efficiency. All work is allocated based on specialized functional capabilities and dedicated to the execution of standardized, product-defined tasks. The design of the jobs and the selection and evaluation of work processes are reserved for the managerial role. These "thinkers" are expected to preplan all doer roles and to evaluate and correct all doer work.

The difference in the continuous improvement design lies in the fact that the rules are generated by the same team that is expected to execute them. Thus, the self-managing work teams of the integrative organization make it both highly formalized and highly decentralized, both organic and mechanistic.

In addition, accomplishing these microtransformations requires the organization to support both extensive lateral cooperation and precise functional control. Team members must be able to evaluate and perform their own work as well as communicate and collaborate across functional and product boundaries to innovate the work processes.

Mass Customization: Dynamic Product Change, Stable Process Change

Mass customizers compete under opposite conditions of continuous improvers. Organizations across a variety of industries agree that customers are making increasingly unique and unpredictable product demands. Customers want the product or service that is right for them, and they want it now. As new competitors arrive and customer preferences change, predicting customer demand and articulating product specifications are becoming more difficult than ever. These are clearly conditions of dynamic product change.

However, these organizations also report that the basic processes that their companies are instituting to meet these demands are more, not less, stable. The rapid and unpredictable process technology changes that the organization first experiences soon evolve into recognizable patterns, allowing the organization to build stable but flexible platforms of process capabilities or know-how over time. As a result, organizations are able to improve process capabilities and know-how on an incremental and continual basis, thus increasing the organization's base of knowledge over time while also increasing process efficiencies. These are clearly conditions of stable process change.

If this scenario of dynamic product/stable process change, as noted on the product–process–change matrix, is indeed one of the realities of today's competitive environment (and our research tells us that managers in leading organizations believe it is), many of today's companies need to be organized and managed not for invention, mass production, or even continous improvement but for something quite different: mass customization.[12]

What is mass customization? It is the ability to serve a wide range of customers and to meet changing product demands through service or product variety and innovation, while simultaneously building on existing long-term process experience and knowledge that results in increased efficiencies. The focus of firms embracing this new business model is on individual customer fulfillment through flexibility and responsiveness. The major distinguishing characteristic of the mass customization model is its capacity to produce product variety rapidly and inexpensively. In direct con-

tradiction of the assumption that cost and variety are trade-offs, mass customizers organize for efficient flexibility, yielding a strategic advantage that
encompasses low costs, high quality, and individual customization.

DYNAMIC NETWORKS

One of the keys to mass customization is what we call the *dynamic network*
form. This is a set of modular process capabilities with a linkage system
that allows them to be brought together instantly for any particular customer order. It is important to understand that these capabilities can be
embodied in individuals, teams, software components, or manufacturing
devices, depending on the critical resources employed by the firm. Whatever the combination, the modular processes must be loosely coupled, i.e.,
not preengineered or prealigned for some known end product.[13]

The dynamic network structure permits a tailored combination of processing steps for any customer order, essentially a customer-unique value
chain. By engineering the flexibility of the processing units and coordinating the flow of materials or service needs between units, the mass customizer can produce a virtually infinite variety at costs competitive with the
mass producer.[14]

Compare dynamic networks with the design requirements for mass
production. Mass producers assume that change in product specifications
introduces higher costs because the change requires resetting production
processes, relearning production tasks, and coordinating fluctuations in
supply and processing requirements. IT is used for single products and
services that are designed to last for the long-run. People are trained and
specialized in known and long-term product or service needs. Today's
mass customizer defies this "old" logic by organizing and engineering
both the processes and the connections between processes for low-cost
flexibility.[15]

Instead of building a single-product, large-volume, focused production process, the mass customizer builds a dynamic network of potentially
infinite numbers of modular (and therefore interchangeable and inter-
compatible) individual production processes.[16] Thus, the challenge of
alignment in this dynamic network environment is to make the unpredictable combinations of processing units function both seamlessly and
efficiently.

It is important to understand that in some ways the mass customization
business model resembles mass production. There is a high degree of centralization in both models, but instead of centralizing all decision-making

for a single value chain, the mass customizer centralizes coordination and control in the hub of a web of loosely linked processing units.[17] The central decision-making function allocates the work necessary to produce the customer's product or service order.

Unlike the mass producer, the mass customizer organizes labor to work effectively in a dynamic network of relationships and to respond to work requirements as defined by customer needs. Whereas labor in the mass production design was organized to perform specialized tasks according to a unitary set of rules and commands, the mass customizer organizes labor to routinely respond to an ever-changing set of rules and commands. This requires that the set-up time—the time to change over between one set of inputs being processed into one set of outputs to a new set of inputs—be drastically reduced or eliminated.

Whether on the plant floor, in the back office, or on the front line, reducing set-up times in the mass-customization organization involves three things: eliminating tasks that do not need to be done, streamlining all remaining tasks so that cycle time equals value-added time, and performing as many of those tasks in parallel with the preceding process operation as possible.

One company that has done all of this is USAA, described in Chapter 3, which focuses on insurance for military and ex-military personnel. USAA completely redesigned its policy services processes through IT, replacing all of the paper files that made their way through the back office in batches with computer images accessible individually by any service representative. USAA accomplished each of the set-up time improvements mentioned above: it eliminated its paper inventory, eliminated waste in the process, brought its cycle time down to its value-added time, and now works in lot sizes of one individual customer, who receives personalized, customized service.[18] As Robert F. McDermott, CEO of USAA, put it:

> [It] changed the way we think. Now when you want to buy a new car, get it insured, add a driver, and change your coverage and address, you can make one phone call—average time, five minutes—and nothing else is necessary. One-stop, on-line, the policy goes out the door the next morning about 4 A.M. In one five-minute phone call, you and our service representative have done all the work that used to take 55 steps, umpteen people, two weeks, and a lot of money. . . . It's a revolution in the relationship between the company and the customers, who now have instantaneous access to and control over their own financial transactions, no matter whom they're talking to. We've got 14,000 employees, but every time you call, you're talking to someone who's got your file in front of them.[19]

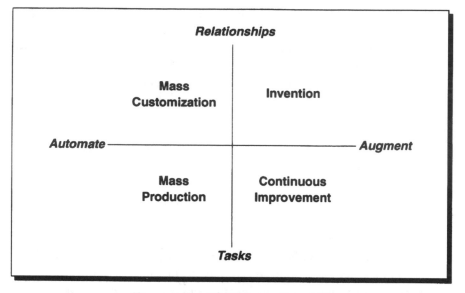

Figure 4.3.   The Primary Use of IT

In summary, the mass customizer combines the product variety of the invention model with the production efficiency of the mass producer. To accomplish this, the mass customizer employs a new organizational design based on a dynamic network rather than the assembly line. While this organization is designed to compete under conditions where product change is highly variable, it does so by maintaining an evolutionary level of stable change in processes.

Aligning IT within Each Model

A concise way of understanding the primary (but of course not the sole) means of aligning IT with each of the business models can be seen in Figure 4.3.[20] The horizontal axis depicts the classic choice in using all machinery since the Industrial Revolution, including IT: it can be used to either augment people's knowledge and skills or to automate them, deskilling and hopefully eliminating people from production. The vertical axis presents a second choice, one less thought about and therefore less understood: IT affects not only tasks (or activities, processes) that must be performed but also relationships. IT can affect and often change the very nature of the relationships among people, as well as between people and the technology itself.

MASS PRODUCTION

In the mechanistic organizations of mass production, the primary use of technology is to *automate tasks,* replacing human labor with mechanical or digital machines. Robots are the latest in a long line of machinery that achieve task automation, and classical applications like general ledger, accounts payable, and inventory control automate complex, information-laden activities.

The end result for mass producers is generally not one IT infrastructure but many, each one dedicated to the needs of each product or service or to each function. There are generally no cross-boundary, horizontal, informational flows but rather vertical stovepipes or silos of specialized information that is accessed on a "need-to-know" basis. Infrastructure is centered around the organization's need for stability and control, to be as efficient as possible (as defined within the narrow confines of each product/ service or function).

A natural consequence of this focus is the belief that people are sources of variation and come at a relatively high cost; these companies, therefore, try to automate as much as possible. This has the further natural effect of reducing labor and deskilling those workers who do remain. When the goal is to produce the same standardized product in the same way over and over again for as long as possible, this makes sense.

INVENTION

In the organic organizations of true invention environments, where process change is dynamic, the exact tasks that have to be performed to innovate a new product or service are unknown. While using IT to better perform whatever tasks arise during the often chaotic activities of invention is important, what is so often crucial for truly innovative acts of creation is collaborative efforts among a team or set of individuals. As Michael Schrage says:

> Collaboration is anything but an assembly-line process. It can't be routine and predictable. People collaborate precisely because they don't know how to—or can't—deal effectively with the challenges that face them as individuals. There's uncertainty because they genuinely don't know how they will get from

here to there. In that respect, collaboration becomes a necessary technique to master the unknown.[21]

Invention, therefore, requires that IT facilitate collaborative activities by *augmenting* people's individual knowledge and skill through collaborative *relationships* with others. This is the precise aim of such new technologies as electronic mail, groupware, electronic chalkboards, and so on.[22]

The IT infrastructure for invention organizations consists of temporary applications that are called upon as the needs of the moment dictate. Tailored, innovative products coupled with rapidly changing processes require tailored solutions and, therefore, generally decentralized application development as well as decentralized information storage and access. Applications, like all other forms of technology, are seen as tools, not replacements for the people who, through collaborative relationships, provide the creative spark necessary for success at the invention game.

It is clear across a number of industries that firms with mass production as their business model are facing increasingly turbulent market environments; it is becoming imperative that they respond faster and with more variety. Many of these firms are doing so by "going back" to invention, providing their professionals with the tools and infrastructure to do more things more quickly. While this can improve the situation for a time, it is doomed to failure if the organizational strategy, infrastructure, and processes still follow the mass production model. These will eventually impair, slow down, and otherwise impede the potential of the technology and people. This underscores the importance of aligning IT with the business. Further, the invention model does not provide goods and services at low costs, which is usually as much a part of the market imperative as faster response and greater variety.

An alternative to going back for mass producers is moving forward to the new competitive strategies. In the integrative organizations of continuous improvement, workers are not only allowed but encouraged to think about their jobs and how the process they execute can be improved. Automation still has its place but only where machines, robots, and computers can clearly do a task more effectively and efficiently than people and where improving that task is not of prime importance. (As a Toyota manager said to us, "Robots don't make suggestions.")

CONTINUOUS IMPROVEMENT

The primary use of technology in continuous improvement companies is to *augment tasks* by enhancing people's deep process knowledge and skills, linking people across functions to provide customer-focused, horizontal, informational flows, and thereby enabling them to continuously improve the processes they execute. Technologies such as measurement and analysis programs, shared databases, videoconferencing, and even machine tools are used primarily as just that—tools for enhancing specific tasks, not as replacements for human labor.

The resulting IT infrastructure tends to provide for a lot of information overlap or redundancy so that information can be shared horizontally across functions and organizations. Rather than accessed on only a need-to-know basis, information is open and accessible to all concerned and helps to focus everyone on the common goal of getting better and better at producing a particular product or service. Also, rather than being isolated in a separate function, IT professionals often participate as equal members of product or quality teams with those from development, production or delivery, and marketing.

For example, Citibank's CPG embraced continuous improvement as its business model in the 1980s. This was to a large degree led by its IS function strategy to build a system that could continually change based on the needs of the business. This was accomplished largely through direct and constant interaction between those in front-line marketing and those in systems. Where requirements used to be handed "over the wall," now they are developed jointly in cross-functional teams. Further, to manage the ongoing business, CPG managers received an enormous amount of information comparing actual figures for each product, brand, operation, and geographic area with prior periods, projections, and goals. This information was the backbone of a common language at CPG, the means of communicating. It was used to focus everyone on a common set of goals, and managers discussed the numbers extensively.[23]

MASS CUSTOMIZATION

In dynamic network organizations of mass customization, technology can still automate tasks, where that makes sense, and certainly must also augment knowledge and skills; but the demands of mass customization require technology to also *automate* the *relationships* or linkages between modular processes, ensuring that people can be brought together to create "instant teams."

For example, networks, common customer views (such as with image processing or shared data bases), computer-integrated manufacturing, workflow management, and coordination software can all be used to automate the linkages between processes and the relationships between people, enabling exactly the right resources to be brought together to service a customer's unique wants and needs. Bally Engineered Structures, Inc., for example, has a database of the skills and experiences of every person in the company, so exactly the right person for any task can be found and contacted instantly (via phone or electronic mail).

However, most of these same technologies can also be used to automate tasks for standard mass production. How they are put to use depends on the mind-set of managers and on the strategy they are trying to execute. Many managers still view the promise of advanced technologies—especially flexible manufacturing systems and computer-integrated manufacturing in production industries and workflow management and expert systems in service industries—through the lens of mass production. However, the promise of technology is not in the "lights-out factory" or the fully automated back office; it is in enabling the full diversity of capabilities that people can bring to bear on servicing customers.

The IT infrastructure of mass customizers must itself be very flexible and responsive to support a dynamic flow of goods and services. Like the products, the systems must be modular and reusable, created very quickly through fast application development so that systems development does not slow down product development. The backbone of such systems is an open, modular architecture that allows for future change, such as that provided by object-oriented programming systems.

Creating a Modular Process Architecture

This IT infrastructure mirrors the modular process architecture that enables the networked organization to dynamically bring together those processes that best satisfy each customer's requirements. This is, in fact, what separates the dynamic network of mass customization from the "traditional" network organization that has been discussed in the management literature for the past ten years or so.

Creating this level of modularity requires two things. First, developing high-quality, flexible, and responsive process modules, which is best accomplished through continuous improvement. In integrative organizations, however, these processes are tightly linked, always the same processes following one after another to create relatively standardized products or services. The second requirement for a dynamic network is to develop linkages—automated relationships—that allow the modules to be combined in unique and even unforeseen ways. At its ideal, this modular linkage system should enable processes to come together instantly, costlessly, seamlessly, and frictionlessly.

INSTANTLY

Organizations must engineer their linkages so that processes can link together as quickly as possible. This means, first, that what product or service each customer wants must be defined rapidly—preferably codesigned by the customer using tools that, rather than overload customers with too much information, present the organization's capabilities in an easy but precise manner. Second, the expressed design must quickly translate into the set of processes that can create it. Third, those processes themselves must fit together instantly. For this to occur, the organization must be certain what each process module will do; part of the linkage is a commitment between processes that the output for one is defined, expected, and matches the input required of the next. Further, part of the commitment is that each process will execute with high quality so that no time is spent in understanding what was done in the previous module or, worse, reworking it.

For example, Bally Engineered Structures discovered over many years of continuous improvement that their administrative processes were the linkages between, and were holding back, their manufacturing processes. By eliminating some activities, reducing waste and time in the remaining, and ensuring high-quality output (e.g., bills of materials), Bally was able to effect very rapid process linkages on its manufacturing floor.

COSTLESSLY

The linkages between processes must add as little cost as possible. Certainly, if a linkage is truly instant, its use (as opposed to the investment required to put it in place) will also be costless. Flexible manufacturing systems can execute any process within the envelope of variety instantly and costlessly because of the investment in technology inherently geared for economies of scope. In services, one of the keys to this is a database that carries all the information known about each customer and the service(s) that customer requires from process to process so that nothing has to be regenerated. For example, USAA uses image technology and a companywide data base so that every representative who comes into contact with a particular customer knows everything about that customer.

SEAMLESSLY

An IBM vice president once said of operating systems, "You always ship your organization." Customers can always see the organizational structure in what programs did not work well with other programs; the organization's seams always show. Since with a dynamic network a new organization is essentially put together for every customer interaction, the occasions for "showing the seams" are boundless. It is imperative to create process linkages that are as seamless as possible. The recent re-discovery of the "case worker" or "case manager" is one way that service companies like USAA and IBM Credit are ensuring that, no matter how many people each customer may come into contact with during the course of a transaction, one person establishes a relationship with the customer and can smooth over any seams that may show.

FRICTIONLESSLY

This attribute of modular linkages is potentially the most difficult to achieve for team-based integrative organizations. Teams are long-lasting, and their effectiveness is generally dependent on the personalities of the team members and their ability to work together, thus providing both the time and need for extensive team-building to reduce friction. With the "instant teams" created for every customer within a dynamic network, there is no time available for team-building; they must be frictionless from the moment of their creation.

While IT is important in effecting each of the above attributes, it is almost mandatory for this one. To be frictionless, the relationships between processes and the people executing them must be automated; information and communications technologies must be used to find the right people, to define their collective task, and to allow them to work together immediately without the benefit of ever having met before, if necessary.

Each of these four attributes is, of course, ideal and can be achieved to a greater or lesser degree depending on the host of circumstances surrounding any particular organization. It is clear, however, that the further the organization goes in creating a modular process architecture with linkages that are instant, costless, seamless, and frictionless, the more effective it will be in mass-customizing products and services.

For example, a significant problem many companies have when they start down the path of mass customization is presenting their sales force—or, worse, their customers—with so many options and so much information that no one can figure out which particular product or service is the right choice.[24] So common is this problem that Trilogy Development Group of Austin, Texas, has created a product configurator that allows manufacturing companies like Dell Computer, Hewlett-Packard, AT&T, and LSI Logic to confer with customers at the level of their wants and needs, essentially

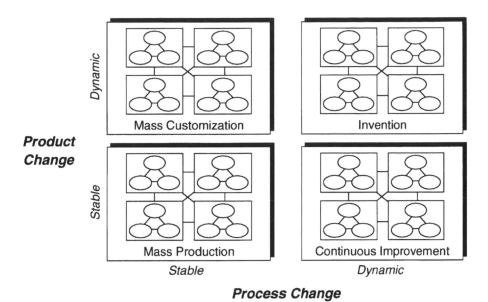

Figure 4.4.   Strategic Alignment in Dynamic Stability

hiding all actual product options. Its product, SalesBUILDER, enables sales reps and customers to work together, detailing each customer's requirements; then, using expert system technology, it automatically generates exact configurations, price quotes, and even graphical representations of the customized products.

SalesBUILDER is an example of using IT to automate the linkages between processes—in this case the linkages between sales, custom product design, and manufacturing specifications—essentially encapsulating it all into one customer-driven process. The same kind of technology could be used in services, where instead of ending with product configurations it would translate customer needs into process execution steps. Further, various companies are working on process management software to coordinate the actual execution of such software, again focusing on automating the linkages.

Conclusion

From this discussion of the differing IT infrastructures and capabilities required by each business model, the problem of alignment is clear. Each model dictates the kind of business strategy, organizational structure, and process required to fulfill its promise. Firms cannot accomplish a low-cost customization strategy with mass-production organizational structures or with an IT infrastructure appropriate to continuous improvement.

To successfully embrace a business model, the company must work to align all of the organizational and IT pieces together into one cohesive and focused package. As seen in Figure 4.4, the choice of business model (related to the strategy execution perspective) must precede the question of strategic alignment. Once that choice is made, the strategic alignment framework can provide the basis for successfully implementing the business model.

Notes

Portions of this chapter are based on work which originally appeared in A. C. Boynton, B. Victor, and B. J. Pine II, "New Competitive Strategies: Challenges to Organizations and Information Technology," *IBM Systems Journal*, 32:1 (1993): 40–64.

1. See K. Clark, "Investment in New Technology and Competitive Advantage," in *The Competitive Challenge: Strategies for Industrial Innovation and Review*, David J. Teece, ed. (Cambridge, MA: Ballinger, 1987); and M. J. Tushman, P. Anderson, "Technological Discontinuities and Organisational Environments," *Administrative Science Quarterly*, 31, (1987): (439–465).
2. D. Miller, "Configurations of Strategy and Structure: Towards a Synthesis," *Strategic Management Journal*, 7 (1986): 233–249; and T. Burns and G. M. Stalker, *The Management of Innovation* (1986).
3. P. M. Blau, P. A. Schoenherr, *The Structure of Organizations* (New York: Basic Books, 1971); and J. D. Thompson, *Organizations in Action* (New York: McGraw-Hill, 1967).
4. F. W. Taylor, *Scientific Management* (New York: Harper, 1911); and Thompson, *Organizations in Action*.
5. M. J. Piore, C. F. Sabel, *The Second Industrial Divide: Possibilities for Prosperity* (New York: Basic Books, 1984).
6. J. R. Galbraith, *Designing Complex Organizations* (Reading, MA: Addison-Wesley Publishing, 1973).
7. S. M. Davis, *Future Perfect* (Reading, MA): Addison-Wesley, 1978); C. A. Bartlett, S. Ghoshal, *Managing Across Borders: The Transnational Solution* (1989); R. E. Miles, C. C. Snow, "Organizations: New Concepts for New Forms," *California Management Review*, 28:3 (1986): 62–73; and C. K. Prahalad, G. Hamel, "The Core Competence of the Corporation," *Harvard Business Review* (May/June (1990): 79–91.

8. I. Nonaka, "Creating Order Out of Chaos," *California Management Review*, 30 (1988): 57–73; I. Nonaka, "Organizing Innovation as a Knowledge Creation Process: A Suggested Paradigm for Self-Renewing Organization," *Organizational Behavior and Industrial Relations Working Papers OBIR-41* Berkeley: University of California, (1989); and P. S. Adler, "Workers and Flexible Manufacturing Systems: Three Installations Compared." *Journal of Organizational Behavior*, 12 (1991): 447–460.

9. D. Leonard-Barton, "Implementing New Production Technologies: Exercises in Corporate Learning," in *Managing Complexity in High Technology Organizations*, (1990): 160–187; I. Nonaka, "Redundant Overlapping Organizations," *Industrial Relations Paper, series OBIR-42* (Berkeley: University of California, 1989).

10. Taylor, *Scientific Management*: R. Florida, M. Kenny, *The Breakthrough Illusion: Corporate America's Failure to Move from Innovation to Mass Production* (New York: Basic Books, 1990).

11. For a description of this activity, see B. J. Pine II, "Design, Test, and Validation of the Application System/400 through Early User Involvement," *IBM Systems Journal*, 28:3 (1989): 376–385. See also R. A. Bauer, E. Collar, V. Tang, J. Wind, P. Houston, *The Silverlake Project: Transformation at IBM* (New York: Oxford University Press, 1992).

12. For a more complete discussion of this new design, see B. J. Pine II, *Mass Customization: The New Frontier in Business Competition* (Boston: Harvard Business School Press, 1993). See also Davis, *Future Perfect*; Piore and Sabel, *The Second Industrial Divide*; A. C. Boynton, B. Victor, "Beyond Flexibility: Building and Managing the Dynamically Stable Organization," *California Management Review*, 34:1 (1991): 53–66; and S. Davis and B. Davidson, *2020 Vision: Transform Your Business Today to Succeed in Tomorrow's Economy* (New York: Simon & Schuster, 1991).

13. Boynton and Victor, "Beyond Flexibility"; Pine, *Mass Customization*.

14. Piore and Sabel, *The Second Industrial Divide*; Pine, *Mass Customization*; Davis, *Future Perfect*.

15. D. J. Teece, "Economies of Scope and Economies of the Enterprise," *Journal of Economic Behavior and Organization*, 1 (1980): 223–247.

16. Boynton and Victor, "Beyond Flexibility;" Davis, *Future Perfect*; Pine, *Mass Customization*.

17. It is important to recognize that the value-chain activities for a mass customizer (or for any other design) do not have to be owned by the company in a vertically integrated fashion. For many companies, value-chain activities are acquired from other firms, thus extending the boundaries of the organization. This has given rise to the "disaggregated value chain" concept or the "networked organization" design. Becoming a firm that relies extensively on external companies for value-chain activities is a critical strategic choice. Given the importance of maintaining tightly connected, flexible, and highly responsive process capabilities for mass customization, the decision to rely on externally owned value-

chain process requirements should be made with extreme caution. This topic deserves more extensive discussion than this chapter allows. For an excellent discussion on networks composed of multiple companies, see C. Snow, R. Miles, and H. Coleman, "Managing 21st-century Organizations" in *Organizational Dynamics*, 20:3 (Winter, 1992): 5–20.

18. M. R. Vitale, J. J. Elam, J. E. P. Morrison, *United Services Automobile Association (USAA)* (Boston: Harvard Business School Case 9-188-102, 1988); and C. A. Plesums and Barties, "Large-Scale Image Systems: USAA Case Study," *IBM Systems Journal*, 29:3 (1990).

19. Quoted in T. Steal, "Service Comes First: An Interview with USAA's Robert F. McDermott," *Harvard Business Review* 126 (September–October, 1991).

20. This figure is adapted from a presentation given by M. Schrage, syndicated innovation columnist for the *Los Angeles Times* and author of *Shared Minds: The New Technologies of Collaboration* (New York: Random House, 1990). This book provides an excellent discussion of how new information and communication technologies can augment people's creative skills.

21. Schrage, *Shared Minds*, 37.

22. Many people use "automation" as a generic term for what IT does, reflecting the success of the mass production paradigm in effecting language. This can be seen, for example, in the paper by D. Sriram, "Design as a Collaborative Process," in *Automation Based Creative Design: Current Issues in Computers and Architecture*, A. Tzonis, I. White, eds. (New York: Elsevier, 1992), where a lengthy discussion of how an intelligent agent-based architecture could support the collaborative process of design is referred to as "design automation."

23. For further information, see A. C. Boynton, B. Victor, M. Eaker, *Citibank Card Product Group*, (Charlottesville: Dardeen Educational Materials Services, Graduate School of Business, University of Virginia, 1991).

24. J. Pine, "Customers Don't Want Choice," *The Wall Street Journal* (April 18, 1994).

5

Building Global Competence

JOHN L. DANIELS and N. CAROLINE DANIELS

Chapter Summary

1 Globalization is the next logical stage in the evolution of multi-domestic or multinational companies, but few companies are achieving it.

2. National companies start on the road to globalization by becoming exporters. Typically they are not customer-sensitive in their export markets, are managed by home country nationals, and have efficient world-wide communication systems.

3. Exporters become multinationals by beginning to source and produce outside their home countries. They still have good communications, but are fundamentally or geographically orientated, and are strongly controlled by the home country headquarters. However, by being closer to their export customers, they do become more responsive to their product needs.

4. Multilocals are an alternative to multinationals. Multilocals are collections of virtually autonomous national business units, who are only loosely co-ordinated by headquarters. As a consequence, the units are much more responsive to customers, but the poor communications prevent learning from each other.

5. Japanese companies exemplify global exporters, American companies the multinational, and European companies the multilocal.

6. Global organizations attempt to 'cherry pick' the positive attributes of all three organizational forms: (a) economies of scale; (b) strong business concept; (c) decentralization of knowledge and decision-making; (d) rigorous attention to cultural fit.

7. IT is the key to becoming global, allowing knowledge to be

shared, processes to be connected, and products to be customized. However, to do this on a worldwide basis means accepting that applications might be short-lived, and that a snap-together, modular IT architecture is essential.

8. Ten attributes of a global organization are listed, ranging from business vision, through management style to implementation suggestions and performance measures. Although the authors admit that no one company exemplifies all these characteristics, they point to many who are on their way.

9. Taken together, the ten attributes form a useful basis for benchmarking your company's current status, and progress towards globalization. As such, they form an important extra dimension to the problem of aligning business and IT strategies.

The Inevitability of Globalization

Waves of change have been rolling over international business. First, there was downsizing, followed by the wave of quality. Next came the wave of customer focus, and today the wave of cycle-time compression as a competitive factor is cresting (see Fig. 5.1). The wave that is building is the wave of globalism and globalization.

Executives who do not find the wave and engage it early—those who do not, to use the surfers' term, get into the curl of the wave, where the best ride lies—are bound to falter as it crashes around them.

Just as the nineteenth-century transition from an agrarian to an industrial economy transformed the lives of people throughout the world, so too the current transition from an industrial to an information economy is transforming our lives.

The first lesson of this transformation is that these very big, real changes in the way we work and live are driven by changes in our base technologies. New technologies allow us to envision new ways to break through previously impenetrable barriers.

Then, once the potentials of a technology become more apparent as applications are invented, a supportive infrastructure, essential to wider adoption, emerges. Business and society become transformed as the infrastructure supporting the adoption of new technologies begins to be set in place.

It is part of a continuous process of evolution. For example, in the

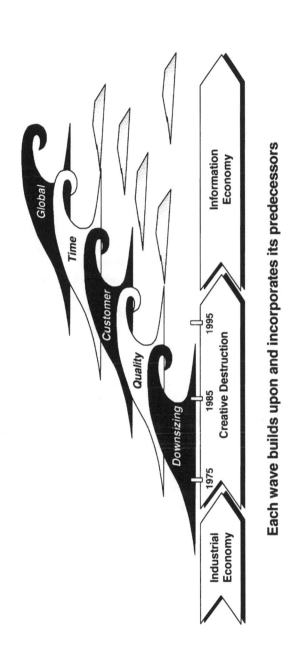

Each wave builds upon and incorporates its predecessors

Figure 5.1. Transformation has been Accompanied by Waves of Change

nineteenth and twentieth centuries, the systematic development of transportation infrastructures allowed companies to move their products further
distances; but the products, by and large, were conceived of, developed,
and manufactured in a limited number of places.

Today, these constraints no longer exist. The reduced cost of transportation allows goods to be produced almost anywhere; and as the information
and communications infrastructure becomes more widespread, companies
can have truly global aspirations. Today, we have satellites and fiber optics,
television and teleconferencing, personal computers and multimedia workstations, local-area networks and wide-area networks, Internet on-line databases, compact discs with read-only memory (CD-ROM), electronic mail
and voice mail, and facsimile (fax) machines. As we enter the twenty-first
century, the world is truly wired.

Globalization represents the next major stage in an evolutionary sequence that first saw domestic companies develop from exporters into either multidomestic or multinational companies (depending on the
company's penchant for decentralization or centralization), but today, despite the rapid developments in the communications infrastructure, only a
few companies are beginning to exhibit some global characteristics.

Why is globalization not a strategic priority? Many managers and executives misunderstand the whole concept of globalization. They do not yet
realize that globalization is important and urgent, and, even when they
grasp the concept and its importance, businesses do not know how to become "global."

This chapter first describes the three most prevalent global business
models that exist and lists their good and bad points from the point of view
of developing truly global competence. The three models are then compared, and a checklist of ten global attributes is proposed for the corporation of the future. Each of these attributes has fundamental implications
for the future alignment of business and IT strategies.

The Starting Point

Companies are attempting to cross the global frontier from three very different starting positions: a global exporter, a multilocal form of operation,
or a multinational form. Understanding where your company is, in terms
of its current business form and global characteristics, is an important first
step in the process of aligning and focusing a company's development as it
moves up the global learning curve. It is also a place to start when creating
a global vision.

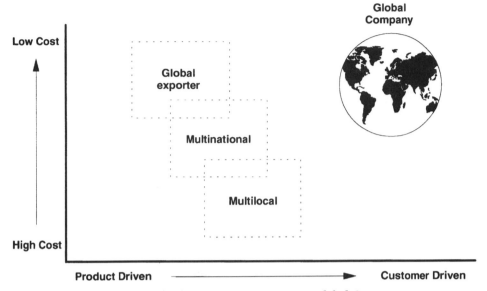

Figure 5.2.   Positioning a Company in a Global Context

Figure 5.2 shows where these three types of company fall on a two-dimensional model, with the ideal being a position at the high end of customer responsiveness and at the low end of cost.

The box in which your company currently sits determines the course it will have to plot to reach the global ideal. Of course, these boxes are generalizations, and you may feel that your company straddles boxes or, especially in large multidivisional companies, that parts of the company fall in one box and parts in another. For such companies, the key to global progress is an understanding that no single approach will work for the entire company's trip up the global ladder. In fact, for some large multidivisional companies, an argument might be made that certain divisions do not even need to "go global," at least not yet.

At the heart of the question of business forms is the question of whether or not the company can grow into the future with its current mindset, configuration of resources, and management practices. Clearly, we believe not. The goal of any business on its quest for globalism is to reconfigure itself, working from its platform of current capabilities and adding to those capabilities to face the business requirements of tomorrow. Unless a business is at least taking its first steps today on the road toward becoming truly global, moving from one of the current, somewhat rigid constructs toward the fluidity and flexibility of a globally run business, that business will face difficult challenges in the twenty-first century.

The process of becoming a truly global company will take years. Changing not only the paper structure of a company but the organizational atmosphere and the mind-set of leadership will probably take a full generation; not until those who have been doing business in "the old way" for so long retire and a new generation of global-thinking leaders comes into being will a company make the complete transition. However, there are concrete steps a company can take in the first five years of planning for and working toward a global company.

With that in mind, it is useful to take a more detailed look at the three operating structures today's internationally active companies take.

The Global Exporter

Companies are motivated to begin international activities when they realize that a market for their products and/or services extends beyond the geographic borders of their country. This expanded perception of the market carries with it the attraction of increased revenues and profits. Companies expand into the international marketplace by pushing domestic product through an expanded distribution channel. Key initial responsibilities include increasing domestic production capacity and finding suitable distribution agents.

Exporters usually develop local sales capacity in new markets by finding trading partners to act as their agents in selling, distributing, and servicing their goods. The initial investment, depending on the choice of local agent, might be very small, while the return is increased sales. Suggestions for suitable partners can come from overseas acquaintances, customers, industry colleagues, or trade departments of the countries in which the company wants to do business or of its own country.

As business develops, the responsibilities of the agent grow as products and services penetrate the market. Ultimately, the reputation of the exporter is in the hands of its trading partner. The partner's ability to manage the local distribution system must keep pace with the increased market.

It is difficult for a company to sustain whatever initial market advantages it has as an exporter in a foreign market. The market typically conspires against exporters to increase the aggregate costs to the customers: the distribution system is not under the exporter's direct control, and its agents often demand a larger cut of the pie; countries express concern about lack of local content; protective tariffs are raised; or local competition, suddenly aware of a market opportunity, emerges.

Characteristics of the exporting company include a product-push view of foreign markets; maintenance of most, if not all, value-chain activities, except sales and service, in the home country, run by home-country nationals; and complete home-country control in management. As Figure 5.2 suggests, the exporter gets its advantage by being a low-cost producer and has great difficulty being highly responsive to the customer. Examples of successful exporting companies, like Hyundai in the late 1980s, are easy to find for short periods of time; but over the long haul the export approach is seldom sustainable.

Exporters often find that success is dependent on expanding local activities early. Companies most often do this in one of two ways. They either increase the human element, by locating expatriate company representatives in the country to act as sales and marketing agents, or they add value to the product itself and make it more attractive to the local market by means of minor modifications or features to fit the local environment. We call companies that engage in such value-enhancing local modifications *global exporters*. They often make extensive forays outside of their home countries to capture knowledge about market and customer requirements. They also study competitors' operations around the world to increase their management knowledge base. While they gather and analyze this market intelligence information from other countries, however, they still run most company operations from home.

As exporters begin to set their sights on globalization, they gradually bow to local pressures and initially deploy local manufacturing activity to support local sales presence. Eventually, perhaps reluctantly, they deploy product-development in selected locations. By doing so, they begin to take on the structural appearances of a multinational.

As Figure 5.3 shows, global exporters tend to treat the world more from a geographic perspective than a business perspective. They do well at managing their companies as world business systems. However, they are very reluctant to move any core activities outside of their home country. Global exporters are not configured to do business anyplace because most of their trusted personnel and talent are concentrated in the home country or major business centers, and they rely on agents and partners to support customers in most outlying regions.

Global exporters are highly integrated, work in multidisciplinary teams, and share a strong common culture, which gets them high marks in holism. The home country is like a high-walled citadel, but barriers in national organizations are permeable, primarily because the national organizations are weak and run by expatriate home-country managers. Global exporters rely very heavily on these home-country nationals for all major decision-making, which reflects little trust in foreign employees.

Global exporters produce products that seek to find the lowest common

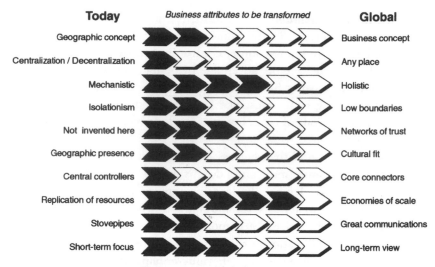

Figure 5.3. Global Exporters

denominators in product appeal so that as little customization as possible has to be done locally. These homogeneous, or "global," products are primarily successful when they are made of extremely high quality because service and support can be a real challenge for the global exporter.

Global exporters rely on very strong control and directives from home-country headquarters. Because of their highly integrated world business systems they have little overlap of resources and consequently get high economies of scale. Outside the home country, global exporting companies communicate very efficiently through formal organizational stovepipes.

Global exporters are very patient and prepared to take a long-term view of such investment decisions as subsidizing a start-up operation in a new country. However, while they do a number of things well, more often than not global exporters find themselves bound by their strongly nationalistic exporter mind-sets, and they have difficulty developing sufficient appreciation and sensitivity to the required openness of a global mind-set, which makes them globally short-sighted.

The Multinational

Being multinational is another option. Most multinationals were once global exporters, and most global exporters will probably have to pass through a multinational phase on the road across the frontier to true glob-

alism. However, that doesn't mean that the trip across the frontier to globalism will be any easier for the entrenched multinational. The trick for the
global exporter will be to pass through the multinational phase as quickly
as possible, without losing the strong attributes of the global exporter and
picking up the bad habits of the multinational.

Multinationalism usually begins with the creation of national sales and
service organizations, often followed soon after by national manufacturing
organizations. Research and development is almost certainly the last function to be moved out from the home country, and basic, or fundamental,
research often never leaves the home country and the centralized organization, while product development is distributed to prime regional market
areas. Significant innovations, however, are rapidly transferred from headquarters to the rest of the world.

The multinational develops relatively homogeneous products or services for the world. Manufacturing is distributed around the world to exploit
economies of scale and to vault barriers to entry. The multinational tries
to maximize the use of resources through strong central coordination,
rather than flexibly integrating resources to distributed competence centers.
By physically moving closer to its customers and taking advantage of scale
economies, the multinational is able to deliver fairly low-cost products to
most customers.

In a multinational company, headquarters plays a strong role in setting
strategies, policies, and establishing standards. While a matrix management
structure may be in place to handle the complexity of product/service offerings in individual locations, major decisions are made by headquarters
and communicated via outbound directives. Sales and delivery channels
tend to be regionally controlled, with some level of autonomy from corporate headquarters, provided fairly rigid revenue and profit guidelines are
met. This concern creates a bias toward the further development of home-
country and major markets since markets are often judged by profit-
generating measures.

The multinational, then, still offers a primarily product-push set of
strategies, while capturing economies of scale. By locating some operations
in countries for cost or entry reasons, the company gathers some intelligence about local customers and is more open to innovation than the global
exporter.

Multinational companies have a very different profile of global attributes than global exporters, as shown in Figure 5.4. With a much more
distributed value chain outside of the home country, they find it a more
complex task than the global exporter to manage their company as a world
business system. The greater deployment of their value chain gives them

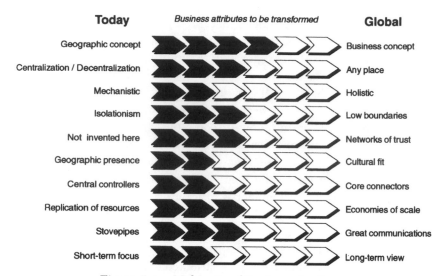

Figure 5.4. Multinational Business Attributes

more cultures and technical resources to draw upon, which tends to make the multinational a more open and innovative company. This deployment of resources also means that the multinational is much better positioned to do business any place than the global exporter.

Multinationals are less holistic than global exporters because they tend to be more bureaucratic and functionally specialized. They decentralize much more power into regional and national organizations, and they spend a lot of energy trying to create multigeographic teamwork. While national barriers are still severe impediments, multinationals are better positioned than global exporters; while they have a long way to go on building trust, they are similarly better positioned on this attribute.

Multinationals, like global exporters, produce homogeneous products for world markets, and they also produce tailored products for specific markets. Because they have much broader geographic presence than global exporters, they acculturate better.

Multinationals have a strong control mentality, but more decision-making is decentralized than in the global exporter. Given their less integrated way of working, their communication is less efficient; while many multinationals have the technology installed for point-to-point geodesic communications, they are frequently held back by their regional hub-and-spoke business-operating philosophy.

The Multilocal

Once a company expands its frontiers beyond export, management sometimes decides to develop markets with less of a strong, centralized approach and to go to the other extreme, *laissez-faire*. This approach allows management to focus on local customer expectations. Customers increasingly want customization of some aspects of products and services. The multilocal specializes in local customization to meet local customer requirements. It is through customization that companies add value to commodity goods. Local sales and delivery offer customized products.

The multilocal is customer-focused, responsive, and flexible to local requirements. The balance of power is with the national organization. These strong national organizations operate as a set of independently operating, self-reliant, and geographically dispersed units. While fostering independence and initiative, the sharing of management knowledge across boundaries is minimal, and such an approach forces unit managers to go up steep learning curves as they continuously reinvent knowledge on how to carry out the business.

The multilocal company tends to duplicate a large portion of the value chain in each country where it does business and sacrifices economies of scale to meet local market requirements. The aggregate global customer pays a high cost for this. The global customer has to deal with several separate operating units of the same company and at times has to sort out its own account administration. In multilocal companies, there is often no assurance of consistency in company policy across borders with regard to price and quality.

Any effort to create synergy by integrating ideas of processes at any great depth encounters high barriers. Since headquarters measures each unit or country by return on investment, or profit, cross-measures are not set and synergistic targets are only achieved with great difficulty. Newer markets may not get the investment earlier markets received since they are expected to "stand on their own." Multilocals take a very different approach to managing themselves and have a very different profile from global exporters and multinationals, as seen in Figure 5.5.

Multilocals do not approach the world as one business system but, rather, as a set of individual markets, each to be approached separately. Because this leads to many separate and distinct sets of operating procedures, the multilocal has more difficulty than the multinational in supporting business anyplace, though it has an edge on global exporters because of the broader geographic scope. It also means that multilocals are much more mechanistic than either global exporters or multinationals.

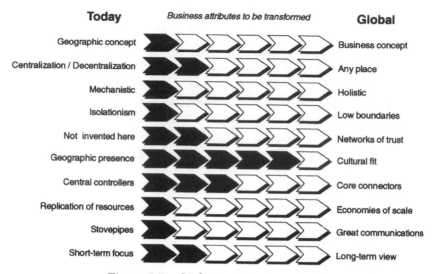

Figure 5.5.   Multi-Local Business Attributes

Multilocals have to contend with high walls built around each country, as well as the strongest case of the not-invented-here syndrome. However, multilocals have a strong advantage over the other current forms in terms of cultural fit, often leading to high-value differentiated services.

Multilocals are much less focused on formal control systems and rigid policies and procedures; corporate headquarters' role is often oriented to connecting different pieces in the organization through personal relationships. There is much less point-to-point communication, however, between operations in different countries than in other forms and much less likelihood that a physical wide-area telecommunications network exists.

Multilocals are long-term-oriented in local markets but have shown little interest to date in taking a long-term investment position in doing business globally.

Comparing the Three Types of Organization

Figure 5.6 shows comparisons in attributes between the three types of organization. As can be clearly seen, each structure has attributes closer to those of a truly global company than the others. The key to becoming global is, in effect, to cherry pick these attributes to form a single entity with all of the strong points, while divesting the company of the kind of attributes that hold it back.

Characteristic	Global exporter	Multinational	Multilocal	Global
Products and services	Homogeneous	Homogeneous, some customized	Customized, some homogeneous	Flexible architecture allowing for mass customization
Value chain activities	Highly concentrated in home country	Distributed but highly controlled by home country	Highly duplicated in each country	Highly networked and distributed around the globe
Basis of competition	Economies of scale in production	Sharing innovations outbound from H.Q.	Local responsiveness	EOS of production and knowledge, and low cost/customer driven
Organization	Home country nationals	H.Q. controls national companies	Strong national organizations, H.Q. plays primarily financial role	Decisions made at centers of competence
Customers	Global or local customers get the same treatment	Local customers supported by national sales companies global customers with difficulty	Local customer focus, global customers only with great difficulty	Supports global and local customers

Figure 5.6. Business Characteristics of Global Exporter, Multinational, Multilocal, and Global Companies

One might say that a quick way to think of the global company would be to think of a company that combines the holistic approach and ability to take advantage of economies of scale of the global exporter, the strong business concept and decentralization of knowledge and decision-making of the multinational, and the rigorous attention to cultural fit of the multilocal.

One could assign the business forms described here to a majority of companies working internationally from the three areas of the world Keniche Ohmae refers to as the *economic triad*—Japan and the Pacific Rim, Western Europe, and North America. By and large, the global exporter model is one we typically see in Japanese companies; the multinational organization is an American phenomenon; and the multilocal format is one favored by Western European companies.

The results of our 1992–1993 study conducted on behalf of IBM reinforce this. This detailed study of ten companies found their current global positions, and their thinking about how to become global in the future adhered to this expected pattern. It is, however, notable that we found that an Australian company and a Canadian company both fit what one might call the European model. The remainder of this chapter provides a summary of the findings and include quotes taken during many of the interviews. Figure 5.7 shows the position of the ten companies that participated in the study on the global chart. It is interesting to note that Pirelli was classified as being in two different positions at the same time. The cable division of the company had a multilocal approach, while the tire division more closely resembled the multinational model.

> In the Tire Sector, vehicle manufacturers are becoming global. The industry is concentrated, competition takes place on an international basis, and innovation occurs in many places around the world. The Cable Sector, on the other hand, has developed products and services to cope with different national specifications from country to country. Customers are happy with their local specifications and care less about globalization. And yet the cable product is everywhere.

Figure 5.8 shows how companies A, B, and C respectively answered the broad question: What are the first-line imperatives you see to becoming a truly global company? Each of these companies is starting from a different point on our global-position map; company A is a multilocal, company B a global exporter, and company C a multinational. The thirteen headings use nine different words or notions—balance, market, system, people, information, organization, service, customer, mind-set—but when they are all boiled down they are remarkably similar.

The simple fact is that it does not matter where your company, or each

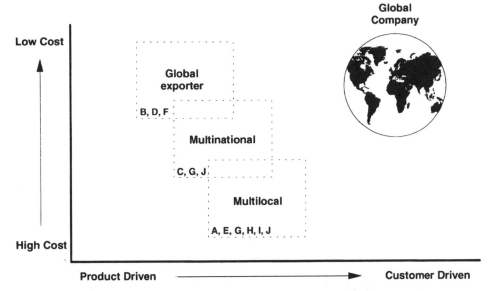

A: European, financial services, Banque Nationale de Paris; B: Japanese, industrial (consumer), Canon; C: U.S., industrial, Caterpillar; D: U.S., service (railroad), CSX Corporation; E: European, industrial (consumer), AB Electrolux; F: Japanese, financial services, JCB; G: European, industrial, Pirelli; H: Canadian, financial services, Royal Trust; I: Australian, service, TNT; J: U.S., service, Waste Management.

Figure 5.7. Positions of Ten Companies on the Global Matrix

part of your company, falls on this map. At the end of the day, every company will have to undertake the same set of basic tasks to get through the first set of hurdles on the way to becoming global.

Developing a company's capability to operate and compete in the global business arena requires an ongoing program of change focused on realizing the company's global vision. That vision is not static; it lives and is kept alive by constant reshaping to reflect the dynamics of the changing business environment.

As a company prepares its global vision, management must take stock of where the company is in its current global development. The company's current position influences the options it can take to create global strategic initiatives that build global processes and programs and to align the company's global efforts. Figure 5.9 offers a calibration for assessing a company's positioning on the global learning curve. We recommend that management use this set of position attributes to assess not only the company's position but that of the competitors.

By understanding where your company is positioned today, manage-

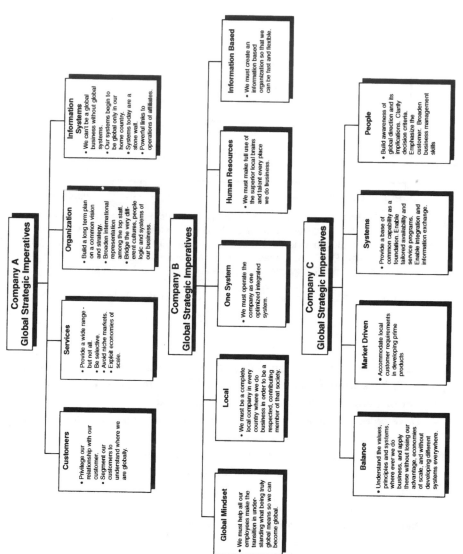

Company A
Global Strategic Imperatives

Customers
- Privilege our relationship with our customer.
- Segment our customers to understand where we are globally.

Services
- Provide a wide range - but not all.
- Be selective.
- Avoid niche markets.
- Exploit economies of scale.

Organization
- Build a long term plan on a common vision and strategy.
- Broaden international representation among the top staff.
- Bridge the very different cultures, people logic and systems of our business.

Information Systems
- We can't be a global business without global systems.
- Our systems begin to be global only in our home country.
- Systems today are a stone wall.
- Powerful links to operations of affiliates.

Company B
Global Strategic Imperatives

Global Mindset
- We must help all our employees make the transition in understanding what being truly global means so we can become global.

Local
- We must be a complete local company in every country where we do business in order to be a respected, contributing member of that society.

One System
- We must operate the company as one optimized integrated system.

Human Resources
- We must make full use of the superior local brains and talent every place we do business.

Information Based
- We must create an information based organization so that we can be fast and flexible.

Company C
Global Strategic Imperatives

Balance
- Understand the values, principles and systems, where ever we do business, and apply these without losing our advantage, economies of scale, and without developing different systems everywhere.

Market Driven
- Accommodate local customer requirements in developing prime products

Systems
- Provide a base of common capability as a foundation. Enable tailored availability and service programs. Enable integration and information exchange.

People
- Build awareness of global direction and its implications. Clarify decision criteria. Emphasize the customer. Broaden business management skills

Figure 5.8.

Global position attributes	Scale		Description
Exploration	Never ● → Always ● ↑		Managers think of the world as one operating environment, exploring the company's depth of presence, business opportunities, and threats.
Commitment to global vision	Never ● → Always ● ↑		All employees are aware of global vision and are thinking globally in the carrying out of both their present and future-oriented (e.g., planning) work.
Building global strategic initiatives	Not at all ● → Throughout the company ● ↑		Multidisciplinary teams are actively involved in carrying out global strategic programs based on the global strategic imperatives of the company.
Appealing to customers worldwide	Never ● → Always ● ↑		The Company understands the global/local spectrum of demand, and is able to meet the needs of global customers, customize offerings, and achieve cultural fit.
Building globally scalable resources	Never ● → Always ● ↑		The Company is deliberately designing resources to be scalable by sharing knowledge, cultivating positive attitudes toward work, and creating synergies.
Managing the connections	Never ● → Always ● ↑		Managers are managing in cultural contexts sensitively, developing global corporate culture, connecting and empowering knowledge workers.
Developing global leaders, teams, individuals	Never ● → Always ● ↑		Global values are permeating the culture, compensation schemes are linked to global behavior, leaders place importance on global.
Leveraging IT to build global capability	Not at all ● → Throughout the company ● ↑		Point-to-point communications systems, portfolios of systems addressing global process, customer, product exist and are running effectively.
Capturing global benefits	Never ● → Always ● ↑		Resources are aligned to global stages and investment returns are realized which support global/local balance.

Figure 5.9.   Estimating Your Company's Global Position

ment can make more effective decisions to build a sustainable program to capture the global payoff. In moving through the global frontier, and ultimately capturing the global payoff, management must first take stock of the company's current and future position and identify leading global processes and projects. Then, it must align the company with globalization stages.

The Importance of Global IT

A company can't become global without making excellent use of a wide variety of IT. Effective use of IT minimizes the negative impact of distance and time and allows sharing of a company's most valuable asset: the collective knowledge of its employees. This connecting of the world through technology enables the adept corporation to operate as efficiently as if all of its employees were in the same building, rather than widely dispersed around the world.

The alignment of IS with the global vision of the company is essential. Just as the transformation from a given starting point on the globalization matrix into a global company is different depending on the starting point, so too will the IT platform in support of these moves be different. Managers in companies going global begin this process by understanding the company's vision and position on the globalization matrix and relating it to the key areas where IT can add value.

Take the example of the CIO who told his executive management team that the company needed a global telecommunications network to enable remote engineers (in Paris, Tokoyo, San Francisco) to send drawings to each other. When the network was considered on its own merits, without considering the added value that would be created in concert with other component programs from the various IT portfolios, the project failed to meet investment/return ratios that would satisfy executive management. The project was quickly shot down. Six months later, after conducting a high-level global architectural study that more fully explored and developed the company's global vision, a much clearer set of justifications for the network was developed. These included enabling new global processes such as global customer support, optimizing distribution activity, and coordinating worldwide manufacturing production schedules. This time the same proposal (in terms of technology and cost), now firmly anchored to the global vision, flew through.

The new global IT platform requires sweeping changes to allow for (1) the coexistence of product, process, knowledge, and coordination support systems; (2) applications becoming much shorter-lived to meet fast-changing customer needs and unpredictable requirements; and (3) having modular, reusable IT components that can be rapidly assembled and disassembled and that take advantage of a shared information and communication resource. These changes require a lot of investment, time, and new management skills and processes.

A Checklist for Globalizing IT

Perhaps the most important first step in achieving global IT is the appointment of the right CIO. Few CIOs nowadays directly manage more than 50% of the firm's IT resources; increasingly, their role is becoming one of influencing rather than managing a diverse set of technologies, which are becoming more and more intertwined with the company's products and processes. Tomorrow's CIO must have the ability to step back and look at problems from a broader perspective and with a global mind-set. He or she needs the skills to coopt every employee in the organization into the successful implementation of IT from the top to the bottom of the company.

Secondly, the senior management team needs to adopt global systems thinking. As a discipline, systems thinking went out of favor in the 1970s and 1980s, but as David Norton comments: "The pressures of restructuring and resystemizing the basic operations of business which are absent in the past 30 years are clearly present. It is time to bring back the systems approach."[1] Systems thinking is an essential precursor to the exciting enterprise modeling initiatives described in Chapter 7.

Thirdly, executives need to drive their business vision down to global IT architecture, which serves as the master schedule for the complex integration required to tie together a wide variety of disparate projects into a unified conception that supports the vision and strategic initiatives. It not only provides the blueprint for integration but also establishes sequences of activity—project C cannot be started until project A is completed, etc.

Finally, global IT resource management and deployment needs to be addressed. In many ways this is a challenge similar to creating a global mind-set in the company as a whole. The IT staff must understand the global vision and be comfortable in multicultural teams working out of a variety of international locations. Their task can be eased by using similar systems development methodologies worldwide, installing international e-mail facilities, and supporting them with individuals highly trained in international project management.

The importance of this kind of global approach to applications development has been proved over and over again, as companies have tried to take the core of a "home" system to another country and to implement it with local adaptations. For example, a major European manufacturing company tried to roll out its U.K. order-processing system into France and then Germany. Unfortunately, to be adapted to the French needs, most of the U.K. system's functional modules had to be rewritten or bypassed. Worse, when they took it to Germany, they tried to capitalize on what they had learned in France by using that version, but they found that the German needs were different again and that they were rewriting the French system modules, which had already been rewritten to bypass the U.K. modules. As the system went from country to country, there was a cascading effect of lost functionality and quality. This is a very typical multinational or multilocal approach; it took the company seven years to finally implement the system into fifteen countries.

An effective approach to preventing this kind of disaster is to adopt a global portfolio management system, which puts every application (and some organizations might have over 100,000 worldwide) into one of five global IT portfolios: product-support systems, process-support systems, knowledge-support systems, control and coordination systems, and IT architecture. This is a useful starting point for sorting out the management complexities of linking IT effort to business strategy, setting funding levels, sorting out priorities, and calculating benefits.

The Cost of Global IT

The upfront investment, particularly in the infrastructural components, of global IT is huge. A global IT architecture design process will prove invaluable in aggregating potential benefits, as well as in understanding the long-term cost advantages of taking a systemic global-development approach over patchwork incrementalism. The company needs to balance long-term investments, however, with a regular stream of short-term deliverables, possibly by selective use of outsourcing resources. This continually reinforces the value of going global to the company's managers and generates enthusiasm and commitment.

So What Is Globalization?

Globalization is more than just doing business in a number of countries around the world. Globalization involves doing business around the world in a new way, balancing the global qualities of product or service and the unique needs of various local customer bases. It involves breaking down

TABLE 5.1.   Ten Global Attributes for Doing Business

1. From a geographic concept (where I do business) to a business concept (how I do business)
2. From a focus on centralization vs. decentralization to doing business "anyplace"
3. From a mechanistic (the whole of the business equals the sum of its parts) to a holistic (the whole is greater than the sum of its parts) view of business
4. From isolationism to low or nonexistent boundaries
5. From "not-invented-here" to networks of trust
6. From mere physical geographic presence to acceptance by the local culture
7. From centralized controllers to core management
8. From duplication of resources to taking advantage of economies of scale
9. From vertical stovepipe[a] communications to communication networks
10. From a solely short-term focus to a longer-term view

[a]A stovepipe is a chimney stack and represents vertical communications within functional hierarchies.

the culturally hidebound ethnocentric qualities most businesses have, whatever their nationality. Globalization involves "recognizing the particular genius" of employees from the company's operations anywhere in the world, whatever the employee's nationality, and rewarding employees for their genius and their efforts at creating a seamless company.

Doing business with this scope involves determining who the "global consumers" or "global customers" are for your products and services. These global consumers may be large customers with operations in many countries who want global contracts for sales and service or they may be individuals around the world who, through their access to the global information infrastructure, have come to desire the same products wherever they live (the global driver, the global parent, or the global traveler, for example). As company after company is finding, certain consumers in Manhattan have far more in common with certain consumers in Tokyo, Paris, or Rio de Janiero than they do with consumers in Queens, the Bronx, Brooklyn, or Staten Island.

A New Global Mind-set: Ten Critical Attributes

Working with large companies around the world over a number of years to explore and apply the global business potentials offered by IT, we have discover ten global attributes that help us understand the essence of the global vision and what it means to be global (see Table 5.1). These global attributes can be seen in juxtaposition to current ways of operating.

These ten global attributes make up the core of the global vision and, more importantly, the mind-set that each individual working in a global corporation must have. It is one thing for corporate leadership to go off into the stratosphere and return with a "vision" of what the company could and should be, but it is far different for every employee to be able to incorporate the components of that vision into the corporate mind-set and culture.

Corporate executives who speak about how they are actively working on making these components part of the company's mind-set say a lot about the difficulty of such an endeavor. A stovepipe is a chimney stack and represents vertical communications within functional hierarchies. During a discussion with an executive team of the Parts and Services Division of a U.S.-based manufacturing company, the following description of being global emerged:

> Being global is to extend your reach and presence, to be broader in scope than only where you have facilities. It means promoting anybody without regard to their country of origin. Being global is trying to adjust your business to the countries you are in. It means taking a basic set of values and business principles and basic systems and tailoring them to the area you're doing business in. It means trying to be more accommodating to the local environment—and still simplify. You need to accommodate and you need to identify the basic needs while you stay with some basic values/principles/systems and still have economies of scale. To be really global, you need to understand the values/ principles/ systems of every place in the world.

FROM A GEOGRAPHIC CONCEPT (WHERE I DO BUSINESS) TO A BUSINESS CONCEPT (HOW I DO BUSINESS)

Many companies confuse the term "global" with "multinational" or "worldwide," but global is a business concept (how you do business) rather than a geographic concept (where you do business).

A company that has a global way of doing business has a sphere of influence that includes all of its potential business relationships. A global company looks at its suppliers, owners, alliances partners, and competitors and asks: What situations and relationships can be leveraged to create a global advantage?

While many companies operate in a number of locations to earn revenue, source material, or distribute goods, a global company stretches beyond its operations to areas of influence, such as exploring potential relationships with third parties or supporting the efforts of a supplier to enter a market that has little to do with the company now but may be of strategic importance later. Many executives recite geographic statistics. When answering the following question: How is your company attempting to become global? "We operate in 117 countries worldwide" usually means that the company has people physically located in those countries operating on its behalf in functions ranging from research and development and manufacturing to selling and servicing.

Sometimes these executives describe such geographic performance measurements as the level and nature of physical asset investment in each country, the number of employees in each country, and the revenues or profits generated in each country; but geographic thinking often encourages the creation of barriers. By dwelling on geography the more intangible and sometimes more important influences of global business are often overlooked.

These geographic descriptors do not indicate, for example, how the company acts; the nature of relationships with customers, countries, suppliers, business partnerships, or alliances; or how frequently and directly the company communicates and bidirectionally shares knowledge across borders and company functions.

In a global business, relationships with suppliers, distributors, and customers are leveraged cross-functionally and cross-geographically. In any particular business system, there may be a number of cross-relationships; a business partner may be a customer for one product or service and a coprovider of another.

For example, Canon supplies chips, print engines, and other products to many high-tech companies in the United States and Europe. The company also acts as distributor for many of these companies in Japan. Canon expands activities with any one company by sharing the knowledge of relationships cross-functionally. Canon's first Global Corporation Plan, launched in 1988, focused on the company's approach to forming relationships with consumers, joint venturers, and technological exchanges in order to move "toward greater equilibrium" by cross-functionally sharing the knowledge gained from its relationships with customers. Canon is expanding its activities and converting these customers into successful alliance partners.

In 1993, Canon entered the second phase of its globalization program. The company used the word *kyosei* as its cultural philosophic watchword; it means "mutually rewarding coexistence." The ideograph suggests relationships between people and people, people and machines, and people and nature. The company crystallizes the global vision in words that describe their operations: "technology for people," "unity in diversity," "borderless contributions," "thinking globally, acting locally," and "across town—or oceans."

In their 1992 efforts, Chairman Ryuzaburo Kaku and President Keizo Yamajii stated:

> Important will be developing products with longer life cycles—a key to lowering demands on the planet's natural resources. . . . We are planning to strengthen our worldwide sales and service system, with moves such as setting up a company for computer sales in the U.S., extending our network in Asia and developing such untapped markets as Eastern Europe. . . . We are preparing to expand our overall imports, with increased use of semiconductors from overseas manufacturers. Tie-ups with companies abroad can also play a significant role in raising imports of parts and products. And we can look to our overseas research laboratories to develop unique products that reflect the character and requirements of their locales.

Just as Canon is exploring its sphere of influence by cultivating relationships in a globally balanced way, other businesses, attempting to become global, are examining who is involved in the flow of goods and services and how these relationships can be leveraged globally by formulating answers to such questions as:

1. How many companies—customers, suppliers, distributors, research-and-development alliances, and others—do you have relationships with?

2. What are the natures of these relationships?

3. Are there any other dimensions to these relationships that can be leveraged?

In producing world-class products with dependent technologies developing in different parts of the world, it is especially important to organize around the context of a whole-world system rather than geography. Activities that combine a crossfunctional, cross-geographic approach, leveraging the company's sphere of influence, produce benefits to the global corporation that are not normally found in the typical multinational corporation.

"Depth of presence" in the multinational form is most often talked about in terms of how much manufacturing capability is located in the region in which a company is selling or in terms of the amount of physical assets and people employed in a particular place. Depth of presence in the global corporation is generated by viewing the world as one market, one source of resources, and a fabric of relationships. We are not only looking at where a company manufactures but at how a company's ideas originate and grow.

The global perspective of business is wider and more sensible than other forms of organization because it begins with the notion of the company's global sphere of influence, which addresses the company's intangible as well as its tangible assets. These intangibles, such as research and development, good will, computer software, serviceability, quality, design, and influence on various players in the global community, are more and more often determining the difference between profitability and lack of profitability, between success in global business and failure.

FROM A FOCUS ON CENTRALIZATION VS. DECENTRALIZATION TO BUSINESS ANYPLACE

Globalization is the ability to do business anyplace, as opposed to being obsessed with which functions are centralized and which are decentralized. To become an "anyplace" company, it is necessary to be able to communicate efficiently and effectively. Today's IT makes it possible to wire the world for any company and to allow members of the company to connect with anyone else in the company as well as anyone outside the company who can add value. For example, Digital Equipment Company engineers in Augusta, Maine, call up a computer-aided design (CAD) drawing on their terminals from a data base in Reading, England, update it, and send it back in less than five minutes. Ford engineers in Cologne, Germany, examine and discuss a failed engine part with a Ford engineering team in Essex, England, using video-teleconferencing, an electronic blackboard, and a fax machine. One of the three video cameras was movable, to provide close-up views of the engine from all angles. These are everyday occurrences.

Increasingly, your customers and business partners will want products and services delivered, negotiated for, and even designed at a place that is convenient for them. They will not care whether you make your decisions centrally or share knowledge cross-functionally or cross-geographically. What will matter to them will be your ability to answer their questions and to deliver your products and services where required.

An executive with the U.S.—headquartered CSX Corporation, a transportation company, believes:

> Today, global companies have no boundaries. A global company is one that undertakes its mission-critical activities wherever it makes the most sense; its research and development can occur wherever the skill or talent for performing it physically resides. We are trying to achieve globalization by making connec-

tions between assets across countries without putting assets on the ground in a particular country.

The fundamental shift in the balance of world economies over the past two decades—away from U.S. dominance and toward equilibrium among the Triad groupings—means that the number of global customers has increased exponentially in that time, and the trend continues. With the collapse of Communism in Eastern Europe, the possibility for a greater distribution of wealth in the Middle East, the growth of the younger capitalist economies in the Pacific Rim, and the possibility of vibrant economies in South America, a generation from now global customers will be doing business all over the world and may be headquartered anywhere.

IBM's recognition of this trend was one of the driving forces behind its decision to study ten global businesses conducted in 1990. IBM found that in 1990 20% of its worldwide revenue stream was generated by 550 international customers. IBM's total customer base is about five million, but one-fifth of the company's revenue was generated by less than one-hundredth of 1% of the customer base. The percent of revenue created by this tiny customer base was growing through the late 1980s and into the 1990s faster than the revenue growth in any "domestic" (single-country) market IBM had.

When IBM developed the Kanji workstation, the aim was at a domestic (Japanese) market; but when IBM salespeople went to sell the product, they found that Japanese companies needed the product sold, supported, and serviced in Detroit, where a number of subcontractors to Japanese auto companies are located.

A European consumer-durables executive categorized all individuals who live in industrialized countries as having one of four global life-styles and determined that urban or suburban professionals who live in the Boston area have more in common with urban or suburban professionals in Paris or Tokyo than with people who may live only a few miles away. The company has begun to revolutionize its business to cater to a global market segment rather than to people with national characteristics.

FROM MECHANISTIC (THE WHOLE OF THE BUSINESS EQUALS THE SUM OF ITS PARTS) TO HOLISTIC (THE WHOLE IS GREATER THAN THE SUM OF ITS PARTS)

A global business acts as an organic whole rather than as something with a number of disconnected elements moving in different directions. Making progress toward becoming a global business means moving from a mechanistic organization, where the whole of the business equals the sum of its parts, to a holistic organization, where any part of the business reflects its "genetic code" and the whole is greater than the sum of its parts.

Jacques Henri Wahl at BNP put it best when he said,

> A corporation is global like a human, living structure. In one cell is all the description of the whole. The cell allows the corporation to reconstitute the whole being.

For employees, global holism means the organization has shared beliefs, attitudes, and values. This creates a consistency in the way you treat customers, vendors, other business partners, and each other, wherever business is being done.

As John Mullen, CEO of TNT Express Worldwide, says:

> We try to project a corporate culture worldwide. Managing directors travel widely, and each middle manager is driven by a similar set of requirements and a short-term focus on results. They all talk the same language. We move managers around a lot. We use profit incentives—all parties benefit from an international deal.

Holism also defines the way the functional pieces of a global company fit together. Rather than seeing things as sequential, or "happening somewhere else," the global company sees all of its internal functions as a closely choreographed operation. An executive with CSX says,

> It makes sense to look at manufacturing, marketing, and logistics holistically and think of them and treat them as a single system or entity. Sourcing may be worldwide but driven by the mind-set of a global system.

An executive of an American service company chides his organization for its lack of such ability:

> We still react to requests as though there are other parts of the company who take care of such things; we don't have the holistic feeling or approach to universally handling a customer's needs on a universal basis. Our attitude is that we have made the introduction, now it is someone else's problem. In other words, the barrier we have to going global is how to work together.

Whether you offer the same or different products in different countries, customers carry a holistic expectation of the quality of your products and services and an idea of your company wherever they go. Whether you are organized as an integrated global company or a set of distinct multi-domestic enterprises, your customers' experience is holistic. How any one part of the company operates has an effect on the company's global image.

We like our American Express and Visa cards because we travel constantly. We have the convenience of needing local currency only in small amounts, for cab fare and tips, because every hotel, restaurant, and major store we visit accepts our "anyplace" plastic. We realize that we sometimes get a better rate of exchange from the cards than we do by converting cash at local banks, and at the end of each month, all of the charges from around the world have been pulled together on one statement.

For American Express, global holism means that its other customers can expect a certain quality of convenience and service wherever they travel. American Express cards and traveler's checks provide customers with convenience and standard methods of payment anywhere in the world, while the company offices provide worldwide and local travel information and services, as well as a place to convert local currency. American Express realizes that the customer has a global, integrated view of its business—that if you have a bad experience with the company in Brisbane or Brussels, you are likely to switch providers when you get home, wherever home may be. American Express personnel around the world must have a similar level of expertise and set of standards for treating customers.

FROM ISOLATION TO LOW OR NONEXISTENT BOUNDARIES

To be global is to have the ability to act as if boundaries are low or do not exist at all. It means eliminating the isolationism that precludes sharing. Barriers between functions, divisions, or locations of your company are powerful impediments to process effectiveness, innovation, and flexibility. A global company eliminates the isolationism that gets in the way of sharing.

To believe that if a company stays home and sticks to its knitting business will do well just doesn't fit the way the world works. The truth is, if a company has a good product in a healthy market with good margins, someone else will want to introduce a product in that market and get at those margins. Another company may figure out how the product is made and make it better or more efficiently or more precisely tailored to the customer, or it may come up with a new idea that addresses the market in a way that makes the first company's product obsolete. With global competition, these things happen every day. When the Berlin Wall fell in late 1989, most people on both sides of the wall were astonished. They had not conceived that what they had so recently regarded as a permanent barrier to trade and human interchange could give way so easily. East Germans brought down the wall because they finally woke up to the reality that their economic system could not work in isolation from their close neighbors to the west. They wanted the goods and services, as well as the jobs, that they could see just over the frontier.

Western business perspectives about the possibilities of doing business in Eastern Europe changed almost overnight. Well-laid business strategies went out the window as companies rethought basic principles and scrambled their resources to adapt to the expanding European market, which went from 160 million people to over 350 million with the addition of the Eastern European countries.

As the world economy opens into a broader playing field and more and more companies are able to offer global products and services, the value of physical barriers such as the Berlin Wall and conceptual barriers such as protectionist "local-content" practices will have less and less meaning.

FROM "NOT-INVENTED-HERE" TO NETWORKS OF TRUST

Being global means creating relationships built on trust. By trusting other managers to act as reliable entities in a corporate organization, you can reduce the amount of time and effort required to accomplish anything. If someone trusts you, you don't have to spend all of your time getting "buy-in" from that person.

Global companies gain trust by focusing on similarities rather than differences. By sharing the responsibility for the development of ideas wherever they come from, global companies create a powerful advantage. To move flexibly and quickly, therefore, your business must have a well-woven fabric of mutual trust upon which it can depend.

Many companies hold worldwide management meetings at least once a year for all levels of management. During these meetings, team-building exercises are run to create bonds among the group and to encourage people to share expertise. Groups are arranged to solve particular issues the company will face in the coming year.

Solutions must consist of global-action programs in which management is willing to engage. Not only does the company gain powerful insights into issues from many perspectives but individuals gain contacts within the company. They learn alternative ways to solve problems by sharing process issues. Many companies, holding these meetings in exotic places, say that the return from such sessions can be exponential.

FROM MERE PHYSICAL GEOGRAPHIC PRESENCE TO
ACCEPTANCE BY THE LOCAL CULTURE

Globalization means more than merely having a geographic presence in a country or region. It means that the local customers and business partners recognize your company and perceive you as appealing. Further, it means that your company and your products are accepted by the culture and perhaps are identified as part of the culture. This usually means that you are a "good citizen" in those countries where you do business and that your global products and services reflect the local culture and tastes.

Yatsutaka Obayashi, Deputy Senior General Manager of Corporate Strategy and Development at Canon in Tokyo, put it this way:

> In order to prosper, to succeed long term, we must be perceived wherever we do business as a good member of society, accepted as a good, respected manufacturing company. This requires our being a total company, a complete company, wherever we do business.

"Local look and feel" describes your company's products, services, and presence when they are tailored to achieve cultural fit. The most obvious example of local look and feel is the ability to speak your customer's language.

Apple Computer reaps benefits by providing different keyboards, as well as software packages, in many languages for its globally consistent personal computer processors. Operating with a "local face" by providing local languages has increased the ease of use and diffusion of Apple products in many countries.

As Michael Spindler, Chief Operating Officer of Apple Computer, Inc., says:

> The concept of global business does not allow for a company that is based in one country or location to look at the rest of the world as one big market. It must have a truly international perspective. The new global company starts with a clear vision behind a product and then adjusts or adapts that idea to products uniquely suited to each country or market. It not only manufactures and markets worldwide, it interacts culturally in a dynamic way so that the original idea or product becomes part of the local society.

In the process of setting a new course, companies need to consistently tinker with their global–local balance, reevaluating which elements of their business have to be the same so that all other elements can be different as they create a proper balance between global economies of scale and local responsiveness.

As companies enter countries, often the initial impressions formed are the most long-lasting. Local good citizenship can ease the tension of entry or expansion. As Dr. Diane Wilson, a researcher on strategic alliances and investment in IT at the Massachusetts Institute of Technology, states:

Cultural fit is all about realizing that there will be conflict with the local culture, planning for it, and taking some form of action that demonstrates a long-term interest in the community (Interview, 1992).

An executive with Waste Management put it slightly differently when he said:

The global company must learn to deal with the issues of unity (being one company) and disparity (being many companies). Regarding disparity we need to learn how to respond to local needs. This is very important in a service company. We need to learn how to be an Italian company in Italy. We have to be "local" wherever we do business. We have to have business processes that allow that behavior. We have to internalize and adapt to/in our processes everything going on in local markets served with regard to competitive behavior and translate that into our behavior.

Turning conflict into accord, diversity into strengths, is a necessary concern for the global corporation.

FROM CENTRALIZED CONTROLLERS TO CORE MANAGEMENT

In a global business, the management core of the organization functions as a connector of the many operational areas, as well as an amplifier and interpreter of the communications between those groups. This is in marked contrast to the center functioning as the controller of the entire network of operations.

Core connectors recognize a responsibility to solve problems rather than to merely assert status by being remote from the work. In knowledge-worker dominated industries, where technical expertise is as valued as management expertise, management acts more and more as a coordinator and connector.

At the IBM Consulting Group, the senior partners act as connectors to the local practices by providing information about engagement results and industry expertise being developed in different parts of the world. Local practice managers are responsible for the running of their units, as well as connecting the people within their units.

On the shop floor at Nissan Motors plants, management joins in on the assembly line when there is a problem. They see their job as managing the contingencies, assisting the line with problem-solving resources. Connecting the shop floor to the resources for solution is one of their primary duties, and their attitude reflects that.

Bill Harker, Chief Operating Officer of Royal Trust in Toronto, sees

the need for the whole organization to become connected in how it goes
after business and in how individuals are rewarded for group success.

> Mutuality of interest is a key global value. The firm seeks to build this mutuality
> of interest by exchanging shares of stock. This gives everyone a stake in the
> game. Executive bonuses are issued in stock. Decisions are therefore made with
> the long-term impact on stock price and customer service in mind, not this
> year's objectives. This builds and sustains the company network worldwide. We
> have given up control to get control. It is the common understanding of where
> we are going and how we will get there that keeps it working.

From Duplication of Resources to Taking Advantage of Economies of Scale

Global companies take advantage of economies of scale without overly rep-
licating resources, and increasingly knowledge is the source of many of
these economies of scale. Individuals are responsible for sharing relevant
information with others who will benefit from knowing, without creating
so much "clutter" that everyone constantly has information overload. Individuals can't be passive receptors of other people's communications. This
is part of the shared trust that makes it possible for global companies to
function efficiently.

A chemical company we studied is a good example. As one executive
says:

> Having access to a central pool of skills and knowledge is key. For example,
> we had a disaster in Taiwan. A typhoon came through and virtually wiped out
> the operation. We were able to fly in operational and technical specialists as
> well as staff for a period of four to six months in order to get the situation
> restored. They had no problem working together or working in that local en-
> vironment as they shared the same values and knowledge base.

More than twenty years ago IBM created the RETAIN system, a knowledge repository that gives customer-service engineers anywhere access to
vital information about how to fix especially difficult hardware and systems-
software problems. Over the years engineers have built the data base of
problems they have encountered and solutions they have found or created,
and the system has been upgraded to make it easier for customer-service
representatives to get into the data base and find useful information.

At Bain & Company, a consulting firm, "librarians" travel from project
to project to document progress and create a data base of the company's
experiences. Without good mechanisms for keeping others informed of

what work is being done, redundancies such as the following can happen. A team of financial-market dealers in London was, unbeknownst to it, competing with a team from its own company in California to make an offer to a Japanese client. By studying the patterns of purchases and other client behavior, both teams were trying to develop the most attractive combination of global financial instruments to offer. Because of their limited views of the client's holdings, neither team felt that it had a great chance of winning.

In the initial stage of the deal, the California team had a database of only the client's equity positions, while the London team had access to a database of the client's debt-instrument positions. When a senior company executive discovered the fact that the two teams were competing, he urged them to work together. They readily agreed, but it took the back-office staff much time to find a way to link the two databases so that the teams could share information, ideas, and solutions to the client's needs.

In the area of waste disposal, with a company becoming global by acquisition, there are unique problems and opportunities. An executive at Waste Management says:

> Since most of the costs of doing business are incurred locally, we can't see how to achieve global economies. However, there are some good examples of how we can achieve global synergy if we consider some of the technologies we export. Our big advantage is that we know how we can move the knowledge and technical know-how to the local operator. We need to drive the company to where it is a local company for one global customer.

FROM STOVEPIPES TO COMMUNICATIONS NETWORKS

Being global means having anyplace, anytime communications with anyone in the organization, not communicating vertically up stovepipes within specific organizational functions.

Field forces at most companies are well aware of the lag time predicament in hierarchical decision-making. What field force has not taken an action, deciding to deal with the consequences later rather than send the request up the stovepipe and wait for it to come back down? You cannot be truly global without being connected.

In fifteenth-century Spain and Portugal, this meant having fast ships. Today, it means having great telecommunications facilities, knowledge repositories, and windows into those repositories in the form of microprocessor-based workstations and other information-processing tools.

Jacques Henri Wahl of BNP explains:

To accomplish the strategic imperative of privileging our relationships with customers with global needs we have to have the highest amount of information on our customers. Information systems are central to our vision.

It also means having an organizational culture that permits direct communication from any person to any other person in the organization, a culture that calls for true communication and not merely following a chain of command.

A global business does not have one center but multiple centers, located around expertise and competence. Communications need to be outbound and node-to-node as well as inbound, i.e., from anyone to anyone.

An executive with Pirelli sees one of his company's chief objectives as "taking a global perspective in designing products and positioning brand names." To do this, the company must

> develop the means to update drawings and coordinate design, engineering, and manufacturing activities in real-time; increase headquarters knowledge of market trends within and across countries to help it track the development of, and changes in, global lifestyles.

We've seen this concept in operation, as bond traders in London, Tokyo, and New York, all watching multiple digital and video inputs on their desks and talking on multiple phone lines to clients, at the same time monitor a shared internal "hoot-and-holler" system[2] that allows them to stay in touch.

Communications are also of utmost importance in how global customers interact with the company. An executive with CSX states:

> We need to start with information closer to what the customer really wants. Moreover, we need to provide a common interface for linking electronically to the customer throughout the domain of where they do business.

FROM SHORT-TERM FOCUS ONLY TO A LONGER-TERM VIEW

You can't become global without adding a long-term financial view to a short-term focus. To do this, you need to understand the worldwide economics of your business, including geographic and competitive forces and opportunities. Effective trade-offs can be made only if there is sufficient information available to make global decisions.

Adding a longer-term view can be accomplished only if there is full commitment to and acceptance of your global business vision. To enter a new market, for example, it may be necessary to use cross-subsidies from other parts of the business rather than looking for a one-year return on investment. A company will handle different parts of its business in different stages of development in ways that are appropriate to each situation and enable them to effectively develop their resources.

Taking a longer-term view does not mean formulating an extensive strategy and set of implementation plans that cannot be changed in the future. On the contrary, long-term means putting a stake in the ground as to the identity of your company, around which your customers, business partners, and employees can act.

Royal Trust's Bill Harker describes how his company has become more global over time:

> Our operations are around the world, but quite independent. The way we got into each country was different. Management did not think of it as an attack on the globe. Product niche has been the main focus, as opposed to geographic concern. In the future our configuration is likely to contain more nodes in the galaxy . . . and it is a galaxy, not a pyramid. There will be more focus on building the core values by design, rather than by accident.

The ideal global company is both a low-cost producer and customer driven. It balances global consistency with local diversity. It has a flexible product and service architecture that allows for a high level of customization. It has a highly coordinated value chain that utilizes multiple centers of excellence distributed throughout the world in the most appropriate locations.

The global company can support both global and local customers with balanced global/local sales and support channels. It operates like a geodesic network that enables and encourages its employees to communicate point-to-point rather than through the hierarchical chain of command.

These attributes may seem too good to be true. Certainly, no one company has come close to realizing all of them, but many companies have already implemented some of these ideas. If we were to assemble an all-star company out of exemplary global practices of companies around the world, we could create a single entity pretty close to our target.

Benchmarking Your Company's Global Progress

Initially, exploring the global frontier involves finding out just how much discussion is currently going on in a company about the globalization of business and creating forums for further discussion. Concerns about globalization will bubble up in different ways from different functional and geographic areas.

Marketing may be concerned about serving global customers and the lack of integration in serving these clients; manufacturing may be concerned about integrating worldwide capacity for production; and research and development may be concerned that there are various parts of the world that are developing competing technologies faster than one or two centers can manage.

By integrating a few of these concerns around a common issue—such as examining the state of world-class competition, tracking global trends in new technologies, and/or finding the company's emerging global business opportunities—management may find that there are several people who already have ideas about how to become global. By pulling together these various people and parts of the company that are already concerned with global issues, management can develop the roots of global change already occurring in the company's culture and cultivate the process more organically.

Focusing discussion around the ten global business attributes is one way to further develop ideas within the company. By exploring the forces driving your company and others to become global, the management team can generate a set of global themes.

At a heavy-equipment manufacturer, for example, an executive team discusses the difference between isolationism and low boundaries; the team determines that functional barriers are an important global issue to the company. While the company possesses strong functional expertise in its managers, there is a lack of cross-functional, multicultural business perspectives. Assigning accountability is done on a functional basis, creating roadblocks to multidisciplinary objectives. Serving global customers will become more and more difficult if these functional barriers remain intact. The company's managers have to learn to think more globally. The company has to invest in developing managers who are more aware of the company's global direction and its implications. By discussing the forms of international business—global exporter, multinational, and multilocal—and the pros and cons of each type within a forum, management can determine what type the company currently is, as well as key strengths and weaknesses of the company in its current business form and what must be done to become truly global. Management may learn that many of the perceived obstacles to becoming global can be overcome in the short run by sharing existing knowledge across organizational and national boundaries, while other issues must be addressed by longer-term efforts.

Developing a shared global vision and a set of global strategic initiatives adds depth to current global thinking. Creating a global vision and mandate involves going through three phases:

1. The initial phase is discovery: creating the right team and mandate, developing a vocabulary to discuss problems, and identifying major issues and themes.

2. The next phase involves making the global vision as tangible as possible: visualizing the global objectives, adding flesh to the bones, and coalescing the issues and themes into direct action of value statements about the company's attitudes and beliefs in becoming global.

3. The third phase involves the actualization of the global vision, developing a call for action and commitment throughout the company, and "passing the torch" to the rest of the organization.

Global vision and global strategic initiative processes ultimately must involve all levels of the organization. Crafting global strategy takes advantage of the experiences of many members in the company to make decisions to cope with a global environment of discontinuous change. By constantly revisiting the global vision and global strategic initiatives to keep them current, management steers a course for the global company.

The globalization of the marketplace is a complex phenomenon. The process of becoming a truly global company will be no less complex. Only through the cross-pollination of ideas from different geographic and functional areas of a company will globalization occur. Executives are challenged to think about business in new ways that meet the future global business environment with success. You have to live in the future to get to the future.

Notes

This chapter is based in part on John L. Daniels and N. Caroline Daniels, *Global Vision, Building New Models for the Corporation of the Future* (New York: McGraw-Hill, 1993).

1. David P. Norton, Stage-by-Stage 9, *Nolan Norton Journal* no 2 (1989).
2. "Hoot-and holler" is an internal, informal system of communication. This particular reference refers to a voice-activated intercom that connects multiple traders across multiple offices around the world.

III

IT Strategy

6

Do You Need an IT Strategy?

❖

PETER G. W. KEEN

❖

Chapter Summary

1. A central contention of this chapter is that the unnecessarily complex language used to discuss IT, prevents many business executives from understanding the fundamental strategic issues which they must address in order to use technology effectively.

2. The problems began in the 70s, when IT specialists were just beginning to understand how IT worked, and developed their own jargon to explain it to themselves and non-experts.

3. Nowadays, knowledge about IT has matured to the point where nearly everyone can comprehend its value, without needing to grasp complex detail about how it works. An analogy is drawn with the electrical supply, which is even more important than IT, and as complex, yet no one needs to know much about in order to plug in an appliance.

4. What business executives really need to grasp about IT (and electricity) is its power to connect. Much has been written about data, even how to transform data into information. This is not as important as how to *share* data or information, who it is shared with, and what happens as a result.

5. The technology which underpins this sharing is business networking (or telecommunications). Telecommunications has a dramatic impact on anything it is applied to, as it removes traditional barriers of time and location in getting things done. Effectively, by transforming business logistics, telecommunications make time a new form of capital—although its value varies between industry sectors.

6. The problem facing IT and business executives is often going

beyond aligning strategies, and actually *fusing* together the key imperatives which drive the company, with the appropriate strategic response. This fusion should occur on three levels: processes, culture
and technology.

7. An eight-stage process for achieving fusion is described,
which depends on understanding the 'knowledge-anchors' of the business. These are a mix of facts, assumptions and axioms which underpin the direction of the company, and which should evolve over time;
they need constant testing.

8. In effect, this chapter advocates applying the 'strategy execution', 'technology potential', or 'IT infrastructure fusion' perspectives of the strategic alignment model, where considerations of
business strategy define the organizational and IT structure of a business.

9. An important driver of technology strategy for telecommunications is the concept of 'reach and range'—how far, and how much
information can be distributed? Once this is determined, the technological implementation should be left to the specialists, not business managers.

10. Telecommunications is an effective way of understanding
how IT can bring the elusive, but nowadays essential 'quality and
service' dimension to a company's product offerings, but at an afford-
able cost. As such it provides an alternative route to justifying IT
spending that business and IT managers may be able to agree on.

11. The concepts introduced in this chapter are drawn together
in a quality-profit-engineering framework, that sets out to provide a
creative and practical solution to how to get payback from IT investments.

Leading vs. Managing IT

This chapter aims at helping senior managers lead the deployment of IT
without having to know how it is managed. The fusion map it presents
shifts the focus of management attention from strategy, which addresses
the "how" of action, to the issues of "what" and "why" that precede and
enable strategy. It uses a business language that does full justice to technical issues, instead of following either of the two extremes most common
today: relying on a technical language whose terms, such as "architecture,"
"standards," and "integration," puzzle or put off executives or arguing that

technical issues are irrelevant to business executives, thus obscuring the key policy decisions that must drive technical choices. This is consistant with the alignment enablers and inhibitors presented by Luftman in Chapter 3.

Some of the views presented here amount to heresy. For example:

1. We need more computer illiteracy.
2. Aligning IT strategy with business strategy is too late and is like closing the gate after the cattle are out.
3. IS methodology is increasingly a blockage to progress. It keeps IT "different" and imposes an artificial structure and way of thinking on business participants.
4. The main problem in turning executive monologues into effective dialogue is language; the language of IT strategy was needed to help the field of IS evolve but is now largely irrelevant to business.
5. Computers and "information" are secondary, not primary, elements of IT. The driving force is telecommunications. By removing barriers of time and location on coordination and service, telecommunications has made business networking in core logistics a major destabilizer of entire industries. Point of sale in retailing, airline reservation systems, EDI, and customer–supplier links are a few instances.

Together, these assertions add up to a commonsense approach to handling IT as a business resource, using business, not IT, language.

The Irrelevance of Computer Literacy

Managers need not be computer-literate. Most business executives routinely travel on airplanes. How many of them are Boeing 747–literate? Would in-depth knowledge of airplane planning and technology make them more effective travelers?

The CEO of one of the world's largest electrical power generation companies recently told this author that he is computer-illiterate and hence, of course, unqualified, unable, and unwilling to deal with IT. The obvious and immediate reply was "I'm electricity-illiterate but that doesn't stop me knowing how to use your product." Fluency in decision-making and use is far more empowering and necessary than literacy in technology.

The electrical utility is a useful analogy here to the firm's IT platform. Understanding how electricity is generated in no way empowers its users. The need instead is to understand a few key rules about how to connect to the system. The electricity industry has evolved to an extent where the rules make the system invisible and remove the need to know about the strategy. There is autonomy on each side of the wall plug that is the interface to the utility. The user is free to design and employ devices on the "user" side of the interface. The generator is free to install new capacity and manage the power grid on the other side. This coordinated devolution rests on a small number of policies and regulations and a clear set of standards for the interface.

The electrical utility is the direct equivalent of what firms are trying to develop in their IT infrastructures. The political arguments about decentralization vs. centralization of IT and the cries to "break up corporate IS" or "outsource the lot" mainly come from the tension between coordination and devolution. This tension also sets the limits of IT strategy. Lack of clarity about imperatives and corresponding policy and suitable regulation block coordination of what is recognized as a key business resource are really what "integration" and "architecture" mean or should mean.

Forces pushing for devolution of decision-making combine with technical forces pushing toward distribution and localization of computers and telecommunications. The result is at best an ongoing tension and more often a mess of technical incompatibilities that prevent the development of a platform and make "systems integration" firms rich as they fix up the mess. Business choices should obviously drive technical decisions, but technical decisions increasingly affect business options, too. Imperatives are the business drivers and policy rules, the hinge for swinging from business requirement to technical platform.

The field of electrical power is immensely technical, with a jargon at least as obscure as that of IT. Business and society depend on it even more than on IT. Yet, managers are comfortable in their intuitions about the electrical utility. The IT field has not yet evolved to that point, largely because the IS profession has had to scramble to learn how to manage the technology, its uses, and relationships with its own clients and colleagues, whom they generally have seen as an abstraction called "users." Many of the problems of dialogue and language were created in the 1970s, when the IS field was trapped by its own technology, which was cumbersome, expensive, and hard to make work; by its own bureaucracy, where the management information systems (MIS) department became notorious in almost all firms for lack of service, monopolism, and minimal understanding of, or interest in, the business; and by its own economics, with "charge out" and cost allocations adding up to a property tax, which those paying it saw as not only providing little value but as something they could not influence.

The Irrelevance of IS Methodology

The information services field spent most of the 1980s trying to redress technology, bureaucracy, and economics. IS managers took the lead in building bridges to the wider community. As they tried to bring business managers into the planning process, they naturally began from the technology and extended the bounds of their own planning. They used the language of IT and added a business flavor to it. They explained their strategy, relying on methodology. Much of this process was an essential and partly remedial step for IS to get its own act together. For instance, many of the most useful methodologies examined the fit—or lack of fit—between where IS was placing its resources and the business needs. Examples are Critical Success Factors, introduced by John Rockart; the work of Richard Nolan, which in many ways created the professional field of IS; and various approaches to creating steering committees, assessing the IS "applications portfolio," and "alignment" between business and IS strategies. Later, many methodologies emerged that aimed at creating comprehensive IS plans— e.g., IBM's BSP (Business Systems Planning), stages studies, enterprise data models, business process reengineering programs, and the like.[1]

One of the main arguments underlying the recommendations in this chapter is that the reliance on IS methodology to communicate with the business community is no longer necessary and does not work anyway. It makes a subject that is complex in its details and almost entirely opaque to outsiders; imagine a business discussion that required managers to understand electricity at the level of strategy and in the language of power generation. Of course, for both electricity and IT, the technical issues are vital and highly complex. That is why the need in both instances is to lead so that others can manage, to sharpen the policy drivers and business imperatives that remove the need to know about the strategy. The model for action must be the investment adviser, not the doctor. Methodologies, especially ones focused on business integration and reengineering, will remain as core to the discipline of the IS professional as capital asset management and tax planning techniques are to the financial adviser. They will be used in context, though, not as the context for business/technology planning and dialogue.

The Significance of Business Networking

The central concept in the traditional view of IT is obviously information. The organizing element of IT here is the computer, initially defined as a large and expensive room, off-limits to most staff, containing a complex of machines. Most recently, it is defined as decentralized personal computers (PCs), off-limits to none as part of a sort of technological *glasnost*.

Both the computing and information paradigms are less and less useful in explaining IT and assessing it as a business resource. The traditional emphasis is on computing, with telecommunications as an add-on. Data are seen as the raw material from which information is refined. "Information" is distinguished from "data" in this traditional viewpoint as a vital corporate asset, computers as equivalent to the information age, and information as almost axiomatically the core of a new industrial or postindustrial revolution.

This traditional view emerged from the early history of computers and database technology. It is incomplete and outmoded. Computers had little impact on the basis of business until the 1980s. The office of 1980 looked very much the same as that of 1950. PCs were an economic rather than a technical innovation and had only marginal impacts on core organizational processes. The glut of information in this information age has not prevented the erosion of student test scores or U.S. competitive losses to often less information-intensive nations. The Japanese in particular have been high-tech providers and low-tech users of PCs. In 1992, there was an estimated one PC for every twenty schoolchildren in the United States and one for every eighty in Japan.

The primary and radical element in IT is what is here termed for lack of any suitable and available alternative "business networking." Combined with computers and information stores, telecommunications has literally transformed the basics of industry after industry and is sure to continue to do so. Obvious examples include:

- airline reservation systems, where the core logistic is distribution, with the reservation system becoming the base for marketing, pricing, ordering, and many aspects of forward planning.

- ATMs, cash management systems, and foreign exchange trading systems, which are the new core of banking.

- point of sale (POS), which is the base for electronic streamlining of merchandising, ordering, distribution, and fast management analysis and response to trends and problems.

- customer–supplier order entry systems and EDI, a major element in supporting just-in-time operations.

Information, expert systems, the jargon of IT, and PCs are only the visible trappings of business networking in the core logistics that constitute the foundations of organization and competition. It is this that business managers need to know about; the trappings obscure the radical nature of IT and the extent to which it must be a central element in their understanding of their business and their markets.

Redefining "Information"

The concept of information needs a fresh perspective. Information is not an artifact but a process by which people become informed. It is the product of the interaction between a person, a network, and an information store. At its simplest, this is you, your eyes and mind, plus a book. Next, it is you and a face-to-face conversation. Next, you and a phone instead of another face. Each addition of networking extends the range of sources and vehicles for you to be informed, far more than does the addition of information stores per se.

POS creates information, but that is not enough for being informed: that comes from the telecommunications network that moves the data, the software that filters them, and the screen that displays them in meaningful form. Meaningful is in both the eyes and mind of the beholder. For example, sending a digital image of a CAT scan to this author is to send meaningless data. Sending it to a consulting physician in a Massachusetts medical practice or to an expert at Mass General Hospital via NYNEX's MBS (Media Broadband Services) network is to transform many aspects of consultation. Images need no longer be printed on film and transported between facilities before doctors can review them. This is not a change in information per se; the image moved by business networking is identical to the physical film; information movement transforms the process of being informed.

These points may seem academic (and indeed form the basis of much of academic cognitive psychology, philosophy of language and hermeneutics, and computer science), but they have practical implications. The IT professional's almost axiomatic conception of information as an artifact is not a very helpful one. The management issue is less one of "What information do we need?" as "How do we make sure we are well-informed and act intelligently as a result of this?"

When this question is asked, business networking becomes a powerful new force, not so much in terms of information but of core business logistics and of the ways business is done; being informed more quickly and moving information to people who need it are part of this. Telecommunications is the driver here; without it, the network for being informed is more limited and slow. Conversely, of course, telecommunications without data is just an open line.

The "Re-" Phenomenon

Together, data, hardware, software, and telecommunications—business networking—change the rules of many business games. If you look in the index of any business book that was published more than five years ago, you will find very few terms that begin with "re-," in the sense of "try again." If you go to a business conference today or skim through a recent article, the odds are high that "re-" is everywhere in it—restructuring, redesign, renewal, reengineering, reorganizing, repositioning, realignment, and the like. Something is happening out there.

Business networking is closely associated with that something and is fueling many of the changes that are part of the "re-" phenomenon and thus part of business that is not considered as usual. This may seem an overassertive statement, but it is easy to justify. Stripped of the technological language and trappings, telecommunications networking simply removes barriers of time and location on service and coordination.

The basics of organizations and industries are based on time and location: departments, documents, branches, reporting systems, administrative procedures, managing across time zones, much of division of labor and management hierarchies, and organizational structures. This is drastically, if not visibly dramatically, changed by business networking; going to work is complemented by bringing work to people and location-independence. An obvious instance is the 800 number. When you phone customer service, you have no need to know where it is located. EDI streamlines time- and location-dependent, paper-dominated processes. Payment systems turn money from physical to symbolic currency. None of these is dramatic, but they change the very nature of organization, distribution, service, and becoming informed.

IT is thus now intrinsically about basics. It has infiltrated into just about every element of the basics, but the old language of IT obscures this. That is why we are seeing not just the "re-" phenomenon but an IT-influenced shift in the very language of business, including the networked organization, the learning organization, knowledge work, and "just-in-time" everything. The something happening is that IT has moved from being an important but separate element of business management to being right at the core of everyday business and social life, but we do not yet have a reliable way of managing this shift. The "re-" words and the new language of organization indicate that we cannot easily fit the something into our old discourse and set of distinctions.

However, we must find a way of doing so; in every industry, where business networking has transformed the core logistics of service and operation, 50% of firms disappear within ten years. The same pattern emerges in financial services. Surely, there is no plausible scenario for 1999 that has the same number of banks and security firms in New York City as there are today. While real estate loans and foreign debt are part of the reason for the banking industry's shaky position, the massive overcapacity created by IT—in terms of transaction processing, outlets, products, and commoditization—have contributed heavily to a radically new competitive environment.

Time is the New Competitive Asset

Time is the new imperative or even cliché of competition. The new differentiator in commodity markets is time and its concomitant convenience and ease of access, not product. For example, if the average time for processing a loan, restocking shelves, filling an order, or any other key activity averages thirty days in an industry, there is little competitive advantage in cutting this to twenty-five days and little disadvantage for a firm that takes thirty-five days. If, though, a leader cuts it to two hours, the rules of the game change at once. This is not so much a matter of gaining competitive advantage as of avoiding being put at a sustained disadvantage.

In retailing, the leaders' response times in core logistical chains are under a week and sometimes under a day. Dillard, for example, sends information on sales from each store to headquarters every two hours. Wal-Mart uses quick response systems to automate just about every step in the sales to reordering to delivery cycle. JC Penney's buyers meet through videoconferencing, and its suppliers in the Far East send and receive high-resolution photographs of fashion goods specifications electronically. Each of these firms has competitors whose merchandising, replenishment, inventory, costs, and ability to spot and respond to short-term trends have been badly hampered by lack of what is now an essential component of business operations. IT is no longer new technology but as much part of the business fabric as money, materials, and human resources.

Of all major industries, retailing is perhaps the one where competitive leaders drop out of the game fastest. Of the top twenty discount stores in 1980, only six were still in business in 1990. The list of department and fashion stores that have filed for bankruptcy includes such well-known names as Zayre, Bloomingdales, and Jordan Marsh. The pile of debt through leveraged buy-outs explains only part of their demise; failure to match the new leaders in core business logistics is the difference.

The key issue here is IT's impact on core logistics. In some industries, it has had little if any impact and is thus not a redefiner of basics, even though it may be heavily used. In the pharmaceutical industry, a core logistical chain is time to market, beginning with research and development and ending with the certification of a new drug. This averages around a decade; the contribution of IT has been small in cutting this, so it has not yet had any major impact on the basics of competition. However, the combination of electronic document management technology and changes in procedures for submitting data to the Food and Drug Administration (FDA) could slash the time dramatically; if this happens, IT will shift from the periphery of management and planning to part of the basics. (This is becoming apparent in one of the pharmaceutical industry's other core logistics, the testing process, where IT has significantly sped up the process.)

This means that CEO's interests, attitudes, attention, and responsibilities will—and should—shift with the impact of networking on core logistics. The automotive industry is an example here. It falls between the extremes in time frame of retailing and pharmaceuticals. One of its key logistical chains is also time to market. Until very recently, as in pharmaceuticals, IT did not contribute directly to reducing the seven-year time frame. Now, however, networked computer-aided design and manufacturing, parallel engineering, computer-aided logistics, and many other uses of IT are cutting into that significantly, with Ford leading the U.S. competitors, except for the Japanese, who are way ahead in their use of IT to automate manufacturing and engineering processes. Senior executives in automotive firms are paying far more attention to IT as a result.

Representative figures that show how the industry's critical success factors have moved from styling and fuel consumption to time to market are shown below:

1. Vehicle manufacturing takes fourteen to thirty days for a Western firm and two to four days for a Japanese one.

2. Time to market (1990) is four to six years vs. two and a half to three.

3. The average age of a product is five years vs. three.

This author recalls with a sense of shame his experience in management education programs and his failure to interest top managers of European and U.S. car makers of the relevance to themselves of IT as a source of competitive opportunity. The easy explanation was that they didn't understand. Perhaps a better one would be that they did understand that IT was important to aspects of running the business but not that it was fundamental to leading the business. Only when it transforms a core business logistic and makes time a new form of capital do they need to divert their attention from other important business issues to IT as an urgent one. It now is urgent to them, and they pay appropriate attention to people who talk to them in appropriate terms.

When Time Doesn't Matter

Top managers in oil companies or timber firms still pay relatively little attention to IT as a business fundamental and can afford to do so. Exploration and development of new fields takes decades; IT has not even hinted how and where it might cut those decades to years. Growing and harvesting trees takes up to a century for hardwood timber. IT is thus unlikely to change the dynamics of the basics of competition here, though biotechnology may.

It is not that IT is unimportant in any of these industries. Automotive firms rely on IT for just-in-time inventory and production and for electronic links to suppliers. Pharmaceutical firms invest heavily in IT to leverage research. Timber companies use it for planning, project management, and geographic mapping. IT supports existing activities but does not destabilize the industry status quo.

The same line of analysis applies to location as well as time, but the trends are more recent. The most striking instances of location independence relate to how cities are using networking to gain a geographic advantage, with companies offshoring work electronically to places like Ireland, Omaha, Heathrow (Florida), Mauritius, and India. We are seeing the emergence of the 800 number organization. Firms are exploiting telecommunications to look for opportunities to operate in places that offer a combination of a skilled labor force and low real estate costs.

For timber or mining companies, basic operations are totally location-dependent; they have to cut a tree or dig out coal where it is physically placed. They can put their customer-service units wherever they want, however. They can consolidate regional units nationally, as Conrail has; its 1991 press announcement stressed that the 90,000 square foot customer-service center incorporates "the latest fiber optics and telecommunications technology." A more accurate statement is that it is these that make it possible to get the advantages of central coordination, while keeping close to the local customer. "Local" here means physically remote but effectively as close as next door through the network.

Airlines have to fly planes from airports. They can locate their reservation centers literally anywhere they choose. Banks and insurance firms can put their claims processing in Ireland; customer service in cities like Omaha or Heathrow, which have first-rate telecommunications infrastructures and first-rate supplies of labor; and data entry in the Caribbean. When they do this, their telecommunications network becomes their effective organizational structure in that it, far more than bricks and mortars and boxes on the organizational chart, determines operations, communication, work flows and relationships.

When a company builds its business processes afresh and assigns its people to new roles and activities in this way, it is obviously changing its basics of structure, strategy in action, communication, and management. This, not information, is why IT and "re-" go together and why it is increasingly impractical to handle IT as different and technical; as part of the basics, it has to be meshed into everyday management. That needs a new map, not so much one of "re-" but "fresh"—a fresh look, a fresh design, and a fresh structuring. We are rapidly approaching the end of the era of MIS and rapidly entering one where general management includes managing IS as part of managing just about every element of business. Most importantly, there has to be the same degree and style of leadership for IT as for the other major areas of business and organization.

The Fusion Map

Figure 6.1 presents a fusion map showing the great management divide between leading and managing, between imperatives and strategy. The key to the business/technology dialogue is at the imperatives stage. Identifying the imperatives depends on *knowledge anchors* (a mix of assumptions, facts, axioms, and opportunities) and on vision and strategic intent, a clear and focused commitment to a long-term direction of effort, with opportunistic and situational responses that help the firm plan when it cannot predict.

The term "vision" is widely used in the IS literature; it is a useful code word for a new style of thinking and ambition, but visions are not contagious and easily become foggy or only so much fantasy. At its weakest, vision is "We have a dream" or "Wouldn't it be wonderful if. . . ." Many of us have a vision for ending the federal deficit or improving education; the impasse in our political and social system here seems more one of strategic intent. In this chapter, vision and strategic intent are linked together to

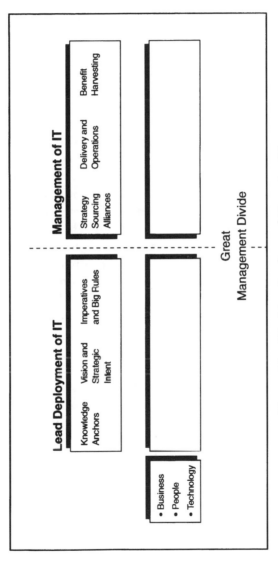

Figure 6.1. The Map: Leading and Managing IT

indicate a combination of ambitious thinking and commitment to ambitious action.

The map presented here is not a reality but a guide. Just as a road map abstracts from the details of houses, shops, traffic lights, bends, and signs that mark physical reality, behind the map are many complex details of activity and operations. The map puts them into a context that can help firms move from *compartmentalization* (the design and management of complex processes through separate functions and discrete stages) to *integration* (the coupling and streamlining of stages and crosslinking of functions) through to fusion.

The map has two dimensions, one of structural elements and one of temporal steps. At each step, the three elements of structure—business processes, culture, and technology—need to be fused. In parallel, so too must the temporal elements link to each other: knowledge anchors, business vision, and strategic intent; management imperatives and policy; strategy, design, delivery, operation, and benefit harvesting. The latter are temporal in the sense that they involve discrete stages in which the output from one is the needed input to the next. The sequence is bi-directional, however. Strategy may lead to a fresh look at the knowledge anchors and business vision on which it is based; that is inherent in the constant fresh thinking as well as rethinking that today's environment now constantly demands. Tomorrow is not a simple extension and extrapolation from yesterday. Any assumption taken as a given is a likely pitfall.

Eight Key Issues in Applying the Fusion Map

1. Include technology as part of the *knowledge anchors.* Most of the problems senior business executives and IS managers report in building an effective dialogue come from technology not being included at the start. Aligning the IT strategy with the business strategy is then too late.

Lack of attention to knowledge anchors is so often why the 50% of firms that disappear when business networking changes the basics of competition includes several of the previous leaders. It is very hard for any firm to challenge the assumptions and principles that made it successful.

For example, many retailers, including the industry power player Sears, did not spot how POS and telecommunications provided an entirely new base for merchandising and backward integration of the entire distribution chain. Toys "Я" Us, Wal-Mart, Dillard, and others that were minnows when Sears was the leviathan did spot it.

When a firm is successful without IT playing a central role in that success, it is reasonable for business managers to delegate it to a support role, not part of leading business change. When IT meant mainly computers, that was in general a safe approach. Business networking, however, may relatively suddenly redefine an industry core logistic, and such delegation can be myopic and mean loss of business freedom. If IT is not fused with business at the stage where basic assumptions are created and basic strategic commitments defined, IT-fueled change will generally be an enemy, not an ally.

Given that IT often allows companies to use their delivery bases to intrude on other industries' traditional territories, the comfortably successful firm may not recognize early enough that its real competition will be from outside, not inside, the sector it understands and monitors. This may be why such an outstanding hotel company as Marriott was preempted by British Airways (BA).

BA spotted that travelers who make international plane reservations by phone do so before they make hotel reservations, so BA decided to add hotels to its existing IT platform at a very small cost. When it did so, none of the major American hotel firms had any on-line international reservation capability, relying on telex and telephones. Marriott, Hilton, and others had to spend well over $100 million over five years to try to match BA, using American Airlines as its technical partner. The project was a fiasco, leaving Marriott with no practical strategy for countering BA.

Marriott is first-rate in terms of service and quality. It recognized in the mid-1980s that it would soon face a demographic nightmare, where service firms would have only two qualified applicants for every three jobs. It used this knowledge anchor to establish new incentives and programs, such as rewarding promising staff who had dropped out of high school by sending them back to get their diplomas. Here, Marriott fused business and culture along the entire chain from knowledge to action. In the mid-1980s, however, there was not the same link between its international business strategy and IT. After all, Marriott was in the hotel industry and none of its main competitors had a computerized reservation system capability, so there was no stimulus to move. BA saw itself as part of the travel-related industry and took an opportunity that historically had "belonged" to the hotel business.

The above example highlights the fact that it is not incompetent or failing firms that neglect IT as a knowledge anchor or fail to include it in establishing imperatives. Indeed, it appears to be the leading firms that are often the most frustrated by the management process. Perhaps the explanation is that they may be handling the pieces well individually but not fitting them together. The business strategy is clear. Human resources (HR) understands its role in facilitating change. The IS strategy is sound and supports the business, and IS delivers on its promises. Yet the critical fusion is missing. Success and failure in competing in the electronic marketplace occur well before strategy is set.

2. Identify *business imperatives* (concrete targets for action) that implicitly or explicitly begin "Regardless of how we do it, it is absolutely vital that we. . . ." These imperatives are closely linked to the firm's vision and strategic intent.[2]

3. Link these business imperatives to *technological imperatives*: "If these are our 'must dos' for the business, then to achieve them it is absolutely vital that our IT resource. . . ."

4. Review the technological imperatives; if they have common dimensions of *reach and range* (Fig. 6.2), they establish the business requirements for the firm's IT platform. This process defines architecture, integration, infrastructure, and standards inductively from business-first principles in business language. The logic here is: "These are our business imperatives. Here are the corresponding technical imperatives. We see the link and also see that they share the common requirement of reach—who can we connect our own processes to—and range—what information can we directly and automatically share across processes? Obviously, then, we must have a coordinated IT platform as a business priority." It is the inductive process that leads business executives to add the "obviously."

5. Define the organizational policies needed to ensure appropriate coordination and appropriate devolution. The lever here is to establish a small set of *big rules,* each of which must have a sound business reason. These provide the basis for selecting technical standards that have the force of organizational law. For instance, a big rule for one electrical utility is "All departmental systems must be able to connect to the firm's corporate telecommunications network." The business reason is the economies of cost, expertise, and capacity this ensures.

The big rule here requires several technical standards and recommended products, including token-ring, Systems Network Architecture, Transmission Control Protocol/Internet Protocol, and X.25. The standard is not the rule, however. There is a substantial difference in terms of political and organizational legitimacy, business logic, and quality of dialogue between saying "Our standard is X.25 and all local area networks must adopt token-ring" and "The big rule is that departmental systems must. . . ." Given that choice of technical standards is absolutely central to building the platform, this shift to an inductive sequence of steps that are all in true business language but that directly lead to identifying standards is, in the author's experience, a genuinely empowering and liberating force for dia-

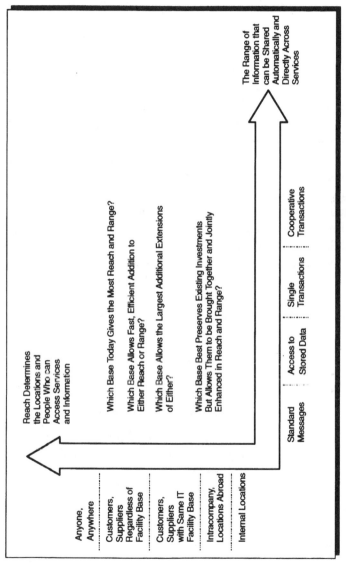

Figure 6.2. Reach and Range: Explaining Integration

logue that is welcomed by both business managers and IS managers and planners.

6. Make the business case for the platform and key applications that use it in terms of *quality profit engineering*. The quality profit engineering framework provides a convincing economic framework that senior managers will recognize and appreciate.

"Convincing" means just what it says, not "clever," "analytical," or "original." The simple need of executives for something they can understand, calibrate, monitor, and trust will not be met by a consultant's two by two boxes; complex formulae "proving" IS payoffs; IS methodologies with their own business-flavored language of "gray cells," "iron cross," or "benefit/beneficiary matrix;" or elegant equations based on theoretical assumptions. All of these have a role within the old tradition of IS as "special" but not in the new context; IT is half of capital investment and just another way of spending money, so IS has to show it will pay its way and justify diverting scarce money from other business opportunities.

7. Establish oversight mechanisms for managing IT and *get out of the way*. This removes any need for computer literacy among managers; they need instead to be fluent in setting the criteria for IT investments. The strategy process can then be left to professionals. Increasingly, strategy for IT mainly addresses multisourcing (of which outsourcing is a suboption) and alliances.[3]

8. Make sure there is a *constant rechecking of knowledge anchors*. That change is now the norm is a cliché of business life. It means that today's assumptions that have led to success may be invalid for tomorrow.

Practical Uses of the Fusion Map

Too often, there is a separation between business and IT thinking and action. The circles and triangles in Figure 6.3 indicate either "We are in good shape here" or "This is a problem area," respectively. The lines that connect the circles and triangles show if the relevant processes are well connected. Each example in Figure 6.3 is a real company.

Firm 1 in the diagram is very typical. Its business leaders spend time and imagination scanning the business environment (knowledge anchors). The vision is clear and the intent firm. Management is clear in its business imperatives. It links business issues to issues of culture—HR planning, recruitment, management development, and incentives. However, there are no corresponding imperatives for IT, even though the IS group understands the likely impacts of IT on business and updates its own knowledge anchors

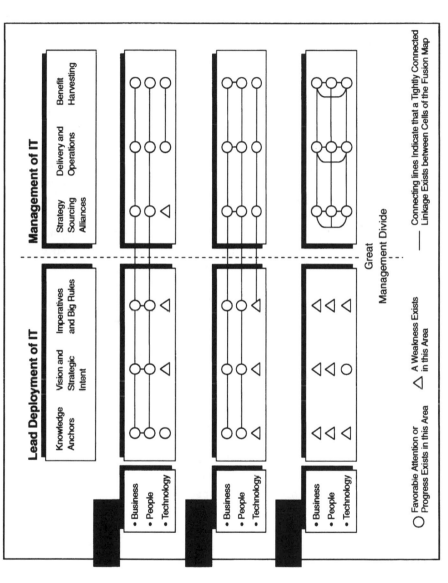

Figure 6.3. Examples of Lack of Fusion

about technology and competition. The technology anchors are not connected to those for business and culture. This company is a pharmaceutical firm. Its business managers do not know what they do not know; technology is not part of their focus. The company is overlooking the importance to itself of EDI for linking to major health care authorities worldwide and of image processing as a key element in faster time to market. The importance has been explained by the CIO but in terms that do not resonate for the business leaders. The language is wrong, not the content.

Firm 2 is also typical. It is a manufacturing company, whose business planning and implementation are aggressive and tightly coupled along the full sequence of leading to managing, from what and why to how. Its IT planning and implementation are similarly well coupled but disconnected from business and culture. The firm has a strong CIO, with a clear technical vision and commitment to providing a competitive edge through IT. He is likely soon to join the many CIOs being fired at twice the rate of other senior executives, according to a number of surveys.[4] The CIO has made many efforts to communicate, but the CEO remains, as are many, an "agnostic" about IT. The business units are going their own way and see the CIO's corporate vision as just a disguised form of the old MIS monopoly.

Firm 3 is also typical. Here, there is a tight linkage across business, technology, and culture from strategy on. The firm is Mutual Benefit, introduced in Chapter 3, the insurance company that was an early leader in business process reengineering and whose success in cutting the time to issue a life insurance policy from twenty-four days to four hours is one of the most widely publicized success stories in reengineering. It fused business, culture, and technology imaginatively and effectively.

It also filed for Chapter 11 bankruptcy soon after it reengineered the policy process. The head of IS has moved on and the IS group has been broken up and reduced in size. Mutual Benefit's problems were ones of knowledge anchors. It misread the implications of the depression in real estate prices and the corresponding impact on public confidence in Mutual Benefit's financial position.

Strategy in general does not compensate for errors and omissions of knowledge anchors, ambiguity, incompleteness of vision and intent, or inappropriate or mispositioned imperatives. This is not an attack on strategy since ineffective strategy and implementation make knowledge, vision, and intent irrelevant. The issue is fusion, attention to what precedes strategy, and above all, recognition that IT is part of business basics now and must be included in the basics of the management process right from the start.

The "Have a Nice Day" School of Service

Companies that achieve structural fusion create, in effect, a coin where the heads side—service and quality—and the tails side—technology—look very different but the result is literally seamless and inseparable. An obvious and well-known instance is Federal Express's legendary level of service. Federal Express promises that it can tell any customer where his or her package is within half an hour or the customer gets his or her money back. Is that service built on people or on technology? Heads, it is people: culture, attitude, training and management. Tails, it is technology: bar code scanners, mobile communications, and data bases. Hidden in the middle are business processes that are markedly different from most firms' attitudes to operations.

Federal Express does not promise to try to deliver or locate any package; it promises to do so. There is no fine print about "provided there is no fog over Memphis airport." One anecdote from a financial services firm, whose accuracy was confirmed by its chief operating officer (COO), was that over a three-month period the company's Federal Express bill suddenly soared. The explanation was that people had discovered that it was faster to send a memo or file from the thirteenth to the fifth floor by having Federal Express pick it up and transport it to Memphis, where it was sorted and transported back to the same building, than to send it through the firm's internal mailroom. This is business networking in action. It is also technology and it is also people. It is also a major new level of service made possible only through time- and location-independence.

The firm that has the people but not the technology is part of the "have a nice day" school of service. Federal Express's staff would be able to say only "Sorry, I don't know. I'm sure we'll find it for you. Sorry. Have a nice day." The firm that has Federal Express IT capability but not its culture is part of the school of technology known as bureaucracy. Most banks in the 1960s and 1970s used technology to automate existing processes, with the people element being forced into patterns of administration rather than service.

The firm that has people and technology but has not thought out its business processes afresh probably has too high a cost base. Much of the disappointment managers in firm after firm report about the lack of payoff from IT investments—which is becoming the single largest concern of CEOs about IT—seems to reflect using it to automate existing processes, create minor variations on existing products and services, and retain the existing organization and levels of staffing. For instance, one major bank

calculated that it obtained about $50 million of incremental annual reve-
nues from its ATM network, for an incremental operating cost of $35 mil-
lion plus a capital investment of at least $300 million. Management was
very disappointed. Further analysis showed, however, that it had avoided
cost increases of $185 million a year in terms of staff savings, the ability
to handle large additional volumes of transactions, real estate expenditures,
and so on. The CEO accepted the figures as accurate. The firm's profits
had remained relatively constant over the prior three years. The cost avoidance and incremental profit from ATMs added up to an annual $200 mil-
lion. Bank teller productivity had soared, measured in terms of accounts
per teller, cost per transaction, and errors. The obvious question then was
why were these gains not showing up as increased operating profits?

The answer was just as obvious. The bank had kept its old structure,
numbers of supervisors and middle managers, and reporting and administrative procedures. Supervisor productivity had plummeted, using the same
measures as for tellers. The bank was grossly overstaffed. It finally took
action to change this, but many other banks and security firms have not
done so and are paying the price, as is apparent in New York City. The
mid-1991 announcement of the merger of Manufacturers Hanover and
Chemical banks, for example, included an estimate that the combination
would cut out sixty thousand jobs, with no loss of revenues. Reliable analyses show that the entire back office processing of all Wall Street firms
could be handled by the spare capacity on Merrill Lynch's or Shearson's
computer and telecommunications systems. The banking system in New
York has gross excess capacity, is overstaffed, has neglected foreign competition, and has wasted its often vast investments in IT made over the past
two decades.[5]

That so many firms have not received value from IT does not mean
that the value was not there to grasp.[6] That systems have been technical
successes but organizational failures does not mean that the technology
was the problem (or the solution). If business processes, people, and technology are handled as separate compartments, no one should be surprised
that the result is less than the sum of the components.

The New Service Equation

The pattern of seamlessness between people, processes, and technology is
apparent in just about every company that is best known for quality and
service. Wal-Mart, for example, has the right goods on the shelf, well-
designed stores, and first-rate staff. How do the goods get there? Through
POS technology and quick-response logistics, which link Wal-Mart to its

suppliers and manufacturers. Toys "R" US, Dillard, Dayton Hudson, and the other leaders in retailing similarly have fused people, process, and technology so that the technology is, as it should be, invisible. In the airlines, American Airlines and BA stand out in the same way, as does Banc One of Ohio in banking, USAA in insurance, and *USA Today* in its quality of service in publishing. (A rhetorical question that illustrates the power of telecommunications to become better informed and the emerging new core logistics of newspaper publishing is: How does *USA Today* manage to print sports scores of late-night West Coast games in its East Coast editions, when the suburban editions of *The Washington Post* and *New York Times* often do not even include evening games played on the East Coast?)

One of the contributions senior business executives make as leaders of the fusion process is to regard knowledge anchors as their own responsibility and business imperatives and policy as their own priority. Imperatives define the purpose and set the criteria for priorities. Policy ends the thinking sequence and establishes commitments: "Since this is the imperative, we need a policy; policy means simply that this is the way things will be done around here. Here's what must drive strategy. This is a big rule." Very few senior managers set the policies and business imperatives for IT. Instead, they operate through reaction; they rely on case-by-case business proposals, cost displacement, or immediate competitive or operational necessity as the driver and on annual budgets as the financial mechanism.

This approach is dominated by delegation.[7] It makes investments in comprehensive IT platforms close to impossible. It provides no statement of the business imperatives that help define technological imperatives; instead, IT planning generally begins with strategy, bypassing the preceding temporal steps of knowledge anchors, vision, and policy. This means that these vital components of innovation do not mesh processes, people, and technology. Looking at the firms that are at the same time acknowledged leaders in business and in their use of technology, there is ample evidence that much of their edge comes from embedding IT into the left-hand side of the fusion map.

There is also evidence that their IT strategies are often less sophisticated than many of their competitors'. They do not need to rely on state-of-the-art technology but can exploit technology which is "good enough." Of the many examples of the use of IT to change the competitive rules of an entire industry, only one rests on the technical state of the art: USAA's creation of a new image-processing technology in cooperation with IBM.

All of the other exemplars were based on technology that was widely available to every major player: this is true for American Airlines's SABRE computerized reservation system, Otis Elevator's diagnostic and service maintenance systems, Mrs. Fields Cookies' store automation and management aids, Benetton's store management systems, Merrill Lynch's Cash Management Account, American Hospital Supply's customer–supplier links and lock-in, and Frito-Lay's hand-held computers. (While the technology was widely available, however, Frito-Lay had to make sure it worked in a heavy-duty environment of coffee spills, hot weather, and "Whoops, sorry, I didn't mean to drop it.")

From Action Back to Knowledge

The knowledge/action drive is the natural one for businesses: think, then act. Begin from the business environment and move via strategy to action. The emergence of "re-" words is a reminder that looking back has become a new business priority. Think, then act, then think again—i.e., rethink continuously. Without this constant scanning of knowledge anchors, IT can at best support the business status quo, even as it may in that very process transform that status quo. The "re-" words have their place in business language when "look again" is a management imperative.

One of the implications of business networking is that the real revolution in IT is that there is no revolution, that technology is really no big deal. Managing it is. Leading it is well within the experience and ability of any senior executive. In many instances, all the executive has to do is to stop doing dumb things. It is dumb to have an aggressive technology plan without an organizational plan, for instance, or to create a business strategy that depends on fast and easy coordination, cross-selling of products, and globalization of operations without ensuring that the firm has a technological platform with the needed reach and range.

Using "Reach" and "Range" Concepts to Decide on IT Platforms[8]

Justifying IT infrastructures has become one of the major priorities of IS managers who see a critical business need for a shared resource, defined through a technical "architecture" and technical standards. From the perspective of IS, the architecture is the strategy and technological integration is increasingly regarded by leading and informed practitioners and consultants as a cornerstone for business integration: the linking of previously independent services and operations.

Very few managers see this as a priority for the firm. By and large, they are not hearing a compelling business message about the need for a coordinated IT platform rather than for a set of independent technical systems and "applications." Increased management awareness about the business importance of IT largely leads to increased delegation and pressures toward systems disintegration. The process is fueled too by the shift from centralized mainframe computers as the cornerstone of the IT resource to a much more economically attractive combination of "distributed" computing, where PCs and local area networks comprise the base, downsizing or "rightsizing" of IS organizations, outsourcing of more and more aspects of development and operations, and a general suspicion of centralized IS units as bureaucratic. Roughly one-sixth of top executives in large firms see a need for a coordinated corporate IT platform.[9]

The paradigm of IT as essentially equivalent to computers encourages senior corporate executives to allow individual business functions, operating units, subsidiaries, and national operations to make their own choices about IT because just about every trend in computing favors small vs. large and distributed vs. centralized. This makes business sense and organizational sense; a decentralized business philosophy demands decentralized IT planning and implementation. Decentralized technology—PCs, workstations, local area networks, departmental systems, and the like—supports decentralized operations.

The argument is attractive. It is also deceptive. It overlooks the business trends generated, stimulated, or supported by business networking: the importance of sharing data across products, services, locations, companies, and countries and the shifts from largely independent business functions to interdependent ones and from product- to relationship-based services and cross-selling, plus the expectation that information will move as fast as goods and transactions.

In this context, the decision about the need for a coordinated vs. local view of IT must rest on the firm's business imperatives. If these do not point to technical imperatives that require a shared platform, then decentralization makes sense. If not, then the lack of a corporate platform becomes a business issue. In the era of business networking, there are very few firms that can afford to ignore this issue.

The platform is a shared business resource and services delivery base, whose business functionality is defined in terms of two dimensions of reach and range:

1. *Reach* determines the locations to which the platform can link, from workstations and computers in the same department (through local area networks) to domestic customers and suppliers to international locations or to anyone anywhere.

2. *Range* determines the information that can be shared directly and automatically across services and systems. At one extreme, systems built on exactly the same software, hardware, and telecommunications can only process messages and data created by each of them. At the other extreme, not yet practical but the main target of vendors and users, any computer-generated transaction, document, and even telephone message can be accessed and used by any other system, regardless of its technical base.

Common sense demands that senior managers make sure that there is no contradiction between the business imperatives, the lifeblood of the firm, and the IT base if IT is critical to turning those imperatives into action. In practice, many business managers have not even thought about the link. Obvious instances are the firms whose imperatives relate to international distribution and coordination but lack international reach in their telecommunications networks; financial service firms committed to relationship management and cross-selling but whose data bases and processing systems cannot interlink; or manufacturers whose systems are built on so many different hardware, software, and telecommunications bases that they cannot share information. The manufacturer's opportunities for improving quality, costs, and lead times are thus greatly constrained. The financial service firm does not know its customers and what products they use. The international firm has to run a "just-in-time" business across multiple time zones without adequate alerting systems and "just-on-time" communications.

It makes no sense to create such a contradiction between business needs and technical resources. When a leading CEO increases the gap instead of narrowing it, there has to be a reason. The most typical reason is simply that the logic of decentralization dominates considerations of coordination. In 1991, the recently appointed head of a major international petrochemical company dismantled the firm's corporate IS group and totally decentralized IT decisions. He is a vocal public enthusiast for IT, but as application not as platform. The consequences are already apparent: significant problems in international coordination, major difficulties in developing manufacturing and procurement systems, frustration about poor information across countries and business units, and rapidly escalating IT costs everywhere.

The CEO is obviously not a fool or anti-IT, but in this organization IS did not have a strong corporate executive as advocate and the issues addressed in this paper of links between business and technical imperatives have been overlooked. What is happening looks like a major blunder; the cause is the compartmentalization of business and IT thinking and strategy.

This is not a defense of centralization. Just like the electrical utility, the IT platform balances coordination and devolution as well as shared capability and independent use. The technical features of the IT platform are defined through an architecture and standards. As with the electrical utility, this is an immensely complex task, involving many trade-offs, uncertainties, problems of meshing new components into the existing base, vendor relationships, and details of operation. The entire logic of the fusion approach is to make sure that the business imperatives are clearly stated and equally clearly related to technical imperatives. The translation of those imperatives into needs for reach and range in a shared platform provide the basis for translating business functionality to technical strategy.

The key step in the transition from leading to managing is to establish big rules. These are policy statements that clarify what must be coordinated and what is entirely a local option. There can and should be debate about the rules, in much of which senior management need not directly be involved; a suitable oversight committee can do this in the same way that capital investment committees or compensation policy groups do. The logic should be that a big rule should be approved only if it is essential to building the platform that is in turn essential to meeting business imperatives. The rule must have a sound business reason. A technical standard may fall out of the rule. If there is no rule, business units are free to make their own choices. There is no need for lots of little rules and IT bureaucracy; units may establish such rules as they see fit, but within the big rules.

This process may seem simple and so it should be. In practice, the entire discussion of architecture, infrastructure, and integration has become very complex in most organizations because the issue of choice of technical standards is inherently complex and always will be so. The bewildering and escalating rate of change in technology make uncertainty, innovation, acronyms, hype, and technical detail a challenge to the very best IT professionals. For them to do their work and for managers to be sure of the business criteria for that work, the management process has to change so that the language can change and real dialogue can replace monologues.

When this is done, senior business managers can get out of the way. They do not need to know or approve the specifics of the technical plan. This plan will mainly address multisourcing and alliances. Strategy and sourcing are increasingly interrelated in IT.

The Economic Target: Quality Profits

Technology is a means to a business end, not an end in itself. The purpose of fusion is to help an organization, whether private or public, achieve its aims and make IT a multiplier in the sense that it significantly leverages its ability to meet them. Those aims may include customer service, maximizing shareholder value, market growth, and so on, but they rest on some economic base. It may be unfashionable in today's world of partnership, service, and total quality management to state that profits are the purpose; but, in Peter Drucker's phrase, "profits are the cost of staying in business."

The view taken here is that profit is no longer the bottom but the top line and that firms have to face up to four economic realities that will dominate the 1990s and almost certainly beyond:

1. The margin crunch will continue; profits, not revenues, are the top line of management concern.

2. Quality and service cannot be charged for but must be provided as the entry fee to the competitive game.

3. Revenue growth will not in itself ensure profit growth.

4. IT investments will consume an increasing fraction of scarce capital, with no short-term guarantees of payoff.

The economics of IT are a frustration for just about every manager. There is no evidence of real payoff for major IT investments in any industry. IT budgets continue to increase faster than business growth. IT now amounts to half the incremental capital investment in most large firms.[10] This is a worry for any responsible business manager.

Responsible IS managers worry about lack of investment in IT as a core protector of future business health. Their most common frustration is that they are often unable to justify major investments unless they can promise direct cost savings. They see business executives as too focused on the short term—the Wall Street disease, where only next quarter's earning seem to matter. In turn, the most common frustration expressed by their business clients is that IS does not offer them a convincing economic justification and has repeatedly failed to deliver promised profits and productivity improvements.

As a result of the overselling of claims about IT creating competitive advantage, there has been a growing skepticism in business about the payoff from IT. Study after study by academics and consulting firms shows that productivity has not been improved in financial services or white-collar work as a whole by the massive investments made in PCs, telecommunications, office technology, and electronic banking. Given the disastrous condition of the banking industry in the early years of this decade, many business executives have closed their ears to the claims. They are looking for ways to outsource networks and computer operations and to drastically cut costs. They see IT mainly as a necessary cost but not as a potential value. The IS field has entirely failed to address the need for a convincing economic model decade after decade. Changing this has to be its priority.

The quality profit engineering framework is a starting point. It faces up to the responsibility to show how IT investments will improve the firm's profits and cost structures. It identifies five categories of economic opportunity: (1) improve margins, (2) improve traditional costs, (3) provide a quality premium without adding a cost premium, (4) provide a similar service premium, and (5) generate "good" revenues—i.e., ones that reuse an existing delivery base and thus do not require major new investments. In this framework, profit is the top line and revenues the bottom line, reversing the traditional order on the profit and loss statement.

Profit as the Top Line

The focus on profit as the top line, not the bottom line, is not a gimmick. The economic reality of the 1990s for U.S. and European corporations is one of increasing margin erosion and, for public sector organizations, increasing budget pressures. Historically, profits were a by-product of revenues. We call profit the bottom line because, in the expansionist economy of the 1950–1980 period, if a firm increased its sales and kept its costs reasonably well under control, profit flowed to the bottom line. Inventory was an asset: if you made something, you could expect to sell it. Revenues drove growth. Management reporting systems were largely sales-based.

The leading firms in the airlines, retailing, car rental, supermarket, telecommunications, and banking industries are increasingly shifting toward a very different economic model, one which emphasizes "yield," a term invented by the airlines and referring to the operating margin of a flight. Airlines frequently discount fares, which decrease unit revenue, to maximize profit margins. They can do this only because their technology base—computerized reservation systems—provides the means to monitor market performance and trends and update prices on a real-time basis.

In 1986, when Continental Airlines launched its Maxsaver discount fares, industry prices dropped by over 40%. The profits of the top airlines increased 36%. This is how to manage profit as the top line. The leaders in yield management, most obviously American Airlines in the United

States and BA in Europe, monitor every individual flight for a year before it actually takes off, fine-tuning prices as traffic patterns become apparent.

The same shift to on-line alerting systems is found among retailers. In the 1970s Sears stood out as the dominant force, mainly through its massive purchasing power; central head-office buyers negotiated contracts with suppliers, and decisions about stocking individual stores were made centrally and/or regionally. In the early 1980s, Kmart led its industry through low prices, again through central merchandising and stocking. By the late 1980s, Wal-Mart had used superior networked logistics to overtake Kmart, creating one of the main success stories of modern business. The individual store became the focus of both operations and information.

POS technology both ensured up-to-the-minute store data on inventory and purchasing patterns, up-to-the-minute pricing adjustments, and up-to-the-day information for central buyers, product line managers, and business unit executives. Wal-Mart first streamlined ordering and distribution and then transformed it. Historically, retailers have closely guarded information about sales to maintain an edge in negotiations with manufactures. Wal-Mart opened up access to its POS data to Levi Strauss, which now supplies directly to the store, with Wal-Mart paying for the goods only when sold.

Through the early 1990s, Wal-Mart had a lower gross margin and offered lower prices than Kmart, yet made far higher operating profits, with telecommunications and POS a key factor in optimizing its information, pricing, merchandising, purchasing, and distribution. Through 1991, Wal-Mart's gross margin was 5% lower than Kmart's, but it sold an average of $250 a square foot of store space vs. $190 for Kmart. Retailers with networked logistics are able to have the right goods on the shelf at the right time and at the right price. Kmart frequently had empty shelves for fast-moving items and boxes on the floor holding items that were not selling. In the recession of the early 1990s, profit growth continued for the networked leaders, even though revenue growth was flat or two to three times lower than profit growth.

In the fashion apparel industry lead times from design to sale are typically six months. In this highly seasonal and volatile business, each element in the chain writes off or writes down 25% of its inventory. In the decade since JC Penny started to use business television for its buyers to meet electronically as needed, several times a week, it has so shortened its reaction time that it has never had an inventory write-down sale. The extension of its network reach to its Far Eastern suppliers similarly cuts out delays in a time-dominated competitive arena; the design process is handled by digital fax and videoconferencing instead of by air freighting samples and documents thousands of miles and back.

Of course, neither retailing, manufacturing, financial services, nor airlines are only time-dominated. They are more and more quality- and service-dominated. In retailing, "discount" used to mean "crummy." Now, it means the best price, best inventory, and best level of service, including after sales. Firms cannot trade off price and service, and there are very few areas of business where a firm can neglect quality and service. Obviously, if it has to increase its own costs to provide them, without being able to pass those costs on in the form of higher prices, it faces yet another pressure on margins.

This is a major reason why revenues no longer ensure profits. The main economic justification for diverting scarce capital to IT has to be its role in helping a company dramatically improve its cost structures, profits, and, sometimes, revenues.

The Economic Realities of the 1990s

There is no major industry where profit margins per unit of revenue are likely to increase in the next decade. Firms will have to learn how to manage as if they were under a permanent recession. Deregulation, globalization, and overcapacity mark most industries. Individually, these erode margins. Together, they guarantee a margin crunch.

DEREGULATION

Deregulation cuts margins by around 20%. This estimate is based on the experiences of the U.S. airlines, securities, and long-distance phone industries and of European financial services. In every industry where deregulation has occurred, unit prices drop fast. The U.S. long-distance telephone industry illustrates this. The price of a typical call has dropped 40% since the AT&T divestiture of 1984. The local telephone industry remained a regulated regional monopoly in this period and prices went up. In Britain, competition in the telecommunications equipment market reduced prices 30% in two years. Airline seat prices on individual European routes dropped by as much as 60% in 1991 once the national carrier's monopoly was relaxed. The average commission on securities dropped by 15–30% first in the United States in the 1970s, then in the United Kingdom, with its radical Big Bang deregulation; the Dutch market; and, most recently, the major Asian markets.

The pattern of deregulation cutting margins is clear and unstoppable. In general, the customer gains (though many critics of both airline and telecommunications deregulation argue that the price cuts were offset by a reduction of service). This obviously puts pressure on any firm, especially where the industry has historically had high costs of administration and overhead. Improving cost structures is an immediate priority when deregulation changes the rules of competition. The U.S. telecommunications industry has cut over one hundred thousand jobs since divestiture. It had no choice. Regardless of one's individual opinion on the political and social issues of deregulation, there can be no question that it puts immediate and sustained pressure on firms to rethink their basics of operation and to recognize that they can no longer pass on their costs to customers.

Deregulation is thus a major driving force for networked logistics. Any hint of a move toward deregulation should alert business leaders to an opportunity for the firm. The basics of the industry will change, and IT will be a factor in who gains or loses from that change.

GLOBALIZATION

Globalization also cuts margins, by up to 30%, partly through its being a form of deregulation that breaks the hold of large and often lazy domestic firms, but mainly by raising the base level of service and quality to that provided by the leading transnational supplier; this might be termed the Sony, Toshiba, and Toyota phenomenon. Companies can no longer charge for service and quality; these become the entry fee for being players in the game. A striking example of this is the car industry. In the era of yuppies and junk bonds, the car of choice for the hotshot was a BMW or Porsche, costing $60,000 and up. The best German cars were highly engineered and high priced.

The Japanese Lexus is highly engineered and low priced, with a level of after-sale service that matches the manufacturing quality. American customers are used to getting letters that announce a recall of their cars, where the message is essentially "We messed up again. The government has made us recall your car. Bring it in and we won't charge you. If you don't bring it in, that's your problem." Lexus handled matters very differently. A small number of customers in 1990 reported a minor problem. Toyota arranged to pick up every car it had sold in the United States to date, drop off a spare, take the owner's car back to Toyota, check the fault, carry out a tune-up, clean the car inside and out, and then return it. One Toyota employee had to drive three hundred miles each way to carry this out.

QUALITY

The Lexus story stands for the new base level of service needed to compete in a marketplace of global excellence. Quality is just as much a new requirement. The total quality movement (TQM) that has become an established priority for most firms, and is represented by the Baldrige Award, has moved quality from being an add-on feature to an integral element of, first, manufacturing, then services, and, most recently, education and government. While much of the quality movement has been a defensive response to the erosion of U.S. firms' market position by Japanese competitors, many American companies have thrived through quality in every market.

For example, Motorola dominates the cellular phone equipment industry, partly through its early commitment to "six sigma" quality, a term borrowed from statistical quality control, which means error rates of less than one part in a million. U.S. retailing is moving aggressively into Japan and Europe. Toys "Я" Us led the United States into Japan, in the face of massive restriction on foreign retailers, and is now in the United Kingdom, offering a range of quality products at prices no British firm can match. Land's End, the catalog clothes seller, has also moved into Britain. Of the top ten securities firms in Tokyo in terms of 1991 profits, six were American.

It is almost certainly not a coincidence that the firms most noted for service and quality are also advanced in their use of IT, ranging from the first-rate telephone service of a Hewlett-Packard or Dell when you have a query or problem with a software or hardware product they provide to Land's End and L.L. Bean shipping goods to you by UPS or Federal Express—thus offering, through electronic service prices, quality, and range of inventory what only a few mall-based retailers can exceed—to USAA electronically approving a loan and issuing an auto insurance policy by fax to the car dealer's office five minutes after the customer phoned. It is intriguing how often IT, which was used in the 1970s and 1980s to depersonalize service, has now made many aspects of non-face-to-face service much more personal. A phone call to USAA is answered with the service agent saying "Hello, Mr. X," and since Mr. X's records, including copies of such documents as handwritten letters, are being pulled up on the screen at that very moment, the conversation is not blocked by "Sorry, I don't have that information. You need to contact. . . ."

Underlying the examples above are two points that are central to quality profits:

1. Quality and service are competitive necessities in the globally driven marketplace.
2. IT is an essential option for providing them.

There are three ways to afford quality and service, in the sense of providing it within decreasing margins per unit of revenue. The first is to charge customers for it; that is not an option in more and more industries. As Compaq found out in the PC market, a Dell or AST will provide a cheaper version of a commodity PC with top-level quality and service so that "cheaper" goes with "better." Compaq later successfully fought back by building better computers but making them cheaper this time and re-thinking distribution. USAA's service is the best in the business, as are its prices. It is becoming harder and harder for any firm to trade off service and quality against price. The high end of the pharmaceutical industry, professional or legal services, and entertainment are exceptions; but the pattern in computers, telecommunications, banking, securities trading, air-lines, retailing, distribution, manufacturing, and publishing over the past decade strongly suggests that this is part of a long-term fundamental shift in business, not a temporary correlate of a recession.

The second way to provide quality and service is to add people. That is what helped get American banking and manufacturing into trouble in the first place. U.S. firms in these and other industries became greatly overstaffed through the 1980s, to the extent that just about every company in the Fortune 1000 has been able to reduce its middle management by 20%, with no loss of efficiency. Firms are aggressively trying to control benefits and health care, which have become a heavier and heavier burden for them and for society as a whole.

If a firm cannot afford quality and service by charging for it or by adding people, the third option is really the only one: use IT to add a quality and/or service premium without adding a cost premium. This does not mean that IT guarantees quality and service, only that it is hard to find any solution that does not rest heavily on IT.

This is a very new situation for most businesses. "Quality" and "total quality management" will not be found in the indexes to top management books of 1982. "Telecommunications" is almost entirely missing. Even in leading books on time-based competition, total quality management, and global competition, the topic is rarely mentioned.

Globalization of business is yet another factor fueling margin erosion. It is highly correlated with overcapacity in many industries, including man-ufacturing, financial services, transportation, and distribution. Much of this overcapacity is the direct result of technology. Manufacturers across the world have reduced the labor component of their goods, shortened time to market, and reduced ordering and delivery lead times, much of this through on-line processing and communication links. They are producing goods to-day with a fraction of the labor and inventory of ten years ago. All of this has led to high productivity and high capacity. There is a similar oversupply of transaction capability in the credit card industry, in bank payment sys-tems and ATMs, and in the securities industry.

How can margins hold up in this era of deregulation, globalization, and overcapacity plus the commoditization that each often accelerates? Obviously, they cannot hold up, even for pharmaceutical firms, which for decades have been able to exploit lengthy patents and premium prices for new drugs. They now face the same pressure to cut time to market and the same customer power in pushing prices down as do manufacturing, retailing, and financial services.

Reinventing Cost Structures

Businesses are having to reinvent their cost structures. That is not the same as cutting costs; anyone can do that just by laying off all of the firm's employees. The challenge is to advance the business while changing the relationship between revenue growth and cost growth and by rethinking profits as the top line, not the bottom line.

Here is the main opportunity for IT in the 1990s. Computer-integrated manufacturing, EDI, customer-to-supplier links, POS, and electronic payment systems open up the chance to change the cost structures of service and quality and thus help rebuild margins. EDI offers the most obvious example of combining service, quality, and improved operating margins per unit of revenue. For instance:

1. 1992 estimates show that electronic claims processing and payment of medical bills cut health care providers' costs of paperwork from $4.85 to under $1 a claim; the industry generates five billion paper claims a year. Payment is much faster, typically two days instead of several weeks.

2. Levi Strauss's Levilink system reduced replenishment time from fourteen to three days for a major chain of stores and cut the time for Levi Strauss to deliver orders from nine days to three.

3. The Port of Rotterdam clears goods through EDI in fifteen minutes vs. the typical two days. Every export order typically has twenty-five to thirty documents. Of these, 50% have to be sent back because the information is inaccurate. Electronic movement of documents has led to greatly reduced error rates and time to correct errors.

4. Super-Valu, the largest U.S. grocery wholesaler, directly saved $100,000 a year on purchase orders and $2 million on inventory carrying costs. In addition, disputes about reconciliation, discounts, and allowances dropped by over half.

The figures here are less important than the underlying issue of directly relating key IT applications and technologies to quality profits: transforming cost structures and quality and service at the same time. The specifics will vary by firm and industry, and effective implementation will depend on the successful fusing of business, culture, and technology. EDI and image processing, for example, involve dramatic organizational change and rethinking of entire business processes. We can expect many firms to introduce them but see a technical success that is an organizational failure.

IT is a key enabler here. Some of the targets of opportunity are:

1. Manage profits, not revenues.
2. Contribute to improvements in traditional costs.
3. To help provide the needed quality and service premium without adding a cost premium.

Tactically, these principles provide the base for assessing where and if IT offers a more likely source of economic benefit than other contenders for a share of scarce capital; if not, then there is no reason to protect IT budgets, let alone continue their historical growth rate at two to four times that of business growth.

Traditional Costs

Traditional costs include the obvious elements of labor, materials, and real estate. IT can contribute to profit engineering in three main ways.

BUILD LOCATION-INDEPENDENCE

Bring work to people, not the other way around. Given the decline of education in the United States and consequent problems of labor demographics, this is sure to be one of the driving forces for international business networking. Cities, states, and even countries are recognizing the opportunity here. There is a common pattern underlying Omaha's becoming the 800 number capital of the United States, Ireland's capturing the back offices of financial service firms in New York for electronic processing, and the many comparable moves to exploit business networking for economic development: (1) a recognition among business and government leadership of the new opportunity location-independence opens; (2) a coherent plan to shift education, especially at the junior college and high school senior levels, toward building skills that can be marketed in relation to that opportunity; (3) close cooperation by the local or national telecommunications providers to ensure fast installation of facilities and service; and (4) a policy and strategy to put in plan an IT platform ranging from "intelligent buildings" to teleports to fiber-optic networks to satellite hubs.[11]

RECREATE ORGANIZATIONAL SIMPLICITY

EDI and image processing have dramatically streamlined overcomplex administrative processes so that American Express cut its billing costs by 25%, USAA improved productivity per employee by a factor of six, and Northwest Airlines increased efficiency in revenue accounting fiftyfold.

Much of today's emphasis for consultants and managers in the IS field is on business process "reengineering," "redesign," and other of "re-" words. These share two underlying common principles: questioning the basics of the process, including why it should exist in the first place, and meshing process, people, and IT, rather than "applying" IT. These principles almost invariably result in streamlining and simplification. They also, over the longer-term, contribute to a reduction in the levels of hierarchy and administrative staff. These can sometimes be dramatic: purchasing departments lose two levels and 80% of people since image processing, EDI, e-mail, and creative thought about the basic activities take out much work that is not worth doing and is better eliminated or handled electronically. Our organizations are too often frustratingly complex. Recreating simplicity seems a vital part of strategic organizational intent.

IMPROVE THE COST DISCIPLINES FOR IT ITSELF

IT is typically the third largest expense for service firms, after labor and real estate. In most companies, the accounting system and management processes do not capture the nature of the costs accurately. A reliable rule of thumb is that the apparent price is really just 20–25% of the full cost.[12] It costs $4 million over the first five years of use to operate and maintain a $1 million systems development. A $5,000 PC takes $8,000 to $18,000 a year to support. While it is outside the scope of this paper, improving the tracking of real costs and their inclusion in business justification is a central responsibility of IS and its business clients.

Quality and Service Premiums

Quality and service premiums have already been discussed several times in this chapter. The core premise of quality profit engineering is that firms have no choice but to ensure ever-higher levels of both quality and service, which will inevitably erode margins unless they can be provided without adding labor costs, managerial layers, and administrative overhead, which in themselves add more of the organizational complexity that has been a barrier to quality and service.

Improving Revenues

Improving revenues is not the same as increasing them. "Downsizing" often means "We can't afford these revenues; they are hurting our profits." This is, of course, the natural outcome of erosion of margins for the reasons of deregulation, globalization, and overcapacity discussed in earlier sections.

IT may be able to help add revenues that do not disproportionately add costs. One emerging trend among the leaders in many industries is to exploit their occupancy at a point of event and operation of their IT platform to change the economics of innovation. For example, as mentioned earlier, it was cheaper for BA to add hotel reservations to its platform than for Marriott and Hilton to build their own infrastructures. McKesson's ownership at point of event of the pharmacist's office for ordering and distribution made it easy to add insurance claims processing and thus become the third largest processor in the United States, business that it took away from the insurance industry.

Point of event and platform open up new opportunities and correspondingly new competitive threats. One key reason why IT has to become part of the knowledge anchors, along with business and culture, is that failure to observe trends in business networking in core logistics in other industries can easily mean overlooking coming intrusions on one's own traditional industry. In addition, if a firm must spend substantial money on telecommunications, information, and transaction processing, it logically ought to maximize the revenues it can gain from the platform that is already largely paid for. The network and data base then becomes a true business asset.

Summary: Quality–Profit–Engineering

The above summary of quality–profit–engineering is, of necessity, brief and the topic demands detailed attention by IS managers, business leaders, researchers, teachers, and consultants. It is now the core element in getting payoff from IT. It is the largest single frustration of business executives. The quality–profit–engineering framework is just that, a framework for thinking creatively and practically about how to resolve the most difficult single problem in IT and the one that has dogged its progress: getting real payoff.

The phrase "quality–profit–engineering" is cumbersome, of course, but was chosen to highlight the following points:

1. Quality profits are not the same as profits, nor are profits the natural bottom line outcome of revenue growth. IS has to focus ruthlessly on helping solve the dilemma of quality and service as essential in an era of eroding margins.

2. Profits are the main issue. The competitive advantage model for justifying IT has largely missed that.

3. This is not an issue of reengineering. We never did the engineering in the first place. IS, as a field of research and practice, has focused on technology, development methods, project management, and most recently competitive advantage. It has neglected the practical economics of managing IT capital.

4. The term "engineering" is useful in that engineering is the discipline most analogous to the aim of IS. It is a profession, with a clear tradition and body of knowledge. Its core is design and project management. It has to keep up with new technology while operating and updating existing technology.

As a profession—or if it wants to be seen as a real profession—IS needs to shift its perspective and build the new disciplines and principles which every senior executive is demanding, principles for ensuring that IT contributes directly and reliably to the top line.

Conclusion: Leading IT

Several conclusions emerge from experiences in applying the fusion map in approximately a dozen firms. The first is the entirely different nature of each case. This point is not as obvious as it may seem. The technical strategies and even technical architectures were fairly similar. Indeed, knowing the industry and a few aspects of the business plan, one can generally predict the architectural blueprint; the sensible range of choices is relatively narrow.

In most of the companies, the focus was on the IT strategy. The strategy did not in general clarify priorities; imperatives do that. The priorities were not ones of detailed applications but of the degree of urgency, the issue of big rules vs. local decisions, and most of all senior business management's emphasis on factoring IT into its own discussions early in business innovation.

The second lesson is that language really is the key. The author's field notes and detailed notes from interviews in all of these firms are full of top managers' comments about "relevance," and "the IS people try to get their message over but they are not on our same wavelength." This applied in every company, even where the IS group was very business-focused and had credibility with the business leadership. The two groups wanted to work together and tried to do so, but they did not connect. The author's strong view is that an overfocus on strategy is the main cause of the problem. In addition, traditional methodologies do not help. All of the companies had brought in consultants for in-depth studies. Some of the reports had led to action, but none seemed to have changed the nature of the mutual planning process or of the dialogue.

The third major conclusion is that the simple idea of business imperatives, reach and range, and big rules were empowering new contributors to language and dialogue. In many instances, these created a response of "Ahha!"

The fourth conclusion should be no surprise: senior managers are urgently concerned about how to assess the economic payoff from IT. This is in the back of their minds, no matter how much of the foreground discussion is on competitive positioning or business opportunity. The quality–profit–engineering framework is not an adequate solution to the question of justifying major IT investments or measuring the business value of IT, but the emphasis on viewing profit as the top line plus the categories the framework uses seem both to make sense and to be useful in evaluating recommendations and trade-offs concerning platform and big rules. The nature of IT cost dynamics, especially the many hidden costs and cost multipliers is "news," including to many IS managers.

The fusion map has been applied to a number of organizations. It seems to work in that it makes sense to business executives, has led to radical initiatives, and has helped make IT a more central and recognized part of a real business dialogue. The issues the map addresses are key ones for IT and for business.

The obvious issue it addresses is leadership so that others can manage. This is critical. It is also practical. One of the main lessons learned from developing, testing, and applying the fusion approach is that we have made IT unnecessarily complex, obscure, and forbidding. As one outstanding IT specialist comments: "Let's make it simple again—please." IT is not nuclear physics. It does not need to retain its own special language. Business executives are as well qualified to handle it as they are other technically centered business resources, such as research and development, other long-term capital investments, and other contributors to business and organizational change. The main principles for this are the vital need to include IT in the process of building and applying knowledge anchors, to be clear about both business and technical imperatives, to have a convincing economic framework for IT, and above all to recognize that in the end leading IT is the business executive's responsibility. Delegation is not a strategy. Abdication is a cop-out.

Notes

Portions of this chapter originally appeared in *IBM Systems Journal* 32:1 (1993): 17–37.

1. J. F. Rockart, "Chief Executives Define Their Own Information Needs," *Harvard Business Review* (March–April 1979): 81–93; R. L. Nolan, C. F. Gibson, "Managing the Four Stages of EDI Growth," *Harvard Business Review* (January–February 1974): 76ff; R. L. Nolan, "Managing the Crisis in Data Processing," *Harvard Business Review* (March–April 1979): 115–126.

2. The term "strategic intent" is taken from an article with that title, written by Gary Hamel and C. H. Prahalad, *Harvard Business Review* (May–June 1989): 64–73. They cite as classic examples of strategic intent President Kennedy's Apollo program to put a man on the moon, Komatsu's "Encircle Caterpillar," and Honda's aim to become a second Ford. In each case, the company "envisioned a desired leadership position and established the criteria the organization will use to chart its progress." A major point made in the article is how frequently the companies best positioned in their industries in terms of revenue and resources in 1970 lost ground in the 1980s through a lack of clear and consistent strategic intent, even though they often had detailed strategies.

3. Outsourcing has become a major "either/or" topic of argument in the IS field. In practice, every large organization uses a combination of sourcing, such as outsourcing network operations but keeping network management in-house, joint ventures with vendors for some system development plus in-house development, plus alliances with other members of the industry. The clearer the statement of imperatives and policies, the more strategy, the "how" of action, becomes an issue of sourcing choices.

4. Most of these surveys are anecdotal. They all point to the same general trends that led *Business Week* to define CIO as standing for "career is over": a dramatic shortening of the tenure of the average CEO to about 18 months, an equally dramatic increase in firing rates, and a growing reliance on bringing people from outside the IS mainstream to head IS.

5. The wealth of literature on this topic and reaching this conclusion includes R. H. Franke, "Technology Revolution and Productivity Decline: The Case of US Banks," *Technology Forecasting and Social Change,* 31 (1987); and P. A. Strassman, "Management Productivity as an IT Measure," in *Measuring Business Value of IT* (ICIT Press, 1988).

6. P. Weill convincingly demonstrates that unless what he calls a "management effectiveness conversion factor" is included in the analysis, just about every study shows no relationship between investment in IT in manufacturing companies and payoff from it. See *Do Computers Pay Off* (ICIT Press, 1989).

7. Detailed examples and support for this assertion are provided in P. G. W. Keen, *Shaping the Future Business Design through Information Technology* (Boston: Harvard Business School Press, 1991). The analysis is based on in-depth interviews with top managers in twenty-seven large U.S. and European firms, their senior management teams, and their heads of information services.

8. A fuller description of the IT platform and reach and range is provided in Keen, *Shaping the Future,* chapt. 7, see ref. 11 therein.

9. See Keen, *Shaping the Future,* chapt. 1, for data and discussion.

10. See Keen, *Shaping the Future,* chapt. 6, for a detailed discussion of IT costs and principles for managing them.

11. These are described in P. G. W. Keen, "Planning Globally: Practical Strategies for Information Technology in the Transnational Firm," in *The Global Issues of Information Technology Management,* S. Palvia et al., eds. (Idea Group Publishing, 1991).

12. See Keen, *Shaping the Future,* chapt. 6, for detailed examples and figures.

7

Managing by Wire: Using IT to Transform a Business from "Make-and-Sell" to "Sense-and-Respond"

❖

STEVE H. HAECKEL and RICHARD L. NOLAN

❖

Chapter Summary

1. Enterprise models can represent the behavior and environment of a business in the same way that the latest generation of commercial aviation systems represent an airplane and its environment to pilots. Both "Fly-by-Wire" and "manage-by-Wire" capabilities are necessary if humans are to serve-and respond quickly enough and well enough to survive and thrive in times of turbulent, unpredictable change.

2. Running a business via an informational representation of it, a model of "what's going on out there and 'how we do things around here' is already a reality in some organizations. It may become the only way of managing in a complex future of rapid, discontinuous change, where the key to success is 'sense and respond', rather than 'make and sell'.

3. Implementing managing-by-wire may be the only way that big companies can match small company flexibility, and speed of response. It provides policy-makers with a replacement for large central planning staff as the mechanism for coordinating the activities of the parts of a company to produce optimum performance.

4. An important aspect of building enterprise models is to see them as learning systems, not automation systems. Successful fighter

pilots are known to have faster 'OODA' loops (observation, orientation, decision, action), which enables them to sense-and respond more quickly. Businesses will similarly stand or fall on their ability to sense, interpret, decide and act, using their corporate information system.

5. Enterprise modeling tools have been around for over 25 years, but they have suffered in the past from an inability to represent human accountability and unstructured work. They also took too long to convert into computer code. New tools, however, have changed this, and made it possible to specify both aspects of business processes (human accountability) and predetermined procedures.

6. While managing a business by managing information that describes it is now possible—illustrated by numerous convincing case studies in this chapter—it does not absolve management from any of their traditional responsibilities. In fact, the onus is even greater on leading and setting strategic direction, as the system frees up time formerly needed to process and collate information, or micromanaging implementation.

7. Because the information system is so intimately bound up with managing the company, "alignment" does not do justice to the extent that IT decisions must be an integral part of business strategy.

The Future of Strategy

IT has introduced new critical success factors for many businesses, such as time-to-market. The resulting compression of product and market cycle times inevitably reduces the premiums that core products or services can command. Added value shifts downstream from development and production to distribution, logistics, and service functions. As this happens, flexibility and responsiveness replace efficiency and predictability as the hallmarks of successful companies.

Coping with the dynamics of an information-intensive economy requires a capacity to react strategically in "real time." Indeed, for many firms, the time available to adapt to environmental change is becoming so short that reengineering the business isn't enough: continuous reengineering is required. This translates into an imperative for leveraging IT to permit very rapid design, implementation, modification, and execution of business processes.

Even as IT renders industrial-age strategies obsolete, it is enabling a fundamentally new type of strategy. Rather than a specific long-term plan to get from where we are to where we want to be, strategy will become an information-intensive structure that provides rapid implementation of any strategy, the duration of which will become shorter and shorter (Fig. 7.1). In particular, strategy becomes a firm-specific integration of people, hardware, software, and information resources orchestrated by an enterprise design model that provides context for the behavior of the business. This model is a high-level representation of business processes in terms of data flows, procedures, and human accountabilities. As discussed below, its purpose is to codify and institutionalize management's design for sensing change earlier and responding to it better than the competition.

From "Make-and-Sell" to "Sense-and-Respond"

The concept of how a successful company operates is undergoing a historic shift: from "make-and-sell" to "sense-and-respond." Make-and-sell is an industrial-age model centered on transactions, capital assets, mass production, economies of scale, and margins. Sense-and-respond is an information- and service-age model, emphasizing client relationships, intellectual assets, mass customization, economies of scope, and returns on investments (see Fig. 7.2).

The fundamental disposition of a *make-and-sell* company is to prepackage and shrink-wrap as much as possible to take advantage of economies of scale and then to offer persuasively what has been made. It thinks of service as a way of enhancing the attractiveness of its products (be they hamburgers, loans, insurance policies, or computers), and it pays sales or manufacturing representatives on the basis of their contributions to its own business outcomes.

A *sense-and-respond* company will concentrate on assembling modular elements into a customized response to a specific customer's specific request. It thinks of products as components of a complete service response, and it pays "relationship managers" on the basis of their contributions to customer outcomes. Large system integrators such as Bechtel and IBM's subsidiary, are quintessential sense-and-respond firms. In a survey of one hundred and ten senior executives attending courses at IBM's Advanced Business Institute (ABI) in 1993, only 11% described their companies' current orientation as sense-and-respond, but 78% of them, representing a wide span of manufacturing and service industries, felt that their firms would have to become sense-and-respond organizations by the year 2001.

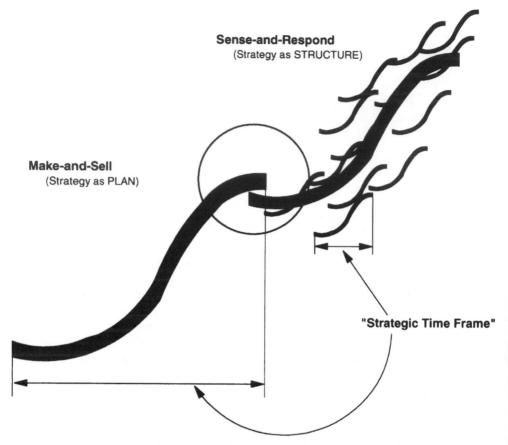

Figure 7.1. The Future of Strategy

These executives shared a conviction that radical change was inevitable and a sense that technology would be a crucial tool in managing the necessary transformation. Virtually all of the respondents (94%) stated that institutionalizing learning and adaptiveness would be increasingly important, 44% calling it a critical success factor.[1] This input, buttressed by a 1994 survey of two hundred and fifty executives, 70% of whom described the future of their companies as "discontinuous," led the ABI to establish a curriculum that focuses on the strategy, structure, and principles of adaptive enterprise design.

   IT is driving the transformation to sense-and-respond, creating a new competitive dynamic that rewards institutional agility.[2]

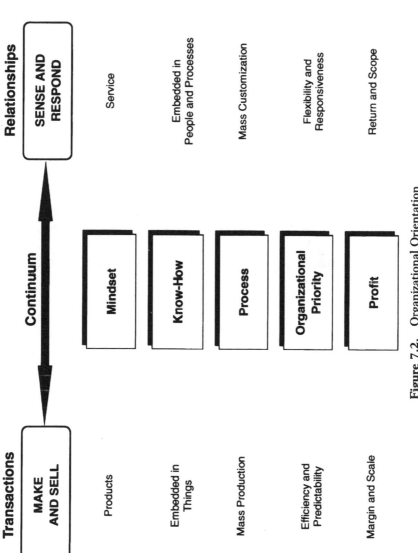

Figure 7.2. Organizational Orientation

An Analogy: Flying by Wire

The advent of jet engine technology in the 1950s had a similar impact on aviation, increasing the speed of fighter planes to a level that made it impossible for pilots to keep up with external events. The response to this technologically induced phenomenon was itself technology-based: using technology to help humans assimilate information and react in time.

The United States Air Force uses the acronym "OODA Loop" to describe the iterative mental process of a fighter pilot. *OODA* stands for observation (sensing environmental signals), orientation (interpreting the meaning of the signals captured), decision (selecting from a repertoire of available responses), and action (executing the response selected).[3] Fighter pilots with faster OODA loops tend to win dogfights, and those with slower OODA loops get more parachute practice.

Today, piloting an airplane is a technology-based operation. *Heads-up displays*—computer-generated pictures projected onto the pilot's helmet visor—present selected abstractions of a few vital environmental factors captured and presented by the technology to assist a pilot in apprehending "what's going on." Instrumentation and communication technologies aid in evaluating alternative responses, and when the decision is made—say, to take evasive action by banking sharply to the left—it is technology that intercepts the pilot's action and translates it through software into the myriad of detailed, nuanced orders that orchestrate the plane's behavior in real time. It is no longer the pilot who knows the detail of "how we do things around here."

Today's fighter pilots do not fly airplanes; they fly informational representations of them. In the aviation business, this is called "flying by wire."

It is important to distinguish *fly-by-wire*, which augments a pilot's function, from *auto-pilot*, which automates it. Auto-pilot systems are much more limited in the number of situations that can be handled and are used only in stable environments. Fly-by-wire systems, in contrast, integrate the pilot's accountabilities and ad hoc activities with software that translates pilot decisions into the instructions that actually modify the plane's behavior. This integration is the product of a design that incorporates responses to both foreseen and unforeseen events. A wide degree of freedom in pilot behavior, including override capability, is a standard feature of such designs.

Flying a modern jet airplane is a complex, sophisticated operation. More than twenty million lines of computer software are required for the current generation of fly-by-wire systems. The fact that an information model can successfully capture this level of dynamic complexity raises the following question: How close are we to *manage-by-wire*—the capability of managing a business by managing an informational representation of it?

Imagine an enterprise design model that defines the behavior of an entire business. Imagine making this model a part of the corporate informational infrastructure, implementing it on technology that connects all relevant sources and users of information and affords maximum sharing among all parts of the firm. In theory, it would then be possible for an executive crew to "pilot" the organization using controls in the information cockpit of the business. Managers could respond to the read-outs appearing on the console, modifying the flight plan en route based on changes in external conditions, monitoring the performance of delegated responsibilities, sending coordinated directions to subsidiary functions, and experiencing exhilaration (or an occasional bout of nausea) upon their execution. Of course, if the model represented some other reality than the one intended, or if it were incomplete, out of date, or operating on bad data, the outcome could be catastrophic—like putting the engines in reverse at thirty thousand feet. Managers must have confidence that the model they design reflects "how we do things" robustly enough to let people make decisions based on it. To the extent that such a model captures the essentials of how the business should operate, it constitutes institutional memory and intelligence, which augment management's ability to run the business. The word "run," rather than "simulate," is used advisedly. The distinction is analogous to that between computer systems that simulate the behavior of an air frame in a wind tunnel to help engineers improve design and computer systems that take off, fly, and land airplanes in response to pilot direction. Such a model is, therefore, neither automation nor simulation. It is an integration of human accountability and preplanned procedure into a dynamic serve-and-respond system.

As with fly-by-wire systems, an enterprise design model should not be a blueprint for automating the behavior of the firm. It should be a coordinating mechanism to ensure that its automated, manual, and ad hoc processes are all carried out in a coherent manner consistent with management's intent. This goal requires codification of that intent, which means rendering explicit those things management thinks important—policies, processes, informational flows, accountabilities, and so forth. A well-designed model operates as a subconscious context-provider that influences the decisions and activities of the human beings accountable for the business.

When people direct an enterprise, or part of it, by changing its codified representation, they are "managing by wire." The value of this capability is directly proportional to the size, speed, and complexity of a company's operations.

The Need for Institutional Intelligence

In today's fast-moving marketplaces, decentralizing operations is crucial; but empowered, networked teams require a unified view of what's happening and a way of coordinating their responses. Coherent behavior must, therefore, be governed by something that codifies the intent of the institution and "the way we do things around here"—most importantly, "the way we change the way we do things around here."

This "something" can be thought of as a kind of corporate mind with institutional intelligence. It establishes the potential and limits of behavior by the individual parts of an organization, while still allowing considerable freedom of choice and creativity of action. Without such a unifying mechanism to guide decisions at the operational level, suboptimized and counterproductive behavior by the constituent units is virtually guaranteed.

In small firms, the coordinating mechanism can reside in the brains of a few people who run the business. In large firms, something else is required, something that institutionalizes the parameters that govern, without dictating, corporate behavior. Whether individually or collectively, executives in firms with hundreds of millions in revenue and tens of thousands of employees cannot "get their minds around their business." Human beings simply cannot keep track of all that happens in and to a large organization, much less coordinate millions of elements into a timely, coherent response. They never could, which is why central staff and hierarchies were created to coordinate and institutionalize behavior. These mechanisms, however, were designed for a relatively stable and increasingly rare make-and-sell business; they cannot cope with the dynamism of today's sense-and-respond environment. Consequently, the traditional large firm can no longer modify its structure and processes in synchronization with marketplace change.

Coping with Size and Complexity

The functional hierarchies and command-and-control systems that were built in and for more stable environments seem to be inevitable casualties of the new sense-and-respond dynamic. However, must companies relinquish the benefits of large size along with the structure that supported it?

Why shouldn't market power, rather than bureaucratic clumsiness, once again become the dominant quality of being big?[4] Since large companies stand to be the major beneficiaries of a manage-by-wire strategy, how important will size be in the future?

Even posing these questions is a fairly new idea. Since the advent of the Industrial Revolution, large organizations have had important competitive advantages—economies of scale and scope, staying power, purchasing clout, deep pockets, and market presence.

Today, big firms are struggling to keep up. The number of employees in U.S. companies with more than ten thousand workers dropped three times as fast in 1991 as did total employment. Revenues of the largest Fortune 500 companies fell from 61% of gross domestic product (GDP) in 1980 to 40% in 1991. Reflecting on "the decline in the advantage of being big" in the *Wall Street Journal*, Peter Drucker declared: "No new theories on which a big business can be built have emerged. But the old ones are no longer dependable." [5] In General Electric's (GE) 1992 annual report, Chairman Jack F. Welch, Jr. told stockholders: "Size is no longer the trump card it once was." Still, he affirmed the value of bigness in giving GE and other companies staying power.

In fact, certain undertakings—such as building power plants, supersonic planes, or the 128-megabit chip—can be effectively pursued only by large firms. Further, the reach of multi-nationals like Royal Dutch Shell, Nomura Securities, and IBM provides indisputable advantages in the emerging global marketplace. For these reasons, GE's relentless pursuit is not to become smaller but, as Welch said, to "get that small-company soul and small-company speed inside our big-company body." He, like Louis Gerstner, IBM's CEO, "wants it both ways." We believe that size is worth saving and that management by wire is a promising strategy for doing so. Organizations must create and codify an information-driven, technology-enabled intelligence with the ability to deal with complexity and dynamism on a much larger scale than heretofore possible. This corporate intelligence will be an informational representation of the business and will replace the functional hierarchy with its command-and-control systems as the institutional coordinating mechanism by which a large firm senses and reacts to change.

The Corporate Mind that Learns

In his book *The Fifth Discipline*, Peter Senge cites Arie de Geus, former Coordinator of Group Planning for Royal Dutch Shell: "institutional learning . . . is the process whereby management teams change their shared mental models of the company, their markets, and their competitors."[6]

A similar view of institutional learning has been a guiding principle in Xerox's business transformation. In a 1993 presentation to the Marketing Science Institute, John Seely Brown, Vice President of Technology for Xerox and director of its Palo Alto Research Center, described the results of several years of research by a team of anthropologists on how learning occurs at Xerox. Based on their work, Brown concludes that organizational learning occurs on the institution's periphery, where intellectual outlyers, renegades, closet philosophers, and others who think "outside the dots" experiment and speculate. He is convinced that learning is a social, rather than a private, process and that the mechanism by which it occurs is story-telling. It is the swapping of stories that causes mental models to change and learning to take place. A primary function of technology should, therefore, be to facilitate storytelling among people with common interests throughout the organization. Accordingly, Xerox will deploy mobile tech-nology to enable continuous networking and the archiving of acquired knowledge among individuals grouped into "communities of interest."

What about institutional learning? How much does the organization know when the people go home? Most organizations would still know how to process payrolls. Some would know how to dispense cash and others how to replenish stocks. These firms can be said to "have learned" certain things through automating them, but it would be a stretch to describe them as "learning," which suggests a dynamic, ongoing process and the capacity to sense and adapt to change.

A company that must integrate many diverse assets, skills, and pro-cesses to accomplish its mission can be thought of as a complex adaptive system—i.e., an adaptive organism. All learning organisms have the OODA loop's four essential processes: sensing, interpreting, deciding, and acting (Fig. 7.3). This adaptive cycle is known in control theory as a closed-loop feedback system. It is important, in designing such systems, to keep them "closed" in order to ensure control. Therefore, a great deal of attention is paid to isolating the system from the external environment.

In a sense-and-respond world it is crucially important to capture as many environmental signals as possible. Instead of a closed system, what is needed is an open system that can deal with ill-structured business sit-uations. We believe that, if well designed, an adaptive loop can become the kind of self-reinforcing cycle that scientists say is requisite for order to emerge from chaos—i.e., an open system. The outcomes of actions taken in one cycle of the adaptive loop become part of the observations of the next. Favorable results reinforce the tendency of the system to take the

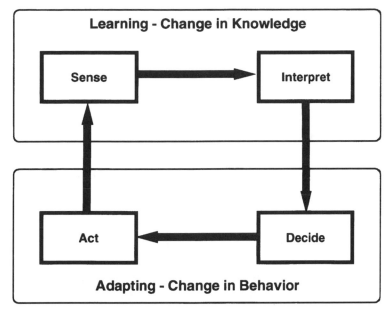

Figure 7.3.

actions that led to them; poor results weaken that tendency. Learning systems interpret feedback in terms of better/worse, good/bad, or adequate/inadequate, then make decisions based on their predictions of what actions in their repertoire are most likely to improve their situation.[7]

Sensing

Every organism captures a species-specific subset of all of the signals present in its environment. There are sounds we cannot hear, sights we cannot see, pressures we cannot feel, odors we cannot smell, and flavors we cannot taste. Similarly, there are buyers, sellers, customs, competitors, transactions, and many other environmental elements of which a business is unaware. If it does not sense enough of the critical components of "what's going on out there," it will perish.

Technology can and does augment both human and institutional sensing. Telephones, microscopes, telescopes, magnetic resonance imaging, sonar, and mass spectrometers are but a few of the devices that extend our sensory reach from the quark to the quasar. ATMs, scanners, POS terminals, PCs, ticketing machines, automated taco-making kiosks, intelligent shopping carts, carburetors, vending machines, and a raft of other devices with embedded digital circuitry are electronic probes in the environment; but if the signals they collect are not remembered and integrated into the corporate intelligence, they remain untapped assets.

Interpretation

Interpretation is the process of assigning meaning to what has been sensed. It involves filters, prioritization schemes, and mental models that structure raw data into recognizable patterns. Mental models come with a variety of labels: perceptions, concepts, constructs, paradigms, gestalts, worldviews— to mention a few of the more common terms. Mental models are good or bad, depending on their relevance, scope, and the degree to which they are integrated with response mechanisms. In every case, however, the trade-off involved is the same: meaning at the cost of completeness. This trade-off is perhaps most obvious in the case of specialists: they see the world in terms of their specific paradigms and miss the meaning that other models might provide. That is why John Seely Brown hired anthropologists to help Xerox "see" itself better.

Deciding

Selecting from an available repertoire of responses on the basis of an interpretation of the signals sensed is our definition of *deciding*. An adaptive organism necessarily has a capacity for predicting outcomes so that it can select an option that improves its situation. Its repertoire may include unilateral, collaborative, or delegation options. Responses may be involuntary and reflexive or conscious and reflective. In either case, to be effective they must exhibit coherence and coordination. Otherwise, they appear as the corporate equivalent of spasms and twitches. An interesting aspect of organizations is their potential for learning by acquisition of other organizations or people. Individuals, of course, do not have this option, but teams of individuals do. The team or organization learns to the extent that acquisition changes the collective mental model.

Acting

Executing a selected response completes the cycle. Since the action changes the real world, there is the potential for sensing that change and factoring it into a modified interpretation of the environment. Deciding and acting comprise the response mechanism of an adaptive system. The mechanism for coordinating responses defines "how we do things around here." We emphasize again that creating an intelligent corporation is not an exercise in automating a business. It is, instead, a strategy to specify and centralize only the essential mechanisms that govern a firm's behavior, including:

- the strategic intent of the firm
- the rules and authorities (legal, logical, policy) that establish the boundaries of "how we do things around here"
- the models that enable consistent interpretation of environmental events
- the specifications of human accountability for key organizational outcomes and the processes that produce them

An example of an institutional learning loop at work is the system that Wal-Mart and its apparel suppliers use to replenish stocks. Every evening, Wal-Mart transmits five million characters of data about the day's sales to Wrangler's, a supplier of blue jeans. The two companies share not only the data but also a model that interprets the meaning of the data and software that acts on that interpretation to send specific amounts of specific sizes and colors of jeans to specific stores from specific warehouses on specific trucks. The result is a win–win outcome of lower logistic and inventory costs and fewer stockouts. Every time the data model is changed to reflect a new fashion season or pricing pattern, both Wal-Mart and Wrangler's learn and adapt.

Using technology to integrate information into a coherent institutional view of "what's going on out there" (sensing and interpreting) and linking that view to a sufficiently rigorous model of "how we do things around here" (deciding and acting) is a strategy for creating an adaptive enterprise. If the loop uses IT to keep in tempo with the rate at which the environment changes, it becomes the basis for implementing a manage-by-wire strategy. As the tempo increases, it becomes more important to employ technology in each of the essential functions of the adaptive loop.

Institutional Intelligence and Corporate IQ at Two "Smart" Companies

A firm's intelligence, like a human's, must function within a physical structure. This can happen only if presently isolated and fragmented technology

is integrated into an institutional central nervous system. In this technological infrastructure will reside the information and organizing principles
that define how the firm senses, interprets, and adapts to its environment.
Figure 7.4 depicts the capacities that define a firm's corporate "IQ":

- the comprehensiveness of its information sources; how much does it
  sense of what it needs to sense

- the degree to which it can identify important relationships in the data
  and thereby interpret the meaning of what it senses

- the number of elements it can integrate into a shared, coordinated
  response to environmental change

A corporate intelligence must deal with real-world entities (such as
competitors, customers, employees, regulations, products, services, and
capital assets), their attributes, and their relationships. A large company
may have hundreds of these categories and tens of thousands of entities,
each a source of information that may change daily or even hourly. Their
sheer number is compounded by the dynamic nature of their relationships.
The resulting complexity is far beyond the capability of managers, even at
a very high level, without assistance from technology.

Computers already play an important role in helping management cope
by automating many applications of the business. In fact, a small, relatively
uncomplicated company may be able to build a robust, hard-wired corporate intelligence from these automated processes.

Mrs. Fields Cookies: A Hard-wired Approach to Manage-by-Wire

Debbi Fields captured in software the ingredients that she believes make
for success in the cookie business.[8] In 1978, when she opened her second
store in San Francisco, forty-five miles from Palo Alto, she experienced the
logistics problems of maintaining hands-on management at remote locations. Furthermore, she and her husband Randy had ambitious expansion
plans that would make her personal oversight at each store impossible. They
needed a strategy for becoming big that would enable them to understand
what was going on in hundreds of dispersed locations and ensure that local
management responded to daily challenges in the same way she would.

Some of the fundamental things that make Mrs. Fields "Mrs. Fields"
are a thorough articulation of "how we do things around here," the conviction that quality must be centrally controlled, and the recognition that shar-

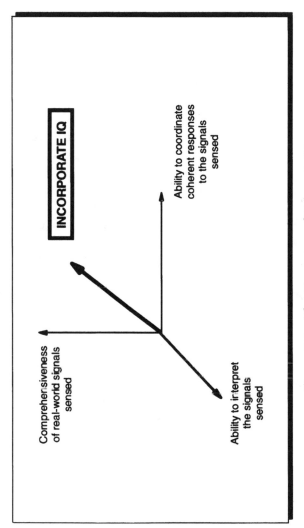

INCORPORATE IQ

Comprehensiveness
of real-world signals
sensed

Ability to interpret
the signals
sensed

Ability to coordinate
coherent responses
to the signals
sensed

Figure 7.4. The Dimensions of Corporate IQ

ing knowledge between herself and the store managers is of central importance.

Drawing on her own experience making and selling cookies, Debbi Fields abstracted, and Randy Fields then codified in computer programs, the essentials of running her business. Software is the form in which Mrs. Fields issues instructions and advice to store managers and thereby makes herself virtually present in every one. Each morning, local managers project sales for the day and enter information into the computer—e.g., the day of week, season, weather.

The software analyzes these data and responds with hour-by-hour instructions on what to do to make the day's objectives—how many batches of different cookies to mix and make, how to adjust these mixtures as the actual pattern of customer activity unfolds, when to offer free samples, how to schedule workers, when to reorder chocolate chips, and so on. The program also advises on nonroutine activities, such as how to react to a malfunctioning piece of equipment, how to interview applicants, and how to administer benefits.

As a matter of policy, the company relies on just one database and one set of principles about how things are done the Mrs. Fields way. Because her vision is so complete and unambiguous and the business niche in which she operates is relatively well defined and stable, Mrs. Fields has been able to automate a remarkable portion of operations—in effect, cloning herself in her stores.

Since the software had hard-wired behaviors for store managers in America, it required reimplementation when Mrs. Fields moved into Europe and Asia. After a troublesome period of consolidation, the company has resumed its expansion. In early 1993, Mrs. Fields owned four hundred stores and franchised three hundred and eighty others, with plans to open another one hundred by 1994. The company employs five thousand full- and part-time people, only eighty-seven of whom work at headquarters. Proforma profit at Mrs. Fields was $2.1 million in 1992, a year in which the company announced the sale of its complete store management system, called Return on Investment, to Burger King.

Most larger firms compete in more complex, diverse, and dynamic environments than Mrs. Fields. If anything, their management is heading in the opposite direction from hard-wiring operations. Rather than specifying explicitly to "do it this way," many executives are empowering employees to "do it the best way you know how." However, without coordination, accountability, and shared objectives, this approach can lead to "management by letting go of the reins."

Brooklyn Union Gas: Using Technology to Institutionalize Flexibility

In 1987, after the failure of a $2 million effort to upgrade a badly obsolescent 1971 Customer-Related Information System (CRIS) and after several years of feasibility studies and prototypes, executives at billion-dollar Brooklyn Union Gas approved a $46 million proposal by its IT department to completely redo the system. Approval for the three-year project was given with a mandate: the new system should be designed to not become obsolete, even in an environment of deregulation, new regulation, and an increasing need for micro-managing the business.

The IT staff codified in the new system (CRIS-II) a great deal of the customer side of its business—everything from meter reading and cash processing to credit, billing, and customer field service orders. Brooklyn Union's corporate intelligence now contains ten thousand appropriate actions that people or systems should take in eight hundred distinct business situations. The ten thousand processes are incorporated in CRIS-II by specific combinations of seven hundred modular software building blocks, an implementation that institutionalizes flexibility.

These programming "objects" are linkable in accordance with parameters of law, logic, and business policy that broadly define the scope of acceptable corporate behavior. At present, control of these parameters is not directly in the hands of business managers. They are embedded into the system by the IT department based on its interpretation of management intent. Like Mrs. Fields Cookies, the intermediation of IS professionals is required to reflect new management policies in the software that determines business behaviors. Establishing new policy is not, therefore, a part of either company's manage-by-wire capability.

Still, after an investment of $48 million and four years of successful operation, CRIS-II has brought many benefits to Brooklyn Union. New capabilities can be created by making extensive reuse of existing objects and adding only those required for specific additional functions. For example, 30% of the objects required for a proposed new engineering system already reside in CRIS-II. Senior management views the major payoff as the ability to react to market change and opportunity in a timely way and with costs that are commensurate with the nature of the change or the size of the opportunity. In other words, at Brooklyn Union, IT is being used to cope in an environment of discontinuous change.

CRIS is living up to the mandate given to the IT department not to deliver a system that would become obsolete. Because of its modular architecture, it is adaptable enough to respond in time to an accelerating pace of marketplace change.

How smart are these two companies? We define the IQ of a firm as the extent to which it demonstrates an ability to cope in each of the dimensions of Figure 7.5: the comprehensiveness of what it is able to sense; the extraction of meaning from the data sensed; and the integration of shared information, logic, and policy into coherent behavior.

At Mrs. Fields, there are comparatively few informational sources and people's roles are quite clear. Therefore, corporate IQ can be characterized as very high in the dimensions of comprehensiveness and sharing in an environment of relatively low complexity.

At Brooklyn Union, CRIS-II captures a smaller percentage of the total business, albeit in a much more complex industry. Its ability to share information and logic is high, as is the comprehensiveness of environmental signals sensed in one important area—customer-related activities. Data models codify the way the company interprets the meaning of the data that it senses, which raises its IQ.

Because Brooklyn Union has no enterprise design model, it has no mechanism for managers to directly modify the hard-wired policies contained in CRIS-II and no business design that relates CRIS-II to the engineering side of the business. Nevertheless, compared to many other companies, Brooklyn Union is an institutional genius.

Mapping a Business into an Information Model

In the new world of empowered, networked teams, management must provide and codify intent and policy. Managers require, therefore, tools that let them specify objectives, human accountabilities, high-level processes, measurements, and policies without having to directly manage the details of implementation—just as an individual can bound up a flight of stairs two at a time without consciously instructing nerves and muscles to do so.

Human mechanisms for sensing and responding to outside events constitute a useful model of how an organism, as opposed to an organization, institutionalizes such a capacity:

> We react to our perceptions of particular objects and events (a noise in the night . . . an unexpected reaction by a neighbor to some innocent question) by trying to map them into some pre-existing concept that has a linguistic representation (a burglar . . . paranoia). In other words, our moment-to-moment

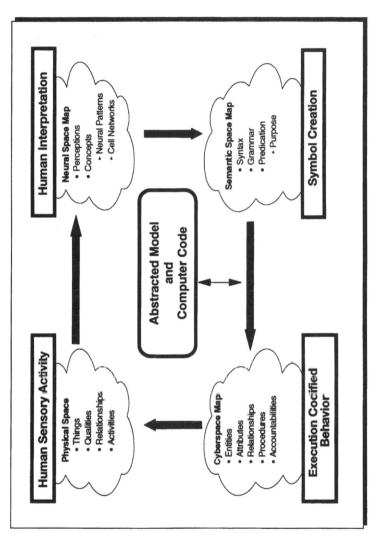

Figure 7.5.

functioning in the world relies, unconsciously but quite implicitly and completely, on our having the equivalent of a map of reality which includes all the things that, at least for our species, are in it. This map enables us to orient ourselves rapidly to the fluctuations of the environment and to prepare appropriate responses to them.[9]

Human sense organs capture signals from real-world things and events, as well as their qualities and relationships, then map them into specific neural patterns that constitute our perceptions and concepts (Fig. 7.5). When reality is mapped into neural space, some things are lost—sounds we cannot hear but dogs can, sights we cannot see but infrared sensors can, pressures we cannot feel but cockroaches can. What is captured, however, clearly suffices for humans to function and evolve as a species.

Mapping from neural space into semantic space translates perceptions and concepts into a form that can be shared by others. Another portion of reality is lost in this transition, as evidenced by the universal experience of being unable at times to satisfactorily express what we feel or think. Again, the loss is minor compared to the advantage gained—the means of communicating with others to coordinate behavior. An important attribute of semantic space is its explicit structure, provided by the rules of predication, syntax, and grammar. These rules govern, but do not dictate, the permissible paths through semantic space: phrases and sentences.

Human beings carry out these mapping processes continuously, often automatically. Why should their analogues not be applied to a business? In fact, there are many similarities. Like humans, businesses fail to capture some information (about customers it doesn't have, for example). Companies also lose information as reality passes through successive filters before being captured in "cyberspace," a term coined by William Gibson in his novel *Neuromancer* to describe a world created by computers and inhabited by symbolic abstractions of people, places, and things that are accessible through a terminal.

Unlike human beings, a business system can be designed. A firm's intent and purpose can be specified, as can its ability to sense, interpret, and react to the external world. Such a design would seem prerequisite to "institutional learning," if the term is ever to mean more than the aggregate learning capacity of people in the firm.

A Tool for Designing a Corporate Mind: Enterprise Modeling

An *enterprise design model* is a goverance mechanism. It maps a business and its functions from semantic space into cyberspace, a process completed by writing computer code. Once represented in computers by specific bit patterns and machine states, the model becomes "real." The computer's memory and speed can then be leveraged to track and relate millions of events, responsibilities, attributes, and relationships simultaneously; to allow selective sharing of information and logic; and to initiate physical processes—in other words, "to keep a mind" around a large, complex organization.

Enterprise modeling methodologies have existed as tools for IS professionals for more than twenty-five years. Because of their origins, they are typically high-level flow charts that capture procedures and data flows. As management tools, they suffer three major drawbacks:

1. They fail to adequately incorporate the elements of commitment and human accountability in business processes, which is a particularly important omission because procedure without accountability is bureaucracy. Process is more than procedure.

2. They cannot deal with unstructured work and ad hoc processes, which is the nature of most managerial work in any business and the essential element of adaptive behavior.

3. They take years to map into computer code, by which time the model is usually badly out of date. The reason for this is that process description languages were not rigorous enough for computers to execute directly from the model.

Enterprise models have typically been prepared by IS professionals based on their interpretations of what business people tell them about the processes and policies of the company; but if it is to represent the institutionalized understanding of "how we do things around here," an enterprise model should be specified by the conscious part of the corporate mind—the people running the company. It should be expressed in business language, not IS terminology, and be rigorous enough for information systems to interpret accurately. Only then can management have confidence that processes will be executed with integrity—i.e., as designed.

To completely and faithfully represent management's design, any modeling notation must be able to:

- unambiguously and consistently characterize any process, at any scale, from individual to enterprise
- account for all possible outcomes of every process
- show the accountabilities and commitments—as well as the procedural components (tasks and decisions)—of business processes

A representational schema based on theoretical work by Fernando Flores and extended by Allan Scherr, a former IBM fellow, has been verified to have these properties. In an early test, it was applied to a product–change process that IBM's Vice President of Manufacturing considered the best in the organization. Representing the process in this schema revealed multiple opportunities for procedural improvements, but most startling was the accountability gap it made clear: in the entire process, not a single commitment by people was made—only forecasts, estimates, and targets. Because there had been no way of representing accountabilities, the lack of commitments in this process had never before been realized. Certainly, it had never been realized that the best process was in fact a bureaucratic one because only its procedural elements and data flows had been defined.

This schema is a universal and general protocol. It is capable of representing the entirety of an organization's behavior, which is nothing more (or less) than the execution of its business processes, both ad hoc and formal. Each business process is comprised of two components: the accountabilities of humans for specified outcomes (who owes what to whom by when) and the procedures that produce these outcomes (who or what does what to what in what sequence; see Fig. 7.6). The procedures may be automated, documented, or simply informal traditional behavior. Each procedure, as well as the roles and accountabilities of the humans involved, can be represented by the protocol in an unambiguous way and with sufficient rigor to allow computers to faithfully execute processes represented in its notation.

The art of business process design lies in knowing the correct balance between accountability and procedure that is appropriate for a given process. In general, the amount of accountability that should be designed into a given process increases with the amount of adaptability required.

Because of the rigor of this schema, business people can change the way their businesses operate by changing the models that represents them.[10] At Brooklyn Union Gas, for example, its use would make possible a shift in responsibility for designing the way the company relates to its customers from the IS department to business professionals.

Management's Role in Creating the Enterprise Design Model

Having adopted a sense-and-respond strategic intent, management should formally determine the highest level at which coherent institutional behavior adds value. This means deciding which business units, if well coordi-

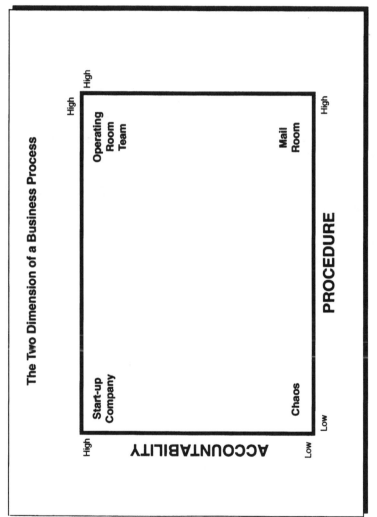

The Two Dimension of a Business Process

High
High
Operating Room Team
Start-up Company
High
ACCOUNTABILITY
Low
Chaos
Mail Room
Low
High
PROCEDURE

Figure 7.6.

nated, could together create more value than the sum of their individual parts. There is no pat answer to this question, and widely divergent views can exist within the same industry. For example, McGraw-Hill's strategy is to treat its IT infrastructure, and certain editorial contents, as assets to be shared among multiple units. Dun and Bradstreet, however, deliberately emphasizes the separateness of its various informational services because management believes there is more cost than synergy associated with sharing.

Once the target level is identified, economies of scope can be pursued to leverage common assets. This is the level from which the enterprise design model will eventually orchestrate subordinate activities.

Management should also select and use one business design language and insist on its use throughout the organization. In many companies, a variety of first- and second-generation enterprise modeling techniques have already been used to capture key procedures in different functions or operating units. It is important that these be recast into a common business language and that the accountability dimension be added. Then, there can be one way of talking about "how we do things around here," and future integration of presently autonomous organizational units will be facilitated, if that should ever make strategic sense. This does not mean that the existing procedural work has to be redone. It forms a necessary base, to which specification of accountabilities and protocols for ad hoc activity can be added.

The technological infrastructure should be assessed in terms of the parameters discussed below to ensure that these are sufficient to accommodate coherent behavior at the target level. To support a modular, responsive business, the software that implements the informational business model will have to be reengineered into reusable modules, or "objects." Object-oriented programming systems are an IS implication of the manage-by-wire strategy.

Of course, it is business management, not IS professionals, that should design the business. Management should make the strategic decisions regarding the environmental data to be sensed—where and what probes should be positioned where, the level of detail to be captured, and how often to sample. It means business people getting involved in, and understanding, the design of data models because if they reveal irrelevant or insufficient patterns, the business will experience institutional delusions about "what's going on out there."

If realized, managing by wire a significant spectrum of a firm's activities will redefine the practice of management, just as fly-by-wire systems redefined the skills needed to fly an airplane. However, management's collective understanding of the business and its environment will remain the major determinant of success. The quality of management's abstraction, the accuracy with which it is mapped into the informational infrastructure, the placement and sampling rates of its informational probes, and the skill with which the model is manipulated and modified will become critical success factors by the year 2000.

Of course, even an elaborate model that accurately specifies the parameters of organizational response to environmental stimuli and management intent will not guarantee predictable outcomes, much less success, any more than a DNA map can predict an individual's golf scores.

The IT Infrastructural Capabilities that Determine Corporate IQ

Restructuring information, rather than organizational units, is part of the manage-by-wire scenario. The ability to change reality by modifying an informational model of it is possible only with the requisite underlying technological infrastructure. As depicted in Figure 7.4, the degree of corporate intelligence varies directly with the number of sources comprising the information, the extent to which it is shared, and the amount of its structure (or context). Accordingly, the key parameters of an organization's technological infrastructure are connecting, sharing, and structuring (Fig. 7.7).

Connecting (Sensing)

As an infrastructural function, *connecting* determines what the firm can institutionally sense—i.e., "what's going on out there." It is measured by the degree to which the technological architecture links informational sources, media, locations, and users. This attribute defines who and what can be accessed and determines its capacity to perceive its environment. How many points of presence to establish in the marketplace, where to place them, and how often to sample them are, therefore, strategic design decisions.

As the advantages of extended connectivity became obvious and the cost of communications technology declined rapidly in the 1970s, networks sprang up in multiple places for multiple purposes. As a result, many companies today are criss-crossed by dozens of independent networks that are incompatible technically and thus actually inhibit, rather than promote,

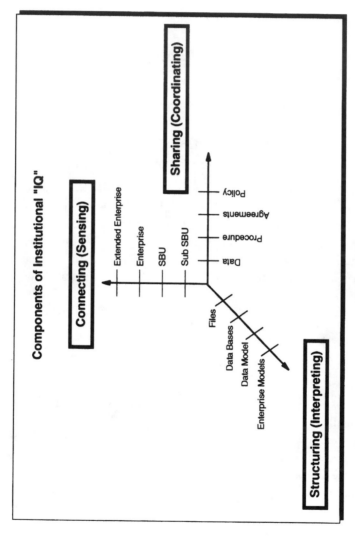

Figure 7.7.

information sharing. Separate networks reinforce the tribal mentality that exists in functional hierarchies, with the result that in many organizations the left hand rarely knows what the right is doing. This lobotomization of the corporate intellect remains perhaps the single largest impediment to realizing the potential of technology to help manage large companies.

Structuring (Interpreting)

Structure is created by information about information—e.g., how data are classified, organized, related, and used. Tables of contents, indices, and "see also" references are familiar examples. Structure provides context, and context yields meaning. Structure can be quite elaborate, even for "hard copy" information. *The Encyclopaedia Britannica,* for example, devotes an entire volume (the *Propaedia*) to describing the overall organization and relationships of the information in the other twenty-nine volumes.

Humans interpret environmental signals by structuring information and ideas into constructs, paradigms, conceptual diagrams, gestalts, and worldviews to create context and extract meaning from what we experience. These structures act as filters of the data bombarding us every day. The corresponding filters for a computer-based corporate mind are called *data models.*

The value that structure provides can be dramatic because when information from previously unrelated sources is integrated in a meaningful way, human beings become capable of thinking thoughts that were previously unavailable to them. When computers use their speed and memory to reveal patterns in raw data, they complement the extraordinary capacity of humans to recognize and assign meaning to patterns.

For example, using spectral analyses and mathematical equations that model the red shift, a computer can process light signals from a remote galaxy to calculate the distance and size of its component parts. The results can be displayed in a three-dimensional picture and rotated, allowing human beings to see the galaxy from the back or side and to discover, as happened recently, a huge void passing laterally through it. The pattern was implicit in the data, but not until a computer made it manifest could humans recognize and be startled by it.

Using models to structure information can be just as helpful to the brand manager confronted with reams of scanner data as to the scientist inundated with celestial data. Frito-Lay's "data warehouse" was built using data models to structure information in ways likely to reveal patterns of interest to analysts and top managers. Because all of senior management views the same patterns, consensus on action can be achieved much more quickly.

The models in Frito-Lay's data warehouse relate information in multiple databases and extract meaning from the torrent of transaction data that gushes from supermarkets every day. In so doing, the data warehouse has substantially raised the company's IQ in the structuring dimension. Frito-Lay has centralized the management of information as a prerequisite of decentralizing the use of it by managers competing in the field against small, flexible rivals. The greater precision and timeliness of Frito-Lay's information enabled the company to reduce the time to repackage a product from sixteen weeks to two and to move from corporate to regional pricing models, cutting the time to institute a price change from twelve weeks to two and a half days.

Structuring information can be a major advantage, even if it is done for isolated functions or applications. We saw earlier how Wal-Mart extended this leverage by sharing its data models with suppliers.

Sharing (Coordinating Decisions and Actions)

Sharing makes possible coordinated effort and, therefore, the benefits associated with teamwork, integration, and extended scope. The capacity for coordinated, coherent behavior by the elements of a complex organization is a function of the degree to which there exists a common understanding of "what's going on out there" and "how we do things around here." Getting everyone on the same page in a large business requires an institutional capability to share data, interpretations of the data, and specifications of core processes.

Using technology to share data, data models, and application software with its suppliers creates win–win benefits for Wal-Mart and Wranglers, and using technology to share data among multiple application programs was a key functionality of the grandfather of strategic IT success stories. When it integrated multiple applications by enabling them to share data, the SABRE reservation system came to "know what it knows" about American Airlines' business. Then, when inspired marketing minds conceived of frequent flyer programs as a way to improve passenger loyalty, American was able to implement it in a matter of months.

To this day, the automated data-sharing capacity of its IT infrastructure provides American with a persistent advantage over competitors who responded with "unintegrated" frequent flyer programs. Any change in the shared database is available to all software programs using those data, enabling a coordinated response by them. For example, if you are a frequent flyer on American, SABRE knows it before you board the plane and you may be offered a first-class upgrade should one be available, which SABRE also knows. On some other carriers, this information is not simultaneously known by separate applications and is, therefore, never translated into action that creates a customer value.

The added-value that an integrated system may yield leads to a subtle, but nevertheless important, distinction about applications: implementing a breakthrough, such as the automated airline reservation system, may ultimately be less important than how it is implemented. A stand-alone application is less likely to deliver sustainable competitive advantage than one implemented on an integrated technology platform designed for extensive sharing of information. Anyone who receives multiple premium notices on the same day from the same insurance company for different policies is on the receiving end of an informational infrastructure with a multiple personality disorder. These firms have no corporate intelligence about clients.[11]

As defined above, a firm's IQ is determined by the degree to which its IT infrastructure connects, shares, and structures information. Isolated applications and data, no matter how impressive, can produce idiot savants but not a highly functional corporate behavior.

Managing a Large Business by Wire

We argued earlier for a "strategic change in strategy," shifting the emphasis from making and selling products (be they loans, computers, insurance policies, or hamburgers) to providing customized service responses, of which the product is an integral part. Such a shift implies different optimizing parameters for the business and a change in the primary managerial function from resource allocation to value management and context-setting.

As depicted in Figure 7.8, "what we do" is a result of what is understood about customers, other players (e.g., competitors), and the firm's own distinct institutional competencies. The shaded components depict what a modular sense-and-respond firm does physically—create customized responses from modular values provided either by the firm itself or its allies. The design and orchestration of this physical behavior is via an informational representation of the business, depicted on the left side of the diagram. This representation originates in the brains of humans and is then codified as an enterprise design model that defines, enables, integrates, and coordinates the procedures and accountabilities that constitute acceptable business behavior.

Modularizing business processes, data, and offerings is a crucial com-

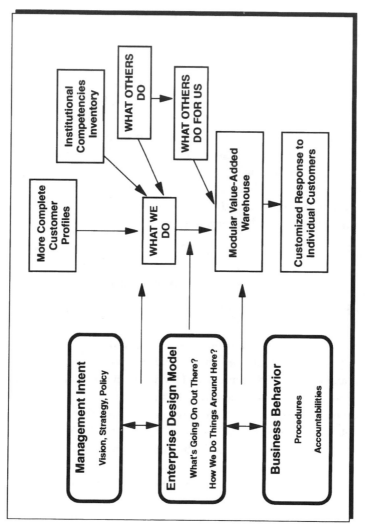

Figure 7.8.

ponent of adaptive behavior. Modular design builds flexibility into the organization and greatly facilitates change management. It avoids hard-wiring the past, present, or any particular future into institutional behavior. These are some of the concepts and convictions that drove the executives of Global Insurance to a manage-by-wire strategy.

Global Insurance: History of a Prototype

Global Insurance, a $78 billion asset company, was suffering under the weight of being big. New policies took two years from conception to consumer, operational costs were 15% higher than competitors, and niche players were luring away customers with innovative offerings. Furthermore, the insurance industry was changing so fast that management had less and less confidence that any action it might take would make a strategic difference. As Global's CEO said:

> There was no way of knowing who our new competitors would be in five years, how the regulatory environment would change, or what financial instruments would be important to customers. How in the world can you justify investing in any long-term strategy under those circumstances? The answer is, you can't.[12]

So, rather than investing in a specific strategy, top management decided to spend $110 million to create a capability to quickly implement any strategy. The CEO continued:

> We had to get rid of the mindset that we were in the business of making and selling policies. That had caused us to organize around products and tie our processes to individual product lines. But products were the things that changed most often, and we were strangling in our own business processes trying to keep up with the smaller players.

Management decided that it must invest in a structure to achieve the responsiveness and flexibility of a small company, rather than in a plan to produce specific products with maximal efficiency. Global implemented the new structure by and in IT. Processes were designed to capture and interpret events in the marketplace; provide analysis and decision support for underwriters, actuaries, and managers; test these decisions for consistency with the firm's practices; and then execute them in an on-line transaction system. One result: agents could customize a policy in a client's living room.

There was, of course, technological risk associated with this project. Even more uncertain was the ability of management to adequately specify the hundreds of procedures and dozens of management policies necessary to ensure that Global's responses coincided with its business goals. The CEO also worried that his IS team, lacking an adequate business context, might misinterpret management's specifications in the process of translating them into the language of their modeling tool:

> Essentially, we had the task of making explicit in the form of models and computer code how we wanted to run the company and at the same time increase the freedom of individuals to act on their own initiative. That was the only way we could imagine making a firm of this size quick enough on its feet to win in alley fights with the small guys. Size helps in the capital markets, but it can be an albatross in a rapidly changing marketplace.

Global's strategic response to smaller, more agile competitors is a harbinger of things to come in the information economy, as large companies come to grips with the switch in mindset from make-and-sell to sense-and-respond. Global's management fundamentally redesigned the way they wanted to run substantial chunks of their business. This meant becoming explicit about what signals they wanted their firm to sense, what data models should be used to reveal the meaning of those signals, what the repertoire of management support options should be, and how to ensure that the decisions made were consistent with management intent and policy. Finally, it meant completing the institutional adaptive loop by linking decisions directly to the company's on-line transaction system.

For example, if a manager wanted to create a new policy or an agent wanted to customize an existing one for a client, the IT infrastructure would check parameters specified by the enterprise model before implementing the change via the transaction system. This design is a codified abstraction of the business that institutionalizes Global's know-how and amounts to a corporate mind. By specifying management roles and accountability in the "sense, interpret, decide, act" cycle, the firm can make conscious institutional decisions, some of which may be to change the model itself. Because the model also governs behavior, those changes will be faithfully translated into practice, and institutional learning will drive a change in institutional behavior.

Almost all of what Global set out to do technologically has been implemented. The mainstays of the business—the property, casualty, and life insurance lines—have been recast into dynamic combinations of more than two thousand reusable software objects. With a small amount of additional work, management will have the ability to modify underwriting policy on the fly and have these changes reflected immediately in the policies written by agents. The variables that govern delegated pricing are now managed by wire. Their world-class customer information system has become the shared knowledge base at the core of their entire business.

Conclusion: Adaptive Structure as Business Strategy

It used to be a management axiom that structure should follow strategy. That was appropriate and logical when strategy cycles were long enough to permit restructuring before a new strategy was required that dictated yet another new structure. However, strategy cycle times keep getting shorter, and now the choice is often between incrementally improving a strategy that is out of gas and trying to implement a new one in an obsolete structure.

Time is the crucial element, and IT is our best weapon when it comes to doing things faster, especially big, complex things like implementing new strategies and structures. That is why it is increasingly absurd to think about IT as another of the functions that will have to be aligned whenever a new strategy is adopted. In fact, it is increasingly absurd to think about IT as a "function." IT is a strategic resource that, for speed-intensive companies, must be fully integrated into the business strategy. As shown in Figure 7.9, the business and technology components of an enterprise strategy should be fused at the top by a common strategic intent and at the bottom by a common enterprise design model and technological infrastructure.

This is the nature of Global's strategy. It was not a three-to-five-year plan to produce specific offerings for specific markets, nor was it acquisition- or research-based. It was a five-year undertaking to transform the firm into a learning organization that could sense and adapt rapidly to its environment. The strategy was, in fact, a structure that uses a network of electronic probes to capture signals that trigger modifications to a continuous flow of products and services in tempo with changes in the marketplace.

No large firm currently has realized the fully integrated corporate mind, but companies like Global Insurance and Brooklyn Union Gas have demonstrated its promise as a new approach to managing size and complexity. They and a growing number of other firms are showing that large and complex domains of a company's operations can be codified and captured in the technological infrastructure, then used to govern business behavior. The payoff now is significant improvement in response time and a substan-

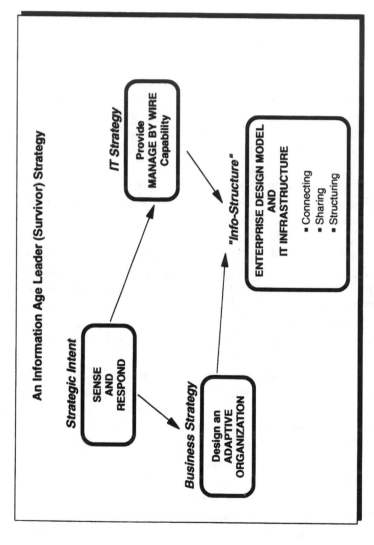

Figure 7.9.

tial reduction in the cost of developing the applications that comprise new products or services. The promise in the future is for something much greater: the potential for managing by wire.

For large firms, creating a corporate mind is a journey that will never be started if management doesn't know or think that it is possible to design and implement manage-by-wire adaptive behavior, but those managers attuned to the nature and implications of an increasingly information-intensive economy will realize that it is not a question of "if" but "when."

The new news for them is the imminent arrival of a new generation of modeling tools that make this strategy plausible. The old news is that it will be management's skill in using them to codify "how we do things around here" that will make a manage-by-wire strategy successful.

Some Guidelines for Managing by Wire

For managers who find the logic of a manage-by-wire strategy persuasive, the following guidelines can help initiate the required changes:

1. Change the executive mindset from "make-and-sell" to "sense-and-respond."
2. Commit to an integration of business and IT strategy development, which means acknowledging that IT cannot remain a spectator sport for senior management. Technological knowledge must join financial and operational know-how in the repertoire of policy-making executives, or crucial trade-off decisions will be delegated by default to the IS department.[13]
3. Formally determine the highest level at which coherent institutional behavior adds value. This means deciding which business units, if well coordinated, could together create more value than the sum of their individual parts.
4. Move from functional toward process, or "capability," management as rapidly as the organization can absorb the shift. Make explicit decisions about which processes are, or must become, the firm's core capabilities.[14] Use the adaptive loop as a design template for change-sensitive processes.
5. Make a comprehensive survey of existing and prototype enterprise modeling tools and select one as an organizational standard. This model will become the common language for expressing "how we do things around here" and interpreting "what's going on out there." It should be used to articulate business strategies, policies,

decision processes, and implementation plans. Insist that the tool be capable of representing commitments and accountabilities.

6. Use the common language to codify the core processes of the business. Incorporate the automated, automatable, and non-automatable (i.e., ad hoc) elements of these processes. After the core processes have been defined and codified, use the same language to integrate them into higher levels of institutional behavior, until the level defined in point 3 above has been attained.

7. Be sure that the process work is not limited to defining procedures, which only creates bureaucracies. Focus on the accountabilities of people and the desired balance between accountability and procedure in every process.

8. Elevate to a strategic level decisions about what operational and environmental data should be sensed, where and what kind of probes to place in the marketplace, the level of detail to be captured, and how often to sample. Because inappropriate or insufficient data models are the institutional equivalent of hallucinations and delusions, business managers must understand and participate in their design.

9. In parallel with points 3 and 4 above, assess the firm's corporate IQ along the three dimensions of connecting, sharing, and structuring. Force policy decisions about the distance that the technical infrastructure should extend in each direction. Insist on a definition of the strategic options that must be preserved and see that these are explicitly mapped into the architectural specifications of the infrastructure.

10. Develop an integrated technology/business plan to move in digestible stages from the existing infrastructure to a platform for the "corporate mind." Create a governance process to propagate the boundaries of acceptable behavior for each of the core business processes.

Notes

1. CEOs, who made up approximately 15% of the sample, had a slightly different profile: 64% classified their present companies as make-and-sell; 73% thought that sense-and-respond would be an imperative by the year 2001; and 79% stated that organizational learning/adapting was becoming increasingly important, with 20% terming it a critical success factor.

2. See Rashi Glazer, "Marketing in an Information-Intensive Environment," *Jour-*

nal of Marketing, 55, (October 1991): for a thoughtful discussion of the management implications associated with becoming a more information-intensive firm.

3. T. M. Hout, M. F. Blaxil, "Making Decisions Like A Fighter Pilot," *New York Times* (November 15, 1987).

4. See Alfred D. Chandler, *Scale and Scope: Dynamics of Industrial Capitalism*, (Cambridge, MA: Belnap Press of Harvard University Press, 1990). *Scale* economies realize market share and low unit costs. *Scope* refers to economies realized by spreading the same resources over multiple product lines and markets.

5. Peter Drucker, "How to be Competitive Though Big," *Wall Street Journal* (Feb. 7, 1991).

6. Senge, Peter, *The Fifth Discipline* (New York: Doubleday, 1990).

7. Complex adaptive systems are the subject of a body of theory that has emerged over the past few decades called *complexity theory*. Its scope includes biological, economic, and cybernetic systems. See H. Mitchell Waldrop, *Complexity: The Emerging Science at the Edge of Order and Chaos* (New York: Simon & Schuster, 1992) for an overview of its current status and multi-disciplinary applications.

8. The primary source of this description is research commissioned by IBM's Advanced Business Institute.

9. Bickerton, Derek, *Language and Species* (Chicago: University of Chicago Press, 1990).

10. See Allan Scherr, "A New Approach to Business Processes," *IBM System Journal*, 32: 1 (Feb. 1993). EPM is an extension by Scherr of work done by Fernando Flores in the 1980s. Scherr led the project at IBM to develop a process definition facility and a suite of software tools for executing the processes defined in EPM notation.

11. The sections on connecting and sharing have benefitted from discussions with Peter Keen. They are adaptations of his concepts of "reach and range." Peter Keen, *Shaping the Future* (Harvard Business School Press, 1991).

12. This example is based on the experiences of a large company struggling to manage size and complexity. Global Insurance is a disguised name.

13. Keen, *Shaping the Future*.

14. James Bryan Quinn, *Intelligent Enterprise* (New York: The Free Press, 1992) contains numerous examples of companies that have identified their "what we do" core capabilities and outsourced the other elements of their value chain if outsiders can do them better. See Scherr, "A New Approach to Business Processes."

8

Electronic Commerce and the Extended Enterprise

BENN KONSYNSKI

Chapter Summary

1. Commercial success is increasingly dependent on cooperation between firms and between nations. Inter-organizational systems (IOS) are a critical enabler of this process, but their impact and influence is far more complex and far-reaching than many managers have anticipated.

2. IT transforms the traditional roles, responsibilities and relationships between employees, customers and suppliers. The legal boundaries of enterprises are becoming blurred and individuals are finding that they need to acquire new team-working, influencing and communication skills in order to achieve their objectives.

3. Electronic data interchange (EDI) technology is the best known type of inter-organizational system. However, it does not lead to business benefits if it is only used to transfer information between organizational boundaries. A deeper integration of processes and systems is required if the partners are to achieve significant savings.

4. Electronic linkage can cut out traditional players in some transactions. This threat has had the effect of making all members of supply chains look more closely at the value they are offering their customers, sometimes preventing the electronic bypass from occurring.

5. The claims made for IOS often ignore the true costs of implementing the systems; when fully loaded, they may not be economic

unless conceived as part of a true partnership arrangement, with properly evaluated strategic goals.

6. In the interests of achieving effective alignment, it is important to involve IT organizations from the earliest stage of development of IOS. Although EDI technology is (relatively) simple and cheap, its long-term role as part of the IT architecture needs careful evaluation. As EDI becomes synonymous with the Internet with universal access, this is even more important.

7. IOS can be deployed as a very powerful weapon to restructure and control market sectors, especially in the hands of partnerships between major players. Governments are increasingly intervening, in the interests of protecting the national or public interest, and to try and provide a level playing field for all businesses.

The traditional view of the organization with clear boundaries, limited relationships with other organizations, and a focus on internal efficiency and effectiveness is no longer adequate. Today's organizational boundaries are blurring; partnerships with clients and competitors are commonplace, and quality and efficiency issues extend well beyond the traditional enterprise boundary. The major strategic successes involving IT in the last two decades focus on the redesign of interorganizational relations. The now familiar stories in the airline, hospital supply, and banking industries are not anomalies but merely the tip of an emerging trend in new organizational alliances, boundary redefinition, and market structures. These new organizational and market relationships are made possible through systems that cross organizational boundaries.

When properly executed, IT plays a major role in business process redesign and can enable companies to offer novel products, incentives, and services; participate in new marketing programs; take advantage of multiple channels of distribution; or introduce operational efficiencies and realize revenue enhancements. Such arrangements can make small companies look, feel, and act big, reaching for customers once beyond their grasp, or they can make big companies feel small and close, targeting and servicing custom markets. IT function is being called upon to facilitate the design of these complex, interorganizational systems (IOS) by supporting cooperative, intra- and interorganizational, functional teams.

The challenge of managing in these conditions is huge, messy, interfunctional, and takes a long time to stabilize. It is also rich in operational and strategic threats and opportunities. For example, the upside potential offers an opportunity to change the rules in the marketplace for major competitive advantage. The downside risk, ignoring what is happening, may even be life-threatening to the enterprise, or at least to its market position. In either case, the pace of technological change means that inaction is not a viable option in most industries.

Senior managers are increasingly asking: Where does my company end and my trading partner begin? or How do we share decision responsibility across legal boundaries? Strategic alignment is an essential tool in answering these questions and in designing and managing these new forms of partnership, alliance, and virtual organization.

This chapter is based on the author's experience with more than forty organizations that have pursued IT initiatives to enhance strategic control within the organization, at the boundary, in relations and alliances, and in common practice and industry platforms in the marketplace. It focuses on new ways, deriving value through the leverage of IT to "stretch" the enterprise.

Understanding Boundaries, Relations, and Markets

One way of understanding the impact of the new intra- and inter-organizational systems is to look at them in terms of boundaries, relations, and markets (see Fig. 8.1).

Boundaries describe (or prescribe) roles within and without organizations—e.g., for the purposes of division of labor, conflict resolution, coordination, accountability, authority, and identity. These corporate boundaries can be made "softer" or "harder," more porous or more impermeable, to suit different situations through the use of IT. For example, wireless, handheld, and portable technologies change the potential role of POS, service, or other personnel in their relations with suppliers and customers.

A change of role inevitably changes relationships with managers and the relationship of those managers with other managers throughout the organization. If a customer-service clerk can now handle 95% of all customers' needs with the support of a well-designed IT system, this has a major impact on the role of more senior managers previously employed to manage relations with key customers. Whole areas of functional specialization are disappearing and being replaced with individuals skilled in coaching, mentoring, and team-building.

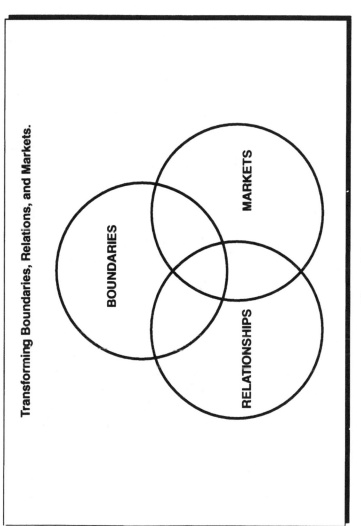

Transforming Boundaries, Relations, and Markets.

Figure 8.1.

Externally, the very speed and efficiency with which transactions can be dealt is transforming previously fragmented markets for goods and services. An analogy can be drawn with the government-backed reforms in the eighteenth and nineteenth centuries, which rationalized financial and securities trading and thereby opened up new possibilities for products, marketing channels, and specialist niche services. Tomorrow's manager needs to pay attention to these boundary-, relation-, and marketplace-transforming issues, just as any general manager in a large bank in the last century had to pay attention to new banking practices, standards, regulations, and controls.

It is no longer possible to look strictly inside when restructuring or reorganizing. Downsizing, delayering, or downscaling the organization involve consideration of outsourcing business functions, possibly purchasing services on a usage-sensitive basis. No business processes is immune from a review that asks the following question: Why are we doing this in-house with this overhead associated with retention of that capability?

Boundary Spanning:
The Role of Competitor Intelligence

Increasingly, as discussed in Chapters 4 and 7, the marketplace is moving from a paradigm of "make-and-sell" to one of "sense-and-respond," characterized by quick, efficient, continuous, fast-cycle customer response. The attention of the enterprise has moved from an internal focus on capital investment, production efficiency, inventory management, and selling to one of hypersensitivity to the market interests and efficient response to perceived market needs in a timely fashion. To support this approach, the enterprise needs to have a new concept of how to extend its "sensing and scanning" activities beyond the legal boundary of the enterprise.

The first step is to change the way the enterprise "touches" or "senses" the market. Identification and evaluation of relevant trends and patterns in the marketplace are critical steps in an organization's business environment monitoring. The successful organization of the next decade will need to invest a considerable amount of resources in "scanning" the external environment. Not surprisingly, the experts who perform this evaluation are seldom skilled in all of the disciplines necessary to accomplish a thorough evaluation of the environmental indicators.[1]

While one expert may be skilled at recognizing the potential for political turmoil in a foreign nation, another may be skilled at recognizing how Japanese government deregulation is meant to complement the development of new products. Moreover, these experts often benefit from one another's skills and knowledge in assessing activity in the organization's environment. Often, the interchange among variously skilled analysts becomes a distributed problem-solving activity that creates the quality of interdisciplinary analysis essential for an effective environmental monitoring activity.

Many U.S. corporations already systematically collect business intelligence. Many have formal environmental monitoring groups. At Westinghouse, for example, environmental monitoring personnel act as information consultants and are involved in all phases of monitoring projects, ranging from defining intelligence objectives to insuring effective dissemination and utilization of results. At General Mills, all members of the organization have been given basic training in recognizing and tapping sources of competitor intelligence.

One director of an environmental monitoring unit said, "It's like putting together a puzzle . . . my people contribute pieces, and after a while a pattern of what's going on out there starts to form." Within the department, insights and conclusions are shared among others; but, as with many activities that require expert assistance, work stops when the expert is unavailable and can't share his or her knowledge. This knowledge extends to questions asked as well as determining and interpreting the answers given. When experts leave the firm, the continuity of aggregate knowledge or expertise available to the firm is interrupted. At other times, the expert may be unavailable to others requiring assistance, making communication difficult.

The extended enterprise involves the use of multiple "agents" (human and system, internal and external) to facilitate the sharing of knowledge in the distributed problem-solving activity of monitoring the business environment. Here, the knowledge to be distributed is not only that which an expert or senior manager uses to identify a pattern of indicators suggesting a threat or opportunity to the organization but also the knowledge of exactly what indicators are particularly pertinent to the classification problem of current concern.

New Patterns of Linkage

The majority of current activities in extended enterprises are related to the establishment of bilateral (dyadic) linkages and other forms of simple, information-based alliances that leverage ITs. EDI,[2] quick response, and standard protocols to support interorganizational relations are emerging in a wide range of industries. The evolution of these (relatively) technically and organizationally simple phenomena needs to be examined in the context of overall IOS evolution and impact.

Partnerships that leverage forms of electronic integration can change the dynamics in the industry. The rules of time, distance, and complexity are changed. For better or worse, there is a blurring distinction in responsibilities and authorities. To the customer, the blurred distinction between Citibank and American Airlines in associating purchases and frequent flyer program mileage credits is unimportant, as long as the benefit is derived. To the partnering organizations, responsibilities, authorities, and coordination need to be clearly identified.

Firms now use electronic data linkages to establish combined marketing programs reaching across traditional industry boundaries to a common customer database. This has been accelerated by dramatic reductions in data storage and transmission costs. For example, airlines, hotels, rental cars, and bank credit cards are now being woven together in a single combined marketing effort. These joint alliances often unevenly benefit the different parties, create barriers for other non-participants in the industry, and represent a new dimension of competition.

What is EDI?

The use of computer and communications technology to support the information exchanges needed to carry out day-to-day business activities is generally referred to as *electronic data interchange* (EDI). Today, EDI is a major IT and communications issue in many U.S. industries:

1. The U.S. Treasury Department makes over 150,000 electronic payments per month to vendors. The cost of an electronic check is estimated at four cents per check, compared with the thirty cents needed for a paper check.

2. The EDI Association estimates that over six thousand companies in seventy different industries were using EDI in 1988.

3. Kmart transmits over 60% of its freight bills electronically, amounting to more than two million transactions in 1990.

At its simplest, EDI automates existing paper flows between organizations in much the same way as paper flows within organizations have been automated. EDI can also represent the opportunity to rethink and restructure the relationships between organizations. While the benefits are significant, so too are the pitfalls that can derail EDI initiatives or their business impacts.

Masses of paper documents support the routine interaction between most business organizations. The simplest purchase of office supplies can involve requisitions, purchase orders, sales orders, invoices, packing slips, receiving reports, and checks. Besides the two organizations engaged in this simple exchange, banks and delivery services may be involved. The purchase of raw materials and parts for use in manufacturing or the sale of finished goods for distribution may involve even more information exchange based on paper documents.

Many businesses have long since automated these activities within the boundaries of their own organizations. Transactions are captured at the point of entry into the organization, converted into machine-readable form, and managed with the support of computer-based information systems thereafter. Inventory control systems determine when new materials should be ordered. Order entry systems record customer orders received in the mail or over the phone. Accounts receivable systems record payments received from customers.

From the standpoint of the general manager, EDI, as it is currently known, involves:

- cross-organization information interchange
- application to application communications (system to system)
- form-oriented messages (transaction sets)
- information and commitment exchange (protocols for timing and interpretation)
- few new associations (we are dealing with traditional business functions)

EDI as an Extension of Internal Transaction Processing Systems

All of these transaction-processing systems have traditionally stopped at the boundary of the organization. The machine-readable data maintained within these systems were transcribed onto purchase orders or invoices or shipping notices and then mailed off to another organization for action. On reaching the appropriate destination, the information on these paper forms was converted back into machine-readable form for entry into and processing by the transaction processing systems of the receiving organization. If transaction processing systems reduced clerical costs, improved accuracy, and improved processing speed within the organization, why can't the same benefits be obtained between organizations?

This is the fundamental logic of EDI. The transaction processing systems of the organization would be extended beyond the organization's boundaries and linked electronically with the business and information systems of other organizations. Instead of paper documents linking the organizations, electronic equivalents of the documents would be transmitted. This substitution requires efforts in three broad areas. First, each organization must replace the manual interpretation of incoming documents with computer software. Second, the two organizations must replace the functions of the postal service with an agreement on a telecommunications link. Finally, the two organizations must establish the terms and conditions governing electronically placed orders and agree on the operational details of an electronic link. Often, pressures associated with inventory carrying costs play a role.

EDI as a Partnership Arrangement

Three levels of interdependence occur in decisions involving EDI linkages. Decisions on technical interconnection, business process (application) dependencies, and management practice (multiple business applications) integration may require evaluation. Each aspect may be facilitated by industry or cross-industry standards. The likelihood of the emergence of standards, or the opportunity to influence standards development, often sets competing or cooperating organizations to work together in formulating shared business practices.

Simply providing automation of company border to company border data transport offers little real benefit to the organizations. Speeding the information links with little thought to the restructuring of associated business processes may be more costly than beneficial. The systems in and across organizations have "settled" into certain operating assumptions, and often major changes in one portion of the relationship necessitate a significant review of many other internal systems. For example, a major retailer sends orders to a packaged goods supplier, who takes a printed copy of the transmission and rekeys the information into its order-processing activity. There is little benefit to either party without further integration through application sharing.

Recently, a supplier for a large retail department store chain initiated an EDI linkage for order transmission. The process targeted the speed of order transmission, and little thought was given to the internal impact on the order-processing system, which was designed around the traditional order-handling mechanisms. As a result, the two partners found that neither side could fully benefit from merely automating the order transmission, without a redesign of their respective order-handling processes.

In addition to the business agreement, partnering organizations seek control over the key forms of integration across their organizations—technical, business process, and management practice. If the arrangement is to be successful, these management issues, traditionally handled within the legal boundary of the enterprise, must be examined within the context of an extended view of the enterprise that involves key management participation from all concerned.

The least of these involves the sharing of technological standards (data, communications, etc.) that facilitate an interconnectivity or ability to exchange information. There need be no shared knowledge of an application—say, order processing. At this level, there may be little more than door-to-door shipment of data. As mentioned earlier, many EDI arrangements involve agreements on data formats, key product or other codes, and basic communications protocols.

At the business process level, common procedures and applications mark a higher dependence on coordinated activities within one business application or across a small number of them. In these situations, there is reason to have coordination meetings involving members from each of the partners. The credit card and airline scenarios involve shared business processes.

Management practice refers to arrangements involving a major renegotiation of the business relationship and management control processes, impacting multiple systems in participating organizations and building a significant amount of dependence. When an auto maker establishes a relationship with a supplier to support a "just-in-time" operation, significant commitments in technology, business process, and common strategy need to be accommodated. The negotiation for, and management of, such arrangements is not a simple matter. While major issues of business policy must be shared, the rules of fair competition need to be addressed. To avoid litigation, the parties must be aware of not only the internal impacts among the participants but also antitrust issues that may arise.

Bypass Linkages

A particularly interesting phenomenon is the emergence of bypass linkage situations. Take the situation of a distribution channel that is "losing out" as electronic links bypass the traditional lines of service. Is there any way those being bypassed can add value so that they won't be threatened as much by these electronic linkages? In some cases we've seen the intermediary become the dominant force in the transaction, thus preventing bypass. In other cases we've seen large organizations bypassing their traditional distribution channels by direct client linkages.

Take, for example, travel agencies, where reservation systems services provide order to transactions and allow them to off-load some of the mundane work (ticketing and seating, etc.) to the reservation system provider. Unfortunately for the agencies, the standards brought by the systems have educated the consumer and created an opportunity for customers to bypass the travel agencies. Customers are able to select their product directly through 800 phone numbers, direct mail, advertisement, PC, and network-based access (e.g., EAAsy SABRE).

As another example, consider the issues faced by a large West Coast appliance distributor. The CEO is concerned that manufacturers could create a bypass situation, marketing directly to his customers. His response is to use IT to enhance services to customers and to lock himself in with them. IT created a "golden thread" across to their IT organizations, making it very hard for them to switch or bypass.

Figure 8.2 shows that while the appliance distributor (top left corner) was considering his investment in linkages with vendors and retailers, they realized that increasing the value in one link without an understanding of the impact on other relations could be both foolish and wasteful. The problem was how to:

- maximize the value (++) in the distributor–retailer relationship and the distributor–vendor relationship
- reduce the potential value (−−) in the stronger vendor–retailer link and prevent vendor–customer relationships (−)
- facilitate the retailer–customer relationship (+) for revenue enhancement and cautiously build the distributor–customer relationship (+) for direct marketing

The distributor had to account for the full nexus of relationships and make decisions in regard to the establishment of dependencies (compliance with proprietary or industry standards) and effective electronic "integration" of the various players as these systems form the basis for day-to-day operations.

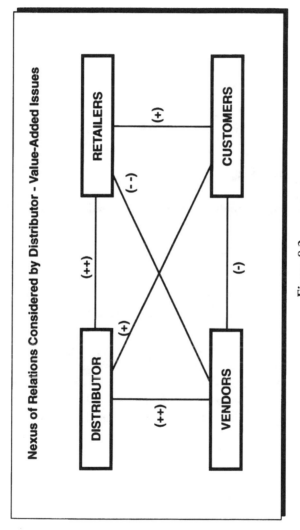

Figure 8.2.

Expected and Realized Benefits from Linkage

The business case for linkage initiatives is often made on the basis of making a significant impact on overall transaction costs (see Fig. 8.3). For example, benefits might include:

- faster order processing
- reduced inventory
- improved cash flow
- reduced order handling
- improved communications
- enhanced coordination
- fewer stock outs
- faster processing

However, an honest analysis of fully burdened costs usually reveals the following.

MODEST ECONOMIC BENEFITS

When costs are fully loaded and the financial record is fully and honestly burdened by the true investment in the needed changes in systems, procedures, and people, the near-term return in transaction economics is seldom supportive of the linkage argument on purely financial terms. One manufacturer found that an investment of over $100,000 was required to respond to the demand of its second largest customer to accommodate proprietary order-handling protocols and procedures. While some portion of the resulting systems and procedures from the development effort are reusable, costs for compliance with other customers' proprietary protocols would be prohibitive.

CHANGES IN RESPONSIBILITIES

Unintended impacts on roles and responsibilities across organizations frequently occur in the wake of linkage initiatives. The normal dynamics that frequently surround order processing and fulfillment events are themselves transformed by the operational changes that accompany the adoption of electronic linkages. Relationships between buyer and seller communities may be restructured in ways that are difficult to control. A manufacturer

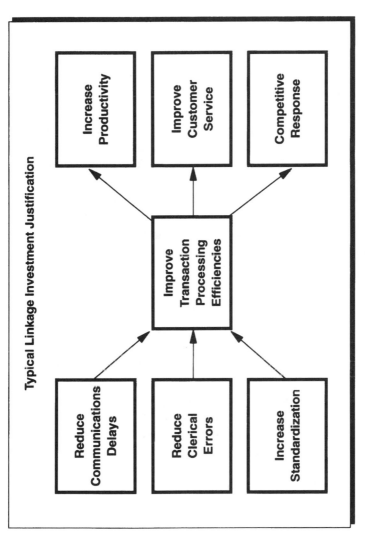

Figure 8.3.

found that, historically, the order-taking activity was their best sales opportunity. Hence, when electronic linkage created new order reception dynamics, the sales personnel lost a significant opportunity to try to influence
the buyer. New procedures, incentives, and responsibilities were needed to
restructure the relationships across the companies to accommodate sufficient contact time.

INDUSTRY EFFECTS

Many general managers are lulled into believing that increased standardization leads naturally to the mythical "level playing field." Indeed, such
initiatives often result in the "leveling" of the playing field to either a lower
common denominator, which inhibits market innovation, or to a raised ho-
rizon, which sets standards that only deep pockets or existing practice can
accommodate. In either situation, the channel practices are biased in ways
that exclude previously viable participants or stifle innovative market transforming initiatives. The debates surrounding the reservation systems in the
airline industry or the insurance carrier to agency "interface" design reflect
these tensions.

How the IT Organization can Help Linkage

While there are many examples of how investments in technology have
yielded significant competitive advantage, there are also many examples
where such investments have resulted in no measurable impact. In many
cases, this failure stems not from an inappropriate vision but from the
inability of the organization to effectively integrate the use and the management of the technology into the mainstream of the firm. Successful
partnership and the process of building partnership is a management strategy. Regardless of the level of decentralization of the IS function, there
still remains a critical need to build effective working relationships between
organizations. While some may envision the day in which IS specialists are
not required, trends in technology and the increasing complexity of the
technological infrastructure (such as telecommunications, database systems, and large transaction/application systems) suggest that this is a functional area of the business which is not about to disappear.

   For example, a retailer (a major regional department store chain) is
renegotiating its relationships with certain suppliers. For one of its suppliers
of women's garments, the retailer provides POS information and allows the
supplier to make all merchandising decisions for the fixed display area.

Several other department stores are creating such arrangements, which significantly reduce the buying costs of the retailer.

As another example, a regional food retailer is centralizing its buying force to create a direct product costing management strategy with a centralized buying organization that integrates decisions on advertising, warehousing, and other commitments that affect product costs. The single buying point has a significant impact on the organization's operations from supplier relations to shipment and warehousing to regional and in-store merchandising and marketing support. Yet another parallel group is concerned with the profitability of the products. It is expected that once these two functions are integrated a full direct product profitability (DPP) program will have a significant effect on the various arrangements with suppliers that will develop.

Partnership describes a working relationship that reflects a long-term commitment, a sense of mutual cooperation, shared risk and benefits, and other aspects that are consistent with concepts and theories of participatory decision-making. Among the key elements are:

- stability of the relationship
- sustained over time (no explicit end point)
- self-maximizing behavior is not optimal
- opportunistic behavior controlled through processes rather than contracts
- significant contract ambiguity
- interdependence of the relationship
- stream of exchanges that are highly interdependent
- joint acceptance of costs/burdens/risks
- flexibility of the relationship
- willingness to invest in the relationship
- mechanism for adapting to uncertain events
- mechanisms of the process
- influence of the relationship
- operational exchange of key information
- economic relationship
- social/political networks

There are many forms of IT partnership; the stated purpose does not always reveal the true nature of, or motivation for, the arrangement. Among the various forms are intraindustry coalitions, customer–vendor relationships, and customer–supplier linkages.

INTRAINDUSTRY COALITIONS

The economies of scale associated with certain kinds of hardware/software configuration have facilitated a very different method of operation. In the airline industry, for example, the economies of scale in developing and managing a reservation system are now beyond the capacities of the medium-sized airlines. In Europe, two major coalitions have been created: the Amadeus Coalition and the Galileo Coalition. Amadeus is built around the United Airlines software and Galileo around the Continental software. Even the largest carriers have acknowledged their inability to handle this problem by themselves and have joined coalitions.

CUSTOMER–VENDOR RELATIONSHIP

The establishment of joint research projects on new technologies through beta sites can provide advantages to both parties. For the vendors, this relationship gives valuable insight into the practical field problems associated with their technology. Further, the ability to resolve these problems in prestige accounts gives vendors highly visible reference sales. For the customer, the relationship is a cost-effective way to learn and participate in new technological developments that may be beyond individual skill and financial resource levels. On both sides, considerable care must be taken to select the right partners to ensure good relationships.

CUSTOMER–SUPPLIER LINKAGES

These joint efforts potentially provide better service to both parties, enabling them to better control investments in inventory, storage facilities, and operating costs. Sensibly architected, these linkages can give both parties a competitive advantage. If the two firms are of unequal size, however, a risk exists that the larger party can force its standards upon the smaller party. Such a major power transfer can potentially destabilize the relationship.

IT partnering arrangements, whether to leverage or to acquire a technical competence, involve review of both organizational and technical cultures. In addition to the normal factors that a general manager considers, the compatibility of the technical architecture plays a significant role in the partnering decision. Arrangements often involve the need to share: capital infrastructure, technical architecture, information resources, established software, and technical expertise.

Rationalizing Fragmented Markets

The role of IT in the rationalization of the many fragmented markets is the final theme of this chapter. Fragmented markets are those that involve many buyers and sellers, often governed or supported by trade associations. Whether in insurance or automobile parts, a significant portion of transaction costs have to do with identification of trading partners and coordination of transaction execution and settlement. The class of IOS that I call a *virtual system* is the most primitive form of these shared platforms, involving agreement only on data interchange protocols and basic operating procedures. However, other shared platforms involve direct support for transactions, introducing new economies and disciplines to the market.

Several individual, or groups of, stakeholders (trade participants, trade or industry associations, vendors, etc.) may take the initiative to influence the direction of rule changes in the market through the leverage of ITs to create integration effects, build dependence, and otherwise impact the pattern of exchange practice in an industry. Internal and external market forces trigger these unilateral or collaborative initiatives.

- *Individual initiatives* A market leader or innovator seizes the initiative and establishes a climate for participation in alliances. The airline initiatives of American and United illustrate such unilateral initiatives that resulted in a shared platform.

- *Competitive response* In response to a significant move in a market, an organization creates, in the name of defense, a partnered environment. Johnson & Johnson developed the COACT system, partially in response to previous initiatives by American Hospital Supply.

- *Collaborative effort* A coalition of medium-sized players collect the capital and skills required to create the technology infrastructure for an industry. Several cases in the ATM arena illustrate such coalitions.

- *Professional organization* Trade organization serves as a fair broker in specification and management of a shared platform. IVANS was an initiative of ACORD in the insurance industry, while Transnet resulted from actions by MEMA in the motor equipment sales market.

- *Distribution channel consolidation* Intermediaries defend their distribution status. Efforts in the travel agency arena in the 1970s illustrate a failed attempt at a consolidation for creation of a shared reservations platform.

- *New entrant* A new entrant to a market may lay the groundwork for IOS initiatives. Sears' move into new markets, leveraging its distribution channel services, is one example. A technology vendor may bring its technology electric information services and automatic data processing, which provide EDI platforms in specific industries.

Where the intermediary attempts merely to create a level playing field and reduce transaction costs for all parties, these relations are called *industry platforms*. Where the intermediary defines market rules for buyers and sellers and performs more and more significant market activities, these relations are called *electronic markets*. While both involve shared technology platforms, the electronic market involves a major intervention into the practice of the market. These classes of extended enterprise initiatives are summarized in Figure 8.4, where the dark areas reflect the level of policy control.

Linkage and Industrial Policy—IT Role in Design of Markets

Vertical market EDI systems that tie together production systems of particular industries, such as between manufacturing companies and their suppliers, are relatively uncomplicated socially and politically. Such linkages can be built through agreements among the parties involved without much controversy. This is especially true when these information linkages enhance current bilateral arrangements through cost reductions and improved coordination. With the exception of situations in which buyers leverage extraordinary power to reduce logistics costs, such arrangements are frequently the result of amicable agreement and expectations of mutual benefits.

However, electronic linkages that cut across industries, especially industries characterized by strong competition, are much more difficult to construct and usually never get started, nor advance, by simply leaving things "to the market." Often, governmental and quasi-governmental entities can and do play a key role in facilitating the development of such

Forms of Interorganizational Systems

MARKETING and LOGISTICS systems involve bilateral linkages of buyers and suppliers, often using proprietary protocols (communications, product identifiers, data formats, etc.). Such linkages offer significant product or service differentiation (MARKETING, e.g., Levi Strauss LEVILINK, Haggar HOTS) or influence inventory and ordering procedures (LOGISTICS, e.g., many EDI initiatives like K-Mart). The intent of these forms of IOS linkages is COOPTIVE.

VIRTUAL SYSTEMS arise when national, or international, standards are selected by a community of market participants. The "policy" for selecting the appropriate protocols is owned by the community, and each individual entity (supplier or buyer) is responsible for their own systems that implement those standards. For example: UCS codes, X12 or EDIFACT standards, GEIS value-added network services, etc., might be adopted by an industry to prevent the dominance of one or more proprietary standards. Pressures for this approach often arise from the emergence of multiple proprietary standards that reduce the overall efficiency of the participants. Several industries have undertaken such initiatives: WINS (warehousing), TALC (textile), etc. Such forms of IOS linkages are COLLECTIVE.

INDUSTRY PLATFORMS represent the initiative of one, or more, players in a market to provide a common "platform" for the industry. Often these platforms emerge from trade associations that wish to leverage the transaction economics of the collection of participants to bring economics of scale to reduce the costs for all participants. Thus, standards are set to raise the level of the industry's efficiency (ex: TRANSNET in auto parts, and IVANS in insurance). The intent is to establish a relatively level playing field to the benefit of the entire participating community. Further, the information sharing opportunity may offer important coordination that is essential to the operation of the market (e.g., airlines reservation systems). Such IOS linkage arrangements are COLLABORATIVE.

ELECTRONIC MARKET ACCESS FORUMS refer to environments where the intermediary offers more than transaction economics, actually performing many essential market functions. These functions include seller and buyer identification, matching, negotiation, settlement, etc. In these trading environments, the third party intermediary sets and enforces the rules of the trading environment. The EMAF facilitator has the responsibility to reduce the risk of participants in the market. Horizontal market trading is often enhanced in these environments. Examples include: American Gem Market System (gemstones), TELCOT (cotton), Inventory Locator Service (airplane parts), Autoinfo (auto dismantlers), Reuter's INSTINET, etc. The intent is often the promotion of fair, competitive markets. These IOS arrangements are COMPETITIVE.

Figure 8.4.

systems. Examples in Finland, Singapore, Norway, and Hong Kong high-light the range of possibilities and opportunities—whether it is leveraging a product portfolio, improving technology or service capabilities, or estab-lishing unique skills or market presence.

In the cited cases, government is contributing through a range of in-terventions from declaration of standards to operation of the facilitating market information mechanisms. The issues of partnership, benefits, fair-ness, and control illustrate the challenges that arose in determining the appropriate level of influence for the government in defining market prac-tice.

SINGAPORE'S TRADENET SYSTEM

At the extreme, an interindustry partnership may be actively led by govern-ment initiative. The Singapore government has spent a significant amount to link trade agents with relevant government agencies at the port—freight forwarders, shipping companies, banks, and insurance companies with cus-toms and immigration officials. Clearing the port, which used to take a vessel two to four days, now may take as little as ten minutes. This startling reduction has more than halved the time any ship has to remain in port and is believed to be a key to ensuring that Singapore remains a port of choice in the Far East, where competition is clearly growing. TradeNet itself involves the partnership of a unique assortment of government agen-cies, bureaus, statutory boards, private agencies, and companies involved in all aspects of the shipment of goods.

FINLAND'S FINNPAP/FINNBOARD SYSTEM

The TradeNet initiative is in sharp contrast to the initiatives of the Finnpap/Finnboard (paper and wood products associations) effort in Finland. The role of the government in the Singapore initiative was significant and prob-ably critical to the success of the endeavor. The broad range of stakeholders required incentives to coordinate and cooperate. The trading environment for Finland in the international wood and paper products was no less sig-nificant. However, in Finland's situation, the government opted to play no significant role in the coordination of the eighteen mid-sized paper com-panies. The paper companies jointly developed a global electronic infor-mation system to link themselves with hundreds of key customers and international sales offices. In spite of the critical contribution to the coun-try's manufacturing GDP, the government played no significant role in the formation of standards and the investment in, and establishment of, the system.

In Singapore there was a total commitment, with the government playing a critical role in setting deadlines and coordinating resource allocation. Another factor was the leverage of interlocking directorates that are important to the patterns of public–private business practice in Singapore, contributing also to a knowledge transfer that is associated with rotation across the various directorates. The Tradenet initiative did not just "speed up the mess." Rather, it redesigned the forms and procedures that make up trade document processing. Strict change control processes and unique accounting arrangements contributed to the effort.

HONG KONG'S TRADELINK SYSTEM

Like Singapore, Hong Kong is a trading center that depends greatly on the vitality of its trading companies for its welfare. Visionary leaders in the trade sector saw early on that EDI offered a promise for improving trade. Hong Kong actually began a project to create EDI for trade *before* Singapore. Yet today there is no EDI system for trade in Hong Kong. In 1983, the Hong Kong government helped sponsor a special council to improve trade practice. Public and private sector representatives made up the council, which, after some deliberation, proposed the creation of an EDI system, a data base of consignments to facilitate trade. The proposed system, called Hotline, looked promising.

However, the council did not have the means or the charter to pay for the system. The council made a report to the Hong Kong government, suggesting that the government build the system. The government's reply was that the system would be of benefit mainly to business and, therefore, business should pay for it. A council-led survey of trading companies provided another argument for government sponsorship, noting that business people would feel uneasy if competitively sensitive trade data were stored by any organization other than the government. Again, the government argued that it was not in the business of providing information-processing services that could well be done by other value-added network suppliers.

Several companies decided to start their own firm, Tradelink, to support a consultancy study investigating the commercial viability of a trade-related EDI system. The resulting report indicated that such a system would probably not be a moneymaker. Meanwhile, TradeNet was turned on in Singapore. Suddenly, it was clear that such a system could be built, that it had real advantages, and that some kind of partnership between government and private businesses would be required to make it happen. The Special Project on EDI (SPEDI) was created. SPEDI was to come up with a framework and a general plan for building a trade-related EDI system in Hong Kong. SPEDI recommendations are now being implemented.

NORWAY'S TVINN SYSTEM

Norway successfully implemented the TVINN system for automated clearance and control in its Customs Department. This system is significant as an early arrival on the trade-related EDI scene, coming on-line in August of 1988, four months before TradeNet. The system (not a comprehensive trade-related system) focuses on customs and represents an intermediate solution to trade documentation efficiency. The Norwegian government's Customs Department took the lead in 1985. The project was managed by the Norwegian computer consulting and design firm Avenir, and the TVINN system was built in about two years (similar to TradeNet). Unlike TradeNet, TVINN was designed to allow routine intervention by customs officers to watch the documentation process and modify it as necessary. Like TradeNet, the project has been very successful, and Norwegian customs claims significant labor savings, improved accuracy, and faster turnaround.

Government Role in Electronic Commerce Policy

Generally speaking, competition in the private sector is likely to result in more innovative and effective systems than will the monopoly function of government. However, there are times when the public sector might take the lead in order to move the creation of an electronic linkage system forward in a timely manner. When should the public sector take the initiative and influence through policy and regulation? Under the following conditions:

1. When cross-industry conflicts develop due to incompatible business procedures that could be standardized but that no one business wants to bear the costs for standardizing. The public sector usually intervenes to find ways to facilitate standardization and to ensure that the costs of coming into compliance are fairly borne by the various parties that will benefit.

2. When the competitive posture of the nation or region is threatened (e.g., a competitor installs a capability that puts one at a genuine

disadvantage, and a response in kind is called for) or when particular windows of opportunity exist that might be exploited quickly.

3. When key elements of an EDI capability require construction or use of "natural monopolies," such as the local telephone network or specialized government data resources.

4. When key functions to be served by the EDI network require the actions of a government agency.

There can be little doubt that EDI in areas like the trade sector will grow rapidly in the coming years. There is also little doubt that government can take an active, and often leading, role in the creation of trade-related EDI systems. The inevitable involvement of customs and possibly other government agencies in the trade process makes this a certainty, but what about other cross-cutting EDI systems that do not necessarily involve government agencies? Can we expect the government to play major roles there as well?

The answer is yes because the government has an abiding interest in ensuring that systems built to facilitate business among competing companies are not designed or used in ways that give any business unfair competitive advantage. This principle has been enforced with much controversy in the United States, where the airline companies that own and operate computerized reservation systems have come under government orders to alter the ways their systems perform in order to eliminate systematic unfair competitive practices facilitated by the designs. We can expect similar concerns to arise with respect to horizontal EDI systems, and in many cases, government agencies are likely to look upon such systems as analogs of "common carrier" networks, such as the telephone system. While such systems can be privatized, as is the Singapore TradeNet system, the government will probably be required to have an ongoing role, ensuring that key social objectives are upheld in the actual functioning of the systems.

Conclusion

This chapter has taken an ambitious sweep in reviewing the IT role in extending the enterprise from external scanning at the boundary to EDI and buyer–supplier relations to partnership arrangements, marketplace strategy, and governmental issues in policy setting for electronic commerce. This sweep of technology employment, boundary, relationship, partnership, and market transformation is intended to underscore the need to prepare for the "sense-and-respond" environment.

This chapter has challenged the traditional view of the organization with clear boundaries, limited relationships with other organizations, and a focus on internal efficiency and effectiveness as no longer adequate. To-day's organizational boundaries are blurring, partnerships with clients and competitors are becoming commonplace, and quality and efficiency issues extend well beyond the traditional enterprise boundary. New product and service offerings, channel systems capabilities, and target marketing initia-tives are enabled through these partnerships, alliances, and information interchange arrangements.

This chapter has also looked at the internal structure of the enterprise; corporate boundaries are transformed often through employment of these ITs. Culture and practice are interdicted. Organizational structure issues are profoundly impacted—division of labor, conflict resolution, coordina-tion mechanisms, accountability, authorities, identities. New relationships with organizations outside the enterprise are of operational and often stra-tegic concern to the general manager. Relations with suppliers, customers, competitors, and other forms of partners and affinity groups have earned significant management attention. Many forms of partnership arise—in-traindustry coalitions, customer–vendor relationships, customer–supplier linkages, and other market-transforming relationships. These alliances, when properly executed, change the balance of power and create new pat-terns of behavior in the marketplace.

Organizational boundaries are being transformed by these new linkage relationships. Where one company ends and another begins is no longer easy to see, if it ever was. Distinctions associated with legal definitions and formal authorities and responsibilities are being challenged as the new ar-rangements defy traditional boundary tests.

The internal structure of the organization is not immune from impacts associated with these linkages. An interesting emerging phenomenon is that an organization's entire transaction set is potentially subject to EDI. Therefore, the organization needs to establish and design a new architec-ture. Internal, interdivisional transactions will be treated as if they were cross-organizational. A new organizational agility is required to make the decisions on the location of processing, even outside the organization.

Management needs to play a significant role in the development and maintenance of policy that relates to electronic linkages involved in rela-tionships with suppliers, customers, and competitors. These initiatives have a high potential for radically transforming the organization, its market po-sition, and overall market practice and balance of power. When senior managers think about "linking," there is a higher potential for the enterprise when they recognize that these issues involve more of a business innovation than a technical innovation.

Notes

Portions of this chapter originally appeared in *IBM Systems Journal* 32:1 (1993).

1. G. Elofson, B. Konsynski, "Delegation Technologies: Environmental Scanning with Intelligent Agents," *Journal of Management Information Systems,* 8:1, (Summer, 1991): 37–62.
2. J. McGee, B. Konsynski, "A Note on Electronic Data Interchange," Harvard Business School work. 9-190-022 Rev 7/19/89.

9

Benchmarking IT Strategic Alignment

❖

PATTI PRAIRIE

❖

Chapter Summary

1. Benchmarking is now a widely used management tool; this chapter shows how it can be applied to measuring the alignment of IT and business strategies.

2. The IT alignment benchmark concept has been rigorously tested in two major projects, carried out by IBM in 1992/3 with the cooperation of over 50 large companies.

3. The first exercise--the American Express Benchmark Study--resulted in the identification of a number of key factors which must be managed effectively in order to achieve IT transformation.

4. A common theme linking the factors was the need for a new understanding of how IT created value in a business. Companies who had a clear vision, and who brought together IT and business executives to jointly manage the challenge were most successful in leveraging long-term benefits from their IT investments.

5. These factors formed the basis of the second (ongoing) exercise: the IBM IT Transformation Benchmarking Project. At the end of the first phase, seven areas of IT best practice stood out: the management of human resources; IT architecture; legacy systems; strategic alignment; governance; value delivery and company culture.

6. Participating companies were able to gain immediate benefits from the first phases of the benchmarking project, and to begin a continuous process of assessing and reassessing the IT competencies which were most appropriate for their businesses.

7. Both projects are best practice examples in their own right of how to carry out benchmarking in a way that is relevant to all companies involved. They are also interesting examples of collaborating rather than competing in order to survive turbulent market change.

What Are IT Strategic Alignment Benchmarks?

As many chapters in this book testify, sweeping advances in IT hold out the promise of new ways to compete. In pursuit of the technological dream, aggregate investment in IT continues to grow faster than corporate revenues. Yet, as many executives will attest, the relationship between their investments in IT and business profitability is tenuous.[1]

Our experience with dozens of clients in the United States, Europe, and Japan is consistent: only companies that achieve effective alignment between business and IT strategies will maximize the value realized from investment in IT. It is, as American Airlines' Max Hopper points out, not possession of new technology but effective management of it that makes the difference.[2] Achieving alignment between business and IT continues to top the priorities lists of executives[3] and so does the key question of *how* to do it.

One approach that has proven quite effective is the use of IT strategic alignment benchmarks. By studying the management processes of firms that have achieved a high degree of alignment between business and the IT organization, management can identify proven processes that can be implemented in their own organizations.

The concept of benchmarking is familiar to most IT managers, who are regularly presented with "feeds and speeds" benchmark data from IT product vendors; but the application of benchmarking techniques to the strategic management of IT itself is a new approach.

Limitations of Conventional IT Benchmarks

After starting in manufacturing, benchmarking has expanded into many other sectors of industry. Once viewed as a last-gasp improvement program for floundering companies, benchmarking is now standard procedure for many major organizations, including Alcoa, AT&T, IBM, Motorola, and Xerox. Over two-thirds of large companies have established some sort of benchmarking program,[4] and by 1995, most U.S. companies will be using benchmarking as a part of their total quality management programs.[5]

Recently, cost-based benchmarks of IT performance have become popular as managers struggle for a reliable way to gauge the true business value of IT. Frustrated by the difficulties associated with quantifying the strategic value of major information systems and confronted with IT expenditures that are ratcheting upward significantly faster than business revenues, senior managers are benchmarking IT costs against other firms to drive a financial stake in the ground. Many management consulting firms offer sophisticated methodologies for comparing internal IT costs with other companies.

IT cost benchmarks are certainly a valuable tool for management, but these benchmarks—focused on cost-per-MIP (millions of instructions per second), budgets, and related operational measures—are of limited use to managers seeking to maximize the strategic value of IT. Assume, for example, that you conduct an IT cost benchmark exercise and learn that you are spending 1.2 times the industry benchmark on IT. Is that good or bad? Should you slash spending, stay the course, or open your wallet even wider?

The answer, of course, hinges on another set of questions: On what is the money being spent? In particular, how much is being spent in support of initiatives that are of strategic importance to the firm? What is the expected strategic value of the investments? Asked another way, are the IT investments providing true value to the business? The question facing managers today is not necessarily how to minimize the cost of IT but how to align IT expenditures with business strategies to maximize IT's strategic value.

Enter the IT strategic alignment benchmark. By establishing a baseline view of how an organization's IT strategic processes should support the business strategy and then comparing these processes to other leading companies via an IT strategic alignment benchmark exercise, management can uncover new techniques to increase the IT organization's ability to transform IT into competitive advantage and business value.

IBM began its work on IT strategic benchmarks with a benchmarking exercise carried out for American Express Travel Related Services in 1992, involving seventeen companies and focusing on IT strategy and planning.

The American Express IT Benchmark Study

American Express is a widely recognized leader in innovative use of IT. Yet, top management of Travel Related Services (TRS), the company's flagship credit card business, knew they could do even better by more closely aligning the IT organization, TRS Technologies, with the company's business strategies. TRS decided to benchmark its IT management processes against a select set of world-class organizations. By first identifying the best IT management processes and then incorporating the best applicable practices into its management system, American Express expected to strengthen IT's strategic alignment with the business, resulting in higher quality, higher morale, lower project risk, and greater productivity.

Using an international team of consultants, American Express conducted an extensive benchmark study to identify and describe the best practices for IT strategic processes in large, complex companies. The study focused on the management processes involved in maximizing the value of IT to the business, particularly those processes associated with developing strategic plans that align IT with the business under conditions of significant market turbulence.

At a structural level, the IT strategic alignment benchmarking process resembles other benchmarking exercises: a project is defined, company data are collected and analyzed to identify superior practices, and the insights gained are applied back home (Fig. 9.1). However, senior management from TRS, TRS Technologies, and American Express's corporate strategy organization very wisely invested additional upfront time to reach a shared vision of not only the issues to be addressed but how the company would use the benchmark findings that the study would produce. By building executive commitment early in this way, the study team ensured that action would be taken on the results from the project. Issues they discussed included:

- How can IT best be responsive to business needs?
- What processes secure strategic alignment with the business?
- How do we maintain alignment during changing business strategies?
- What is the best culture for change?
- How do we adapt the people and the organization?
- How do we manage the transition from legacy systems to systems that are more suited to today's user needs?
- What is the best governance or ownership of different parts of the process?
- How can we best assimilate new technology?
- What are the best processes for managing vendor relationships or alliances?

1. Define Objectives	Identify what management processes are to be studied
2. Define Analysis Approach	Determine the Criteria for Assessing the Performance of the Processes to be Benchmarked
3. Understand Yourself	Establish a Baseline for Comparison by Studying within the Company First
4. Identify Partners	Select Other Companies to be studied
5. Collect, Analyze, and Process Data	Conduct Site Visits to Benchmark Partners to Understand How Their Management Processes Work and Identify Best Practices
6. Determine Gaps	Understand Company Performance Relative to Best Practice
7. Identify Applicable Practices	Select Practices from Other Companies to be Modified and Implemented
8. Implement	Secure Executive Commitment and Install Practices in the Company

Figure 9.1. Benchmarking Steps

Management Processes Chosen for Benchmarking

As a result of this period of consultation American Express ended up by defining eight management process issues to be studied during the benchmark (Fig. 9.2).

TECHNOLOGY FORECASTING

Technology forecasting is the process of identifying promising new IT, testing those technologies to determine their business value to the firm, and transferring proven technology into productive use throughout the organization. The key questions are:

- How are potentially valuable technologies identified?
- What steps are taken to evaluate the real value of technology and the risks associated with it?
- How are potential end users of technology involved during the pilot phase to validate results of the test?
- What techniques are used to transfer valuable technology into the business units?

COMPETITIVE ANALYSIS

Competitive analysis is the process of studying how other companies (sometimes not direct competitors[6]) are using IT. This benchmark homes in on the process of understanding how other companies are using IT. We asked:

- What competitive data are collected for analysis?
- What data sources are used?
- What type of analysis is performed?
- Who is involved in the analysis?
- How are the results of the analysis translated into action?

ARCHITECTURES

Architecture is the process of building, maintaining, and using an IT infrastructure that promotes effective information sharing. By some estimates, IT architectures can amount to 50% of the capital investment in large

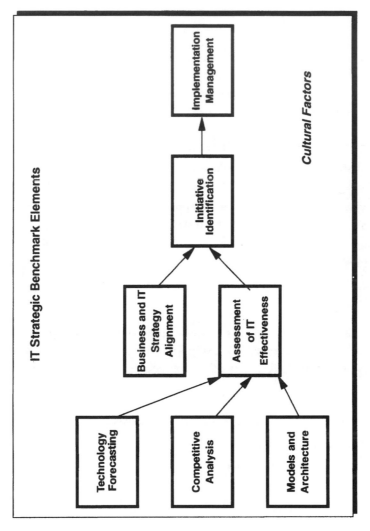

Figure 9.2.

firms.[7] Too often, senior management lacks an effective process for directing this spending and ensuring that it is directed toward achieving competitive advantage. We asked:

- How is the current infrastructure analyzed to identify requirements?
- How are architecture initiatives identified?
- What techniques are used to fund infrastructure?
- What approaches are used to address conformance to architecture?
- What approaches are used to measure the business value and effectiveness of existing architectures?
- What techniques are employed to enhance the architectures over time?

ASSESSMENT OF IT EFFECTIVENESS

Assessment is the process of evaluating IT service levels. This strategic element includes assessment of IT infrastructural performance, applications adequacy, human resources (HR), and operations management processes. In this area, the IT strategic alignment benchmark establishes the best practice for understanding how the current IT is positioned to meet current and future business requirements. We asked:

- How are measurements defined?
- Why are they chosen?
- How are IT effectiveness measures translated into business results?
- How are performance gaps translated into action plans?

BUSINESS AND IT STRATEGY ALIGNMENT

Alignment is the process of ensuring that the IT strategy fully supports the business strategy. This concept is easy to understand but often difficult to implement, as many CEOs and CIOs will attest.[8] We focused on the communication and management processes used by firms:

- How does the IT organization develop an understanding of the business strategy?
- What are the most effective processes for ensuring two-way communication between user management and IT management?

- What techniques are used to enable the IT organization to influence the business plan?
- What are the best techniques for maintaining alignment of the business and IT strategies over time?

INITIATIVE IDENTIFICATION

Initiative identification is the process of defining IT projects, estimating their business value, and establishing project investment priorities across the business. As IT use expands throughout organizations and as businesses expand globally, the need to effectively manage the trade-offs between various IT initiatives has never been stronger. By benchmarking this area, managers can understand how to effectively prioritize projects across business units and on a global scale. We asked:

- How are initiatives identified?
- What techniques are proven effective for prioritizing initiatives across business units?
- How are organizations dealing with the complexities of global scale?
- What are the best approaches for negotiating agreement on initiative priority?

IMPLEMENTATION MANAGEMENT

Implementation management is the process of delivering functions that meet user requirements while maintaining schedule, quality, and financial controls. As seasoned IT managers know, for every spectacular IT success story, there has been an IT debacle. According to Richard Walton of the Harvard Business School, IT implementation problems result from management's failure to fully appreciate the interdependence of technology and organization.[9] An IT strategic alignment benchmark in this area highlights the systematic approaches applied successfully by leading companies to ensure project success. We asked:

- How are projects managed?
- What processes are used to balance resources?
- What techniques are used to measure the actual benefits from initiative implementation?

- What is the best process to ensure that the organization learns from the experience of past projects?

CULTURAL FACTORS

Cultural processes encompass the intangible organizational qualities that shape and direct the IT strategic processes. While not a discrete process themselves, cultural factors are often the most important element in determining the success of IT strategic planning. Consider the relationship the CIO has with the other senior managers.

- Is it one of partnership?
- What is the nature of communication between them?
- What mechanisms are used to encourage effective dialogue between IT and users?
- How can management create the proper cultural environment?
- What communications programs are most effective?

Choosing the Benchmarking Partners

A further outcome from the upfront work was a profile of the corporations to be invited to participate in the benchmark. The target corporations had several characteristics in common: they would be world-class and have complex relationships with multiple business units operating in multiple countries. Moreover, the companies would have experienced success in the following areas:

- aligning IT strategy with business goals
- quickly assimilating new technologies into the organization
- replacing older legacy systems with state-of-the-art systems, while preserving key portions of previous investments
- delivering highly responsive IT solutions during periods of rapid change

The study team assembled an initial list of over two hundred companies for consideration. Nonfinancial as well as financial industries were considered because American Express understood that the best practices from these other industries could be found and applied within TRS Technologies. The company list was sequenced based on the selection criteria developed by the study team. Then, starting at the top of the list and working down, American Express executives made personal contact with their peers in the candidate companies.

In short order, seventeen of the top companies eagerly agreed to participate. One of the reasons for the participants' enthusiasm was the study's focus on qualitative strategic alignment issues instead of the more typical IT cost approach. For example, the study team investigated how an organization's IT infrastructure aligned with and supported strategic business processes. Also, the study proposed to look beyond processes to understand the relationship of the top business executives with the CIO and other key IT managers.

Measuring Excellence

One of the challenges faced by the study team was how to measure excellence. When comparing IT strategic processes from different companies, it is useful to be able to quantify the effectiveness of each process. Ultimately, the benchmark must determine which process (or subprocess) is the best practice. Managers will want to know the size of the performance gap between their process and the best practice. Moreover, specific metrics can be used to establish performance goals and to track performance improvement over time. Unfortunately, agreed-to measures of performance don't exist for many IT processes. Revenue and cost savings attributable to a process can provide overall measures of process effectiveness, but these measures do not provide sufficient information for managers seeking to improve their processes.

To address these issues, best practice criteria were developed for each IT strategic process to be benchmarked. These criteria are similar to the criteria used for the Malcolm Baldrige National Quality Award.[10] The best practice criteria were then transformed into metrics that were scored based on interviews and other process-related data collected as a result of interviews. Multiple metrics were used to assess the performance of each process, then combined to establish a single performance metric for each process. With this approach, processes from different companies could be compared (Figs. 9.3, 9.4).

Not all of these metrics were relevant to American Express; what was best for one company could not be assumed to be right for another. For example, best practice for a company focused on expense reduction may be radically different from best practice for one experiencing rapid growth.

To understand applicability of the identified best practices, the study

Summary IT Strategic Alignment Criteria

Example	Business and IT Alignment
Business Strategy	- Business Strategy and vision are agreed to and well communicated
IT Strategy	- IT strategy and vision are agreed to and well communicated
Business Procedures	- IT expenditures are controlled by needs of the business
IT Procedures	- IT consistently addresses the needs of the business - Key IT people are trained in and understand the business functions
Partnership	- Business and IT strategies are integrated - Goals are shared between IT and business personnel

Figure 9.3.

Sample IT Strategic Alignment Metrics

Control

	Subprocess Ownership	Objectives / Procedures
High	☐ Agreed	☐ Agreed and Communicated
Medium	☐ Stated	☐ Defined
Low	☐ No Owner	☐ Not Defined

Input

	Business Strategy	Understanding of Competitive Analysis	Technology Impact	IT Assessment	
High		☐	☐	☐	Participants Well Informed
Medium		☐	☐	☐	Limited Understanding
Low		☐	☐	☐	

Activity

	IT Structure	IT ???	Governance	Funding Level
High	☐ Meets Current and Future Requirement	☐ Mapped to Business Strategy	☐ Strategic Evaluation	☐ Reflects Strategic Requirements
Medium	☐ Meets Current Requirement	☐ Defined by Competitors IT	☐ Operational Consideration	☐ Going Rate
Low	☐ No Awareness	☐ Defined by IT	☐ No Consideration	☐ Funding Not Part of ITSP

Resources

Execute Management   IT Management   Business Planner   IT Planner

Man-Months/Yr

Output

	IT Strategy
High	☐ Documented, Communicated, Covering Technology Technology Vision, Core Competencies, Priorities, Governance, and Funding
Medium	☐ Documented with Partial Coverage
Low	☐ No Documented Strategy

Figure 9.4.

team assessed the situational context within which each best practice operated. Among the issues considered were:

- Does senior management express a shared vision for IT?
- Do cooperation and mutual trust exist between departments and divisions?
- How is hiring, training, and motivation of staff accomplished?
- Who has authority to take action?
- Is risk taking encouraged and are failures allowed?

Eventually, the study team developed a set of over fifty metrics that were meaningful for American Express. Each participating company's processes were rated using these metrics, and the IT management processes from the higher scoring companies were documented in detail to American Express management with a solid understanding of what made the best processes best.

Results of Benchmarking Study

One of the specific findings that could be implemented immediately was that users must be involved in strategic projects very early in the game, especially in reengineering projects that cut across functions. As a result, the company has become much more proactive in its relationship with the user community.

Another was the conclusion that poor IT strategic alignment was often caused by major transition—e.g., moving from a growth situation to cost containment because of changed market conditions. Even the best companies had problems maintaining IT/business alignment under these circumstances.

In the best companies, senior management in both business and IT displayed significant vision, provided strategic directions, and were committed to rigorous planning and execution. All across these organizations, including the relationships between departments and divisions, there was a feeling of trust and a team orientation. HR were emphasized, and in the IT organization motivation and training were considered very important.

The benchmark found that change, especially change precipitated by crisis, was a major influence on the IT function. Over half of the companies benchmarked had experienced a crisis in the last seven years brought on by a competitive threat, a financial upheaval, or a dramatic change in executive leadership style. Each of these companies had reorganized and realigned its IT function in response to the crisis. Their success in weathering the storm came in part from a successful alignment of IT and the new business processes.

The study team's findings reinforced American Express's perception that change is a constant and that the proper alignment of IT with business strategies and processes is a continuous endeavor.

A Continuous Benchmarking Process

Although this particular benchmarking exercise is now over, the process that it initiated is not. In addition to implementing the recommendations to further improve its IT strategic planning process to better realize its business goals, American Express and some of the other companies involved were keen to continue the study.

Many of the companies commented that they had never before received such useful data on the effectiveness of business processes. They wanted to see the project continue on a regular basis and to include a number of new topics each time it was run.

The IBM IT Transformation Benchmarking Project

As a result the IBM IT Transformation Benchmarking Project was created—a multicompany global search for best IT transformation management practices, now comprising thirty-three companies from North America, Europe, and Asia. Rather than being part of a one-shot study, the consortium members mutually participate in a series of benchmarks over a period of years; build relationships; and share knowledge, ideas, and IT approaches. This project was constructed to assess how IT functions within companies were responding to a new set of critical issues confronting business executives today, which were defined as:

- inadequate quality
- shareholder impatience
- cost pressures
- skill shortages
- global competition
- compressed product life cycles

- organizational inertia
- market fragmentation

These issues are forcing multi-faceted responses in most organizations (see Figure 9.5), including defining a radically new role for IT. At the same time, technological advances are continually improving, and changing the ability of IT to support and enhance business strategy (see Figure 9.6). The project set out to understand how people, technology and value had been combined to produce business transformation in some of the world's leading companies. Five fundamental questions were asked:

- What are the best practices associated with each critical success factor?
- What makes a best practice best?
- What are the effect of cultural and other factors on the implementation of best practices?
- How do each of the benchmark companies compare to best practices?
- What are each company's strengths and weaknesses relative to best practices?

Consortium Benchmarking Process

In order to answer these questions, a three-phase approach to the project was taken but constructed so that it could provide immediate feedback and action points for all the companies involved. Phase I identified appropriate benchmark companies; Phase II, collected qualitative and quantitative management process data; and Phase III, analyzed the findings to determine best practice (see Figure 9.7a, b).

PHASE I: SELECTION OF BENCHMARK COMPANIES

Multiple filtering criteria were applied to identify a select group of comparable companies from an initial target population of the top 1000 companies worldwide. In descending order, we filtered first by size, followed by industry mix, the role of the CIO, the company's status as a technology leader, and finally by its overall status as an industry leader in its sector.

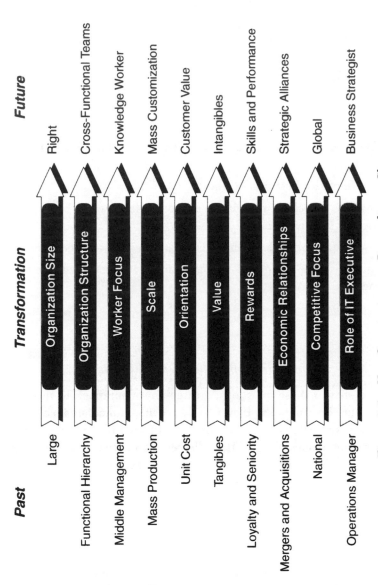

Past	Transformation	Future
Large	Organization Size	Right
Functional Hierarchy	Organization Structure	Cross-Functional Teams
Middle Management	Worker Focus	Knowledge Worker
Mass Production	Scale	Mass Customization
Unit Cost	Orientation	Customer Value
Tangibles	Value	Intangibles
Loyalty and Seniority	Rewards	Skills and Performance
Mergers and Acquisitions	Economic Relationships	Strategic Alliances
National	Competitive Focus	Global
Operations Manager	Role of IT Executive	Business Strategist

Figure 9.5. How Organizations are Responding to Change

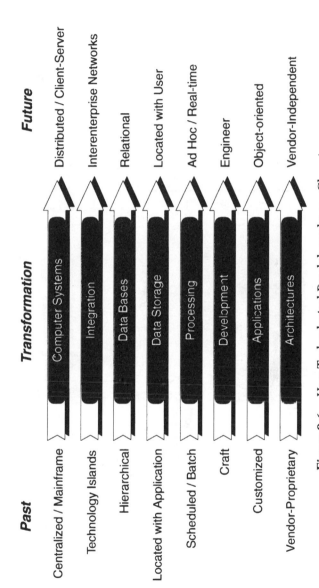

Figure 9.6. How Technological Breakthroughs are Changing

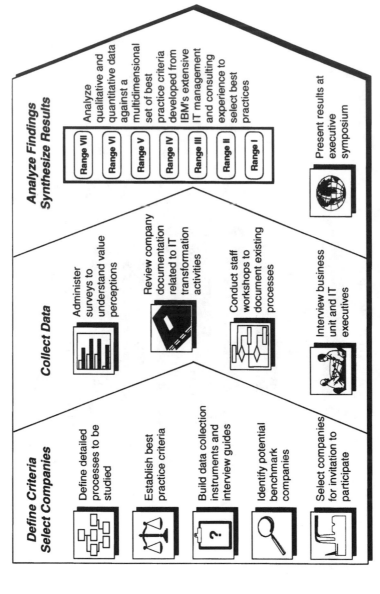

Define Criteria
Select Companies

- Define detailed processes to be studied
- Establish best practice criteria
- Build data collection instruments and interview guides
- Identify potential benchmark companies
- Select companies for invitation to participate

Collect Data

- Administer surveys to understand value perceptions
- Review company documentation related to IT transformation activities
- Conduct staff workshops to document existing processes
- Interview business unit and IT executives

Analyze Findings
Synthesize Results

Range VII
Range VI
Range V
Range IV
Range III
Range II
Range I

Analyze qualitative and quantitative data against a multidimensional set of best practice criteria developed from IBM's extensive IT management and consulting experience to select best practices

- Present results at executive symposium

Figure 9.7a. IT Transformation Benchmark Consortium Approach

Range VII — Outstanding sustained effort and results in all elements throughout the organization. Excellent integration with other processes. World-class.

Range VI — Effective efforts in all elements, world-class in some. Good integration, good to excellent results. Fully deployed. Industry or national leader.

Range V — Evidence of effective effort in most categories, outstanding in several. Strength in deployment and results, but some efforts lack maturity.

Range IV — Evidence of efforts in many elements. Some outstanding. Good prevention base, but efforts lack maturity. Need further deployment and sustained results.

Range III — Some effort in several elements, but poor integration, little preventive activity.

Range II — Slight evidence of effort in any category. IT transition activities receive low priority.

Range I — Virtually no evidence of attention to any of the elements.

Figure 9.7b. IT Transformation CSF Scoring Ranges

The resulting initial group of twenty-one benchmark companies (subsequently expanded to thirty-three) represented in aggregate over $220 billion in revenue across nine major industry segments.

Fifteen companies were based in the United States, one in South America, three in Europe, and two in Japan and provided a broad range of new ideas for IT transformation with their very different stages of revenue growth and organizational structures (Fig. 9.8).

PHASE II: COLLECTING THE BEST PRACTICE DATA

Our international team of consultants spent a total of seven weeks with each of the twenty-one companies, collecting data through questionnaires, process workshops, interviews, and company documentation (Table 9.1).

PHASE III: ANALYZING THE DATA

Individual IT transformation scores were labeled to protect confidentiality and then processed through a further four stages of analysis before best practice descriptions could be derived (Figs. 9.9, 9.10).

Consortium Feedback Process

As a result of the on-site visits, companies could immediately begin to achieve near-term benefits by analyzing the consultants' interim report and modifying current practices where applicable. For example, they did the following:

- reviewed process documentation developed during the process workshops and used it to identify ways they could streamline current processes

- conducted role and responsibility analysis for key processes, using process documentation to help clarify roles and responsibilities to streamline decision-making

- prioritized improvement opportunities identified in the interim report and formed quality improvement teams to generate improvement initiatives that capitalized on current strengths and needed improvements

TABLE 9.1.   Data Gathered during the Benchmarking Process

Interviews:

Two-hundred thirty-five IT and two-hundred twenty business executives were asked over two-hundred twenty questions to gather qualitative information on process performance and satisfaction with process results. Each company's processes were scored using a comprehensive set of process metrics, and best practices were selected and documented.

Questionnaires

Four-hundred ten IT and two-hundred ninety business executives completed five-hundred–question questionnaires, providing over 395,000 quantitative data points for analysis. The questionnaire data were correlated, with detailed process characteristics identified in the interviews, and then discussed and documented during the workshops.

Process workshops

Three-hundred sixty IT and two-hundred business executives participated in process workshops, covering five CSFs and twenty process areas, to provide information on workflow and stakeholder participation.

Company documentation

Six-hundred seventy documents were assembled to provide data on IT processes and programs, including deployment and results.

Taken together with documentation, interviews, and questionnaires, the company was given a score on a scale of 1–7 (7 being the highest score), indicating the extent that IT was successfully integrated with the business, resulting in good performance (see Fig. 9.7a, b).

- assessed gaps in perception between the business and IT units using the perceptions survey feedback, improving communications programs in critical areas of significant perception gaps

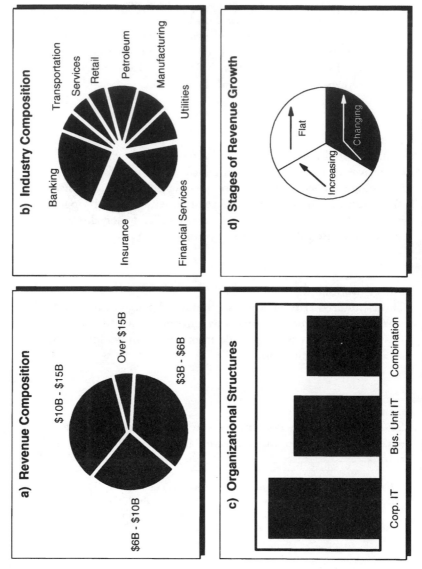

Figure 9.8. IT Transformation Benchmark Consortium Profile

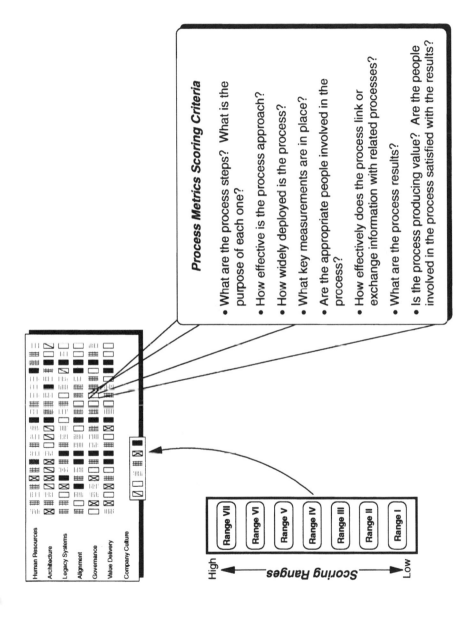

Figure 9.9. IT Transformation Benchmark Consortium Scoring Process

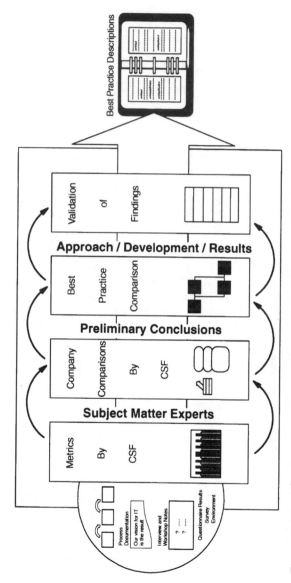

Figure 9.10. The Four-Stage Analysis from Individual Scores to Best Practice Definitions

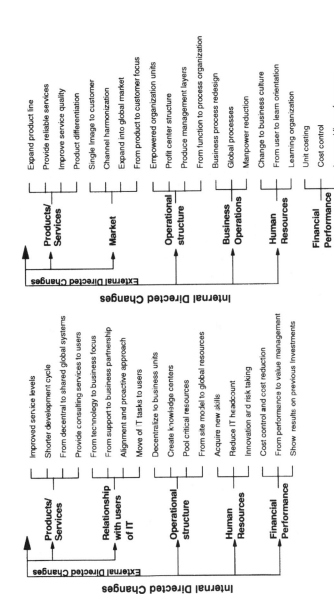

Business Changes

Technology Changes

Figure 9.11. How Organizations are Responding to Marketplace?

Further follow-up comes at a postbenchmark symposium, where the participants discuss each study's results and have a chance to interact and become part of a network of IT executives interested in best practice. At the symposium meeting IBM Consulting presents a best practice aggregate report (individual company findings remain confidential) to the group and opens the floor for discussion. In the evening, each company is briefed on its individual findings. On the following day, companies with like interests get together in a workshop setting to swap information and opinions. Any companies wishing to present their findings to the group and get the benefit of feedback are given the opportunity.

One multidivisional company with a typical *stovepipe* or *silo* organization, where each line of business has its own IT department and systems, knew that it was running redundant IT activities on the order of 35% and recognized the problem but never found a way to crack it. However, thanks to initial benchmarking against another multiproduct company that did not stovepipe, its IT organization was able to develop new cross-business systems and increase efficiency and lower operating costs dramatically.

Another had never measured the value of its IT function. It was viewed more as an expense rather than an asset to the business that would, say, help make decisions sooner or be more reactive, like with just-in-time ordering. In the course of benchmarking, it got to network with a company that has done a phenomenal job of understanding and measuring the value of IT. So, it changed its IT organization into an autonomous information provider, with its own CEO and even a new chief financial officer, to measure its IT better.

Results of the IT Transformation Project

The first iteration of the consortium study found that enterprises were making radical and far-reaching changes to respond to a dynamic marketplace and to propel themselves into the twenty-first century (Fig. 9.11). While management processes vary by individual company context, a common set of critical issues in managing transformation emerge from best practice companies:

Understand the effect of culture
- The business's willingness to partner with IT is directly related to the importance of IT in the business strategy.

Get the strategy straight
- Benchmarked companies with a strong business vision tend to have a strong IT vision.
- Most companies do not understand the full costs of their legacy systems and do not employ a systematic process for portfolio assessment.

Develop a balanced set of customer-centric measures
- Fifty-five percent of companies consider service their primary focus, with price, speed to market, and customization being secondary considerations.
- Companies measure performance technology costs, with 60% of the companies also measuring customer satisfaction or quality.

Pick the spots for change
- Sixty-five percent of companies are concentrating on IT to achieve dramatic cost savings, while 35% are considering IT as a strategic weapon to accelerate corporate directions and goals.
- Thirty-five percent of companies are undergoing major restructuring: if centralized, they are decentralizing to provide more rapid response and flexibility; if decentralized they are centralizing to drive toward a single view of the customer and to increase the cost reduction focus.
- While all companies have a legacy of mainframe skills, the top technical skill sets are being driven by the business; architecture, networks, client/server, and open systems are in short supply and impacting the business.
- Instill a corporate wide view of the importance of technology.
- Companies with a corporatewide view of the importance of technology as well as senior management sponsorship are significantly more satisfied with their technology investment and processes.
- The business's willingness to partner with IT is directly related to the importance of IT in the business strategy.
- Companies with a technological model or high-level view of the enterprise realize a 30% greater value in increased productivity, cost saving, better decision-making, and increased profitability.

Fit IT processes and skills to the business objectives and expand
the business objectives through IT processes and skills

- Effective communication between business and IT emerged as one
  of the primary factors associated with value delivery.
- IT has a 30% higher value to the business in companies which consider IT competencies as technical, business, and consulting skills
  which are directed to business needs.

IT is everyone's business—recognize the roles

- Companies with the strongest peer relationships between business
  and IT executives enjoy the highest value delivery.
- Significant IT executive turnover has occurred in these companies,
  with over half of the senior IT executives less than two years in the
  job and sourced from business backgrounds.

These critical issues form the three fundamental components that organizations need to address if they are to transform their IT organizations
for optimal performance: people, technology, and value (Fig. 9.12).

People

Managing people is perhaps the most critical skill in achieving alignment
between business and IT. Successful companies in our benchmarking exercise saw it as a continuous circular process, starting with an HR (Human
Resource) strategy based on the concept of people as valuable assets. This
strategy generated policies and practices aimed at deploying those assets in
the most effective way for the company. Measuring the effectiveness of the
resulting performance shed new light on the critical IT competencies
needed for the business and thus influenced the next iteration of the strategy formulation process.

Establishing an HR Strategy for IT

The best practice firms not only viewed people as valuable assets but had
a very clear understanding of the core competencies and services required
right across their business. For these relatively few organizations, determining HR strategy for IT personnel was a matter of ensuring that IT competencies strengthened and supported business competencies, especially in
business areas with a high technological requirement. Noncritical IT activities could be outsourced as a result, though most organizations monitored
this policy closely to ensure that they did not lose control of an activity that

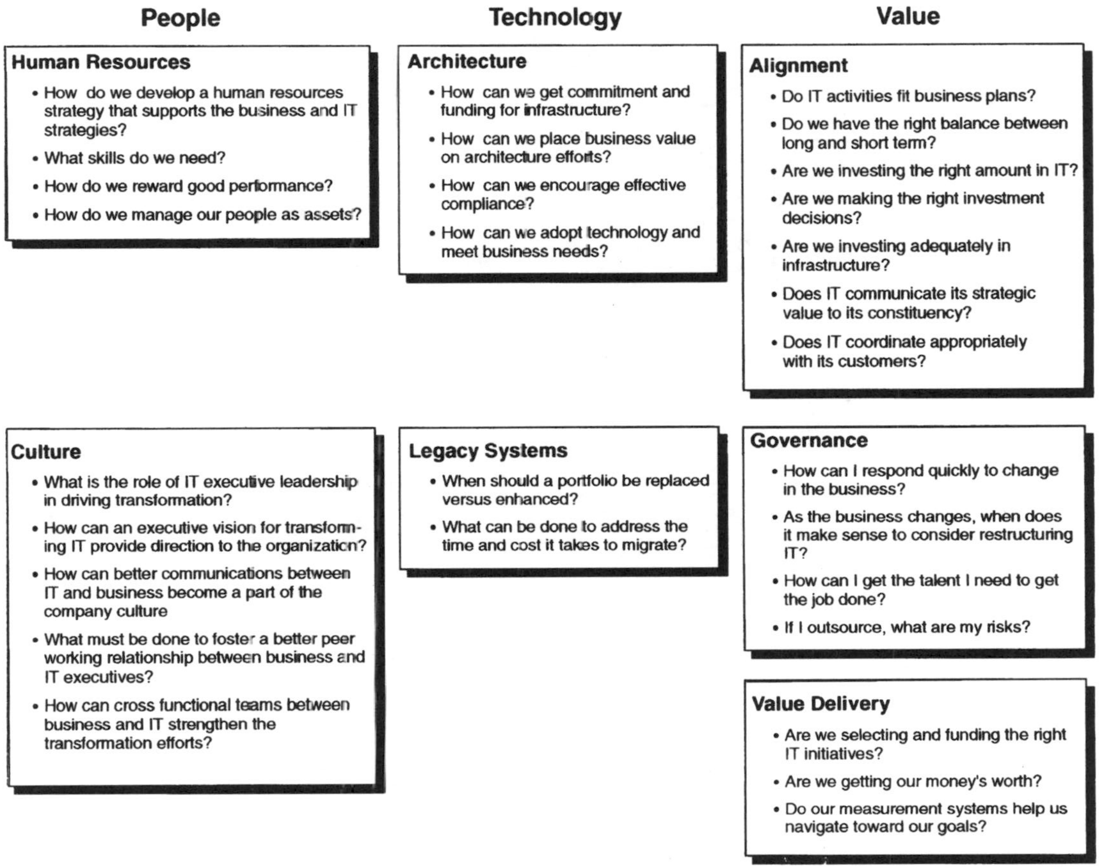

People

Human Resources
- How do we develop a human resources strategy that supports the business and IT strategies?
- What skills do we need?
- How do we reward good performance?
- How do we manage our people as assets?

Culture
- What is the role of IT executive leadership in driving transformation?
- How can an executive vision for transforming IT provide direction to the organization?
- How can better communications between IT and business become a part of the company culture
- What must be done to foster a better peer working relationship between business and IT executives?
- How can cross functional teams between business and IT strengthen the transformation efforts?

Technology

Architecture
- How can we get commitment and funding for infrastructure?
- How can we place business value on architecture efforts?
- How can we encourage effective compliance?
- How can we adopt technology and meet business needs?

Legacy Systems
- When should a portfolio be replaced versus enhanced?
- What can be done to address the time and cost it takes to migrate?

Value

Alignment
- Do IT activities fit business plans?
- Do we have the right balance between long and short term?
- Are we investing the right amount in IT?
- Are we making the right investment decisions?
- Are we investing adequately in infrastructure?
- Does IT communicate its strategic value to its constituency?
- Does IT coordinate appropriately with its customers?

Governance
- How can I respond quickly to change in the business?
- As the business changes, when does it make sense to consider restructuring IT?
- How can I get the talent I need to get the job done?
- If I outsource, what are my risks?

Value Delivery
- Are we selecting and funding the right IT initiatives?
- Are we getting our money's worth?
- Do our measurement systems help us navigate toward our goals?

Figure 9.12. Critical issues for Companies Transforming their IT Organizaitons

might be required in future by the business or become too dependent on outside suppliers.

However, in most firms the process of HR strategy definition was not as straightforward, due to lack of clarity on core competencies or other problems relating to historic reward structures or the corporate culture of the IT organization. Nevertheless, most acknowledged that the critical impact and increasing cost of IT HR meant that matching IT competencies to activities that added the greatest value to the business was essential.

HR POLICIES AND PRACTICES

Most traditional IT HR policies emphasize technological skills over consulting and business skills, but the composite best practice findings stressed that recognizing and rewarding a broader mix of skills was more appropriate. Particularly effective policies ensured that IT professionals were motivated and rewarded as part of mixed business and IT teams dedicated to achieving common objectives.

Technological skills are, of course, important but only in terms of what the business is setting out to do. Encouraging greater communication and consulting skills improves both the application of IT to business objectives and the business understanding of the potential of IT. It also provides a useful basis for evaluating IT training requirements, as they can be more directly related to business performance.

Aligning IT reward systems with business objectives has enormous potential for achieving business transformation. It not only allows business executives to properly measure the contribution of IT to particular projects but it gives IT personnel a new sense of status and a source of motivation. Best practice companies that we interviewed had well-developed policies for providing continuous feedback to IT staff on the development of their technical, consulting, and business skills and the relevance of those skills to current business targets and objectives.

HR PERFORMANCE ASSESSMENT

IT performance assessment is difficult without a clear concept of how business value is delivered across the company. Best practice companies had concluded that there was a direct link between employee satisfaction and customer satisfaction, and thus eventual profits. They therefore assessed their HR policies for IT in terms of how they improved IT personnel's understanding and satisfaction in achieving business objectives.

In the process of discussing these issues with IT staff, they gained a clearer understanding of how IT skills and competencies could reinforce business objectives and used these insights to drive their HR strategy for IT.

Company Culture

Company culture can be a catalyst or an inhibitor of IT transformation. In many instances IT is more generally aware of the need to change than the business, and the conflict which then arises between IT executives and their companies is evidenced by the high turnover of IT personnel in our bench-marked companies (Fig. 9.13); increasingly, senior IT positions are being filled with people with business backgrounds.

The best practice companies controlled this situation through strong leadership, linking business and IT visions into coherent strategies and maintaining strong communication with all of their employees. The effect of creating cross-functional teams and strong working relationships in these companies was a much higher perception of the value of IT to the organ-ization (Fig. 9.14).

Technology

Building an IT Architecture and Dealing with Legacy Systems

Best practice companies proactively develop architectural blueprints for IT tied to business strategies and goals and skillfully manage the migration of legacy systems to support these objectives. However, the process for doing this is heavily influenced by two main considerations: whether they are trying to achieve cost savings or marketplace differentiation (Fig. 9.15).

Cost-focused companies benchmark themselves against competitors to ensure that they are the lowest-cost providers of IT in their industry, whereas differentiation-focused companies actively research and exploit technology to position themselves in their marketplaces.

ARCHITECTURE

The role that IT architecture can play in supporting either of these strat-egies is addressed at four levels in the organizations we studied.

Firstly, the board and other senior executives must be convinced that

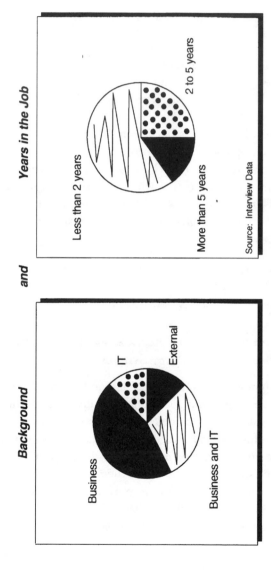

Figure 9.13. Mortality Rate of CIOs

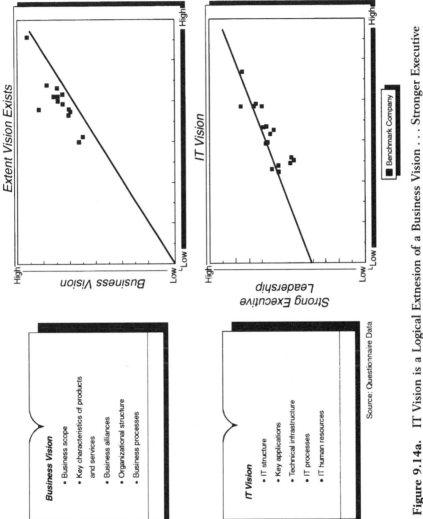

Figure 9.14a. IT Vision is a Logical Extnesion of a Business Vision . . . Stronger Executive Leadership Drives a more Effective Vision of IT

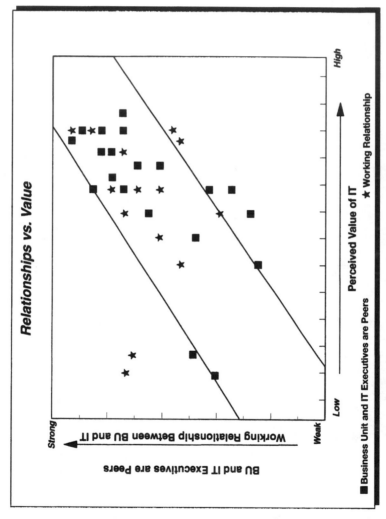

Figure 9.14b.   Strong Working Relationships Directly Contribute to the Perceived Value of IT

Focus Attributes	Cost	Differentiation
Strategic View of Technology	Low cost	Strategic weapon
Focus of Blueprint	Increased service at lower cost	Total value chain: company, suppliers, and customers
External Options	Reduced cost	Increased core competencies
Technology Assimilation	Dramatic cost savings	Acceleration of corporate directions and goals
Technology Change Driven	Evolutionary, based on continuous improvement	Revolutionary, based on repositioning of business and process reengineering
Role of IT Organization	Central provider of low-cost services	Change agent and information utility for self-sufficient business units

Figure 9.15.   How Cost-Saving or Differentiation Goals Influence IT Strategy

Source: Questionnaire Data and IBM Consulting Group Analysis

Figure 9.16. Effectiveness of Gaining Senior Management Commitment to IT Architecture

IT architectures *do* indeed play a key role in achieving business objectives. This is difficult in many companies, and the most effective strategies we saw involved the spontaneous creation of cross-functional "inner circles" of executives, who were able to clearly see the value of IT architectures to their individual areas of responsibility. These inner circles were often represented by a "champion," whose role was to gain top-level sponsorship for their ideas.

When commitment had been obtained, the inner circles were often the basis for cross-functional steering committees, who took over responsibility for reviewing IT architectural plans, prioritizing projects, and approving funding. Most best practice companies had abandoned contentious SBU chargeback schemes and accepted that the IT architecture was a central corporate responsibility. Figure 9.16 illustrates the effectiveness of this approach.

Secondly, best practice companies have developed a comprehensive IT

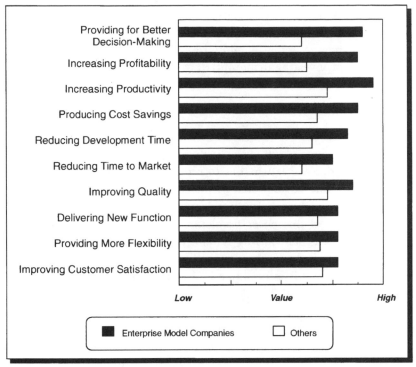

Source: Questionnaire Data

Figure 9.17. How Blueprints Help Realize the Business Value of IT Architecture

architecture blueprint based on an enterprise model of the company to manage and guide future IT investment. James Martin has described such models as "high level views of the enterprise, its functions, data and information needs . . . grounded in top management goals and critical success factors." The great advantage of such blueprints is that they provide a detailed management guide to realizing real benefits from IT (Fig. 9.17).

Thirdly, having gained commitment and designed a blueprint, best practice companies must address the issue of achieving compliance to the model across the organizations. Few companies had effective procedures for doing this, preferring to encourage and reward compliance rather than to actively punish offenders. A valuable approach was to support the use of common systems and tools to solve new applications and problems.

Finally, especially for firms interested in differentiation rather than cost-saving, the IT architecture needs to address the issue of how it can help the firm assimilate and evaluate new technological developments. The best practice here was to formalize research and development procedures and to involve the business units in systematically evaluating, prototyping, and piloting new systems to minimize the risk of either missing a new development or investing inappropriately.

LEGACY SYSTEMS

One of the most important uses of an IT architecture is in helping define what should be done about legacy systems. The fundamental question that needs to be addressed is whether to replace or enhance existing systems; this can only really be answered by looking at the gap between legacy systems and the IT architecture blueprint.

However, even this poses problems, as few companies have comprehensively reviewed their existing systems and have a full picture of the costs of maintaining and developing them. The best practice companies we interviewed did have this information and, moreover, had instituted a regular review process with their business units to look at future options and costs.

Where it had been decided that existing systems were inadequate and that migration to new systems was inevitable, our benchmark companies expressed universal dissatisfaction with the time and cost of this exercise.

Techniques used in best practice companies to manage the process successfully were based on classic project-management prescriptions. First and foremost, business objectives, processes, and costs were analyzed and clarified before undertaking the assignment and realistic deliverables planned into the project from the start. Secondly, great care was taken in breaking the project into manageable chunks, employing dedicated teams, and making sophisticated use of tools and techniques to simplify and save time (Fig. 9.18).

Many best practice companies identified long cycle times for migration as fatal—even the best run projects could become redundant as the business conditions which dictated the migration changed again—and suggested a completely new direction in terms of systems and architectures.

Value

Alignment

Alignment between business and IT strategies is consistently ranked by our benchmark companies as their top issue. Best practice companies are exceptional in that they develop a synergy between planning, funding, and

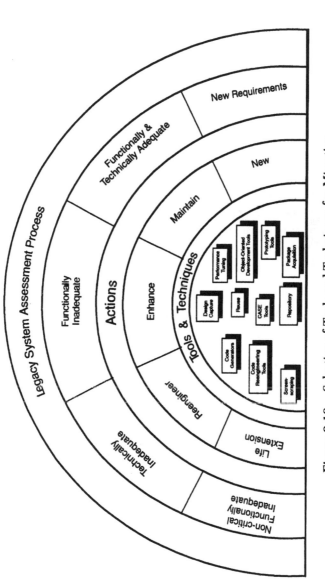

Figure 9.18. Selection of Tools and Techniques for Migration

communications, whether they are taking a long-term, strategic approach
to alignment or a short-term, operational view (Fig. 9.19).

PLANNING

We found that very few companies planned alignment over the longer term.
Even where there were such plans, they tended not to be fully executed
and instead developed into rolling plans, heavily influenced by external
events. Interestingly, some best practice companies actually built in a two-
quarter time lag within an eight-quarter cycle to give their business and IT
functions a realistic chance of achieving short-term coordination within a
longer-term plan.

However, the longer-term approach made a conscious effort to include
all stakeholders (business, IT, and partners) and tended to result in a well-
integrated plan, with a strong IT component, which the partners executed
jointly. The operational approach, in contrast, while depending on a good
relationship between business and IT, was much more driven by the short-
term tactical requirements of the business unit.

FUNDING

The problems of achieving alignment become particularly acute when making IT investment decisions, and no company that we investigated had
moved beyond a historical trends approach to valuing IT for this purpose.
Most, however, had found that some mechanism for earmarking funds for
specific purposes helped.

In the case of an operational planning approach, the immediate business unit needs tended to identify specific IT requirements quickly and to
get equally quick approval of the funds needed to solve them. In some
instances this would include some necessary spend on infrastructural items.

A more strategic approach to funding involved rolling, multiyear spending on particular plans, and cross-functional teams allocating the money
and resolving disputes. Infrastructural spending tended to be taken more
seriously in these situations.

COMMUNICATIONS

We found communication about IT strategy and its relation to business
strategy to be very poor in many companies. In 50% of organizations, the
IT vision was not articulated or was used to inform decisions on a day-to-
day basis. In best practice companies, by contrast, great stress was placed

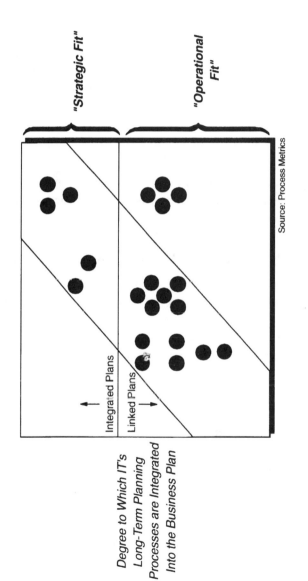

Figure 9.19. Short and Long-Term Approaches to Achieving Alignment

on explaining how each IT project linked to business strategy, to the extent of appointing dedicated communication specialists and relationship managers to major projects (Fig. 9.20).

As might be expected, the longer-term approach to planning resulted in a deeper-rooted relationship between IT and business personnel, with senior IT executives becoming part of the inner circle of strategic policy-making individuals and a collaborative working style developing at all levels. However, even the short-term, operational approach relied on good communications between IT and the business unit and good practice at "instant teaming" to meet fast-changing requirements.

Governance

Managing the integration of IT and business strategy requires a complex mastery of the roles and responsibilities of the various participants. Our best practice companies were winning by:

- extending their boundaries through a network of creative outsourcing partnerships
- using a single view of the external customer to build consensus for change among its players
- responding to externally driven changes in the rules by redefining roles and responsibilities and moving faster

ROLES

In general, we found that the willingness of business units to work with IT depended on how much their strategy depended on IT. Where IT was core, the secret of successful integration was to introduce shared accountability for both problem-solving and project-execution. However, this process was hampered in many companies by the difficulty of releasing IT staff to new business-critical applications. In over 50% of organizations, the majority of IT staff were still tied up with ongoing application maintenance work, instead of being free to address, for instance, client/server, LAN, WAN, and open systems issues.

In a great many companies, therefore, there was a clear need to restructure IT organizations, redefine roles, and clarify mission (in fact, this was happening in 35% of our benchmark organizations). The problem was whether to centralize or decentralize IT operations (Fig. 9.21).

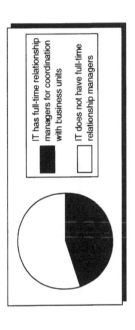

When Objectives Were...

- To increase the involvement of business unit executives in IT activities and decisions

- To make the relationship managers both empowered and accountable

- To improve cross-business unit technology sharing without usurping business unit authority

- To prevent the relationship from becoming a bureaucratic substitute for appropriate business unit involvement

The Actions Were...

- Increased the status of the IT relationship manager position and assigned senior-level personnel who knew the organization well

- Assigned the relationship manager ownership of a portfolio of production and development projects. Responsibility was assigned to him for pricing, staffing, and results

- IT issues "opinions" about planned initiatives that suggest ways business units could share costs and/or adopt successful techniques

- Implemented peer-to-peer project managers within the business unit who have coordinated responsibilities

Source: Benchmark Company Interview Documentation

Figure 9.20. The Use of IT Relationship Managers in Best Practice Companies

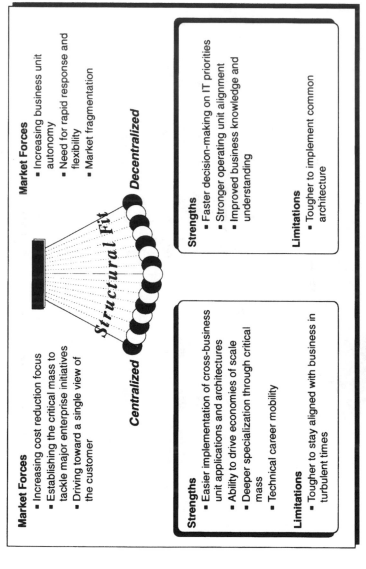

Figure 9.21. Fitting IT Structure to Business Needs

OUTSOURCING

A small but growing number of best practice companies have learned that the way to outsource is to strengthen their internal IT core competencies and to manage as though the outsourced players were their own (Fig. 9.22), but these are still in the minority. Most companies have yet to master relationship-management at the level necessary for successful outsourcing.

Value Delivery

The goal of value measurement is to render explicit IT's contribution to business results through linking IT activities more firmly to business strategy. Our survey showed that this is far more likely to occur when the business units are actively involved in the selection and justification process and have robust measures for monitoring customer satisfaction, continuous improvement, and verification of results.

Nearly every company we examined had implemented a set of performance measures, but few were satisfied with their ability to link them convincingly to business results. The problem was usually that the measures were too internally focused, did not reflect the breadth of their IT objectives, or were used only as part of a total quality program. Best practice companies routinely optimized value by embedding technological projects within business initiatives, defining service quality indicators in customer terms, and using market comparisons to evaluate competitiveness and to establish sourcing strategies.

Conclusion

During the 1970s and 1980s, as Max Hopper, Senior Vice President for IS at American Airlines, points out,[11] companies who were the first to build proprietary information systems garnered huge competitive advantage. American Airlines' SABRE reservation system and American Hospital Supply's ASAP order-entry described by Luftman in Chapter 3 are, perhaps, the two most cited examples of successful implementation of this strategy. Technological changes are forcing this strategy to change as well.

Phenomenal advances in computing price/performance and compatibility have transformed the rules of the game for competing with technology. Today, high-function information systems are available from a variety of vendors. Competitive advantage stems not from having these systems,

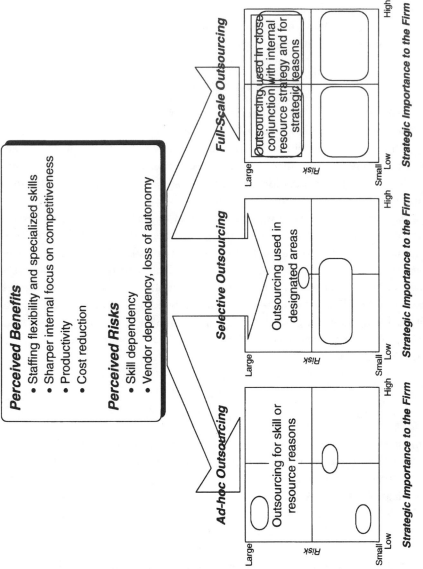

Figure 9.22a. Issues Driving Outsourcing Decisions

Ad-hoc Outsourcing	Selective Outsourcing	Full-Scale Outsourcing
Use of External Options	**Use of External Options**	**Use of External Options**
• Supplement internal staff to provide specialized skills or handle peak workload periods • External options primarily considered based on timelines, available skills, and cost.	• Supplement internal resources • Outsource low-risk commodity project	• Contractors • Outsourcing agreements • Equity partnerships/alliances
Linkage to IT Core Competencies	**Linkage to IT Core Competencies**	**Linkage to IT Core Competencies**
• Building awareness of internal services' competitiveness	• Evaluation of outsourcing commodity services on a project-by-project basis • Limited linkage to human resource practices	• Tight integration of IT and business unit core competencies • Human resource practices center around strengthening core competencies • Sourcing strategies are consistent with competencies being developed
Management/Practices	**Management/Practices**	**Management/Practices**
• Contractor/consulting management • Broadening perspective on available alternatives • Sharpening internal IT competition	• Longer-term contract management • Risk management • Confidence and trust in working with external firms • External relationship-building skills	• Redefinition of internal competencies based on market forces • Integration of internal and external human resource practices • Partnership management

Figure 9.22b.

for they are equally available to competitors, but from being more adept at using them.

IT strategic alignment benchmarking, then, is right for the times. By learning from the best in the class, managers can build the competencies necessary for survival in increasingly competitive global markets. It also represents a new spirit of cooperation taking root in American industry. The era of rugged individualism is over. Organizations are beginning to realize that they exist in a network of relationships, both internally and externally, that are far too complex for any one management team to fully comprehend.

Notes

1. For a comprehensive discussion of the relationship between investment in technology and business profitability see Paul A. Strassmann, *The Business Value of Computers* (New Canaan, CT: The Information Economics Press, 1990).
2. Max D. Hopper, "Rattling SABRE—New Ways to Compete on Information," *Harvard Business Review* (May–June 1990): 118–125.
3. Cite CIO magazine here Martin James, *Rapipid Application Development,* (New York: McGraw-Hill, 1992).
4. Alexandra Biesada, "Benchmarking," *Financial World* 160 (September 17, 1991): 28.
5. Jeffrey A. Schmidt, "The Link Between Benchmarking and Shareholder Value," *Journal of Business Strategy* 13 (May/June 1992): 7.
6. Robert Camp, *Benchmarking: The Search for Industry Best Practices that Lead to Superior Performance* (Milwaukee, WI: American Society for Quality Control Press, 1989).
7. Peter G. W. Keen, *Shaping the Future: Business Design through Information Technology* (Boston: Harvard Business School Press, 1991).
8. Jeffrey Rothfeder, Lisa Driscoll, "CIO is Starting to Stand for 'Career Is Over,' " *Business Week* (February 26, 1990): 78–80.
9. Richard E. Walton, *Up and Running: Integrating Information Technology and the Organization* (Boston: Harvard Business School Press, 1989).
10. D. Garvin, "How the Baldrige Award Really Works," *Harvard Business Review* (November–December 1991): 80–93.
11. Max D. Hopper, "Rattling SABRE—New Ways to Compete on Information," *Harvard Business Review* (May–June 1990): 118–125.

IV

Organizational Infrastructure and Processes

10

Business Culture: The Key to Regaining Competitive Edge

❖

JANET C. CALDOW and JOHN B. KIRBY

❖

Chapter Summary

1. Understanding corporate culture is critical to the success of most major management initiatives. The "skills" components of the strategic alignment model's infrastructure boxes encompassed the cultural concept presented in this chapter. Four categories are suggested to help comprehend its scope: (a) traditional cultural components; (b) organization design components; (c) HR program components; and (d) capability components.

2. In each of these four areas there are extremes, which are useful indicators of how far a company is evolving towards a new business form. At the well-understood, traditional level (a), the mission and values might embody many statements about caring for customers, employees and the environment. In terms of organization (b), the company may have a high-involvement or network structure.

3. These styles and structures are unlikely to have come about without new forms of leadership, (c), for example, embodying coaching, enabling or orchestrating skills. Finally, these advanced organizations are likely to have identified new competencies (d), concerning what employees need to know in the future, how that knowledge is to be acquired, and how it can be shared around the company.

4. It is particularly important to understand the sort of culture which is likely to support certain types of strategies. Strategic initiatives such as network-supported business communication will not succeed in strongly hierarchial command and control cultures.

5. In fact, as earlier chapters in this book have shown, the problem is even more complex, as business strategies might require more than one type of culture in different parts of the business. A detailed breakdown is given of the culture models appropriate to the four business strategies outlined in Chapter 4 (invention, mass production, continuous improvement and mass customization).

6. The four cultural forms which emerge from this classification are labeled (a) entrepreneurial; (b) hierarchical; (c) partnership and (d) modular. While all of these can be effective in different business environments, the authors issue a general caution as to the myopia induced by any strong culture, and the extent to which it prevents consideration of alternative strategic options.

In the face of global competition, accelerating change in information and process technologies, and quick shifts in customer demands, firms are turning to a myriad of new programs to transform their organizations and regain their competitive edge. Some of the more popular approaches include total quality management (TQM),[1] reengineering,[2] empowerment,[3] job redesign,[4] and new compensation schemes.[5] Most of these businesses are discovering that the implementation of these programs is not an easy task: few efforts deliver sustainable increases in speed, productivity, and profitability.[6]

In part, these failures may be a function of how extensive an implementation is undertaken—that is, are these efforts focused on only one or two aspects of the business, such as compensation, vision, or structure, gaining them the reputation of "program of the year"? Or are they comprehensive implementations which significantly transform those components which define the firm as a unique entity—its *business culture?*

The Multiple Components of Business Culture

As detailed in Table 10.1, transforming business culture focuses not on one or two aspects of the organization but aligns multiple components to provide a framework for organizing and directing employee performance. A useful metaphor for understanding this relationship is the weaver's loom. As many threads create an intricately woven fabric, so do the multiple components create the business culture, with its own unique design and character. To repair or change the pattern requires reweaving multiple,

TABLE 10.1. Components of Business Culture

Component	Definition	Ref. No.*
Traditional cultural components	These components capture the anthropological aspects of business culture, the underlying set of key values, beliefs, understandings, and norms shared by employees.	Duncan, 1989; Smirich, 1993; Sathe, 1985
Vision	A mental image of a possible and desirable future state of the organization.	Bennis & Nanus, 1985
Values	The true culture: the intangible, underlying assumptions, beliefs, and thought processes of the organizations.	Schein, 1991, 1985
Cultural symbols	Observable symbols of culture: ceremonies, stories, slogans, behaviors, dress, and physical settings.	Schein, 1991, 1985, 1984
Organizational design components	The control and coordination of the organization, encompassing structural form, technology, and control systems, HR policies, and linkages to other organizations. Culture is often considered an element of organizational design.	Daft, 1992
Structure	Formal and informal structures including the formal organization reporting relationships, interactions leading to effective coordination and control, and informal relationships, networks.	Nohria & Eccles, 1992; Baker, 1993; Child, 1984; Ranson, Hinings & Greenwood, 1980; Wilmott, 1981
Leadership style	How a manager influences others to attain goals. Styles include charismatic, authoritarian, coach, and orchestrator.	Potts & Behr, 1987; Bass, 1985; Galbraith, 1982; Fielder, 1967
Employment contract	The formal relationship between employer and employee, such as employment-at-will, contractual, commodity, or individualized.	Youngblood & Bierman, 1985; Schwoe'rer & Rosen, 1987; Williamson, 1991
Decision-making	The actual process by which organizational decisions are made. Types include consensual, simultaneous, functional, and collaborative.	Hart, 1992; Shrivastava & Grant, 1984

continued

TABLE 10.1.   continued

Component	Definition	Ref. No.*
Communication network	Process by which information is exchanged between members of the organization. Types include bottom-up, top-down, and formal and informal networks.	Nonaka, 1991; Davis, 1968; Foltz, 1985
Tolerance	Ability of the organization to change. Types include none or resident, first-order or incremental, second-order or generative, and continual.	Argyis & Schon, 1978; Watzlawick, Weakland & Fisch, 1974; Miller & Friesen, 1980
HR program components	The formal systems for selection, motivation, and management of employees.	Schuler, 1984; Meyers 1986
Employee morale	How employees are motivated: extrinsically through rewards/punishment, recognition, or "collective actualization" or intrinsically through "self-actualization."	Lawler, 1986; Skinner, 1953; Deci, 1975; Manz, 1992
Evaluation	Assessment of employee job performance, based upon various factors including productivity, number of defects, service time, knowledge, and patents, depending on the work comprising the job.	Bernardin & Beatty, 1984; Schiemann, 1987
Compensation	Program of employee compensation comprised of pay, rewards, and benefits. Plans can be based on individual, group, or organizational performance measures. Pay can be time-, productivity-, or knowledge-based. Some or all can be at risk.	Milkovich & Newman, 1987; Stayer, 1990; Savage, 1981
All other HR programs	Compromised of other HR programs such as recruitment, training and development, termination, succession planning, as well as work at home, child and elder care, and flex-time. Characterized as rigid, flexible, innovative or cafeteria-style.	Schuler & Jackson, 1987; Gatewood & Field, 1987; Schneider & Schmidt, 1986; Jannotta, 1987; Reibstein, 1986
Capability components	The skills of an organization's workers and the translation of those skills into competitive advantage.	Ulrich & Lake, 1991

continued

TABLE 10.1.   continued

Component	Definition	Ref. No.*
Organizational capability	What an organization is good at— its competitive strength, particularly related to how an organization learns.	Prahalad & Hamel, 1990
Individual competencies	The skills of the work force ranging from broad to narrow, knowledge- or procedure-based.	Miles & Snow, 1986, 1983; Reich, 1992

*See notes 83–106 to this chapter for complete citations.

individual threads into new patterns. Similarly, to recast business culture multiple, interrelated components need to be altered.

Business Culture's Anthropological Foundations

First and foremost, business culture is the intangible, unwritten, feeling part of the organization: the set of values, guiding beliefs, understandings, and ways of thinking shared by its members.[7] If strong, it provides members with a sense of organizational identity and generates a commitment to corporate excellence.[8]

Although no longer considered the only driving force for the organization's culture, a strong, appropriate vision plays a key role in defining the organization's guiding values, beliefs, and assumptions.[9] Three competitive battles of the last decade—GM vs. Toyota, RCA vs. Sony, and Wal-Mart vs. Sears—illustrate the importance of a clear vision to corporate success. Each of the winners had a unique vision for its organization: to beat the number one firm in its industry by redefining the rules of the game.

This vision enabled these organizations to radically alter the basis of competitive advantage by focusing the efforts of their organizations on radical innovations in products, inventory systems, or production systems; but vision doesn't have to be entrepreneurial (one which stretches the organization) in scope.[10] It may be important to maintain the status quo, which led many Fortune 100 organizations to success in earlier decades, or to achieve high-quality products and services, on which many of these same organizations are focused today.[11]

Vision is not the only visible aspect of culture in an organization. Culture can also be discerned in the firm—the symbols, ceremonies, stories, heros, dress, and language that members share. For example, the enthusiasm for clean, pressed uniforms and behavior according to strict protocols in the army illustrates an authoritative, status quo culture, whereas Apple Computer's policy regarding jeans and taking risks encourages a more informal, innovative culture. Tupperware's weekly sales rally and Mary Kay's annual sales celebrations exemplify the importance of employees to their firm's success much more than a statement on paper would ever do. Stories of how corporate heros often worked in secret on innovative products are repeated by top managers at 3M to strengthen the rebel, entrepreneurial spirit believed to be instrumental to the organization's success.

However, these observable symbols and behaviors are only the tip of the cultural iceberg; they reflect deeper values, assumptions, beliefs, and thought processes that are the "true" culture.[12] Organizations often attempt to change these observable behaviors without considering the underlying values driving them. These efforts are often as successful as those of the doctor who treats symptoms without attacking the root cause of the illness.

As with many causes, values are not readily quantified, but they can be derived from the observable behaviors, myths, ceremonies, language, and stories of the organization. For example, caring about employees and customer service are two values which are easily discernable at such organizations as Nordstrom, Inc. and Levi Strauss. Levi Strauss shows its concern for employees through the efforts of management to empower the workforce, communicate more effectively, take advantage of diversity, and balance work and family lives.[13] Nordstrom draws an organizational chart, with the customers on top, supported by the employees, who are in turn supported by the management, to illustrate how "customers are king" and managers are there to assist the employees in achieving this goal.[14] The values of caring about employees and customers are seen through a no questions asked returns policy, a retraining/transfer rather than layoff program, and a valuing of long-term employee loyalty.

Other values may also be prevalent in organizations. For example, innovative companies such as 3M stress invention and risk-taking, whereas others, such as Toyota, reinforce stability and efficiency. Values may also reflect independence and competition in order to win at all costs. An example of this value set is found in highly competitive companies, such as Wall Street trading firms or consumer products businesses.

These firms' values reflect the desire to become number one. Fierce competition is the rule of the game—even at the company picnic. Careers can be made or broken on one-tenth of a point of market share and managers change jobs frequently. Rather than long-term loyalty, executives may average only 10 years, as is the rule at PepsiCo.[15]

Business Culture Reflected in
Organizational Design

Business culture is more than its anthropological underpinnings; it is also the reflection of these basic assumptions and values in the organizational design of the business.[16] Key aspects of design include structure and processes, including decision-making and communication networks, leadership style, the overall employee relationship, the HR practices and policies used to select and motivate the employees, and the flexibility to respond to fluctuations in environments—i.e., the tolerance for change.

An example illustrates how the values and beliefs are revealed through the organization's design. Consider the business culture of organizations in the former Soviet Union before perestroika.[17] They were characterized by authoritative, centralized control, a strong bureaucracy, top-down communication networks, a lifetime employment contract, and a stable but inflexible organization. This orientation reflected the values of stability: risk-taking, and innovation were distrusted and beaten down at every opportunity. Compare this to the same organizations today. Their values regarding efficiency and innovation have altered as reflected in decentralized decision-making, top-down/bottom-up communication networks, leaders as coaches of entrepreneurs, and a much more flexible organization than before.

Key components of organizational design are its structure and processes: the formal reporting relationships as depicted on an organizational chart and the informal interactions among employees that are essential for coordination and control. Various structures have been identified by academic and popular research, each reflecting a unique set of values, assumptions, and beliefs.

Bureaucratic Structures

One such form—the mechanistic form, or bureaucracy[18]—reflects the values of status quo and efficiency.[19] It is characterized by hierarchical structure, top-down communication, and centralized decision-making[20] and so is found primarily in businesses requiring strong coordination and control for effectiveness, such as the military or emergency units of hospitals.[21]

Organic Structures

A second structure, the organic structure, is in stark contrast to the mechanistic form. Reflecting the values of flexibility and innovativeness, this design is characterized by an informal, entrepreneurial style which is less rigid in all respects.[22] It is difficult to capture the essence of this business on an organizational chart. Network analysis[23] will show that job holders have broad responsibilities that change as the need arises and that communications occur bottom-up and top-down as advice and information is required, rather than through rules and orders. Decision-making is decentralized and informal, where expertise and judgment are highly valued.[24]

High-Involvement Structures

New organizational structures are emerging in businesses today, including the high-involvement form[25] and the network form.[26] The high-involvement, or self-leading, form[27] is found in companies as diverse as General Mills, Federal Express, Microsystems, Aetna Life & Casualty, Volvo, and Compaq Computer. Such organizations create a structure reflecting the value of adaptation, one which enables them to tolerate incremental change.[28]

In contrast to temporary cross-functional project or quality circle teams, these teams assume managerial duties, such as work scheduling, ordering, and hiring and firing team members. They are given access to resources needed to complete a whole task, including materials, information, equipment, machinery, and supplies, and are empowered with decision-making authority and the ability to eliminate communication barriers existing between departments, functions, suppliers, and customers.[29]

Network Structures

The network is the second new design emerging in organizations today.[30] Incorporating a free market style rather than a vertical hierarchy, team, or guild structure, it disaggregates major functions or production components into separate companies or individuals. The form reflects the value placed on continuous transformation—a component of the network is easily replaced with a cheaper, more reliable, higher quality, or quicker supplier.

More loosely connected than the team or hierarchical form, decision-making is empowered—either individuals or specialized groups simultaneously solve any problems or issues that arise during day-to-day operations in accordance with broad directions. To keep costs at a minimum, cross-functional communication is less extensive than in other forms—only essential information is passed through the authorized networks.

The Importance of Leadership Style

Leadership is one of the most influential components of organizational design. Through different styles of leadership, managers are more or less successful in influencing others to attain the organization's goals.

Charismatic Leadership

This style, exhibited by leaders as diverse as President John F. Kennedy, Napoleon, Lee Iococca, Thomas Watson, Alfred Sloan, and Steve Jobs, is often seen to be instrumental to organizational success. These leaders are dominant and self-confident and have a strong conviction in the moral righteousness of their beliefs.[31] They articulate a vision for their organization and create a sense of excitement and adventure.

Research suggests that charismatic leaders are most effective in innovative organizations or those that require radical transformations. These leaders can inspire trust, confidence, unquestioning acceptance, and willing obedience in such situations.[32]

Authoritative, Functional Leadership

However, charisma is not the only effective leadership style. In situations requiring strong hierarchical coordination and control, such as the military or an emergency situation, authoritative, functional leaders who take charge and give orders will be most effective.[33]

Coaching, Enabling Leadership

In other situations, such as when a team is attempting to identify a problem and test alternative situations, a more democratic, participative style of management is appropriate. Often labeled coachers or enablers, these leaders advise empowered, cross-functional teams in their problem-solving activities.[34]

Orchestrating Leadership

A fourth leader type is emerging in today's new organizations: the orchestrator[35] or broker.[36] These leaders coordinate the web of interrelationships of the network businesses or individuals, each of whom specializes in a necessary aspect of the business, such as supply, distribution, design, or production.

Leaders and Employees

Often leadership style is key to defining the employment contract of the organization. For example, an authoritative, take-charge leader defines the contract that has existed in many organizations for most of this century: a predictable, stable work environment, where people worked hard but were well rewarded. Most of these "commodity" employees traded loyalty to the union for regular promotions, an increasing standard of living, and a secure future.[37]

Today, few, if any, firms can guarantee employees career stability, advancement, or even a job as they adjust to the changing competitive environment. For most employees, downsizing has ripped apart the social contract between companies and their employees. A number of new contracts are being established in their place.

Employment-at-Will Contracts

One such contract is based on mutual understanding, or *employment-at-will*.[38] Under this contract the old promise of cradle-to-grave careers is replaced by more versatile jobs, the chance to use a broader base of skills, and greater participation in decision-making. GM's Saturn plant and Toyota/GM's joint venture NUMMI have relationships best characterized as this type.

Guild Contracts

A second form of contract is defined by the charismatic leaders of entrepreneurial firms: a *guild*. In a guild, craftsmen or experts at a specific, broad set of skills trade loyalty to their work for high pay, broad responsibilities, and freedom in their approaches to their work, as long as they achieve results consistent with the firm's goals.[39] Many high-tech and basic research firms develop guild relationships with their employees.

Contractual or Market-Type Contracts

In the new network forms of organizations, a third type of contract is taking shape: a contractual or market-type.[40] Based on employability or marketability of skills, employees are contracted and paid for work performed only when needed and, hence, are free to contract with more than one business at a time. One of the largest software houses in the United Kingdom, the FI Group,[41] has implemented this type of contract. Most of their employees are freelancers, who work offsite about twenty hours a week. Strategic direction and coordination support is provided by a small core of permanent, central staff.

HR Policies

HR practices and policies define, communicate, and reinforce the employment contracts set by organizational leaders. For example, authoritative leaders implement HR strategies which are rigid: all employees are selected, trained, developed, evaluated, and compensated similarly. Job designs are by the rules; compensation for narrow, often mind-numbing, tasks requiring specialized skills and motivation is based on rewards and punishments rather than on recognition of any intrinsic, self-motivating characteristics of the work.[42]

However, entrepreneurial leaders look toward HR practices which stress flexibility and motivate employees to innovate.[43] Adaptable policies rule in regard to job designs, benefits, compensation schemes, and even the hours of work. Employees are evaluated on their output—are they creative? did they achieve their goals?—rather than on their input—how much did it cost? did they follow procedures? Compensation often includes a share in the business unit's profits. Intrinsic morale drivers are necessary; it is assumed that employees do their work well because they enjoy it.[44]

High-involvement, empowered work teams require HR practices and policies which are creative in that they are based on specific requirements of the business employees.[45] Diversity is celebrated rather than denied, leading to innovations such as job sharing, work at home, flex-time, child and elder day-car—sometimes on site. Training and development are customized to the needs of the team and include problem-solving, decision-making, and leadership education in addition to multiple job skill instruction. Compensation is based on team achievement of improvements in quality, safety, and defect rates and often includes a limited amount of pay at risk.[46] Promotions and evaluations are skill- or knowledge-based.[47] These programs are consistent with morale drivers of recognition of team-based success and gains in employees' skill base.

Networks Require New HR Policies

Novel HR practices, each of which is consistent with the new contractual employment relationship, are seen in networks.[48] With the morale driver "collective actualization,"[69] evaluation is based on aspects key to individual or group reputations: quality of service, time of delivery, and ease of linkage to other parts of the network. Compensation is knowledge-based and dependent on a mix of individual, group, and organizational results. If any benefits are offered, cafeteria-style plans are utilized which permit employees to individualize packages of medical and dental insurance, dependent care, life insurance, or cash. Finally, training and development are the responsibility of each group or individual, not business headquarters.[50]

Change Management

One of the most important aspects of a business culture today is the reflection of its underlying values in its ability to tolerate change. Only in extremely stable customer and technological environments can a business culture reflecting the values of business as usual, or status quo, be successful. Instead, businesses must determine which point on the stability/flexibility continuum they must occupy to meet the requirements of their chosen competitive arena. Some organizations create a culture supporting incremental change, whereas others build one which allows more radical or generative change. Metamorphic change, or continuous transformation, is a third level of flexibility that some organizations, such as those pursuing customized strategies, work to achieve.

Individual and Corporate Competencies

As illustrated above, organizational design is a key aspect of business culture in that it reflects the values, beliefs, and assumptions which organize and direct employee performance. Of similar significance are the two components which capture the essential skills of the organization and employees and how those skills are translated into competitive advantage: individual competencies and organizational capability.[51]

No longer is it enough to gain competitive advantage using financial, strategic, or technical capabilities. Today, firms must be able to create an organizational capability which fits the requirements of their vision.[52] Such a capability encompasses the definition, development, and maintenance of both a core competence[53] and a learning system,[54] each of which is instrumental to sustaining competitive advantage.

The relationship of core competencies to individual skills is only now beginning to be realized. A good example of these linkages is provided by a microelectronics firm, which, through scenario planning, determined that the increase in mobility of workers would create a demand for the wireless office, similar to that employed by the FI Group. Using its competency in telecommunications, the firm reasoned that a key element of knowledge was missing from its individual competencies: technical know-how in miniature batteries. Once recognized, it could implement a revised recruitment strategy to augment its knowledge in this arena, further strengthening both organizational capability and individual competencies.

Learning Organizations

The learning organization illustrates a second, but equally important, aspect of organizational capability: the ability to learn. The microelectronics company employed an effective learning system when it reasoned that it needed additional skills and competence in miniature battery technology to pursue its chosen goal, but such an outcome is not inevitable. Often, a different learning capability than what is required exists within a firm. For example, entrepreneurial firms focused on creating new products and processes in their chosen core competencies must be adept at translating episodic learning into radical innovations in product and processes, whereas firms focused on providing customized products to each client must develop a capability for metamorphic learning to support continual transformations in products or services.

If a business pursuing customization has a capability in episodic learning but not metamorphic learning, it will be more likely to achieve less effective performance. Similarly, organizations pursuing continuous improvement require a capability in translating incremental learning into improvements in products and processes, which many organizations are discovering is not the learning system that traditional, stable values promote.

To develop and maintain these learning systems, firms must consider employees as critical resources for sustainable competitive advantage,[55] for it is the skills of both current and future employees that constrain the ability of an organization to develop and maintain its core competence. For example, over a decade ago Motorola discovered that many of its employees were unable to perform basic analytical tasks. Lacking these employee skills, Motorola could not create the effective organizational capability in incremental learning required to pursue a continuous improvement strategy.[56]

Motorola took this potential competitive disadvantage and turned it into a competitive resource through creating one of the most comprehensive and effective education programs in the world. To gain broadly skilled work forces, Motorola entered into partnerships with established colleges and universities. It supplies students, equipment, and tuition and brings in outside faculty to teach the fundamentals of reading, writing, and arithmetic in addition to empowerment, quality activities, community, and leadership.

Through these efforts Motorola continues to create a work force which is creative, flexible, broadly skilled, and able to anticipate and adapt quickly to technological change. The creation of these individual competencies and organizational capabilities in incremental learning allows Motorola to anticipate incremental, technological change and to retain its competitive edge.

In summary, business culture is comprised not only of the values, beliefs, and assumptions inherent in the organization but also of the reflection of these anthropological underpinnings in organizational design and the competencies and capabilities of the organization. These components are woven together to create the unique pattern of business culture. Thus, to transform its culture, a business must consider how each part is woven into the fabric of culture and then alter each accordingly.

Case Study: Managing Change in
the IT Department

Consider an organization which decided to implement a major change in its IS unit. Rather than outsourcing these functions, the organization decided that the IS unit would create software for both external and internal clients. Although most of the organization pursued a continuous improvement strategy, market research suggested that the IS unit should streamline its processes to provide more timely, high-quality software customized to individual needs at a lower cost than achieved by the market.

Focused on the idea that leadership is key to transformation, a new CIO was hired, who envisioned the new mass customization approach to doing business. The CIO undertook a major reorganization, creating empowered application–development teams, each of which was focused on a specific customer's needs. To motivate these teams, a new compensation strategy was implemented, adding a bonus based on output drivers, such as customer satisfaction, delivery, and software error measures, for those employees whose teams attained above average performance evaluations.

At first, performance appeared to be effective: costs were never lower. Although first and second quarter new output numbers looked poor, not much concern was voiced; it was expected that this would occur as new roles and routines were learned. Rather than these trends reversing in the next six months, customer satisfaction and quality fell and time to market was worse than under the old system. Once again, the intangible culture was blamed for obstructing the attempted transformation, but was this an inevitable outcome?

This IS business unit attempted to transform itself by making radical changes in its leadership, vision, structure, and compensation plans. One might ask what else was there to change? In fact, other key aspects of the business culture were not altered, which contributed to the failure of this transformation attempt.

First, although organized as teams on paper, network analysis of this business unit's culture depicted a more hierarchical structure. Team leaders, rather than members, defined and allocated work, communicated with customers, and made most of the decisions.

Second, although the new bonus scheme focused on output measures, the performance evaluation plan was based on input measures, such as labor costs and computer usage.

Finally, the reorganization did not consider the new skills required for the group members. Instead of specialized knowledge, employees needed to learn how to work in teams, communicate in a language that customers understood, and make decisions. The lack of individual competencies in team skills was one reason why the empowerment was not being fully implemented.

These inconsistencies contributed, in part, to the lack of success of the transformation effort. No matter how hard the new CIO worked, his hands were tied—the loom could not create a unified, supportive business culture from the inconsistent threads of the components.

Aligning Culture to Strategy

It is not enough to design a business culture to be consistent across each of its components. It must also fit with the selected business goals or strategies. In short, an organization must be internally consistent[57]; its capabilities must match or fit those required to execute its chosen strategy.

Unfortunately, not every business culture has the ability to effectively implement every strategy. For example, some cultures are founded upon values of stability and efficiency, whereas others are established upon the principles of flexibility and creativity.[58] A culture built upon a stable foundation would have difficulty in establishing the organizational designs, HR practices, and organizational capabilities required to execute a strategy demanding flexibility, such as invention.[59] At every turn, the values of consistency, status quo, and low risk would get in the way of pursuing novel, high-risk opportunities.

Aligning culture to strategy (a specific case of the vertical relationship of the strategic alignment model) is particularly relevant today since the old approaches to doing business do not create sustainable competitive advantages.[60] No longer can businesses focus on one strategic goal, such as cost leadership or differentiation in quality, customization, or innovation.[61] Instead, they must pursue strategies focused on several goals, such as cost leadership and quality differentiation or cost leadership and customization differentiation.[62] These multiple strategies require capabilities which combine aspects of stable and flexible cultures. How to create a culture which develops and maintains these contrary capabilities adds a level of complexity to the design of effective culture/strategy fits while accelerating competitive conditions makes it even more essential to discover the most effective match.

A useful framework for considering the myriad of strategic possibilities and the business culture forms which best meet their required capabilities is that described in Chapter 4 of this book. Centered on two types of product and process change, stable and dynamic, the authors consider four classifications of product/process change, each of which is associated with a particular business strategy: invention, mass production, continuous improvement, and mass customization.

As detailed in Table 10.2, unique business culture profiles generate the organizational capabilities required to pursue each of these business strategies: entrepreneurial for invention, hierarchical for mass production, partnership for continuous improvement, and modular for mass customization.

The Entrepreneurial Culture Profile

Organizations pursuing the invention strategy rely on creation of radical change in both products and processes for success. To do so they require corporate capabilities in creative problem-solving and innovation and translation of episodic learning into radical change. A culture focused on stability would cripple these organizations, causing inertia and inability to alter their directions.[63] Instead, they require a culture which reflects assumptions, values, and beliefs of risk-taking and flexibility, including a vision which is entrepreneurial in scope and stretches the organization to radically alter the basis of competitive advantage in their favor.[64] We label this form *entrepreneurial*.

The organizational design which reflects values of flexibility and the entrepreneurial vision is organic in nature, an informal, decentralized, ad hoc organization,[65] in which decisions are made quickly and collaboratively.[66] Accurate information for decision-making must be available to all members so that communication networks do not become entangled; people speak to experts as required, rather than following vertical or horizontal linkages.[67]

HR practices motivate employees to achieve goals set by the charismatic leader. Inventors don't know what type of internal competencies they may require in the future, so their employees are more often bought on the market rather than grown within the organization.[68] Evaluation, compensation, benefits, and termination policies are flexible and often customized to meet the requirements set by talent considered necessary to the future of the organization. They motivate on the basis of achievement and evaluate performance on the basis of creativity and external reputation.

The Hierarchical Culture Profile

A completely different business culture is required for the mass production strategy, one which supports lack of change in products and process. Such a culture must create corporate capabilities of stability and control.[69] The vision will be to remain steady and sure, to retain the status quo, risk-taking and novelty being considered completely outside the scope of a mass production mission. The hierarchical form best meets these requirements.

The organizational design components of the hierarchical form which reflect command and control are mechanistic in nature: authoritative leadership, vertical information flows supporting top-down communication, and functional decision-making processes.[70] Such a design serves to stifle innovation, flexibility, and change. Stability allows work to be highly routinized and controlled through rules and regulations. Few individuals practice decision-making in their day-to-day activities as most issues have been ironed out of the process.

HR practices motivate employees to "go by the book." They import little talent, preferring to develop it within, usually over many years.[71] Extensive training and development programs support these activities and ensure that little corruption from new ideas or approaches occurs within the ranks.

TABLE 10.2. Business Cultures Mapped to Business Strategies

Business Culture Forms	Business Strategies			
	Invention	*Mass Production*	*Continuous Improvement*	*Mass Customization*
	Entrepreneurial	*Hierarchical*	*Partnership*	*Modular*
Traditional cultural components				
Vision	Entrepreneurial	Status quo	Qualitative	Customized products
Values	Innovation	Stability	Efficiency	Adaptation
Cultural symbols	Highly informal	Highly formal	Formal	Informal
Organizational design components				
Structure	Guild	Hierarchical	Team-based	Networked
Leadership style	Charismatic, entrepreneurial, delegate and control	Authoritarian, functional, command and control	Advisory, integrative, cross-functional, coach, enables, team-based	Orchestrators, contingent, interchangeable leader roles, empowered networks
Employment contract	Individualized craftsmen	Commodity factors of production	Employment-at-will, mutual understandings	Contractual, employability, marketability of skills
Decision-making	Chaotic: collaborative	Sequential, functional, top-down	Consensual, cross-functional team, process controls	

Simultaneous, empowered, self-directed teams				
Communication networks	Informal networks	Top-down	Bottom-up	Authorized networks
Tolerance for change	Change generative	Change resident	Incremental	Continual transformation
HR program components				
Employee morale	Intrinsic, self-motivated	Extrinsic, reward/punish	Achievement against process measures, recognition	Extrinsic, collective actualization
Performance evaluation	Creativity	Productivity, unit cost	Defects	Service level: time
Compensation	Individual and organizational performance, some pay at risk	Time-based pay, salary and wages, little or no pay at risk	Team-performance, individualized skills, moderate pay at risk	Mix of individual, team, and organizational performance; knowledge-based
All other HR programs	Flexible	Rigid	Innovative	Cafeteria-style
Capability components				
Organizational capability	Creative, modular, episodic learning	Reactive, change/learning inhibited	Anticipatory, predictive, incremental learning	Metamorphic, change generative, inherent learning
Individual competencies	Professional, expert	Narrow skilled: doer	Skills balanced in teams: thinker and doer	Broad-skilled, cross-trained, knowledge worker

Evaluation, compensation, benefits, and other programs are standardized across employees and focus on ability to do the job the way it's always been done; there's no room for creativity.

The Partnership Culture Profile

Organizations pursuing continuous improvement base competitive advantage on creating radical change in processes for relatively stable product markets. To do so they require a mix of capabilities, including stability in production process and translation of incremental learning into improvements in processes. The balance between stability and flexibility is best met in a culture we label *partnership*, where vision is qualitative and efficiency is valued. Such a mix allows for incremental learning for radical process innovations but stability, not chaos, in implementation of those innovations.

The organizational design components of the partnership culture is the high-involvement form, a participative, team-based structure[72] characterized by consensual decision-making, bottom-up communication, and advisory leadership. This is the organization which values its employees and strives to motivate them to achieve their full potential, as long as they do so in pursuit of the organizational goals.

HR practices focus on creating individual competencies in problem-solving, team-building, and self-management, the skills required to create an organizational capability in incremental learning. Evaluation and compensation programs motivate employees to learn and yet also be efficient at what they do and so are skill- and achievement-based. Training and development are extensive as organizations build the skills required to achieve their objectives.[78]

The Modular Culture Profile

Organizations pursuing mass customization base competitive advantage on capabilities directly opposite to those of the continuous improving organizations: stable processes and flexible products. Such capabilities are supported by a mix of stable and flexible values but in a different configuration from that of the continuous improvers. They require both stability and flexibility in their production systems and stability in the creation of the modules, which can then be recombined to create an infinite number of unique products. The modular business culture creates and sustains these organizational capabilities.

The organizational design for the modular business culture is centered on the values of efficient continuous adaptation, the network form.

Through disaggregating major functions or production components into separate companies or individuals, this form achieves continuous transformation; a component of the network is as easily replaced as a spoke on the wheel. All that's required is that the supplier effectively link into the stable production process.

Leadership is loose in this cultural form; it provides broad direction and coordination to empowered groups. Communication across modules is costly and unnecessary, as each module of the network simultaneously solves any problems or issues that arise. Novel HR practices motivate employees to achieve the goals of quality, speed, and reliability of their components, as well as quick, costless linkage with other components. These employees are the knowledge workers,[74] who are defining a new employment relationship labeled *contractual*. They are employed purely on the basis of the marketability of their skills.

Returning to the IS business unit case study from the perspective of matching business culture and strategy, we note that not only did the management of the group ignore key aspects of business culture in its transformation attempt but it made a number of misjudgments in regard to the fit of its business culture to strategy. Since the IS business unit determined that its key competitive advantage lay in customized, low-cost software products, it needs to create a modular business culture to develop and maintain the organizational capabilities and individual competencies to effectively achieve this goal. Focused on the values of adaptation and efficiency, this culture would allow the IS business unit to develop efficient processes for creating a unique product for each customer.

Such a culture does not rely on cross-functional teams but empowered networks of knowledge-based employees. Leaders are not oriented toward coaching but toward brokering; they provide broad guidelines for linkages across specialized modules. They may be able to effectively lower costs by implementing a work at home program or employing workers on a contractual basis as their skills were required for a particular client. Their primary investment should be in developing a stable, efficient process technology, not a partnership with their employees.

Key to the success of this unit is the recognition that its strategy and cultural form are distinct from those required by the rest of the organization, which is pursuing a strategy of continuous improvement. For all other parts of the organization the partnership form will be the most effective cultural form. Focused on the values of quality and efficiency, this culture values its employees for their ability to develop incremental changes in processes, which add up to sustainable competitive advantages in quality and low cost.

As previously discussed, completely different organizational designs, HR practices, and capabilities will be required for continuous improvement capabilities. It will be difficult for the IS group in this case study to counter the influences of the aggregate culture as it is interfacing with the organization on a day-to-day basis. The IS group will need to create and speak a language different from that of the rest of the organization and develop a different set of priorities and values. Initially, it might be useful to buffer the IS team as a "learning lab" so that it has the freedom to develop a cultural form separate from that of the organization.

Matching Business Culture and Strategy Leads to Effective Performance

The relationships between business culture, strategy, and performance are complex.[75] Both academic and popular literature are replete with stories and studies of how business culture facilitates or constrains the implementation of a chosen strategy. Although these relationships are difficult to discern, it is clear that effective performance results when the underlying vision, values, organizational design, and capabilities of the organization support the attainment of its goals.[76]

Peters and Waterman[77] illustrated how a strong culture might result in organizational effectiveness. However, strong cultures are a two-edged sword, as many of the organizations featured in this book have discovered.[78] On the one hand, they can be a vital asset, serving as powerful, built-in motivational forces for members and guiding corporate goals, policies, strategies, and actions. In many cases, a strong, common culture should ease communication and coordination and provide a common understanding to resolve conflict when it arises. On the other hand, strong cultures can be a liability, particularly when the culture does not support the mission, goals, and strategy of the organization—i.e., when the capabilities inherent in the business culture do not fit with those required. In such a case, business culture can lead to inappropriate strategic thinking and ineffective performance.[79] Often, such a mismatch results when the organization's competitive environment has changed so that the strong culture is no longer effective in light of the new competitive conditions.

Ineffective performance may arise from two forces. First, business cultures can create a serious myopia among top executives by influencing how they envision the present and potential capabilities and external opportunities of the business.[80] These beliefs, values, and assumptions have a systematic quality, developed over many years of successful operations. Managers learn to be guided by these beliefs because they have worked in the past and led to effective performance. Frequently, they miss the significance of changing external conditions leading to new opportunities or threats to current operations.[81] Second, even when managers can overcome such myopia, these strong cultures can create a subtle but powerful resistance to accepting and implementing change required to execute the new strategic intent.[82] The entrenchment of these beliefs, which have been effective guides in the past, is difficult to change; people prefer to stick with what makes them comfortable or what they understand. When top executives don't move to alter their beliefs, ineffective actions are more likely to be taken.

When business culture matches the specific business strategy, these forces facilitate the pursuit of competitive advantage, rather than working against effective long-term performance.

Conclusion

In this chapter we have provided a framework which defines business culture as comprised of more tangible aspects of the business than many practitioners and academics have concluded. We view these multiple components as weavers view the threads for their fabrics: each aspect must be consistently linked to the others to create a business culture with a unique design and character.

Consistent interrelationships among components are necessary but not sufficient to attain competitive advantage. Only when the strong fabric of business culture is matched to the goals and strategies of the firm will effective performance result. To illustrate this point, we have identified four specific business cultures and argued that when these business culture forms are aligned to an appropriate business strategy—entrepreneurial for invention, hierarchical for mass production, partnership for continuous improvement, and modular for mass customization—effective performance will result.

Notes

1. D. A. Garvin, *Managing Quality: The Strategic and Competitive Edge* (New York: Free Press, 1988).

2. M. Hammer, J. Champy, *Reengineering the Corporation: A Manifesto for Business Revolution* (New York: HarperCollins, 1993).

3. E. E. Lawler III, *High-involvement Management: Participative Strategies for Improving Organization Performance* (San Francisco: Jossey-Bass, 1986).

4. R. J. Hackman, G. R. Oldham, *Work Redesign* (Reading, MA: Addison-Wesley, 1980).

5. D. Mitchell, D. Lewin, E. E. Lawler III, "Alternative Pay Systems, Firm Performance, and Productivity," in *Paying for Productivity*, A. S. Blinder, ed. (Washington D C: Brookings, 1990), 94.

6. R. W. Griffin, "A Longitudinal Assessment of the Consequences of Quality Circles in an Industrial Setting," *Academy of Management Journal*, 31:2 (1988): 338–358; C. Placek, "U.S. Manufacturing Executives; Grade Themselves 'C' on Key Quality Areas," *Quality*, 32:3 (1993): 19; T. A. Stewart, "Reengineering: The Hot New Managing Tool," *Fortune*, 128:4 (1993): 40–48.

7. W. J. Duncan, "Organizational Culture: 'Getting a Fix' on an Elusive Concept," *Academy of Management Executive*, 3 (1989): 229–236; V. Sathe, *Culture and Related Corporate Realities* (Homewood, IL: Richard D. Irwin, 1985); L. Smircich, "Concepts of Culture and Organizational Analysis," *Administrative Science Quarterly*, 28 (1993): 339–358.

8. T. Peters, R. Waterman, *In Search of Excellence* (New York: Harper & Row, 1992).

9. J. A. Cogner, "The Dark Side of Leadership," *Organizational Dynamics*, 19 (Autumn, 1990): 44–55.

10. G. Hamel, C. K. Prahalad, "Strategy as Stretch and Leverage," *Harvard Business Review*, 71:2 (1993): 75–85.

11. T. Deal, "Developing a Quality Culture," in *Making Organizations Competitive*, R. H. Kilmann, I. Kilmann, eds. (San Francisco: Jossey-Bass, 1991); W. Ouchi, A. Jaegar, "Type Z Organizations: Stability in the Midst of Mobility," *Academy of Management Review*, 3 (1978): 305–314.

12. E. H. Schein, "What is Culture?" in *Reframing Organizational Culture*, P. Frost, L. Moore, M. Louis, C. Lundberg, J. Martin, eds. (Newbury Park, CA: Sage, 1991): 243–253.

13. R. Howard, "Values Make the Company: An Interview with Robert Haas," *Harvard Business Review*, 68:5 (1990): 133–143.

14. "FYI," Inc., (April, 14, 1991).

15. *Business Week*, 1980.

16. R. F. Zammuto, E. J. O'Connor, "Gaining Advanced Manufacturing Technologies' Benefits: The Roles of Organization Design and Culture," *Academy of Management Review*, 17:4 (1992): 701–728; D. Katz, R. L. Kahn, *The Social Psychology of Organizations*, 2nd ed. (New York: John Wiley & Sons, 1978); R. Miles, C. Snow, *Organizational Strategy, Structure, and Process* (New York: McGraw-Hill, 1978).

17. J. B. Shaw, C. D. Fisher, W. A. Randolph, "From Materialism to Accounta-

bility: The Changing Cultures of Ma Bell and Mother Russia," *The Executive*, 5:1 (1992): 7–20.

18. M. Weber, *The Theory of Social and Economic Organizations*, trans. T. Parsons, A. Henderson (New York: Free Press, 1947).

19. R. E. Quinn, J. R. Kimberly, "Paradox, Planning, and Perseverance: Guidelines for Managerial Practice," in *Managing Organizational Transitions*, J. R. Kimberly, R. E. Quinn, eds. (Homewood, IL: Dow Jones-Irwin, 1984): 295–313; R. F. Zammuto, J. Y. Krakower, "Quantitative and Qualitative Studies of Organizational Culture," *Research in Organization Change and Development*, 5 (1991): 83–114.

20. D. Nadler, J. Hackman, E. E. Lawler III, *Managing Organizational Behavior* (Boston: Little, Brown, 1979).

21. J. Wall, *Bosses* (Lexington, MA: Lexington Books, 1983).

22. R. E. Quinn, *Beyond Rational Management* (San Francisco: Jossey-Bass, 1988).

23. N. Nohria, R. Eccles, *Networks and Organizations—Structure, Form and Action* (Boston: Harvard Business School Press, 1992); W. E. Baker, *Networking Smart* (New York: McGraw-Hill, 1993).

24. H. Mintzberg, *The Structuring of Organizations: A Synthesis of the Research* (Englewood Cliffs, NJ: Prentice-Hall, 1979).

25. Lawler, *High-Involvement Management*.

26. R. Miles, C. Snow, "Organizations: New Concepts for New Forms," *California Management Review*, 28 (1986): 2–73; J. R. Galbraith, "Structural Responses to Competitive Strategies," in *Making Organizations Competitive*, R. Kilmann, ed. (San Francisco: Jossey-Bass, 1991).

27. C. C. Manz, H. P. Sims, Jr., "Leading Workers to Lead Themselves: The External Leadership of Self-Managing Work Teams," *Administrative Science Quarterly*, 32 (1987): 106–132.

28. K. E. Weick, "Management of Organizational Change among Loosely Coupled Elements," in *Change in Organizations: New Perspectives on Theory, Research, and Practice*, Paul S. Goodman, ed. (San Francisco: Jossey-Bass, 1982): 375–408.

29. T. Owens, "The Self-Managing Work Team," *Small Business Reports* (February, 1991): 53–65; J. Kapstein, "Volvo's Radical New Plant: The Death of the Assembly Line?" *Business Week* (August 28, 1989): 92–93; C. C. Manz, D. E. Keating, A. Donnellon, "Preparing for an Organizational Change to Employee Self-Managed Teams: The Managerial Transition," *Organizational Dynamics* (Autumn, 1990): 15–26.

30. Miles, Snow, "Organizations"; R. B. Reich, *The Work of Nations: Preparing Ourselves for 21st Century Capitalism* (New York: Random House, 1992); A. Boynton, B. Victor, B. J. Pine, "New Competitive Strategies: Challenges to Organization and Information Technology," *IBM Systems Journal*, 32:1 (1993): 40–64.

31. M. Potts, P. Behr, *The Leading Edge* (New York: McGraw-Hill, 1987).

32. B. M. Bass, "Leadership: Good, Better, Best," *Organizational Dynamics* (Winter, 1985): 26–40.

33. S. Hart, "An Integrative Framework for Strategy-Making Processes," *Academy of Management Review,* 17; (1992) 327–351; Wall, *Bosses.*

34. Manz, Sims, "Leading Workers to Lead Themselves."

35. J. R. Galbraith, "Designing the Innovation Organization," *Organizational Dynamics,* 10 (Summer, 1982): 5–25.

36. R. Miles, C. Snow, H. Coleman, "Managing 21st Century Network Organizations," *Organizational Dynamics* (Winter, 1992): 5–20.

37. C. Lee, "The New Employment Contract," *Training,* 24:12 (1987): 45–56.

38. S. A. Youngblood, L. Bierman, "Due Process and Employment-at-Will: A Legal and Behavior Analysis," in, *Research in Personnel and Human Resource Management,* K. Rowland, G. Ferris, eds. (Greenwich, CT: JAI Press, 1985): 185–230; C. Schwoerer, B. Rosen, "Effects of Employment-at-Will Policies and Compensation Policies on Corporate Image and Job Pursuit Intentions," *Journal of Applied Psychology,* 74 (1987): 653–656.

39. M. J. Piore, C. F. Sabel, *The Second Industrial Divide: Possibilities for Prosperity* (New York: Basic Books, 1984).

40. O. E. Williamson, "Comparative Economic Organization: The Analysis of Discrete Structural Alternatives," *Administrative Science Quarterly,* 36:2 (1991): 269–296.

41. G. Morgan, *Creative Organization Theory: A Resource Book* (Newbury Park, CA: Sage, 1989): 64–67.

42. Hackman, Oldham, *Work Redesign;* B. F. Skinner, *Science and Human Behavior* (New York: Macmillan, 1953).

43. R. S. Schuler, *Personnel and Human Resource Management* (St. Paul, MN: West Publishing, 1984); R. H. Hall, R. E. Quinn, "Environments, Organizations, and Policymakers: Toward an Integrative Framework," in *Organization Theory and Public Policy,* R. H. Hall, R. E. Quinn, eds. (Beverly Hills, CA: Sage, 1983): 293.

44. E. L. Deci, *Intrinsic Motivation.* (New York: Plenum Press, 1975).

45. Lawler, *High-Involvement Management;* M. R. Weisbord, *Productive Workplaces: Organizing and Managing for Dignity, Meaning, and Community* (San Francisco: Jossey-Bass, 1987).

46. G. T. Milkovich, J. M. Newman, *Compensation* (Plano, TX: Business Publications, 1987); S. A. Snell, J. W. Dean, Jr., "Integrated Manufacturing and Human Resource Management: A Human Capital Perspective," *Academy of Management Journal,* 35:3 (1992): 467–504.

47. R. Stayer, "How I Learned to Let my Workers Lead," *Harvard Business Review,* 68:6 (1990): 66–83.

48. Lee, "The New Employment Contract."

49. Lawler, *High-Involvement Management.*

50. J. W. Dean, Jr., G. I. Susman, "Strategic Responses to Global Competition: Advanced Technology, Organizational Design, and Human Resources Prac-

tices," in *Strategy, Organization Design, and Human Resource Management*, C. C. Snow, ed., (Greenwich, CT: JAI Press, 1989): 297–332; Snell, Dean, "Integrated Manufacturing."

51. D. Ulrich, D. Lake, "Organizational Capability: Creating Competitive Advantage," *Academy of Management Executive*, 5:1 (1991): 77–92.

52. D. A. Garvin, "Building a Learning Organization," *Harvard Business Review*, 71:4 (1993): 78–92; R. Stata, "Organizational Learning—The Key to Management Innovation," *Sloan Management Review* (Spring, 1989): 63–74.

53. C. K. Prahalad, G. Hamel, "The Core Competence of the Corporation," *Harvard Business Review*, 68:3 (1990): 79–91.

54. D. Ulrich, M. A. Von Glinow, T. Jick, "High-Impact Learning: Building and Diffusing Learning Capability," (Autumn, 1993): 52–66.

55. Ulrich, Lake, "Organizational Capability."

56. W. Wiggenhorn, "Motorola U: When Training Becomes an Education," *Harvard Business Review*, 4 (1990): 71–83.

57. Miles, Snow, "Organizations."

58. Quinn, *Beyond Rational Management*.

59. T. Burns, G. Stalker, *The Management of Innovation*. (London: Tavistock Publications, 1961).

60. Hammer, Champy, *Reengineering the Corporation*; Piore, Sabel, *The Second Industrial Divide*; B. J. Pine, III, *Mass Customization: The New Frontier in Business Competition* (Boston: Harvard Business School Press, 1993).

61. M. E. Porter, *Competitive Strategy: Techniques for Analyzing Industries and Competitors* (New York: Free Press, 1980).

62. D. Miller, "Configurations of Strategy and Structure: Toward a Synthesis," *Strategic Management Journal*, 7 (1986): 233–249; D. Miller, "Generic Strategies: Classification, Combination, and Context," *Advances in Strategic Management*, 8 (1992): 391–408.

63. R. M. Kanter, "When a Thousand Flowers Bloom: Structural, Social and Collective Conditions for Innovation in Organizations," in *The Evolution and Adaptation of Organizations*, B. Staw, L. L. Cummings, eds. (Greenwich, CT: JAI Press, 1988): 277–319.

64. Hamel, Prahalad, "Strategy as Stretch."

65. Mintzberg, *The Structuring of Organizations*.

66. K. Eisenhardt, L. J. Bourgeois, "Politics of Strategic Decision Making in High-Velocity Environments: Towards a Midrange Theory," *Academy of Management Journal*, 31 (1988): 737–770; K. Eisenhardt, "Making Fast Strategic Decisions in High-Velocity Environments," *Academy of Management Journal*, 32 (1989): 543–576.

67. R. L. Daft, *Organization Theory and Design* (St. Paul, MN: West Publishing, 1992).

68. R. Miles, C. Snow, "Designing Strategic Human Resources Systems," *Organizational Dynamics* (1983): 36–52.

69. Quinn, *Beyond Rational Management*.

70. Burns, Stalker, *The Management of Innovation*; Mintzberg, *The Structuring of Organizations*.
71. Miles, Snow, "Designing Strategic Human Resources."
72. Lawler, *High-Involvement Management*.
73. Miles, Snow, "Designing Strategic Human Resources."
74. Reich, *The Work of Nations*.
75. T. Deal, A. Kennedy, *Corporate Culture* (Reading, MA: Addison-Wesley, 1982); J. Kotter, J. Heskett, *Corporate Culture and Performance* (New York: Free Press, 1992); A. L. Wilkins, W. G. Ouchi, "Efficient Cultures: Exploring the Relationship between Culture and Organizational Performance," *Administrative Science Quarterly*, 28 (1983): 468–481.
76. Quinn, *Beyond Rational Management*; R. E. Quinn, J. Rohrbaugh, "A Competing Values Approach to Organizational Effectiveness," *Public Productivity Reviews*, 5 (1981): 122–140; R. E. Quinn, J. Rohrbaugh, A spatial model of effectiveness criteria: towards a competing values approach to organizational analysis, *Management Science*, 29 (1983): 363–377; Zammuto and Krackower, "Quantitative and Qualitative Studies"; Ibid.
77. Peters, Waterman, *In Search of Excellence*.
78. B. C. Reimann, Y. Wiener, "Corporate Culture: Avoiding the Elitist Trap," *Business Horizons*, 31:2 (1988): 36–44.
79. H. Schwartz, S. Davis, "Matching Corporate Culture and Business Strategy," *Organizational Dynamics* (Summer, 1981): 30–48; R. H. Kilman, M. J. Saxton, R. Serpa, "Issues in Understanding and Changing Culture," *California Management Review*, 28:2 (1986): 87–94; N. M. Tichy, "Managing Change Strategically: The Technical, Political, and Cultural Keys," *Organizational Dynamics* (Autumn, 1982): 59–80.
80. J. W. Lorsch, "Managing Culture: The Invisible Barrier to Strategic Change," *California Management Review*, 28:2 (1986): 95–109.
81. C. Schwenk, "Cognitive Simplification Processes in Strategic Decision-Making," *Strategic Management Journal*, 5 (1984): 111–128.
82. J. Dutton, S. Jackson, "Categorizing Strategic Issues: Links to Organizational Action," *Academy of Management Review*, 12 (1987): 76–90.
83. W. Bennis, B. Nanus, *Leaders* (New York: Harper & Row).
84. E. H. Schein, *Organizational Culture and Leadership* (San Francisco: Jossey-Bass, 1985).
85. E. H. Schein, "Coming to a New Awareness of Organizational Culture," *Sloan Management Review*, 25:2 (1984) 3–16.
86. J. Child, *Organization* (New York: Harper & Row, (1984).
87. S. Ranson, B. Hinings, R. Greenwood, "The Structuring of Organizational Structures," *Administrative Science Quarterly*, 25 (1980): 1–17.
88. H. Wilmott, "The Structuring of Organizational Structure: A Note," *Administrative Science Quarterly*, 26 (1981): 470–474.
89. F. E. Fielder, *A Theory of Leadership Effectiveness* (New York: McGraw-Hill, 1967).

90. P. Shrivastava, J. Grant, "Empirically derived models of strategic decision-making processes," *Strategic Management Journal*, 6 (1984): 97–113.

91. I. Nonaka, "The Knowledge-Creating Company," *Harvard Business Review*, 69:6 (1991): 49–64.

92. K. Davis, "Success of chain-of-command oral communication in a manufacturing group," *Academy of Management Journal*, 11 (1968): 379–387.

93. R. G. Foltz, "Communication in Contemporary Organizations," in *Inside Organizational Communication*, 2nd ed. C. Reuss, D. Silvis, eds. (New York: Longman, 1985).

94. C. Argyis, D. A. Schon, *Organizational Learning: A Theory of Action Perspective* (Reading, MA: Addison-Wesley, 1978).

95. P. Watzlawick, J. Weakland, R. Fisch, *Change* (New York: W. W. Norton, 1974).

96. D. Miller, P.H. Friesen, "Archetypes of Organizational Transition," *Administrative Science Quarterly*, 25 (1980): 263–299.

97. D. W. Meyers, *Human Resource Management: Principles and Practice* (Chicago: Commerce Clearing House, 1986).

98. C. C. Manz, "Self-Leading Work Teams: Moving beyond Self-Management Myths," *Human Relations*, 45:11 (1992): 1119–1140.

99. H. J. Bernardin, R. W. Beatty, *Performance Appraisal: Assessing Human Behavior at Work* (Boston: Kent Publishing, 1984).

100. W. A. Schiemann, "The Impact of Corporate Compensation and Benefit Policy on Employee Attitudes and Behavior and Corporate Profitability," *Journal of Business and Psychology* 2 (1987): 8–26.

101. J. Savage, "Incentive Programs at Nucor Corporation Boost Productivity," *Personnel Administrator* (1981): 33–36.

102. R. S. Schuler, S. E. Jackson, "Linking Competitive Strategies with Human Resource Management Practices," *Academy of Management Executive*, 1 (1987): 207–219.

103. R. D. Gatewood, H. S. Field, *Human Resource Selection* (Hinsdale, IL: Dryden Press, 1987).

104. B. Schneider, N. Schmidt, *Staffing Organizations*, (Glenview, IL: Scott, Foresman, 1986).

105. J. Jannotta, "Stroh's Outplacement Success," *Management Review* (January, 1987): 52–53.

106. L. Reibstein, "Survivors of Layoffs Help to Lift Morale and Instill Trust," *The Wall Street Journal* (March 13, 1986): 13.

11

Managing the Business Transformation Process

WILLIAM H. DAVIDSON and JOSEPH F. MOVIZZO

Chapter Summary

1. Managing business transformation is an experience which is forced on most organizations by adverse circumstances. This chapter suggests a six-stage process for managing change successfully.

2. The six stages are: (a) strategy initiative; (b) operations improvement and innovation; (c) infrastructure design and deployment; (d) business enhancement; (e) strategy and organization redefinition and (f) operating initiative. The stages are iterative, and tend to take place over a considerable period of time.

3. Each stage is critically dependent on leadership, committment and customer-orientation. Viewed graphically, they represent a steadily broadening understanding of what organizational structure is most appropriate to supporting desired organizational competencies.

4. The essence of managing transformation is communicating vision, and steadily empowering individuals to implement (and own) the new concept of the company. Phases (a)–(c) represent the first iteration of this process, with new system design being driven by the newly determined business vision. However, the authors stress that senior IT executives should be part of the business team that determines the vision, in order to ensure alignment.

5. Transformation moves into a different gear in phases (d)–(f). During this time, the vision either becomes a reality, or must be further adjusted. They are phases in which new opportunities can be identified, which were not previously apparent. The alignment of IT

with business strategy becomes critical to enable the rapid development of new applications and interfaces as required.

6. During these phases it will become important for the leadership to articulate and drive forward the new vision that is emerging. The committment that the whole process takes should not be underestimated, or its toll on the top team's energy and vitality. This may be a good point for the existing management to hand over to a new, fresher team, as the transformation process by this time may easily have been continuing for over 5 years.

7. A six-stage chart concludes the chapter, summarizing the roles and responsibilities of executives involved in successful reengineering initiatives. Managed properly, the process of transformation, initially generated by a crisis, can become accepted as 'the way we do business around here'—possibly a critical competitive competency for the forseeable future.

Successful transformation produces spectacular results, but the process can be prolonged and painful. Transformation occurs over a period of years in even the most agile and nimble organization. It is a sophisticated process involving a series of stages. Each stage of the transformation cycle contains critical tasks and unique issues that must be addressed in order to follow the path through to a successful conclusion. Each stage exhibits unique leadership requirements and barriers that must be overcome. It is a production that, without proper orchestration, cannot achieve its desired ends.

Why then do organizations embark on the path to transformation? A motivating crisis typically triggers the process. Crises may originate from issues of competitiveness, growth, or basic economic survival. A competitor's initiative can lead a firm to pursue a radical change program. American Hospital Supply's success with its on-line hospital procurement system triggered significant change at Johnson & Johnson, for example. Also, demands by key customers may be the catalyst. Toyota and Wal-Mart have driven the adoption of new EDI-based business practices within their supplier communities. Regulatory change can unleash creative programs. Deregulation of airlines and interstate trucking around 1980 fueled innovative transformation efforts in both industries.

Each of these forces feeds the most powerful catalyst for transformation, financial crisis. Most enterprises embark on transformation programs only when they are forced to do so. Such programs are hazardous and require hard work. Yet, transformation is not entirely unexplored territory. The experiences of dozens of firms suggest that the costs and risks of such efforts can be dramatically reduced by approaching transformation as a planned journey. In this chapter, we present a generic framework that addresses the issues, tasks, barriers, and pitfalls found in all transformation efforts. It is intended to serve as a travel guide for transformation.

The experiences of some sixty firms observed in transformation programs suggest that there are six generic phases in this process:

- strategy initiative
- operations improvement and innovation
- infrastructural design and deployment
- business enhancement
- strategy and organizational redefinition
- operating initiative

Transformation initiatives can stall or fail in any of these phases if critical tasks are not performed. Leadership roles in each stage are also unique. Failure to fill these roles at the proper time leaves a vacuum that is difficult or impossible to overcome. The role of the CEO and key senior executives must be sustained over time as success requires a commitment to radically rethinking the business, a demonstrated will to succeed, and pervasive customer value orientation. Each stage also exhibits critical relationships that are essential to progress on the transformation path (Fig. 11.1).

Phase One: Strategy Initiative

In the first stage of transformation, the critical role is played by the CEO, whose principal task is to call the organization to action around a compelling vision. An effective vision utilizes external threats and opportunities to rally the organization around new operating performance goals. At one extreme, the CEO may only sound the general alarm, establish general performance themes and targets, and exhort the organization to increase its efforts to improve performance. In general, specific operating improvements would be developed in the next stage of the exercise. At the opposite extreme, however, program specifics are communicated to the organization

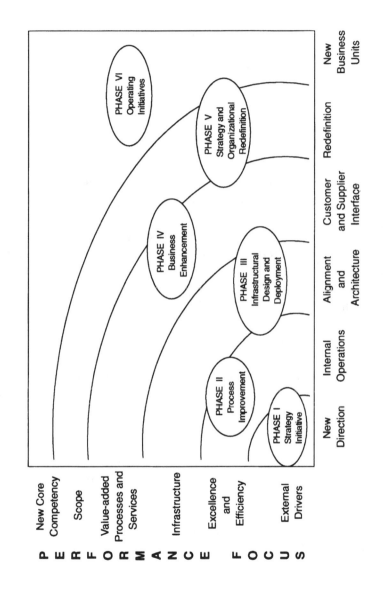

Figure 11.1. The Six Phases of Business Transformation

within the broader strategy initiative. The CEO may design and launch a full-fledged program for operating improvement and transformation. The CEO's personal involvement in these programs has a great deal to do with their success as described by Luftman in the strategy execution perspective.

Turning Around American Standard: A Strategy Designed and Led by the CEO

At American Standard, CEO Mano Kampouris initiated an operating improvement program designed to address a compelling financial crisis. American Standard's management team, with an outside partner and an employee stock ownership plan (ESOP), acquired the firm in 1988. The acquisition entailed the assumption of some $3 billion in debt by the new owners. With recession in the early 1990s, the company faced severe financial pressure to service its existing debt load. Because of the highly leveraged nature of the acquisition, much of this debt carried fixed interest rates of 12–14%, and the terms of these bond issues prohibited debt refinancing.

Kampouris focused on the financial crisis and identified the need to improve cash flow by reducing working capital requirements as the central target for operating performance gains. He assigned Gary Biddle, Corporate Vice President of MIS, to do a global search for methodologies to improve American Standard's working capital and cash flow performance. After a thorough search, a methodology was identified that offered significant benefits to American Standard. Mr. Kampouris and several of his senior officers attended a one week seminar to learn the methods and came away convinced that they had discovered a solution to the company's immediate operating crisis.

Kampouris then announced a formal program called TNT, for Twice the Turns Now, designed to dramatically reduce working capital ratios. This program involved training over thirty thousand employees in new management techniques. In addition, the firm engaged a team of Japanese process planning engineers to implement on-demand production techniques in American Standard facilities. This involved a shift from a traditional *push* model, involving forecast-based production scheduling and inventory management, to a *pull* model that called for production only in response to specific customer orders. The new model fully incorporated many of the *Kanban* and just-in-time techniques used widely in Japan. While these new techniques were being introduced in American Standard production facilities, Kampouris and his management team were actively promoting the

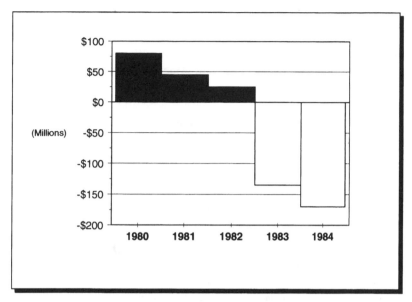

Figure 11.2.   Levi Strauss & Co.'s Plummeting Profitability

program through speeches, communications, and personal intervention in the organization.

In this instance, the CEO not only launched a strategy initiative designed to respond to an emerging financial crisis but was actively involved in the planning, design, and implementation of a highly technical reengineering program that transformed the company's manufacturing and financial profiles. This high level of personal involvement and extraordinary focus on a single program initiative allowed the company to implement this program quickly, relative to the experiences of other large industrial concerns. The TNT program did successfully double inventory turns for the enterprise over a period of three years, and turns almost doubled again in the fourth year of the program. The program's momentum is such that it now appears to hold the potential to cut working capital by as much as 90%.

Levi Strauss: A Turnaround Strategy Started by the CEO

At Levi Strauss, the CEO's role was quite different from the hands-on approach at American Standard. Levi Strauss suffered a series of unprecedented financial losses in the early 1980s (Fig. 11.2). The company had been profitable for a century before experiencing significant losses in 1983 and 1984.

The crisis at Levi resulted in a strategic initiative that was developed in a very different manner from that at American Standard. The principal response to this crisis was the formation of a senior management strategy group by the CEO. The group's mandate was to address the causes of the operating and financial crises, with a clean slate for reviewing different program alternatives. This group, The First Information Resources Strategy Team (FIRST), consisted of twelve senior executives, who focused on potential applications of IT in the business. One of the options identified by this group was the use of bar coding technology. A junior executive was assigned responsibility for exploring potential applications of this technology in the apparel sector. This individual, Paul Benchener, was given a limited budget and staff but was allowed to explore potential applications with few other constraints.

At the time, bar coding was in its infancy in the retail sector and industry standards had not yet been established. Benchener was one of the initial participants in a retail industry consortium to define technological standards for bar coding. He then led an internal effort to attach bar codes to Levi's apparel. This program did not involve any substantial change in Levi's manufacturing or distribution operations. Tags were simply added to garments prior to shipment out of Levi's distribution centers.

The use of bar codes permitted retailers with POS scanners to realize a series of benefits. Bar coding increased the efficiency and flexibility of garment pricing. It allowed apparel to move directly to the retail shop floor without the delays of adding price tags. Data captured at the POS support more efficient inventory management. Benchener group developed a series of services to retailers. The services were largely developed on an autonomous basis. The model stock management program designed to predict sales levels and stocking requirements for retailers was written by a salesman's teenaged son on a home computer, for example.

Over time, these services grew into a package called Levi-Link, a set of enhanced services available to Levi's retailers, including electronic purchase orders, electronic invoices, electronic funds transfer, vendor marking, advance shipping notice, model stock management, and sales analysis and reporting.

Due to the decentralized nature of the program, it took much longer to reach critical scale than might have been the case if it had been driven directly by the CEO. However, over time Levi-Link has moved into the mainstream of the transformation path at Levi's. Where the Levi-Link program initially had no impact on core operations, Levi's now faces considerable pressure from its customers to further build on these capabilities. Customer pressure is resulting in a broader reengineering of production and distribution at Levi's. In 1990, Levi's launched its Customer Service Supply Chain (CSSC) program to align internal operations with retailer needs and expectations. In turn, a new infrastructure plan called LABS (Levi's Advanced Business Systems) is being developed in conjunction with the CSSC program to create a platform for transformation of the business.

The LABS program represents the third phase of transformation at Levi's. This infrastructural design and deployment effort is being led by Bill Eaton, Levi's CIO. The LABS infrastructure program is intimately linked to a series of formal process reengineering projects guided by a senior management team.

The Levi's example shows a very different approach to transformation. It was triggered by a senior executive officer's call to action, but the strategy initiative was left undefined by the CEO. The organization's response to the strategy initiative included a series of programs, and only after some years has the initiative evolved into a focused transformation program.

Results to date at Levi's have been impressive. Retailers utilizing the Levi-Link system report a return on sales more than 50% greater than those retailers who continue to do business in the traditional manner. With Levi-Link, retailers are able to restock in as little as six days compared to a traditional cycle of six weeks. In 1993 retailers on the Levi-Link system accounted for about one-third of total sales. The Levi-Link model has moved into the mainstream of Levi's business and is now pushing in from the outside, from customers to the core of Levi's operations and organization.

The typical enterprise will fall somewhere between these two extremes. It is rare for a CEO to be as involved in the specifics of operational planning and implementation as Mano Kampouris of American Standard. In contrast, the management style and culture of Levi permit an extraordinary level of autonomy and empowerment in establishing the strategic direction of the enterprise. Such a decentralized model may require a longer time to achieve critical mass behind a focused program, but it is likely to provide exposure to a broader range of ideas and alternatives in the early phases of transformation.

The Role of the CEO in Creating a Crisis

Of the firms we've studied, a significant number exhibited extremely strong CEO leadership early in the transformation cycle. At Automated Data Processing's (ADP) Automotive Claims Services Division, new CEO John

Gaulding took advantage of negative trends in the marketplace to create a crisis environment. The Automotive Claims Services Group provides informational services to support automobile insurance claims processing. The division has a dominant position in its industry and an extraordinary record of financial success.

Like the division, the parent corporation enjoys a sterling record of business performance. It has reported double digit quarterly earnings increases for over thirty-six consecutive years. Its record of financial success is unmatched and enviable. With such a track record, efforts to dismantle an existing business model seem unlikely to succeed. Yet that is exactly what has occurred in ADP's Automated Claims Processing Division.

Gaulding emphasized negative trends in the marketplace that were leading to declining auto insurance claims. He projected a 25% decline in the total number of automobile claims over a five-year period. Clear trends in several areas supported this projection. Fewer accidents, higher deductibles, and more uninsured motorists all contributed to the decline. He then emphasized the impact of new competitors in the business. In a single week, two significant ADP customers shifted their business to these competitors. Gaulding seized the opportunity to declare an official crisis.

He launched a series of electronic town hall meetings to communicate the scope of the problem to his organization and to solicit input regarding responses to these concerns. At the same time he assigned two key executives to reengineer claims-processing operations. ADP's Senior Vice President of Marketing assumed the responsibility of COO to oversee design and implementation of a new claims-processing service. Gaulding and the divisions chief technology executive also initiated a complete overhaul of information systems infrastructure during this period. The overhaul of ADP's infrastructure and business processes occurred within only a twenty-four month period.

Gaulding not only identified and escalated an emerging crisis but provided a vision for how the division could respond to new market realities. His vision emphasized a new model for claims processing, utilizing information and communication technologies to revolutionize the process. ADP's new Audatex service is dramatically improving the efficiency and quality of auto claims processing. The company has established an extraordinary database that contains detailed, multilayered engineering diagrams for over thirteen hundred models of car ordered by year of make. This system includes artificial intelligence to calculate repair requirements based on the surface image of the damage. It also includes data on over three-and-a-half million auto parts and standard labor times for every repair job on every vehicle. This system also provides online linkages to twelve hundred auto parts distributors and eleven hundred junkyards to facilitate parts location and delivery at the lowest cost to the appropriate auto repair shop.

ADP is at the forefront of development and utilization of pen-based portable computers. These portable computers provide wireless access to the central data base so that adjusters in the field can access necessary information to facilitate claims processing. This service eliminates the need for a central estimation unit as all the appropriate information and support services are delivered instantly to the field.

With this new system ADP is expanding in several directions. Its Parts Exchange Service facilitates the location and delivery of lowest-cost parts to auto repair shops. It is providing data on specific models to auto insurers so that they can adjust their pricing to reflect the different repair costs of specific vehicles, and it is moving into a central role in overseeing auto repair shop activity. Based on the detailed information available from the millions of auto claims ADP processes each year, it will be able to monitor auto repair shop efficiency and quality so effectively that the claims adjuster role can be eliminated.

In this vision, the vehicle will be delivered directly to the repair shop. The repair shop itself will access the Audatex system to calculate repair cost and locate parts. ADP will monitor labor charges to ensure that costs are within prescribed ranges. It will monitor parts usage to ensure that lowest-cost parts are secured and quality, based on rework, customer complaints, and other inputs. Through this system, ADP will be able to manage an auto repair network in exactly the same way that the Clinton administration is seeking to manage health care.

ADP's transformation program has opened up a series of new growth vistas. Key aspects of the CEO's role in this case were identification of a pending crisis, the creation and communication of a positive vision, engaging key executives in specific roles and responsibilities, initiating an upgrade of infrastructure, and ensuring that these strategic initiatives received the resources and support for effective implementation. These tasks are central to the CEO's role in successful transformation programs.

A CEO-Led Initiative in Customer Focus

Progressive Insurance is a highly profitable automobile insurance company that has thrived in an otherwise dismal business. The automobile insurance industry as a whole has lost money in each of the last thirteen years. Yet, Progressive has reported an average return on equity of approximately 25% during that time period. In the late 1980s, two key events caused CEO Peter Lewis to take drastic action. First, AllState Insurance, a unit of Sears, launched a new insurance unit to imitate Progressive's strategy in auto insurance niche markets. That unit has grown rapidly since its formation. Second, the passage of Proposition 103 in California, which mandates 20% rate rollbacks for auto insurance companies, not only created a financial crisis but signaled a consumer revolt against auto insurance companies. Lewis concluded that customers felt that auto insurance companies were not providing adequate service and value for their premiums. He resolved to address customer dissatisfaction by focusing on improving customer service through innovative operating initiatives.

The focal point for these operating improvements was claims settlement. Lewis believed that claims settlement was too lengthy and adversarial and set about to address both issues. Progressive created a new claims settlement system called PACMAN (Progressive Automated Claims Management) to automate and expedite the claims settlement process. Progressive created an 800 number that can be accessed twenty-four hours a day to insure that customers could initiate claims at any time. In addition, all claims processing personnel were sent through a one-week empathy training course to shift their orientation toward a customer service perspective. This program resulted in significant operating improvements, reducing the claims settlement cycle time to an average of six days vs. an industry average of more than forty. Customer satisfaction measures also increased dramatically.

Progressive is now moving on to a second stage in its customer service improvement effort. A new service, called the Immediate Response Service, was launched in 1992. This service allows customers to call from the scene of an accident, or any other location, and a mobile van will proceed to the scene, where claims estimation can be accomplished by a remote communications link to a central estimation unit. Checks are prepared in the van and offered to the customer within as little as an hour of the accident itself.

The agent's task, however, is not just to write a check and wish the customer good luck. The agent offers to assist in expediting the repair and return of the vehicle. The agent will arrange to have the car towed to a repair shop in the Progressive network. These shops must commit to perform repairs for standard estimates and to meet quality and cycle time standards. As a result, auto repair costs can be reduced by 25% or more, fraud is virtually eliminated, transaction costs associated with communication between the repair shop and the insurance company are minimized because of EDI links and common information systems, litigation costs drop sharply, and customer satisfaction rises.

Nonetheless, Lewis also played the role of architect in designing a formal management structure at Progressive to oversee reengineering of claims settlement and five other core processes. A senior executive was made responsible for each of these core processes. The COO and the CIO also played critical roles in implementing the claims settlement program and the broader program of reengineering and transformation. In this sense the CEO played not only the role of champion for a specific program but also the role of architect in developing a framework to implement reengineering and transformation activity.

Such CEO leadership was central to a second successful transformation effort in the automobile insurance industry. At Progressive Insurance, CEO Peter Lewis personally drove his vision of customer satisfaction through to implementation.

Phase Two: Operations Improvement and Innovation

Strong CEOs often heavily involve themselves in the design and implementation of operating improvements and innovative programs. Ideally, however, a second key executive can assume primary leadership for such activities. These responsibilities are best managed by a strong COO. However, in many enterprises this position no longer exists, and a surrogate COO must be drawn from very senior management. Without strong CEO/COO leadership, many enterprises exhibit highly fragmented, diverse, uncoordinated, redundant, and even self-destructive divisional initiatives in this stage.

Caterpillar

At Caterpillar, operating improvement was pursued in a single large scale program that encompassed all manufacturing and logistics functions. Caterpillar's "Plant with a Future" (PWAF) program involved nothing less than the complete redesign of its manufacturing activities. Responsibility for the overall program, initiated in response to recession and severe pressure from foreign competition, was given to Executive Vice President Pierre Guerindon. As process owner for this manufacturing revitalization program, Guerindon and his team of executives redesigned manufacturing operations from the ground up, incorporating new technologies, methods, and infrastructure in the PWAF program.

Guerindon, with CEO George Shaefer's support, assembled a team of sixteen program managers with backgrounds in each functional area. The group was sequestered with a mandate to formulate the PWAF vision. The group searched the globe to identify and document best practices. It produced a document, referred to as Factory 2000, that outlined best manufacturing practices worldwide. These best practices served as the foundation for Caterpillar's own efforts.

At a manufacturing managers meeting in 1985, the PWAF plan was introduced to factory managers. Each manager was given a mandate to develop a plan for implementing PWAF in his or her facility. Plant funding was tied directly to PWAF plans. The PWAF framework identified seventy-seven specific production/assembly processes and allowed plant managers flexibility not only in selecting processes for reengineering but in methodologies and technologies as well. The sixteen program managers worked as internal consultants to assist in reengineering efforts, but external consultants were also used. Guerindon personally reviewed and approved all PWAF projects.

Management at Caterpillar followed what might be considered classical roles in managing reengineering and transformation programs. The CEO created a compelling case for the program, identified critical external drivers, made the case for significant operating and organizational change, assigned responsibility, and provided support to program leaders. The design and implementation of the program fell almost exclusively to operating executives led by Guerindon, who plays the role of COO in this exercise. Implementation of reengineering efforts takes place at the factory level within PWAF guidelines.

The creation of a structured program is important in this stage. If the CEO simply notes the external crisis and issues a call for action, a variety of responses and programs can be expected in the organization. While it is valuable to consider a wide range of potential paths in planning forums, it is far more difficult to manage a wide array of unique operating initiatives created in response to a broad call for action. Indeed, it appears that unstructured empowerment is a liability in phases two and three of the transformation process. Effective transformation programs create structures to prioritize process reengineering activity, focus scarce resources and attention to high-priority initiatives, and create guidelines for infrastructural deployment.

The Dangers of Uncoordinated Operations Improvements

HEALTH INSURANCE COMPANY

The problem with unstructured empowerment can be seen in the example of a large health insurance company that operates in a highly decentralized manner. This insurance company had over a hundred and twenty operating initiatives that required new information systems in 1992. Each unit within the enterprise was involved in reengineering various aspects of its operations to produce performance gains in response to a challenge from the CEO. This enterprise had found via benchmarking that its overhead costs per policy were three times higher than one of its competitors, and the CEO had called for actions to reduce overhead costs.

A series of divisional initiatives were launched to reduce sales, general, and administrative expenses. How many such reengineering initiatives would be needed to achieve the levels of efficiency already being reported by its competitor? The answer was deceptively simple. It would take one reengineering program to achieve this goal. The greater the number of discreet reengineering initiatives this firm pursued, the less likely it would be able to achieve the higher levels of performance already reported by its competitor.

USAA

As introduced in Chapter 3, USAA has established new standards of operating performance in the insurance industry by reengineering its customer service function. USAA is a full line insurance company, offering automobile, health, life, property, and other insurance services to its customers. It is able to offer a full line of services with much lower overhead costs than its competitors. In the 1980s, USAA reengineered its customer service functions with a striking goal in mind. The challenge in the vision behind the reengineering effort called for the completion of all customer requests and transactions at the first point of contact—i.e., the first person the customer spoke to would be able to answer all questions, address all problems, and complete all transactions in the course of that initial conversation.

USAA reengineered its infrastructure and operating system so that customer service representatives could have access to all of the resources, systems, processes, and information of each of the operating units. This enterprisewide infrastructure, supported by training and development efforts, allowed USAA to complete over 90% of all requests and transactions in the first point of contact with its customers in 1992.[1] The common systems platform established at USAA could not have been created in a decentralized mode. It required a central vision and implementation.

The more discrete reengineering initiatives a firm pursues, the less likely they will be able to achieve the standards of performance implicit in the USAA model. Many of the one hundred and twenty plus projects being pursued at the insurance firm mentioned above involved incompatible data bases, communication networks, software, hardware, and other infrastructural elements. Over thirty-six hundred mainframe databases were already in existence inside this organization, many of them redundant. Senior executives in this enterprise could choose from as many as a dozen different databases to secure an answer to a question about operating performance. The range of responses to such questions would provide ample latitude for misinterpretation of reality.

Examples like this point out the dangers of unstructured empowerment in the early stages of the transformation process. Empowerment can be selective and structured to reduce this problem. It's important to note that in Japanese enterprises, the most effective practitioners of continuous improvement methods, empowerment is highly structured. Most continuous improvement programs in Japan operate under the framework of a *Hoshin* planning focus, which identifies two or three central programs and objectives. The small groups that drive continuous improvement models are managed and coordinated by a management structure that establishes focused guidelines for operations improvement activity.[2]

Continuous improvement, Japanese style, is highly structured and focused. Similar empowerment can be applied within a process reengineering effort, where teams of executives and employees can redesign processes within a framework that incorporates priorities, cross-functional linkages, and common infrastructural guidelines. Process improvement and innovation thus occurs within a larger framework governing the broader transformation effort. Failure to provide this type of structure will lead to a large number of disjointed, uncoordinated operating initiatives that will never be able to achieve quantum performance gains.

The Importance of Process Ownership

Another common failing in phase two of the transformation phase is the absence of effective process ownership. The CEO strategy initiative must be followed by the assignment of responsibility for process reengineering and implementation activities. Caterpillar assigned a very senior executive to this task on a full-time basis. It also tied capital allocation to the PWAF program.

Without credible process ownership, implementation of critical cross-functional improvement programs is unlikely to be successful. In many enterprises, process management is assigned to an ad hoc committee of executives from throughout the company. In most cases these executives are assigned to the team on an incremental basis, with no individual accountability for the outcome of the effort. Such teams can be effective in redesigning processes, but implementation of cross-functional processes requires more substantial commitment and executive authority.

Process reengineering appears to be most effective when a single senior executive is responsible for a specific process from redesign to implementation. At Progressive Insurance, six core processes were identified, and a member of the senior executive team was assigned responsibility for each process. That executive's evaluation and compensation package was tied explicitly to the success of a process reengineering initiative. In most cases the strong commitment of a senior executive will be necessary to overcome the natural resistance to enterprisewide reengineering efforts. Successful process innovation always involves cross-functional and often cross-divisional implementation.

The natural resistance to such efforts can be overcome only through the dedicated efforts of senior executives, with the active support of the CEO. Cooperation can also be insured if senior functional divisional managers are codependent, needing each other's assistance to implement their own process initiatives. Codependence supports horse trading between senior executives in that cooperation insures mutual success in process reengineering efforts. This framework will work best if the CEO actively reinforces the importance of the process reengineering initiatives.

NEW COMPENSATION RULES CAN BE EFFECTIVE

In one large enterprise a new CEO was having difficulty implementing a series of enterprisewide reengineering initiatives, despite a profitability and competitiveness crisis in the business. The lack of progress was not due to middle management resistance but to the inability of senior functional and divisional managers to work together in a highly competitive internal culture. Senior managers viewed each other as rivals and were unwilling to support each other's initiatives. They competed actively for resources and frequently attempted to sabotage or discount their peers' programs. Team-building exercises proved to have little impact on this organization's climate.

Progress occurred only after the CEO terminated the senior executive bonus plan and replaced it with a program that promised to pay a year and half's salary to each senior executive if the organization met a series of objectives in year three of its transformation program. These objectives were tied explicitly to process reengineering initiatives under way in the enterprise. These initiatives required cross-functional coordination to be successful. The new bonus plan held a provision that not a single executive would receive a penny if one of the targets was missed by 1%. This new bonus plan, along with extensive interpersonal guidance from the CEO, appears to have had the desired effect on the organization, and considerable progress has been made in implementing new processes.

The CEO and/or the process owners become the key leaders in phase two of the transformation process, but the CEO's role remains of central importance in this stage. The CEO must reinforce the importance of the transformation program, assure that resources are committed according to established priority, support the leaders of the reengineering efforts in their search for cooperation, and provide the resources necessary to fund those efforts.

Managing Change During Phase Two

A fundamental tension exists in all enterprises during this stage. All organizations exhibit a tension between running and changing the business. Every enterprise has its own set of operating initiatives designed to meet short-term business concerns. Unless these short-term operating initiatives are aligned with the larger reengineering effort, conflict is inevitable. We have found such alignment to be rare. Reengineering programs will always compete and conflict with autonomous operating initiatives. Such operating initiatives are almost always established through some sort of bottom-up effort that culminates in a contentious resource allocation exercise.

Functional and divisional executives make tremendous personal and political investments in these operating initiatives. There will always be competition for resources that support operating initiatives, and business reengineering efforts will be seen as rivals for those resources, rivals that will in many cases attempt to supersede the short-term operating efforts of unit managers. This, of course, does not apply only to capital resources. Imagine a situation where a unit has been asked to participate in a cross-functional process initiative that requires the involvement of key unit personnel. Those personnel, especially scarce software, communications, and systems staff, will also be needed on immediate operating projects. Which set of projects will take priority, and who will establish those priorities? It is very easy for operating managers to shift resources away from longer-term corporate programs to immediate, local efforts.

In one enterprise undergoing a complete overhaul of its operating infrastructure as a result of a CEO strategy initiative, several dozen key software and communications personnel were pulled off of the new infrastructural program by divisional executives and assigned to work on upgrades of existing operating systems that were to be replaced within six months by the new infrastructure! It is imperative at this stage in the cycle to kill or integrate such upgrades and other short-term operating programs that will drain resources away from broader transformation programs.

Most short-term operating programs promise incremental improvements that will never be able to deliver breakthrough performance gains. Yet organizational and business realities will tend, in almost all cases, to draw resources away from transformation efforts to short-term operating activities. Only with a strong governance framework can the organization ensure that resources are allocated to transformation efforts. A strong COO and an effective process ownership framework, with the active support of the CEO, are the primary vehicles for ensuring focused resource utilization.

These pressures are not easy to manage, even with the active participation of the CEO. A financial services company with an aggressive transformation program recently encountered some of these pressures. The CEO called a meeting of the senior executive team to achieve consensus on priorities for the enterprise. After struggling to gain consensus about the importance of the transformation program, one senior executive asked, "If we all agree that this is the most important program under way in the company, is it more important than running the business?"

The consensus seemed to be that running the business was, in fact, more important than implementing this transformation program. Finally, one divisional executive said, "Does this mean I may not get my new divisional accounting system this year? Because if it does, I'm going to do everything in my power to kill that transformation program." The CEO's response to this discussion was, "You can continue to pursue your discrete divisional initiatives but only after you've met your commitment to these high-priority programs." In the end it will be necessary, in almost all cases, to kill or integrate existing operating projects to ensure successful implementation of new processes and infrastructure.

Careful design of the reengineering effort can successfully incorporate many existing operating initiatives or at least address the concerns and objectives of those initiatives. In many cases, however, projects will need to be terminated to free up resources and achieve focus behind the transformation program. Failure to transcend the tyranny of short-term business and operational considerations will stall or kill transformation. The COO, or surrogate, plays a key role in that regard.

Phase Three: Infrastructural Design and Deployment

Significant operating improvements can be achieved without the use of new technologies and operating infrastructures, but radical gains in operating performance will require investments in an advanced infrastructure. The distinction posed by Tom Davenport between process improvement and process innovation is relevant here.[3] Process improvement may involve simplification of existing processes to remove non-value-added steps and reduce cycle times without utilizing new technologies and infrastructures.

Such process improvement activity may realize significant returns with minimal investment, but the potential gains with such efforts are limited. Breakthroughs require new technologies and infrastructures. At Progressive Insurance, the distinction is clear. Progressive's first efforts to improve claims settlement involved establishment of an 800 number and retraining of employees to create a customer-service-oriented culture. These steps involved little new technology or infrastructure. It was only with the development of the PACMAN system and mobile communications that the Immediate Response System became a reality.

Process innovation requires new infrastructure. Implementation of new processes cannot occur until the infrastructure and support systems are deployed. However, it is important that the enterprise goes through the process analysis and redesign effort prior to deployment of new infrastructure. Without the linkage between process reengineering and infrastructural design, investments in new technology and infrastructure are unlikely to realize positive returns. It has been noted by a number of authors that investments in IT have not yielded the kinds of returns anticipated.[4] In many enterprises this pattern can be directly linked to the absence of a bridge between process redesign and infrastructural deployment activities, as described by Luftman cycling from the strategy execution to organization IT infrastructure perspective.

Who Should Design the New Systems?

One of the most hazardous patterns observed in the transformation journey occurs when the strategic initiative proceeds from the CEO to the CIO without active grounding in the operating units of the organization.[5] The CIO is told to create a next-generation infrastructure, without adequate knowledge of operating realities and requirements. While success stories are possible in this pattern, there are many examples of enterprises that have invested hundreds of millions of dollars in such programs only to see a minimal return, if any, on their investments.

How a CIO-Based Systems Initiative Failed

In 1989 one of the regional Bell Operating companies launched a program to completely overhaul its infrastructure. The CIO was given a mandate to redesign the company's information systems from scratch to support improved operations. The enterprise invested many millions of dollars in developing new, integrated order entry, provisioning, billing, and other systems. The design of the new systems architecture was sophisticated, but the effort failed in implementation. The new systems were rejected by operating units that resisted the operating changes enabled by the new infrastructure. Infrastructural improvements are most likely to be successful when they are demanded by operating units to support new processes designed by the operating units themselves. Attempts to force-feed new infrastructure (and processes) via CIO-led initiatives face severe risks of failure.

How Manufacturers Hanover Trust Should Have Involved Its CIO

At the other extreme, even more spectacular failure may occur if the CIO does not play a central role in designing and integrating infrastructure for enterprise transformation. In the 1980s, Manufacturers Hanover Trust Bank decentralized its information management function to four major groups, eliminating the central MIS unit.[6] Each of the four groups aggressively pursued programs to develop new applications and services for its customers. The results were impressive. In the first year following decentralization, dozens of new applications were introduced.

Soon, however, the impact of autonomy on enterprise architecture became apparent. Each of the four groups adopted a different mainframe platform, with unique hardware and software portfolios. The enterprise utilized twenty-seven different communication protocols and a wide variety of application software packages. While autonomy did enable a significant increase in development of new applications, fragmentation of the informational infrastructure caused severe problems for branches and customers. A typical retail branch would offer services from three of the four groups at Manufacturers Hanover Trust. For the branch to access those services it had to operate as many as three different hardware and software platforms, requiring redundant investment and additional personnel at the branch level.

Increased costs were less significant than the customer-service problems that arose for large customers purchasing services from multiple groups within the bank. Customers soon found it very difficult to access services in a seamless manner. In addition, Manufacturers Hanover found it impossible to coordinate across groups in providing portfolios of service to large customers. It also had no central depository of information about customers to assist it in providing customer service. The operating problems associated with fragmentation of information resources were one of the factors that contributed to its acquisition by Chemical Bank in 1992.

Successful Integration at Canada Trust

In contrast, two Canadian financial institutions exhibit the power of focused infrastructural development. Canada Trust is one of the fastest growing and most profitable financial institutions in Canada. It grew from the thirty-third largest financial institution in Canada to the third largest in the 1980s. Its operating infrastructure exhibits a level of integration unmatched in the industry.

One of Canada Trust's product offerings is the Commander account, which allows customers to select from over one hundred different services, including savings and checking accounts, credit cards, brokerage services, insurance, accounting, tax management services, currency trading, futures, options, and other financial services. Commander allows customers to select the services they desire and to configure individual services to their own specifications. The Commander system automates the provisioning of this portfolio of services and provides a single reporting method selected by the customer. Commander is, in effect, a common order entry and provisioning system that allows customers to access all of the enterprise's services in a seamless manner.

The Royal Bank of Canada

The Royal Bank of Canada possesses perhaps the most sophisticated technological infrastructure of any financial institution in the world. Its virtual corporate network (VCN) infrastructure allows any of its hundreds of retail branches to access all corporate information resources and systems instantly. Customers can access these services through dial-up linkages as well. The network is used to download upgrades of all systems software to insure that the entire retail network is utilizing standardized, state-of-the-art systems. In the 1980s the Royal Bank invested over $30 million in the development of its single reference file (SRF), a centralized customer data repository. This central data base contains all information on approximately eight million customers.

The bank's marketing executives are able to access comprehensive customer information instantly to support target marketing for new service offerings. In the course of its SRF efforts, the Royal Bank learned that its average customer purchases three and a fraction financial services from the bank and seventeen financial services from all vendors. It shifted its marketing focus from the acquisition of new customers to increasing the number of services provided to its existing customer base. This reorientation of marketing effort has been supported by the SRF system in conjunction with other data resources.

In contrast to Manufacturers Hanover Trust, customer service levels in these institutions are seamless. This type of seamless service can be provided only if it is supported by a highly integrated infrastructure with common systems and architecture. Such an infrastructure can appear only if the CIO plays a powerful and central role in designing it to support innovative operating practices.

The Right Moment to Introduce Systems Reengineering

The CIO's role is to provide the architecture that will support enterprise-wide operating improvement and innovation, but unless that architecture is closely tied to process reengineering and operating improvement initiatives, it may never provide appropriate returns. At Levi Strauss, the LABS initiative led by Bill Eaton, Levi's CIO, appeared as a formal effort only after the Levi-Link initiative had become a central focus of operating innovation.

LABS itself was not launched until after a formal process reengineering effort was initiated involving senior operating managers and the CIO in discussions to identify, analyze, and redesign eight core processes. Following redesign of these processes, the LABS program could be architected to provide maximal support for implementation of process innovations. Eaton himself played a key role in the process reengineering stage, greatly facilitating the job of infrastructural design and deployment because of strong linkages to the process reengineering effort.

Systems Redesign at Investors Diversified Services

A similar pattern is playing out at Investors Diversified Services (IDS) in Minneapolis, Minnesota. IDS is a highly successful financial services enterprise that is experiencing rapid growth in its core business. In the early 1990s IDS launched a project to dramatically upgrade its field agents' ability to access corporate information resources and operating systems. This project, called IDS 94, was designed to give its financial planners online access to order entry systems, service offerings, and other corporate resources. The project was designed to provide better sales support and superior provisioning and customer service in the field.

At the time of its initiation, IDS 94 was seen by many members of the organization as just one of many operating initiatives. The architects of the IDS 94 plan, including CEO Jeff Stiefler, viewed this as the first step in a broader program. As the IDS 94 plan coalesced and as pilot projects were initiated, IDS launched a major effort to review its information infrastructure. The resulting Strategic Technology Plan (STP) reviewed IDS's information infrastructure and created a plan for overhauling its entire technology base to support IDS 94 and related reengineering programs.

The STP resulted in an overall architecture that incorporates IDS 94 and other process reengineering initiatives in a common architecture. The CIO of the enterprise, Roger Edgar, focused his efforts on insuring that STP, a long term infrastructural vision for IDS, was closely linked to IDS 94 and other immediate operating initiatives. His goal was to bring STP down from the world of visionary architectural planning to a series of immediate projects necessary to support implementation of current initiatives. Such "projectizing" of the broad infrastructural plan supported immediate implementation of the first stages of the new infrastructure. The successful incorporation of short term initiatives into the long term infrastructural plan helps to ensure the emergence of a common, seamless infrastructure for the enterprise.

Achieving Disciplined Integration

The infrastructural design and deployment stage is the most troublesome of the transformation cycle for many enterprises. This stage requires the first substantial commitment of resources. Many millions of dollars must be committed to upgrading and replacing existing systems and facilities. Perhaps more importantly, the infrastructural deployment stage requires extremely disciplined implementation. Autonomy or decentralized design and deployment of infrastructure will not work against the cross-functional and cross-divisional systems needed to promote transformation. In organizations with a long history of autonomy, it may be difficult or impossible to achieve this level of discipline in the design and deployment of infrastructure.

JOHNSON & JOHNSON

These issues were central to Johnson & Johnson's response to the American Hospital Supply's electronic distribution initiative. Johnson & Johnson had a long history of divisional autonomy, with more then fifty independent business units pursuing their own strategies in the extended health care field. Each unit had its own sales force, customer-service organization, and operating systems.

When American Hospital Supply introduced its electronic procurement and distribution system, it offered a single point of contact with the customer that allowed highly efficient procurement from a single vendor. Johnson & Johnson's corporate culture strongly resisted the deployment of a similar order entry system, citing the long history of success associated with its autonomous divisions. At Johnson & Johnson, resistance to the development of such a system required strong action by CEO James Burke, including the termination of a division head. He personally intervened to insure that divisional managers complied with the corporate initiative to create a common order entry system.

CIO MORTALITY RATE

In other enterprises, divisional autonomy may successfully resist efforts to create a common infrastructure, and, as mentioned earlier, ongoing tensions between current operating requirements and longer-term infrastructural programs can also be crippling. These and other reasons make the CIO's job one of the most difficult in corporate America. CIO mortality is higher then for any other senior corporate position. Many enterprises exhibit turnover in this job every two years or so.

This job is particularly difficult if the CIO has been given a mandate from the CEO to create a modern operating infrastructure without the active involvement of operating executives in design and utilization. Without proper grounding of the infrastructure in operating improvement and innovation initiatives, substantial resource commitment (including key personnel), and active, aggressive support from the CEO in the trench warfare of the typical enterprise, it is difficult to successfully complete this stage of the transformation process.

Phase Four: Business Enhancement

Deployment of the new infrastructure permits implementation of new processes that will yield radical performance gains. At the same time the new infrastructure provides resources that can be utilized in a variety of other initiatives. Creation of a central data base, for example, can support a series of new marketing and customer service initiatives. Common systems yield revenue by supporting joint marketing or cross marketing among divisions. In many corporations the opportunity to bundle products and services, to share distribution channels, and to cross-market offers significant revenue enhancement potential.

The Role of Training: IDS

To realize some of these potential gains, cross training is an important issue at this stage in the transformation cycle. At IDS, the new infrastructure permitted customer-service operations for independent divisions to be consolidated in single offices. Prior to the new program, each major division within IDS had its own customer service unit. Mutual funds, life insurance, and other units all processed customer requests and transactions independently.

With the new infrastructure, a single customer service representative could process any or all of these transactions. Cross training of personnel was impossible prior to implementation of the new infrastructure because of the extreme complexity and incompatibility of existing systems. With the new infrastructure utilizing common modules, utilities, languages, and software, cross training of personnel could be accomplished quickly and efficiently, supporting dramatic gains in operating efficiency and customer service.

The Role of Application Development Tools

Even greater gains can be realized if the new infrastructure provides a series of application development tools and utilities to operating units. This type of opportunity is the focus of a new infrastructure being deployed at TRW Information Systems and Services (TRW ISS), one of the largest information services providers in the consumer credit field. It possesses the largest commercial database in the world, with consumer credit histories for over 150 million Americans. This database can now be accessed online by large customers, but the information infrastructure is approximately twenty years old, with a patchwork of disjointed operating systems.

In 1992, the new CEO, Van Skilling, launched a program to simultaneously improve existing operations and to build a new infrastructure for new business development. The Copernicus program is designed to completely replace the business unit's existing infrastructure, to facilitate widespread access to the database, to permit sharing of resources across the three business units in the group, to allow ISS data to be readily combined with other data resources, and to permit customized utilization of data resources.

Copernicus will facilitate sharing of information between TRW's consumer credit business unit and its business credit unit, for example. This permits the files for a business owner to be merged with those for a small business itself, opening up opportunities for more sophisticated credit analysis and target marketing activity.

The Copernicus infrastructure is also designed to allow integration of TRW's databases with data from other sources both inside and outside the enterprise. This capability will permit the introduction of a series of new service offerings that will generate incremental revenue for the enterprise. At the same time that the Copernicus infrastructure simplifies access to data resources, it provides a series of enabling tools to support development of services and applications. It contains a series of utilities such as a "merge/purge" tool that compares entries in databases to eliminate redundant entries and duplication of mailings, for example.

These and other utilities will be used by applications developers both inside and outside the enterprise to facilitate the introduction of new services and marketing initiatives. The infrastructure contains an application module library so that generic elements can be extracted and incorporated into new applications, speeding the development and introduction of new services. This enabling infrastructure provides a platform for business enhancement and expansion.

For such an infrastructure to be effective, substantial investment in training is essential. At TRW, training was provided through extensive joint training sessions between the information systems unit that was developing the infrastructure and the operating personnel who would use them. The transition from infrastructural design and deployment and operating utilization was also facilitated by senior personnel assignments.

The Copernicus effort was headed by Ann Delligatta, whose previous assignment had been in marketing. Her operating experience helped to ensure that the Copernicus system was practical and accessible for marketing applications. The head of IS at this time was Dennis Benner, whose previous jobs had included business development and line experience. Following the successful launch of Copernicus, he assumed responsibility for new business development. Extensive training and effective personal moves of this sort will help to ensure success in the next stage of transformation at TRW.

Financial Justification of Infrastructural Development

Financial justification is often a significant barrier to successful transformation. The creation of the initial enabling infrastructure is often difficult to justify in terms of immediate financial returns. If the infrastructural deployment can be linked to immediate operating improvements, the burden of financial justification can be reduced. However it is important to consider the potential benefits that can be developed on top of the base infrastructure.

BLUE CROSS: A THREE-YEAR PAYBACK

At Blue Cross of Missouri, Ed Tenholder, CIO, built a network to support a new service called Health Care Interchange. This service connected health care providers to insurance claims payers for claims processing settlement. The service uses software in PCs at health care facilities to allow claims to be entered in a standard format. Claims are then converted to the format of the payer, removing an administrative burden from the health care provider and expediting processing and settlement. This new service has been adopted by over one thousand health care providers in the Missouri area. The initial investment in infrastructure will see payback in less than three years. However, once the infrastructure is in place, a series of new services can be offered, creating additional revenue opportunities.

Linkages to health care providers can be used to provide precertification services. In today's health care market, many insurance carriers require that treatment be certified prior to delivery for payment to be assured. Precertification can be provided and automated over the Healthcare Interchange network. Deductible and copayment requirements on the part of the patients can also be determined in real time, insuring that proper credit and billing procedures have been established prior to delivery of service. The network can also be used to provide diagnostic support, medical records transfer, pharmacy and prescription support, and a series of other new business opportunities. The existence of the base infrastructure will support a series of new business opportunities at Blue Cross.

Similar opportunities exist in all enterprises that deploy state-of-the-art infrastructures. Enterprises facilitate the development of new service offerings by designing infrastructures with:

- rapid applications development tools, such as CASE methodologies, application modules, and data utilities
- a natural language service creation environment
- seamless information mobility
- electronic linkages to third-party resources in addition to traditional suppliers and customers

- multimedia capabilities
- user and customer-friendly interfaces

With characteristics of this sort, reasonable security and compliance procedures, and extensive training of potential users, enterprises may unleash ground swells of service and revenue enhancement initiatives.

ENHANCING PAYBACK AT ROYAL BANK

At Royal Bank, field marketing managers have access to an array of tools and resources that they can use to develop local marketing initiatives. Royal Bank provides an electronic tool kit to its field marketing managers. This tool kit is accessed through a PC with online linkages to bank resources. Marketing managers may access the company's comprehensive customer database to identify specific customers for promoting a new product. They may identify a set of customers in their region who exhibit characteristics found in other regions to react positively to specific types of market initiative, for example. Marketing managers around the country are able to share their experiences with different marketing programs so that others can benefit.

HOW A NEW INFRASTRUCTURE LED TO NEW BUSINESS OPPORTUNITIES AT DASSAULT SYSTEMS

In many enterprises business enhancement through the introduction of new services is a fairly systematic exercise. At Dassault Systems, dozens of new enhanced services are added each year to the CATIA CAD/CAM service. Dassault Systems is a prime example of how an operations improvement effort can take on a life of its own as a new business. In the 1960s, Lockheed applied computer-assisted design tools in its aircraft design and development activities both to increase the efficiency and speed of aircraft design and to improve the engineering precision of advanced aircraft.

The application of these new technologies and the reengineering of the aircraft design function made a significant contribution to Lockheed's success in the aerospace sector. As we have seen in other examples, the new infrastructure developed to support CAD/CAM at Lockheed took on a life of its own as a stand-alone business unit.[7] Lockheed created a new business unit, CADAM, to sell these advanced engineering services to other enterprises. CADAM was later acquired by IBM, which partnered with Dassault Aerospace in France to further develop the capabilities of the system.

Dassault then acquired CADAM in its entirety from IBM and established a new business unit, Dassault Systems, to exploit this product line. Dassault's principal CAD/CAM tool is called CATIA. In 1992, Dassault Systems introduced thirty-four new enhanced service modules on top of its existing CATIA platforms. These new service modules included applications such as simulation, materials selection, robotics, machine tool automation, 3D visual presentation, architectural drafting, terrain modeling, and photogrammetric data conversion for turning aerial photographs into 3-D CAD models. The CATIA system has become a vehicle for customer application development as well. Customers may develop custom applications on the CATIA platform and use them internally or allow them to be sold as part of the extended services portfolio.

When a service like CATIA becomes an open platform, it permits not only internal development of new features and functions but an opportunity for customers and third parties to introduce value-added enhancements to the extended product family. Such enhancements not only allow the package to provide a wider range of service to existing customers but often open up new market segments and applications that can grow into stand-alone businesses in their own right. In addition, the opportunity for customers to resell their own custom applications to other users enhances the value of their relationship with the primary product vendor. Such opportunities allow customers to recoup some of their investments in custom application development and, in turn, to accomplish more with a fixed development budget.

VON'S GROCERY STORES

Creative use of the existing infrastructure can lead to substantial new business opportunities. Von's Grocery Store was one of the earlier adopters of POS scanning technology in its Southern California chain. Scanning technologies were introduced principally to reduce labor cost. Scanning significantly reduces cashier and bagger labor requirements, as well as the cost of pricing items on shelves. Scanning offers a series of other operating advantages, such as more efficient inventory management, optimization of shelf space usage, greater accuracy, more timely information, and more sophisticated marketing and promotion activities. Von's realized a series of such operating gains from the introduction of its POS scanning technology.

At about the same time, to facilitate check-out and to provide differentiated customer service, Von's created a second key infrastructure called VonsCheck. This service provides validation for check cashing. A card reader scans the customer's ID and provides approval for check cashing privileges at the counter, radically reducing the traditional check approval process that required managerial approval for individual checks.

The combination of POS scanning and online customer identification technologies provided an unintended platform for the development of a powerful new service. In the late 1980s Von's introduced its Von's Club service. Customers complete an application and receive a plastic card identifying them as members of the Von's Club. At the check-out counter, customers slide their cards through the card reader and are given automatic price discounts on selected merchandise promoted throughout the store. Von's Club members also enjoy a frequent buyer program that allows them to accumulate points toward free prizes. The cashier's receipt highlights the amount of money the customer has saved on that day's transaction and for the year to date.

Von's Club has been a significant marketing success, allowing Von's to differentiate itself relative to its competitors. It also provides a vehicle for target marketing activity. Von's can utilize the data generated by the Von's Club system to support sophisticated micromarketing activities at the level of individual customers. The use of these capabilities by Von's marketing and business development personnel can dramatically enhance its retail business and lead to the creation of new business units. It will allow Von's to deepen and strengthen ties with existing customers by better understanding their buying patterns and needs and to enter new lines of business.

Von's has long been selling its primary POS data to market research firms. In fact, revenue from such sales has totaled a quarter or more of the company's IS budget. Now, with customer identity in addition to product sales data, Von's has established a new subsidiary, Von's Direct Marketing, to provide support to market research and consumer product companies. This unit accounted for a significant portion of Von's total profit in 1994.

In the business enhancement phase, the critical issues are creative identification and aggressive pursuit of opportunities by marketing, product management, business development, and other personnel. For this potential to be maximized, the new infrastructure must be utilized by all operating and business development units. It is also helpful if a series of application development modules and tools are available as well. With such tools, the new infrastructure enables business enhancement and innovation. In that respect, the new infrastructure supports and permits greater empowerment within the organization. Ironically, such empowerment is possible only if tremendous discipline is applied to creating a common infrastructure in the earlier stages of transformation.

Phase Five: Strategy and Organization Redefinition

The successful pursuit of new service and business opportunities will lead to new service offerings, expanded scope of market coverage, new capabilities, new customers, and new relationships with existing customers. Business enhancement will broaden the firm's business profile and portfolio, altering the firm's strategic position without the direction, or even the knowledge, of senior management. The scope of the firm's activities and its capabilities can grow dramatically during phase five. At some point, expansion in these areas must be recognized and addressed in the firm's formal strategy and organization.

Progressive Insurance

At Progressive Insurance, the introduction of the Immediate Response Service opened a range of new business opportunities. The firm could pursue third-party claims processing, for example. The extraordinary levels of customer satisfaction achieved as a result of the Immediate Response Service could provide a platform for new strategy thrusts in several directions. Progressive could use its differentiated service to move from niche auto insurance markets into the mainstream of the auto insurance industry.

During 1992, in fact, Progressive doubled the number of standard auto insurance policies on its books. Heightened customer satisfaction could also allow Progressive to shift from being a specialty auto insurance provider to a full-line provider of insurance and financial services, a pathway followed by USAA over the course of the past several decades. USAA migrated from being an auto insurance firm to a full provider of insurance services, based on high levels of customer satisfaction achieved with its existing customer base.

Progressive could also utilize the infrastructure deployed in support of the Immediate Response System to provide a roadside assistance service to its customers, opening up another array of new business opportunities. These and other strategy options appeared as unexpected consequences of an operating improvement and innovation exercise. Progressive must now formally identify and address those strategy options, recreate or reconfirm its strategic thrust, and make appropriate organizational adjustments.

In many enterprises the strategy and organizational adjustments result principally in the creation of new business units. At Von's, Von's Direct Marketing became the vehicle for the new services and capabilities created in the course of its transformation program. In the best known example of this phenomenon, American Airlines created a new unit, AMRIS, to capitalize on the infrastructure and capabilities that developed around the SABRE system. Such new business units can grow to rival or even surpass the primary core business. AMRIS already accounts for a majority of profits and market value for American Airlines.

France Telecom

In some cases, this phase may involve redefinition of the core business, rather than the creation of a new business unit. At France Telecom, the Minitel initiative has led to a substantial shift in the telephone company's core business strategy. The Minitel infrastructure was introduced in the early 1980s to solve an immediate operating problem and provide a platform for business enhancement. Rapid growth in the subscriber base in the late 1970s and the early 1980s created substantial pressures on the directory assistance function at France Telecom. With millions of new subscribers each year, the average response time for directory assistance exceeded fifteen minutes in 1980. Customer dissatisfaction was not the only problem.

France Telecom operates on a local measured service billing basis; i.e., each local or long distance call generates incremental revenue. A variety of solutions were attempted, but ultimately France Telecom introduced its Minitel system. Minitel is based on a national packet switching network that allows consumers to utilize free terminals to directly access a central directory data base without the assistance of human operators. In 1992, these terminals accounted for over 800 million, or 80%, of total directory requests. Usage of the Minitel system for directory assistance purposes results in net savings in operator staffing and directory publishing and printing costs of $80–$90 million per year.

Unfortunately, the infrastructure for this system required an initial investment in excess of $2 billion. From the beginning, however, the architects of this program envisioned it as not only a solution to an immediate operating problem but a platform for business enhancement. Today more than twenty thousand enhanced services are available over the Minitel system,[8] including a wide variety of financial, shopping, education, and other information services.

France Telecom has created several new business units to capitalize on the capabilities of this system. One unit, IntelMatique, offers videotex hardware, software systems, and expertise to other carriers around the world. Another unit exports information services to foreign users, and a third is creating a global electronic directory data base. The most significant impact of this program, however, may be its effect on France Telecom's core business. It no longer considers itself a provider of voice telephony but as an information services provider. Its shift in focus from carriage to content positions it as a leader in the emerging information economy.

This phase of the transformation exercise focuses essentially on identification and capitalization of opportunities created in the course of the transformation program. Without creative activity in the business enhancement stage and visionary leadership in this phase, the latent potential of business transformation may not be realized. Many firms view services and capabilities developed in the course of these programs as proprietary assets created to support the existing core business. There is a "Cinderella" phenomenon at work here. Such systems are viewed exclusively as internal support mechanisms for the core business, and the full potential of these activities will not be realized. Formal recognition of these new opportunities, through redefinition of core business strategies or the creation of new business units, is the key task of this stage.

Phase Six: Operating Initiative

Phases five and six bring the transformation process full cycle as many of the issues addressed in these stages are somewhat similar to those addressed in stages one and two. The principal difference is that the transformation process is likely to have been triggered by threat and crisis, while phase six is triggered principally by the pursuit of opportunity. Nonetheless, it is imperative that the CEO create a second vision during this period. The new vision, in contrast to the first phase focus, is principally concerned with identifying external opportunities and the vision of a new business profile for the enterprise.

Whether the new vision involves redefinition of the core business strategy or creation of a new business unit, a new operating infrastructure must be established to support the new strategy. That responsibility rests principally on venture management in the case of new business units. The responsibility comes full cycle to the COO or a surrogate in the case of a new core business strategy.

By this stage of the exercise, it is likely that sufficient momentum has been created to overcome most barriers and uncertainties. This may also be an ideal time for senior management succession. The architects of the original strategy may wish to turn over the reins of the enterprise to a new team of executives who can carry through the new transformation cycle to its conclusion. The logic for management succession rests partially on the length of time required to implement successful transformation programs. The first three phases of this exercise alone require at least three to five years for completion. The business enhancement stage could last a substantial term as well, especially with periodic upgrading of infrastructural elements. An appropriate question is whether any manager or management team can successfully complete two full transformation cycles.

Summary

Successful transformation requires an orchestrated plan with structured roles and responsibilities that address specific tasks and issues in each stage of the process. In each stage there are distinct leadership requirements. In the first stage the CEO plays the primary role of program champion and architect. Leadership passes to the COO or a surrogate in the operating improvement and innovation stage. The CIO plays a critical role in phase three. Business enhancement activity can be driven by a more diverse and distributed team of leaders, while strategy and organizational redefinition return the focus to the office of the chief executive. Experience has shown that sustained involvement and committed teamwork by the senior executives are required across all six stages.

An overview of the key tasks and roles in each of the six stages of transformation is shown in Table 11.1. This framework provides the first level of detail in providing a structured methodology for the successful implementation of transformation initiatives. Design of reengineering and transformation initiatives to perform these key roles and address these key tasks will insure that firms maximize their return on investment in reengineering activity. Failure to fill the different leadership roles in each stage has resulted in delay and gridlock, reinforced internal resistance and inertia, and compromised results.

In each stage, a series of key tasks must be addressed. In phase one, critical tasks include creating and communicating a compelling vision that addresses external thrusts while setting new performance targets in a positive vision of the future enterprise. The CEO can leverage a real or perceived crisis at this stage. The CEO must also engage key executives and create a plan and architecture for the transformation effort.

In phase two critical responsibilities include the detailed design and implementation of process improvement and innovation efforts, integration of divisional and functional initiatives, alignment of immediate operating initiatives with the long-term transformation program, appropriate resource allocation, and prioritization. Positioning and structuring empowerment is

TABLE 11.1. Key Tasks and Roles in the Transformation Cycle

			Phase			
	I	*II*	*III*	*IV*	*V*	*VI*
Focus	Strategy initiative	Operating improvements and innovation	Infrastructural design and deployment	Business enhancement	Strategy and organizational redefinition	Operating initiative
Key tasks	Vision, engage executives' set program architecture	Process management transfunctionality	Architecture, management, prioritization	Empowerment, innovation	Exploit new competency	Launch new ventures, restructure core competency
Key roles	CEO	COO, process owners	CIO	Business development, marketing	CEO	Venture management, COO

a crucial role of the CEO at this stage, as is managing the portfolio of change activities. The CIO should, of course, be heavily involved in the process reengineering stage so that an information infrastructure can be created to best support new process models. Line executives must assume process ownership responsibilities at this stage.

The key tasks in phase three include the design and implementation of an enterprisewide infrastructure, enforcement of architectural guidelines, training of potential users, and creation of tools and utilities for business enhancements. Throughout phase three the CEO will be challenged to maintain and prioritize the investments in resources and technology to build the infrastructure.

Key tasks in phase four include empowerment of creative marketing and customer-service activity by a variety of personnel within the enterprise, support and reward for innovation, and maximized use of internal resources to support business and market expansion. In this stage the CEO should be encouraging business units to envision and capture opportunities enabled by the infrastructure. In phase five, the CEO must incorporate successfully developing opportunities into new business strategies and direction for the enterprise, leading to a new vision and new ventures in phase six.

Clearly, transformation represents a continuum of change for which alignment of the executives, priorities, and resources is crucial. Transformation must be planned, architectured, and led through all stages of change. The CEO and key senior executives have to be involved conceptually from the beginning and consistently demonstrate the commitment, will, and customer focus required to stimulate and support the organization throughout the lengthy effort.

Notes

1. Thomas Teal, "Service Comes First," *Harvard Business Review* (September–October 1991): 117–128.
2. W. H. Davidson, "Small Group Activity at Musashi Semiconductor Works," *Sloan Management Review* 23:3 (Spring, 1982): 3–14.
3. Thomas Davenport, *Process Innovation* (Boston: Harvard Business School Press, 1992).
4. C. J. Morrison, E. R. Berndt, "Assessing the Productivity of Information Technology Equipment in U.S. Manufacturing," (Cambridge, MA: National Bureau of Economic Research, working page number 3580, 1991); S. S. Roach, "Amer-

ica's Technologies Dilemma," (New York: Morgan Stanley Special Economic Study, April 23, 1987).

5. J. Henderson, N. Venkatraman, "Strategic Alignment," *IBM Systems Journal*, 32: 1 (1993): 4–15.

6. MHT Worldwide Network, Harvard Business School Case Study 9-185-018.

7. W. H. Davidson, "Beyond Reengineering: The Three Stages of Business Transformation," *IBM Systems Journal*, 32:1 (1993): 65–80.

8. T. Housel, W. Davidson, "The Development of Information Services in France: The Case of Public Videotex," *International Journal of Information Management* (1991): 35–54.

V

IT Infrastructure and Processes

12

IT Value and the Role of IT Infrastructure Investments

PETER WEILL, MARIANNE BROADBENT, and

DONALD R. ST.CLAIR

Chapter Summary

1. This chapter contends that a company's IT infrastructure (as defined in the Glossary in the Appendix), can be its largest, and most unique long-term source of strategic advantage. Constructing and managing infrastructure is one of the most important (and perhaps only) tasks for the corporate IT group.

2. IT infrastructure lies at the base of the IT investment pyramid, and at the heart of a firm's ability to provide IT capability. It can be sub-divided into three components: (a) the hardware—computers and communications technologies; (b) the network services—universal file access, EDI etc and (c) the human infrastructure of knowledge, skills and experience.

3. Corporate IT infrastructures are organized in many different ways reflecting the 'reach and range' vision of the business managers. For example, who needs to receive what information, how quickly, and where. In today's business climate those visions are constantly changing, and this presents a real challenge to IT specialists to create a modular process architecture that can be adopted as required.

4. Understanding infrastructure in this way gives a helpful perspective on ownership. In many ways an IT infrastructure is like a country's infrastructure, providing services of benefit to the whole community. Many carefully conducted studies have shown that judicious investment in public infrastructure stimulates the private sector

economy, and by analogy the same should be true for IT infrastructures.

5. Achieving the right level of investment in IT infrastructure is therefore critical for future success. Three models are suggested which might represent appropriate strategies for firms with different visions of the role IT plays in their companies, which the authors call: (a) utility; (b) dependent; (c) enabling.

6. A utility infrastructure is, as its name suggests, a no-frills service, driven by cost considerations. Dependent infrastructures are driven by requirements of the current strategy. Enabling infrastructures are the most flexible, created with a view to providing a resource to enable fast response to changes in the marketplace.

7. The authors observe that non-alignment between IT and business strategy is the natural state of most firms. The detailed case studies here show how firms have strived to achieve alignment between IT infrastructure and business strategy, Luftmans' IT infrastructure fusion and business strategy fusion described in Chapter 3.

8. One view of infrastructure is not better than the other. The key factor is the strategic context of the firm, indicating how it wishes to compete in its industry. An appropriate vie of infrastructure must be taken for the strategic intent. That appropriate view could be: Utility, Dependent, or Enabling.

The Importance of IT Infrastructure

The purpose of this chapter is to explain the role of IT infrastructure in business strategy through comparing the experiences of three different firms. The chapter draws on international research into the role and payoff of IT infrastructural investments (sponsored by the IBM Consulting Group), conducted in forty large for-profit firms. The experiences of the firms in the study indicate that IT infrastructure, as described in Chapter 2 and Chapter 3, is a critical component to achieve strategic alignment.

IT investment is highly visible in modern organizations. Appropriate investment can add value to a firm in many ways and over differing time periods. Among the IT capabilities required, the IT infrastructure is the largest contributor to long-term strategic business advantage.

The increasing importance of the international business environment and the rise of networked organizations have led to three critical shifts in the application of IT within organizations: a move toward work-group computing, a preference for integrated systems, and a move from internal to interenterprise computing.[1] These developments, together with the pressure on firms to be flexible and responsive, require a purposeful approach to the organization's IT infrastructure.

The role of corporate IT groups is also changing as spending on IT has been dispersed throughout the firm. Perhaps the only role for the corporate IT group in the newly decentralized environment is to provide the IT infrastructure as an enabling base for the business units.[2]

IS managers are becoming increasingly aware of their new role as builders of IT infrastructures. An annual survey of IS executives who are members of the Society of Information Management (SIM)[3] identified building IT infrastructure as sixth in importance and highlighted it as the only new issue in the top ten issues raised in the survey. Development and implementation of IT infrastructure was identified in another study[4] as the most important technological issue for Australasian IS executives. The challenge is to provide a flexible infrastructure at low cost, which is continually evaluated and updated with emerging new technologies.

IT Infrastructure and Strategic Alignment

Strategic alignment requires planned and purposeful management processes within both business and IS disciplines and is short-lived in nature.[5] Nonalignment is the natural state of firms. The achievement of strategic alignment requires a process of continuous adaptation and change[6] in light of strategic intent and current business strategies. Strategic alignment operates at both firm and business unit levels.

The IT portfolio of large firms consists of a myriad of information systems and technologies. Some of this investment is infrastructural, long-term, and focused on achieving the firm's strategic intent. Other investments are aimed at the more immediate and direct benefits allied to executing current business strategies. All investments in IT are not alike, and it is helpful to distinguish between the different management objectives.

Firms invest in IT to achieve four fundamentally different management objectives: strategic, informational, transactional, and infrastructural. These types of IT make up the IT investment pyramid.[7] Figure 12.1 depicts these different objectives and their relationships.

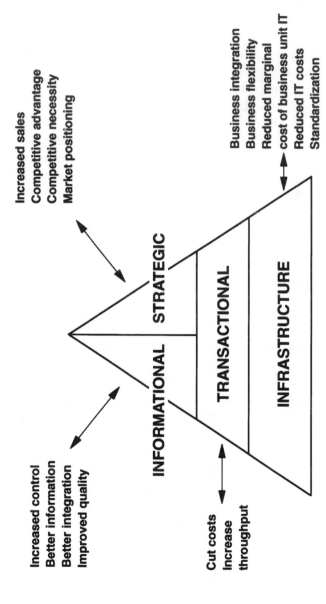

Figure 12.1. Management Objectives for IT

IT Infrastructure

At the base of the IT investment pyramid is the IT infrastructure. IT infrastructure is the base foundation of IT capability in the form of reliable services shared throughout the firm and (usually) provided by the IS function. The IT capability includes both the technical and managerial expertise required to provide reliable services. For example, IT infrastructural services in a firm might include firmwide communication network services, management and provision of large-scale computing, universal file access, management of shared databases, and research and development expertise aimed at identifying the application of emerging technologies to the business. The IT investments which use and sit on top of the infrastructure are the applications which actually perform the business processes.

Transactional IT

The next level of the pyramid is the transactional IT that processes the basic, repetitive, transactions of the firm. This includes systems which support order processing, inventory control, receivables, payables, and other transactional processing. Transactional systems are developed to cut costs, often by substituting capital for labor, or to make it possible to handle higher volumes of transactions. Transactional systems build and depend on the IT infrastructure being in place and reliable.

The apex of the pyramid contains both the informational and strategic uses of IT, which depend on, and are supported by, the infrastructural and the transactional systems. Usually, both infrastructural and transactional systems must be in place before informational or strategic systems are feasible.

Informational IT

Informational IT provides the information for managing and controlling the organization. Systems in this category typically support management control, planning, communications, and accounting. Data for the informational systems come from summaries of the transactional systems and from data on the industry, competitors, and economy external to the firm.

Strategic IT

The objective of strategic IT investments is quite different. Strategic investments in IT are made to gain competitive advantage or to position the firm in the marketplace, most often by increasing market share or sales. Firms with successful strategic IT initiatives usually involve a new use of IT for an industry at a particular point in time (e.g., the first finance company to provide online twenty-four-hour, seven-day-a-week loan approvals in car yards using expert systems technology).

The nature and extent of IT investment for each of these management objectives is determined by the firm's strategic context—i.e., the firm's strategic intent and current business strategies. It is the longer-term component of the strategic context which must drive IT infrastructural investment decisions. IT infrastructure aims to provide the components and services to achieve strategic intent via any number of current business strategies which are consistent with that strategic intent. These current strategies might be unspecified even as the infrastructure is developed.

The strategic intent and current strategy, in combination, drive the other IT investments in the pyramid. Transactional, informational, and strategic systems are likely to evolve with changes in current business strategies. These three types of system can be conceived of as tailored investments to deliver business functionally built on a solid base of IT infrastructure.

Case Study Comparison

The two firms in Figure 12.2 demonstrate the use of the pyramid to assess the alignment of the IT portfolio with the strategic context. Both are single business unit firms and have strong alignment of their IT portfolios with business strategy. The cabinet manufacturer has a strong growth strategy and values flexibility. This is reflected in its IT portfolio with a flexible and extensive national infrastructure and applications which position the firm in the marketplace. The car rental firm has a low-cost, no-frills strategy and a limited, inflexible infrastructure, which supports applications for processing transactions and providing cost and control information. If either firm had the IT portfolio of the other, a poor alignment between IT and strategy would result.

Business Benefits from IT Infrastructure

IT infrastructural investments are typically large, long-term in nature, and underpin the future competitiveness of firms. These investments often have to be made in anticipation of business developments. Returns on infrastructural investments, in terms of business results, are difficult to track directly. IT infrastructural investments typically do not necessarily provide

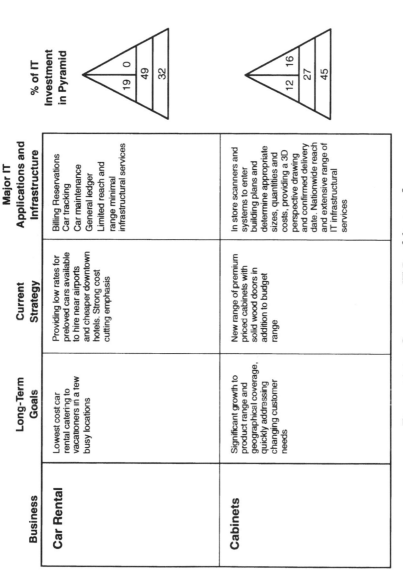

Business	Long-Term Goals	Current Strategy	Major IT Applications and Infrastructure	% of IT Investment in Pyramid
Car Rental	Lowest cost car rental catering to vacationers in a few busy locations	Providing low rates for preloved cars available to hire near airports and cheaper downtown hotels. Strong cost cutting emphasis	Billing Reservations Car tracking Car maintenance General ledger Limited reach and range minimal infrastructural services	19 / 0 / 49 / 32
Cabinets	Significant growth to product range and geographical coverage, quickly addressing changing customer needs	New range of premium priced cabinets with solid wood doors in addition to budget range	In store scanners and systems to enter building plans and determine appropriate sizes, quantities and costs, providing a 3D perspective drawing and confirmed delivery date. Nationwide reach and extensive range of IT infrastructural services	12 / 16 / 27 / 45

Figure 12.2. Comparing IT Portfolio into firms

direct business performance benefits. Benefits are realized by business systems connected to, and enabled by, the infrastructure. However, a highly flexible IT infrastructure can provide direct benefits by enabling economical or rapid implementation of other systems in the pyramid, enabling fast time to market for products or services.

Elements of IT Infrastructure

The elements of IT infrastructure depicted in Figure 12.3 are based on a model from McKay and Brockaway.[9] At the base are the IT components (e.g., computer and communication technologies), which are commodities and readily available in the marketplace. The layer above is a set of shared IT services such as universal file access, EDI, or a full-service network. The IT components are converted into useful IT services by the human IT infrastructure and can then be used as building blocks for business systems. The human IT infrastructure of knowledge, skills, and experience binds the IT components into reliable services, which form the firm's IT infrastructure.

The base of the pyramid in Figure 12.3 contains both the services and the components of the firm's IT infrastructure. The infrastructural set of services is relatively stable over time. Similar services are required from year to year, with gradual improvements over time taking advantage of the new technologies and efficiencies.

The IT for business processes, however, is changed regularly to meet the needs of the current strategy. Often, these changes occur on a yearly basis as business processes are changed to better serve customers.

The objective of the firm's infrastructure is to provide a stable base of reliable services to enable the IT for the business processes to be easily connected and changed.

Who Should "Own" the Infrastructure?

Infrastructures are usually provided at both the corporate and business unit levels. The business unit infrastructure is more tailored to the particular needs of the business unit and connects in a "plug compatible" way to the corporate infrastructure. Some firms have very little corporate IT infrastructure, while others have little or no business unit infrastructure, sharing instead the centrally provided infrastructural services.

Johnson & Johnson Pacific provides an example of infrastructure that

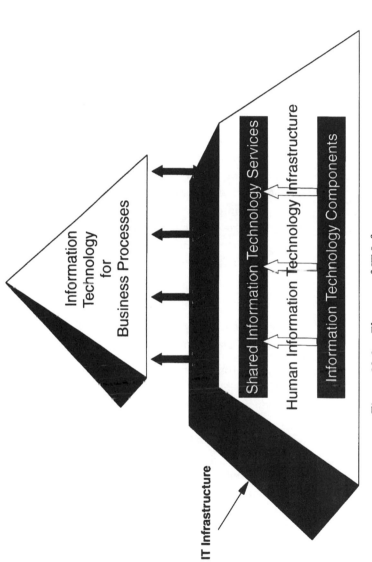

Figure 12.3. Elements of IT Infrastructure

is predominantly corporate. This health care company, headquartered in Sydney, Australia, has two business units. The consumer unit markets and sells the full range of products to distributors, wholesalers, and large retailers. The commercial unit sells non-woven fabric and sun protection products to distributors. Johnson & Johnson IT infrastructural services include:

- corporate telecommunications network, including EDI linkages to clients; large-scale computing services, including a support facility
- electronic mail facilities for local and off-shore communications
- corporate shared application systems, such as the general ledger, manufacturing systems, and the consolidated customer file

The Corporate Information Services Department provides these IT infrastructural services on an AS/400 computer and electronic mail on a Digital VAX computer. These computers are connected via an Ethernet link. Information processing of corporate data is centralized.

Business unit–specific systems, such as sales and retail data, are processed by the Corporate Information Services Department but owned by the business units.

Applying "Reach" and "Range" to IT Infrastructure

The dimensions of the IT infrastructure can be specified in terms of the reach and range,[10] described by Keen in Chapter 6, provided by a firm's infrastructure. *Reach* indicates the extent of locations which can be linked. A firm with a limited reach might be able to link its employees only in a single location, while a firm with extensive reach could link customers or suppliers regardless of their IT base. *Range* refers to the richness of the services provided. This determines the breadth of functionality that can be directly and seamlessly shared across the systems and services. Infrastructure with a limited range would provide the ability to send only standard messages. A more extensive range would provide the capability to perform multiple transactions, which simultaneously updated data bases. The combination of the readily available reach and range is useful in depicting the dimensions of the firm's IT infrastructure.

The extent to which an organization has an appropriate IT infrastructure in place determines its business "degrees of freedom." [13] Having the appropriate technological platform and service set enables other business systems to be produced. This base capability provides improved flexibility and widens the variety of clients or products a firm can handle without increased costs.[12] A comprehensive IT infrastructure provides flexibility in meeting the incipient trends of the marketplace. For example, Otis Elevators revolutionized the service side of the elevator industry with its highly acclaimed computer-based customer-service system "Otisline." [13] Otis Elevators was able to produce Otisline at least four years faster because of the existence of an IT infrastructure including a flexible data base named the Service Management System (SMS).

When the database was first installed, Otisline had not been conceived. Sufficient flexibility was incorporated into the design to enable the production of Otisline in a much shorter time than it would have taken to start from scratch. Valuing the infrastructure before Otisline would have been very difficult. However, the value of the flexibility of the investment is clear in hindsight. The four-year break on the competition was a significant advantage in the marketplace.

Building in flexibility, such as the SMS database at Otis, adds cost and complexity but provides a business option that may be exercised in the future.[14] Otis exercised its option and added the application systems supporting Otisline, generating significant business benefits to the company.

An IT infrastructure of greater reach and range, beyond what is currently required by the business units, provides a flexibility or slack for future needs. Flexibility allows far more rapid response to an emerging business need. One reason firms invest in infrastructure is to buy flexibility.

Thus, the IT infrastructure is a major business resource and perhaps one of the few sources of a long-term competitive advantage.[15] Good infrastructure is not a commodity and is, thus, difficult to duplicate. The human IT infrastructure of knowledge and skills and the IT management vision provide much of the value of IT infrastructure.

Public Infrastructure Analogy

An interesting and useful analogy to help understand the benefits of IT infrastructure is comparing it to public infrastructures such as roads, bridges, sewers, hospitals, schools, and public buildings. While investigating the role of IT infrastructure, Keen studied the development of the railroads in the United States and pointed out the difficulty in directly measuring the business value of the railroads. The business value of applications enabled by the railways is clear: freshness of vegetables, improved production time of newspapers, reduced travel time to market, etc.

The same argument can be made for IT infrastructure.[16] Both infrastructures are relatively large investments with long lives. Both are believed to add to the community in ways that could not be achieved through end-user or private investment. Understanding more about the role and value of public infrastructure is very helpful in understanding the role of IT infrastructure.

National Infrastructure

There have been a number of very careful economic studies of the value of public infrastructure. At the international level, a strong indicator is the relationship between public infrastructural investment (as a percentage of gross domestic product) and the annual growth of labor productivity. A simple regression of these two indicators, for the "G7" countries, indicates a strong relationship. Countries with higher public infrastructural investment have higher productivity. During the period from 1973 to 1985, Japan had both the highest public infrastructural investment and labor productivity while the United States had the lowest of the seven countries on both of these measures.

The rationale for public infrastructural investment is that these services will not be produced by the private market.[19] Private corporations and individuals generally are not motivated or able to provide their own infrastructure, particularly when the infrastructure must exist in other regions. The condition of the infrastructure can be as important as its existence. A highway in poor condition can reduce the productivity of private capital and labor in the form of added time for journeys and wear and tear on vehicles. Maintenance as well as initial capital investment are also critical for infrastructure.

Regional Infrastructure

At the state and regional levels the evidence is equally strong. Munnell[19] studied the differences between regions in the United States. There was overwhelming evidence that public capital has a positive impact on private sector output, investment, and employment. Estimating the size of the effect, Munnell reports that a $1,000 investment of infrastructure per capita resulted in a 0.2% increase in annual employment growth. It is not surprising that the state which goes to the trouble of building roads, sewers, airports, water supply systems, hospitals, and schools will attract more new firms. Thus, public infrastructure matters in firm location decisions and affects employment growth.

Interestingly, the positive effects of public infrastructure are most pronounced in declining regions.[20] Policies can target particular industries, which benefit, and then pass on the savings to the general community. The U.S. federal-aid highway infrastructural investments between 1950 and 1973 had a strong and positive effect on the productivity of trucking.[21] Fierce competition in the industry ensured that these benefits would be passed on to the economy. The benefits of infrastructure are not without limits. Too much infrastructure will deter private investment, and balance and timing are critical.

Comparing Public Infrastructure and IT Infrastructure

The analogy between public infrastructure and IT infrastructure is compelling. There are striking similarities:

1. Both IT and public infrastructure are provided by a central agency funded by some form of taxation.

2. Both types of infrastructure require large investments and are long-term in nature.

3. The central agency in both cases provides an essential service that users would generally not be motivated or able to provide.

4. Both types of infrastructure enable business activity otherwise not economically possible for users.

5. Both types of infrastructure often must be in place before the precise business activity is known. Thus, flexibility is valued in both types of infrastructure.

6. Both types of infrastructure are difficult to cost justify in advance, and it is difficult to show the benefits of each in hindsight.

7. The right amount of investment is a delicate balance for both types of infrastructure. Too little will lead to duplication, incompatibility, and nonoptimal use of resources. Too much will discourage user investment and involvement and may result in unused capacity.

Given the similarities of the two types of infrastructure it is reasonable to expect that many of the benefits demonstrated from public infrastructure can accrue to IT infrastructure. By analogy, it is reasonable to expect that IT infrastructure will improve productivity of user groups, leverage user groups' own IT investment, and enable new business needs to be met more

View of Infrastructure	Primary Value Driver
UTILITY	Cost savings via economies of scale
DEPENDENT	Business benefits for the life of the current strategy
ENABLING	Current and future flexibility

Figure 12.4.   Infrastructure Types and Values Drives

rapidly. What firms expect to get from their IT infrastructural investments depends on their views of the role of IT infrastructure.

The Role of IT Infrastructure

Three different views of IT infrastructure have been observed[22] utility, dependent, and enabling. Figure 12.4 depicts the three views of infrastructure and their primary value-drivers. We describe each of these views and then present case vignettes which illustrate them.

Utility View

The utility view implies that expenditure on infrastructure is seen primarily as a way of saving costs through economies of scale. IT is not seen as a strategic resource but rather as a utility that incurs administrative expenses. It provides a necessary and unavoidable service. The management thrust is to minimize the expense for a desired level of utility service.

Dependent View

The dependent view implies that the infrastructural investments are primarily in response to particular, current strategies. Dependent infrastructural investments are derived from business plans, and thus planning for infrastructure is undertaken after current business strategies have been articulated. This view is consistent with the IT infrastructure fusion perspective described by Luftman. For example, a bank might invest heavily by consolidating previously independent databases into an integrated customer relationship database. This infrastructural investment is dependent on a current strategy of differentiating customer service through relationship banking.

Enabling View

The enabling view implies that infrastructural investments relate primarily to long-term requirements for flexibility to achieve strategic intent. These are often created by expanding the reach and/or range of dependent infrastructure beyond the current requirements of the business.

The resulting infrastructure enables new and as yet unspecified business strategies to achieve the strategic intent. It provides future options for implementing strategies. The flexibility of the infrastructure enables a number of as yet unspecified strategies to be implemented more rapidly than firms with a dependent or utility view of infrastructure. To take an enabling view, senior managers must perceive a flexible infrastructure as an asset of the firm, providing a competitive advantage. This view also implies that the firm values this flexible asset during the project justification process.

Where greater flexibility and business "degrees of freedom" are part of the firm's strategic intent, an enabling, rather than a utility, view of the role of infrastructure provides a higher level of alignment between IT and business strategy. Alignment between firmwide strategic context and an appropriate role for IT infrastructure is achieved through distillation of the implications of strategic intent for long-term IT management decisions on providing information support.

Case Studies

Utility View of Infrastructure—Chemico

Chemico is a leading supplier of industrial and speciality chemicals. Chemico's employees are spread over eighty locations in the Pacific Basin, and total sales for 1993 were over U.S. $1 billion. Chemico is a divisionalized firm with several business units. Each unit develops and manufactures distinct products and serves largely different markets. We examined the Advanced Technology and Chemicals business units.

Chemico aims to be the undisputed supplier of choice for chemicals and related products and services in the market it serves. The company is intent on developing a culture where continuous improvement is sought in all areas to achieve world-class customer service and product quality.

The guiding business principles for the development of IT infrastructure which emerge from Chemico's strategic context seek to reduce costs, support the information-intensive business improvement program, and enable the firm to maintain high standards of customer service and product quality. There is decentralized responsibility for IS functions in Chemico. Business units have full autonomy in the way they manage their IT but are encouraged to seek advice from the corporate IS group and to conform to corporate standards. Chemico has a corporatewide architectural policy which includes telecommunications, preferred suppliers (IBM or DEC), workstation guidelines (IBM PS2), electronic mail, and general ledger controls. Opportunities exist to move outside of these standards with the completion of an exception request, which must be justified on business grounds.

The corporate IS group provides communication services (through a communications network) and processing services (mainframe processing) for all Chemico units. The business units then determine which services they wish to access, usually on a unit charge basis. Use of IT infrastructural services varies considerably among the units. For example, Advanced Technologies controls about 95% of the infrastructure used within that unit and locally supplies processing services using three AS400 IBM computers. All data for the business unit are stored in this system, and only data required for corporate reporting purposes are transferred to the corporate processor.

The Chemicals unit, in contrast, has virtually no local infrastructure and relies almost solely on the corporate IS group for the development, management, and operation of its business systems. Both business units make extensive use of Chemico's firm-wide communications network.

Chemico has a utility view of infrastructure and is heading toward a dependent view. IT planning and development processes are undertaken following from the business strategy. Planning for corporate IT infrastructure takes place with input from the IT managers in each of the business units. The IT managers' estimations of future IT needs of the businesses are used to predict corporate infrastructural requirements. Tracking of the usage of infrastructural services is an important component of the IT infrastructural investment decision. In addition, IT infrastructure is primarily viewed as a utility providing the base IS services at minimum cost. IT requirements are determined in consultation with the business managers to ensure that the strategic needs of the business are being met. This view is consistant with the service level perspective described in Chapter 2 and Chapter 3.

The past five years have seen a major push toward decentralization of management and control within Chemico. IT management has moved from being a centralized function to an activity for which the business units can take total responsibility if they so choose. However, there has recently been recognition of the need for some form of coordination to maximize resources and reduce duplication. An IT council has recently been established, with a major objective to set standards for further direction and strategy. While this may reduce some of the autonomy enjoyed under the present system, it is designed to introduce a more cohesive approach to IT management across the firm.

Dependent View of Infrastructure—Petromark

Petromark is a major manufacturer and marketer of petroleum products to retail and commercial customers. Petromark also has in excess of 15% of the Australian domestic market, revenue in 1993 was well over Australian $1 billion, and it employs over fifteen hundred people. Petromark seeks to "make our customers prefer us to any competing company" and be the most successful downstream oil company in Australia. Success is measured as return on assets.

Petromark's steady financial position has been achieved through a continuing focus on minimizing costs and maximizing operational efficiencies and customer service. In a commoditized industry, Petromark presents a strong corporate image of a quality provider of petroleum products. ITs reimaging project has contributed to a public perception of Petromark as a quality brand, where the retail outlets provide friendly staff and clean facilities.

The focus for the development of IT infrastructure which flows from Petromark's strategic context is relationship building with commercial and retail customers and suppliers in a cost-conscious environment. These relationships require the existence of a firm-wide network and an IT-literate staff.

Petromark has decentralized responsibility for IS functions in each of its business units as well as its corporate IS group. The past five years has seen increased responsibility for IS planning, development, and management at the business unit level, with business units now containing IS staff who report to business unit managers. Petromark has constantly reviewed its infrastructural investments at both the corporate and business unit levels. Major investments at the corporate level have been in the development of communications networks among commercial, retail, and manufacturing sites and suppliers. Petromark supplies extensive communications services through a robust network with an extensive LAN in place at its head office and in capital cities and other major sites. About two thousand PC users have whatever multihost connectivity is required for their business needs.

Business units have undertaken considerable local infrastructural investments, particularly in the commercial area with new distributorship services. The retail group is currently making major investments in upgraded retail and EFTPOS systems. Meanwhile, at the corporate level, the firm is closely monitoring the implementation of the international affiliates systems renewal project.

Planning for IT infrastructure in Petromark is based primarily on current business strategies and thus is categorized as dependent. IT infrastructural investments, as with other IT expenditures, must meet a defined business need, showing clear cost savings and, if part of the customer interface, delivery of a higher level of customer service. This view is consistant with the IT infrastructure fusion perspective presented by Luftman in Chapter 3.

The cost and quality of IT services form a major topic of discussion between business unit managers and senior IT managers. Emphasis on business needs is accompanied by a concern for demonstrating increased operational efficiencies, which usually means providing the service at a lower cost to Petromark.

Petromark has extensive reach through its electronic mail system to send standard messages throughout the Petromark group internationally. Petromark has developed an intercompany communications infrastructure based on X.400 network standards. Increasingly, connections to third-party networks are put in place to facilitate intercompany process simplification. The range of services is being extended by current developments. For example, distributorship systems are extending the range of services to customers and suppliers, and some EDI arrangements are operational. EDI is also currently under consideration as part of a redesign of Petromark's billing process.

The mission and vision of ISD (Information Systems Division) reflect the focus on providing business benefit by exploiting IT for business purposes. The 1993 ISD mission is to provide competitive IT services in partnership with its clients so that the potential of IT to achieve Petromark's business objectives is exploited. In this context, ISD "is committed to being the quality IT service of choice for Petromark in Australia."

Enabling View of Infrastructure—SouthStores

SouthStores is among the world's top fifteen retailers, with revenue in 1993 of over U.S. $9 billion. SouthStores' core businesses are department stores, two mass merchandise store chains, supermarkets, and specialty retail operations. In some segments, such as mass merchandising, its major competitor is another of the SouthStores' business units.

SouthStores aims to continue to grow and develop as a predominantly retail-oriented organization which is innovative, competitive, and dynamic. SouthStores operates as a divisionalized firm, with a corporate group and six relatively autonomous business units. We examined three of these, the department stores unit and the two mass merchandise chains. A newly appointed CEO has indicated a strong desire to utilize the synergies in the company.

The guiding principles for SouthStores' investment in IT infrastructure are based on a strategic intent of growth, characterized by innovation and competitiveness. In a retail environment this includes flexibility to accommodate different and changing markets, connectivity throughout the firm, and synergy to achieve economies of scale and to ensure acceptable levels of profitability. These principles imply the development of a sophisticated communications network and positioning for electronic trading, consistant with the IT organizational infrastructure perspective followed by the organizational infrastructure strategy perspective presented by Luftman in Chapter 3.

SouthStores has decentralized responsibility for IS functions to its business units as well as having a corporate IS group, SouthStores Information Services (SLIS). Corporate level SLIS exists to ensure current and future business leverage of economies of scale, expertise, and scope.

SLIS provides the communications backbone services and manages the operation and maintenance of almost all SouthStores' major data processing services. All large-scale hardware is confined to two sites in the city, which handle the firm's major computing operations. In-store hardware (such as POS terminals and PCs), within-store communications, and applications development are the responsibilities of the business units. The SLIS budget is recouped from payments for services from the business units.

IT usage is integral to all operational aspects of SouthStores' businesses. As a result of firmwide and business unit planning processes in the late 1980s, a set of key requirements for SouthStores' IT were articulated. These included the need for flexibility to accommodate change, connectivity ("anything to anything"), synergies through economies of scale, growth without corresponding cost growth, reliability, and positioning for new services and technologies.

The firm's hardware architecture includes IBM, DEC, and NCR machines. Business groups do not have to limit themselves to the hardware architectures already in place, provided there is a sound business case. SouthStores' communications network is large and sophisticated and is based on a layered approach.

Since 1985 the business units have developed their ITs independently from each other but in association with the corporate IS group. Business units have planning cycles which incorporate IT considerations at the highest levels. SLIS has a consultative and advisory role in these processes. In the late 1980s, SouthStores was an early mover into EDI, and most business units have now established quick response implementation groups. SLIS provided the initial focus, expertise, firmwide strategy, and contacts for EDI for the business units.

SouthStores' IT infrastructure planning is based largely on future business strategies. Desired benefits relate primarily to the flexibility required to meet future and as yet unspecified business needs. Such flexibility is highly valued and is seen to provide a competitive advantage in the retail industry, as well as ultimately lowering the cost of doing business. The firm's IT infrastructure provides a high level of business functionality in terms of reach and range. SouthStores takes an enabling view of IT infrastructural investments.

SLIS's vision statement emphasizes the enabling role of firmwide IT infrastructure for the SouthStores retail group. SLIS aims to be a world class provider of information technology solutions that profitably extends the reach and range of SouthStores retail activities. There was evidence of both dependent and enabling views of the role of local IT infrastructure in the department stores and the two mass merchandise chain business units.

Comparison of the Three Cases

Chemico, Petromark, and SouthStores share some similarities in their IT management:

1. They each have business unit responsibility for IT together with a corporate IS group.
2. Each firm spends a similar percentage of its total IT budget on corporate IT infrastructure (30–40%).
3. All firms have both corporate and business unit IT infrastructures. Differences between the firms focus on aspects and uses of IT infrastructural services and the rationales for these.
4. There is an increasing percentage of corporate IT expenditure which is classed as IT infrastructure from Chemico (utility) through

Petromark (dependent) to SouthStores (enabling). Generally, we have found that, for firms with an enabling view of infrastructure, a higher percentage of corporate IT expenditure is for infrastructural services.

5. A firmwide communications network becomes increasingly important for firms with a dependent or enabling view of IT infrastructure. In firms with an enabling view such networks are used extensively for business processes within the firm as well as between firms and their customers and suppliers. Currently, firms with a utility view use the network more for electronic messaging than as part of inter- or intra-organizational systems for business processes.

6. SouthStores' corporate IS group, with an enabling view of infrastructure, played a different role from Chemico and Petrolink in relation to new technologies, one that was more proactive and anticipatory in identifying new technologies which could be utilized for business purposes.

7. Business units in SouthStores appeared to have higher expectations of access to business-relevant IT expertise in their corporate IS groups than did those in firms with the dependent or utility views.

In Chemico, Petromark, and SouthStores the view of infrastructure can be traced back to the strategic context of each firm.

1. The business value Chemico sought from its infrastructural investment was primarily to reduce costs, to support the business improvement program, and to maintain quality standards. A greater focus on customer service is resulting in a shift toward a dependent view of infrastructure.

2. Petromark has been making use of its infrastructure to link customers and suppliers to build long-term relationships as part of its current strategy. Petromark staff make extensive use of IT within the firm for internal communication and productivity. There is a strong emphasis on a high level of IT-literate staff in Petromark, and the communications network supports this.

3. SouthStores values future flexibility, together with economies of scale, scope, and expertise. SouthStores seeks to be well positioned for new services and technologies.

Each of these firms sees IT infrastructure as a major component of its IT portfolio, though their views of the role of infrastructure differ.

Conclusions

IT infrastructure is a critical component of the IT portfolio. It provides the foundation of IT capability for the development of IS. This IT capability includes both the technical and managerial expertise required to provide reliable services.

The benefits of IT infrastructure are difficult to specify as the value of IT infrastructure is in enabling IS to support business processes. A useful analogy can be drawn between IT infrastructure in firms and public infrastructural investment at the national and regional levels.

The benefits a firm derives from its IT infrastructural investments and the way these investments are justified are related to the firm's view of the role of infrastructure:

1. A utility view is driven primarily by a concern for cost savings through economies of scale.
2. A dependent view is driven primarily by a concern for business benefits from current strategy.
3. An enabling view is driven primarily by the need for current and future flexibility.

One view of infrastructure is not better than another. The key factor is the strategic context of the firm, indicating how it wishes to compete in its industry. An appropriate view of infrastructure must be taken for the strategic intent. That appropriate view could be utility, dependent, or enabling.

IT infrastructural investments are large and long-term in nature. They are linked to the ability of firms to achieve their strategic intents and implement their visions. Implementing an appropriate role for IT infrastructure is a major contribution to achieving strategic alignment between the IT portfolio and business needs.

Notes

1. Tapscott, D., & Caston, A. (1992): Paradigm Shift: The New Promise of Information Technology, New York: McGraw-Hill.

2. Ahituv N., & Neumann, S. (1990): Principles of Information Systems Management, Third Edition, Dubugue, Iowa: Wm. C. Brown. Keen, P. G. W. (1991): Shaping the Future: Business Design through Information Technology, Cambridge: Harvard Business School Press.

3. Niederman, F., Brancheau, J. C., & Wetherbe, J. C. (1991): Information Systems Management Issues for the 1990's, *MIS Quarterly*, 15(4), 475–495, December.

4. Broadbent, M., Butler, C., Hansell, A., & Dampney, K. (1993): Business Value, Quality and Partnerships: Australasian Information Systems Management Issues in 1992, Working Paper No. 5, The University of Melbourne, July.

5. Broadbent, M., & Weill, P. (1993): Improving Business and Information Strategy Alignment: Learning from the Banking Industry, *IBM Systems Journal*, 32(1), 162–179.

6. Henderson, J., & Venkatraman, N. (1993): Strategic Alignment: Leveraging Information Technology for Transforming Organization, *IBM Systems Journal*, 32(1),

7. Weill, P., & Lucas, H. C. (1993): Managing the IT Investment Pyramid for Competitive Advantage, Working Paper No, 11, Graduate School of Management, University of Melbourne, Carlton, Victoria, Australia.

8. Parker, M. M., & Benson, R. J. (1988): Information Economics: Linking Business Performance to Information Technology, Englewood Cliffs, N.J.: Prentice Hall.

9. McKay, D. T., & Brockaway D. W. (1989): Building IT Infrastructure for the 1990s Stage by Stage, Nolan Norton & Company.

10. Keen, Shaping the Future.

11. Keen, P. G. W. (1993): Information Technology and the Management Difference: A Fusion Map. *IBM Systems Journal*, 32(1), 17–39.

12. Weill, P. (1993): The Role and Value of Information Technology Infrastructure: Some Empirical Observations, in R. D. Banker, R. J. Kauffman, and M. A. Mahmood (Eds.), Perspectives on the Strategic and Economic Value of Information Technology, Middleton, Pa.: Idea Group Publishing.

13. Otisline (1990): Harvard Business School Case #9-186–307.

14. Kambil, A., Henderson, J. C., & Mohsenzadeh, H. (1992): Strategic Management of Information Technology Investments: An Options Perspective, in Banker, Kauffman, & Mahmood, Perspectives on the Strategic and Economic Value of Information Technology.

15. Keen, Shaping the Future.

16. McKay & Brockaway, Building IT Infrastructure for the 1990s Keen, Shaping the Future.

17. Aschauer, D. A. (1989): Is Public Expenditure Productive? *Journal of Monetary Economics*, 23, 177–200.

18. Munnell, A. H. (1990a): Why has Productivity Growth Declined? Productivity and Public Investment, *New England Economic Review*, Federal Reserve Bank of Boston, 3–22, January/February.

19. Munnell, A. H. (1990b): How Does Public Infrastructure Affect Regional Economic Performance? *New England Economic Review,* Federal Reserve Bank of Boston, 3–22, September/October.
20. Deno, K. T. (1988): The Effect of Public Capital on U.S. Manufacturing Activity: 1970 to 1978, *Southern Economic Journal,* 55(2), 400–411.
21. Keeler, T. E., & Ying, J. S. (1988): Measuring the Benefits of a Large Public Investment, *Journal of Public Economics,* 36, 69–85.
22. Weill, P. (1993): The Role and Value of Information Technology Infrastructure: Some Empirical Observations, in R. D. Banker, R. J. Kauffman, and M. A. Mahmood (Eds.), Perspectives on the Strategic and Economic Value of Information Technology, Middleton, Pa.: Idea Group Publishing.

Appendix A

Strategic Alignment Research and Practice: A Review and Research Agenda

JAMES B. THOMAS and ROCKI-LEE DEWITT

The purpose of this appendix is to systemically review the work that has been done on strategic alignment through a framework that differentiates the work in terms of "concept building" and "concept testing," as well as the descriptive vs. predictive power of the research. After reviewing the past work, we suggest areas that require attention and present the preliminary results of a major longitudinal project that pushes the study of strategic alignment into new arenas. The objective of the last part of this appendix is to suggest a research agenda in terms of a specific set of recommendations and an overarching guiding framework, which will provide support and guidance for the construction of prescriptive managerial processes.

A Short History of Strategic Alignment

As the chapters in this book and numerous other writings demonstrate, there have been great strides in the conceptual development of strategic alignment during the 1990s. Building on the earlier work of Henderson et al.[1] and others who have written of the business/IT fit,[2] there has been a continual refinement of the critical constructs and relationships that define strategic alignment, as well as its link to other concepts. Work has been done, for example, that documents observations of how strategic alignment and its components are manifested in organizations[3] and how the strategic transformations that mark the changing role of IT have been conducted.[4]

There has also been research that complements the strategic alignment concept, most notably Keen's concept of a fusion map (see Chapter 6) and Konsynski's work (Chapter 8) on the redefinition of the firm's boundary through alignment. Also notable in the development of the concept is its linkage to specific management challenges facing those involved in reconfiguring their organizations.[5]

More recently, this descriptive, developmental work has been supplemented by ongoing research that has sought to provide both predictions and explanations as to what behaviors and contexts lend themselves to an understanding by top managers of the importance and implications of the factors that define strategic alignment.[6] Thomas and DeWitt[7]—discussed in detail below—have extended this work in an attempt to capture how top management teams' understanding of strategic alignment is related to firm action and ultimately organizational performance. This work, coupled with various case reports of the effectiveness of strategic alignment[8] has begun to empirically establish alignment as a cornerstone to growth and success in the 1990s for many industries.

A Framework for Review

A useful way of reviewing the work done on strategic alignment is by placing it in a matrix such as that in Figure A.1. This matrix, based on the work of Snow and Thomas,[9] provides a general framework for evaluating the state of any research topic. When research on strategic alignment is mapped onto the framework, the contributions of existing work, as well as opportunities for future research, become evident. Each cell of the matrix in the figure includes a short description and an illustrative example of the strategic alignment studies that have been conducted.

Concept Development

Concept development involves efforts such as identification of the relevant constructs, explanations for these relationships, and predictions of where and when the relationships will hold. Each of these steps, which we refer to as description, explanation, and prediction, addresses a different research goal. Together, these steps in the concept development process enhance our understanding of what strategic alignment is, how and why it is linked to other phenomena, and under what conditions it is manifested.

	Description	Explanation	Prediction
Concept Building	Research on what variables and concepts compose strategic alignment	Explanations regarding how and/or why certain relationships among variables exist	Attempts to ascertain under what circumstances the relationships hold (when and where are the critical relationships manifested).
	Example: Henderson and Venkatraman	Example: Henderson and Thomas	Example: Luftman, Lewis, and Oldach
Concept Testing	Testing and validation of the variable measures	Documenting the relationships developed earlier usually through statistical testing	Testing competing explanations of strategics alignment's link to other organizational phenomena
	Example: Chan and Huff	Example: Thomas and DeWitt	Example: None

1based on Snow and Thomas, 1993

Figure A.1. Framework for Reviewing Strategic Alignment Research

DESCRIPTION

The main purpose of description is to address the issue of *what*. Description during the ongoing conceptual development of strategic alignment plays a critical role by identifying and refining what the basic building blocks of the theory are and how they relate to each other.

The strategic alignment model, as originally described by Henderson and Venkatraman and summarized in Chapter 2 of this book, is perhaps the guiding framework in alignment research. It establishes the vocabulary and the basic relationships upon which much of the subsequent work in this area has been based. In this sense, the model is a description of what it means to take an alignment "perspective" of the firm. The four domains— business strategy, IT strategy, organizational infrastructure, and IT infrastructure—provide the conceptual grounding. The inter- and intradomain linkages illustrated in Figure 2.1 of this book and described in Appendix B, provide the fundamental relationships that define the model.

The success of this descriptive conceptual development is evidenced through extentions of this initial theorizing by other investigators. This involves extending all or part of the model into related concepts, such as Victor et al.'s (Chapter 4) examination of the structural transformations in the market and the potential role of IT capabilities. Davidson and Movizzo's (Chapter 11) complementary perspective that looks at the role of organizational competencies, enhanced through the use of IT, is another example of descriptive work that has refined and extended the basic strategic alignment model.

EXPLANATION

While the goal of descriptive work is to establish what variables and relationships define, or are informed by, strategic alignment, the goals of explanation are to establish *how* and *why* key variables are related. More precisely, the focus of the strategic alignment investigator in this type of research is to (1) explore the nature and degree of association among major variables (including alignment's antecedents and its link to organizational outcomes) and (2) to offer theoretical and/or observed explanations of these relationships.

One of the best examples of this type of research on strategic alignment is found in the work of Henderson and Thomas,[10] who, building off of the earlier work of Henderson and Venkatraman, provide detailed explanations of the various combinations of relationships found in the strategic alignment model in the hospital industry. Referred to as "planning perspectives," the different relationships that exist between the domains are explained in terms of the roles of key stakeholders, the focus placed on IT by the firm, and the performance criteria that both justify and create a certain perspective (see Fig. A.2 for a summary of this discussion). This matrix is expanded and discussed in further detail by Luftman in Chapter 3 of this book.

Other work that explains how and why key variables are related includes reports of case studies of how strategic alignment was created in a given organization. Examples of these accounts include Edwards'[11] report of how strategic alignment was linked to the revitalization of the Canadian Public Service and Harker's[12] view of strategic alignment's role at Royal Trust in Canada.

PREDICTION

The basic purpose of prediction in conceptual development is to establish the conditions under which the theory of strategic alignment holds. Therefore, the questions addressed by predictive studies involve issues of *who, where,* and *when.* A predictive study incorporates previously identified variables and relationships and then determines the boundaries within which they exist.

There have been a number of studies in strategic alignment that have been designed with prediction as the central research goal. One example is the work of Mayoff and Caldwell,[13] who explored the characteristics of "well-aligned" enterprises to identify the critical organizational and managerial factors that lead to successful alignment.

Taking a cognitive approach, Henderson et al.[7] attempted to identify what activities were tied to top managers' understanding of the relationships characterized by strategic alignment. They found, for example, that managers who have developed stronger partnerships with IS managers had a richer understanding of the relationships between the alignment domains than those with weak partnerships. Increased business and IT planning activities were also found to have a patterned impact on managers' knowledge of the implications of aligning the domains that define the strategic alignment model.

Multiple case study research has also contributed to our ability to build predictions of when and where the elements of strategic alignment are important. These include both intraindustry studies[4] and studies that examine alignment across multiple industry settings.[5] These exploratory studies have been especially important for defining certain types of domain linkage and/or establishing the context in which certain aspects of strategic alignment are manifested or understood. Collectively, these studies have

Planning Perspectives

	Strategic Execution	Competitive Potential	Service Level	Technology Potential
Nature of Domain Relationships	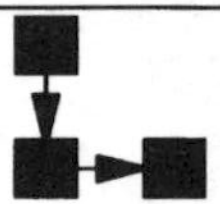	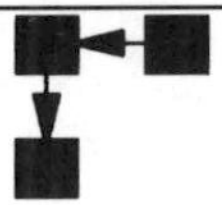	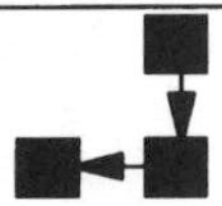	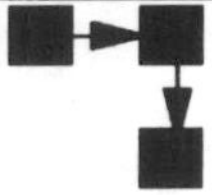
Role of Top Management	Executive Leadership	Business Visionary	Prioritizer	Technological Visionary
Role of IS Management	Functional Manager	Top Management Team	Executive Leadership	Technology Architect
IT Focus	Reactive	Value-added	Business within a Business	Technology based Competitive Advantage
Performance Criteria	Financial	Product/Service Leadership	Customer Satisfaction	Technology Leadership

from Henderson and Thomas, 1992

Figure A.2. Characteristics of Planning Perspectives

focused on the conceptual development of strategic alignment and have strengthened the framework that defines the important variables/relationships of alignment. Yet the ability to make strong assertions about the importance of strategic alignment to organizational performance requires validation beyond the case study or theoretically based prediction. In the next section, we review the work that has tested and/or validated the nature of the findings and predictions from this developmental stream of research.

Concept Testing and Validation

Similar to concept building, concept testing can take on several distinct types or phases (description, explanation, and prediction). Concept testing, however, usually involves larger sample sizes than the more exploratory studies that define concept-building studies. In this sense, concept testing and validation of strategic alignment and its contingencies most often involves some kind of statistical testing across many organizations (or managers).

DESCRIPTION

Whereas description during concept development is concerned mainly with construct identification, during concept testing and validation it focuses on variable measurement. How do we measure the concept of strategic alignment, and, just as importantly, how do we know if we have correctly (and adequately) captured the concept in the questions we have asked or the observations we have made? These are the fundamental questions that must be posed and answered if we are to have faith in the findings upon which prescriptions for managers are to be based.

Generally speaking, until very recently the study of strategic alignment has not devoted much attention to measurement issues. A notable exception to this pattern is the work of Chan and Huff,[14] who focus on developing multiple measures based on different theoretical perspectives of the relationship between business and IT strategies, each of which requires a very different theoretical interpretation as well as a different mathematical model. Their study of one hundred and sixty-four business units across Canada and the United States gives insight to the alternative methods by which the relationships between business and IT strategies can be conceptualized and measured.

Similarly, Reich and Benbasat[15] contributed to the development of alignment measures by utilizing multiple respondents, as well as multiple methods, at each of their research sites. This involvement included interviews as well as the development of written documents by the participants. Findings regarding the linkage between business and IT strategies were then cross-referenced to existing written plans, thereby providing insight to how both the reliability and the validity of the measurement process associated with alignment can be enhanced. Although limited in its generalizability because of the small sample size (ten business units), the study does show the importance of multiple measures in capturing the key dimensions of those aspects of strategic alignment being examined.

EXPLANATION

This aspect of concept testing concerns the documentation of relationships among variables (as contrasted to the specification of relationships in the concept-development study). Explanatory studies are normally well grounded in a theory that posits an association between specific variables. However, there may be inadequate or conflicting arguments about the direction of the relationship or the generalizability of the association across different organizations or managers. The hallmark of the explanatory study thus becomes statistical testing of a relationship across multiple units (business units and/or managers).

Most of the empirical, explanatory work in alignment has focused on the relationship between alignment (or some aspect of alignment) and another organizational concept. For example, Chan's work[16] (see also note 14) examines the alignment between business and IT strategies and its relationship to business performance and IS effectiveness. Results of this study indicate that strategic alignment is positively related to the various dimensions of IS effectiveness, including user satisfaction and IS's contribution to the resolution of certain operational and strategic issues. A link between strategic alignment and business performance (i.e., company innovation) was also found.

Other research of this type[17] focuses on the theoretical and observational construction of organizational exemplars with respect to the "goodness" of alignment in a manner similar to Venkatraman and Prescott.[18] This showed how approximately two hundred firms across multiple industries deviated from the appropriate industry's "ideal profile," which was then used to predict satisfaction levels with IT investments and direction.

The research by Thomas and DeWitt extends the findings of Chan and Huff[16] through an examination of the role of strategic alignment in predicting actions and performance associated with strategic change over time. Using data obtained from a multimethod study of one hundred and thirty-four top management teams in two U.S. hospital systems, an analysis was done of the relationships between strategic alignment, action taken with respect to product and service offerings, and performance outcomes along multiple dimensions. This provided evidence that understanding the importance and implications of strategic alignment is a powerful linchpin in an organization's attempt to compete in market settings that are experiencing dramatic changes and increased information-processing requirements.

Strategic Alignment and Action

One of the overarching research questions of this study was whether attention paid to the domains and relationships that define strategic alignment influences organizational action toward the marketplace. Indeed, study results indicate that when top managers have a heightened understanding of the relationship between business strategy and IT strategy (strategic linkage), it is likely that they are better equipped to identify how IT can promote or facilitate changes in the scope of the business. Specifically, the findings showed that understanding the implications of strategic linkage led to the adoption of more innovative hospital products and services over the subsequent two-year period. Such products and services adopted/implemented included open-heart surgical facilities, organ/tissue transplant, burn care units, neonatal intensive care, and diagnostic radioisotope facilities.

In contrast, when managers focused their attention on, and showed a greater understanding of, the relationship between organizational infrastructure and IT infrastructure (functional linkage), they were less likely to initiate innovative changes in their hospitals' product/service portfolios. That is, they reduced, or did not significantly add to, their product/service portfolio (added services that were not considered innovative—e.g., respiratory therapy, hemodialysis). Clearly, these managers were attempting to identify how IT and organizational structures could be modified to improve implementation of the existing product/service line or, if expansion did occur, that it was for the purpose of including more "basic" services to the portfolio.

Results also show that the two "fit" variables (the business strategy–infrastructure fit and the IT strategy–infrastructure fit) were not significantly related to the product/service change variable. More specifically, IT fit did not enter into the decision of service introduction or reduction; however, business fit was found to be directly linked to hospital performance (profit).

We believe that the lack of relationship between the fit dimensions and product/service action was due to the exclusion of change measures that go beyond the product marketplace (e.g., structural changes, financial decisions, mergers, etc.) and the absence of an IT-specific change measure. These are areas that must be addressed in this type of longitudinal study in the future.

Firm Action and Performance

Findings also suggest that innovative changes in the product/service offering can potentially impact multiple dimensions of organizational performance. For example, the addition of innovative customer services (such as cardiac catheterization in the hospital setting) increased the ability of the firm to serve a diverse group of customers and clients, thereby increasing the scope and overall effectiveness of the organization. Conversely, simply maintaining existing services and focusing primarily on the efficiency of their delivery might result in stagnation of the customer base and revenues.

This research portrays an interesting and somewhat counterintuitive picture of performance changes that accompany alteration in the organizational service portfolio. When organizations in the study (hospitals) changed their service portfolio to include more innovative offerings based on their specific understanding of strategic alignment, traditional measures of efficiency were impacted. Specifically, cost-per-patient and employee-hours-per-patient decreased. However, results indicated that discharges-per-bed and occupancy-per-bed (measures of productivity in the industry) also decreased over the two-year period since the adoption of the new products and services.

What emerges from an analysis of the variation in the multiple measures of hospital performance is a picture of hospitals attempting to reconfigure their portfolios of routine and nonroutine services to improve their overall performance, while at the same time becoming more efficient in the design and delivery of those services through IT.

What is apparent is a trend in the industry to move the routine services of the hospital to outpatient facilities and to utilize the hospital beds to support more nonroutine, information- and technology-intensive service offerings. This, in fact, based on the analysis of financial measures such as profit and return-on-assets, becomes the key characteristic of the hospital that prospers in, or even survives, the turbulent health care marketplace. Given the changes contemplated by the current federal administration, the relationships uncovered here and the critical role of strategic alignment may become even more evident over the next five years.

Overall, an examination of the linkage between strategic alignment, product/service action, and performance provides insight to both the evolution and management of strategic transformation, as discussed by Henderson and Venkatraman. Specifically, findings suggest that the concept of linkage in strategic alignment (i.e., the relationship between business strategy and IT strategy—strategic linkage; and the link between organizational infrastructure and IT infrastructure—functional linkage) is the key determinant of the extent of innovativeness associated with the changes in the organization's product/service portfolio. A focus on strategic linkage is associated with increased innovativeness, while having a top management team that focuses on functional linkage is associated with decreased or stagnating innovativeness.

The extent of innovative products and services introduced into the market was, in turn, found to impact the efficiency by which standard services were provided as well as what processes would be emphasized. The final skill set needed to convert strategic linkage to profit was a high understanding of the implications and importance of business fit (i.e., the relationship between business strategy and organizational infrastructure). This suggests that the perspective called "technology potential" (see Fig. A.2) may be the planning perspective driving success in this industry (hospital), while focusing on a "strategy execution" perspective, to the exclusion of an IT strategy-driven perspective, is detrimental.

This raises the interesting prospect that success in certain industries, and/or within certain life-cycle phases, may be characterized by one of the planning perspectives identified in Figure A.2 as the dominant management "lens" of the successful top management teams. Perhaps even the basic structure of information-processing industries could be defined by the mix of perspectives present in the industry at any given time. These are questions that move strategic alignment to the industry level of analysis and require attention as the concept continues to be expanded.

Prediction

It has been claimed that prediction is the ultimate research goal.[19] Prediction without explanation, however, leaves the researcher with little understanding of the phenomenon in question. As Snow and Thomas suggest, the ideal predictive study would test multiple explanations for a given relationship, similar to the study by Venkatraman and Prescott,[20] who tested the effect on business performance of various theoretical combinations of organizational factors. In this sense, the impact of strategic alignment on the firm needs to be assessed relative to other theories of organizational transformation. Accordingly, predictive, and eventually explanatory, theoretical synergies could be identified.

While we could not identify a study on strategic alignment that met these criteria, we can offer what a study of this type might look like. Using the planning perspectives identified in Figure A.2, multiple theoretical predictions could be constructed regarding the perspectives' relationships to firm action, IS effectiveness, and/or firm performance. These predictions (or hypotheses) would then be tested utilizing a large sample of firms, ideally across multiple industries or even national borders.

In summary, as the above review of the concept-testing studies done in strategic alignment suggests, strategic alignment is a potentially powerful explanation and predictor of successful organizational transformation. However, as the review above also indicates, further support for the utility of strategic alignment for impacting the effectiveness of transformation requires that researchers begin to focus on the following:

- the development of reliable (i.e. able to be duplicated) and valid (i.e. actually measures what it purports to measure) methods for assessing the various aspects of strategic alignment

- the development of theoretical explanations for the relationship between strategic alignment and other concepts and the testing of those relationships across different organizations and environments

- testing competing explanations for how strategic alignment is linked to firm success or even survivability

In the next section, more specific recommendations that facilitate and refine these broader prescriptions are discussed.

Recommendations

Perhaps the primary implication of the review presented above is that research conducted in strategic alignment has been far more developmental and anecdotal than of a testing nature. Given the relatively short history of the concept, this seems understandable. Indeed, most theoretical development begins with an in-depth analysis of the phenomena in question in a single setting, then moves into multiple settings to subject the theory to more systematic scrutiny. However, the rich history of conceptual writings on strategic alignment coupled with the limited empirical work that has been done leaves a vacuum defined by a number of important questions:

1. Does strategic alignment across all four corners of the model make a difference in a firm's performance over time? What factors of performance are important and when?

2. What organizational or cognitive factors influence the relative importance of the various aspects of strategic alignment?

3. Under what circumstances are managers apt to have a more in-depth knowledge of strategic alignment?

4. How can valid measures be developed that allow for the accurate assessment of a firm's strategic alignment?

5. In what manner does alignment evolve over time? Are certain patterns or perspectives more prevalent or successful than others? Under what conditions are they so?

As studies begin to provide prescriptive and normative insights to top managers regarding the planning for, and implementation of, strategic alignment, we need to formulate answers to these critical questions. This requires that we support and refine the conceptual and exploratory developments that have dominated the study of strategic alignment through empirical testing coupled with sound, and even creative, assessment tools and methods. To this end, we recommend the following specific steps:

1. MEASURES OF STRATEGIC ALIGNMENT MUST BE VALIDATED

To date, few studies have rigorously measured the various dimensions of strategic alignment. Those that have used multiple methods for assessing alignment (e.g., Reich and Benbasat) have applied these methods only to the link between business and IT strategies.

It is important to note that alignment is considered from two perspectives in the literature. The first involves assessment of the state of alignment in the organization. Multiple methods for assessing "how aligned" an organization is might be through a combination of questionnaires and an assessment of existing documents, observations, and/or interviews. Also, researchers may wish to explore secondary data sources (existing data bases such as PIMS or COMPUSTAT) with the goal of identifying surrogate measures of alignment.

This unique blend of field and nonfield methods for assessing the extent to which an organization is aligned would greatly enhance the validity of existing alignment measurement tools. Ultimately, the goal should be to identify how alignment is manifested in the behaviors and systems of the organization.

2. Assessing Managers' Understanding of the Model

The second perspective taken in assessing the extent to which managers understand the implications and importance of various aspects of the alignment model (e.g., Thomas and DeWitt, 1993; Henderson, Thomas, and Venkatraman). The tack taken in this assessment is to ask managers (through questionnaire items) the extent to which they understand each of the domains and the linkages that define the strategic alignment model (e.g., "To what extent do you understand the importance of the impact IT strategy has on business strategy?" (see also Luftman, Brier, and Papp)

In addition to this type of assessment, we recommend that questions that take on the form of concrete examples be posed (e.g., "To what extent do you think cutting edge IT such as optical scanning impact the marketing goals of your firm?") and/or questions built around scenarios that represent various combinations of alignment dimensions (e.g., "Please rank the following statements with respect to how well you understand the relationships described").

Depending on the level of analysis (manager vs. organization), selected structured interviews could also be used to assess knowledge of alignment and/or to validate questionnaire responses.

3. The Use of Multilevel and Longitudinal Perspectives

Studies of strategic alignment could also benefit by viewing the evolution of strategic alignment across time as well as across different levels of analysis. For example, while case studies have provided some anecdotal evidence of changes in organizations' understanding of strategic alignment over time, with few exceptions, the concept-testing work to date on strategic alignment has focused on a single point in time (i.e., cross-sectional). How the relationship of strategic alignment to other concepts (e.g., performance, environment) is altered across multiple time periods has important descriptive, as well as prescriptive, implications. Further, strategic alignment is usually considered as an organizational-level phenomenon.

Henderson, Thomas, and Venkatraman take a unique individual-level perspective, while Thomas and DeWitt use the top management team as their focus. Of interest would be how the individual's perception, the team's collective perception, and the organization's measure of strategic alignment are related. Further, studies that would identify how understanding of strategic alignment changes as the researcher moves down or across the organization are also warranted. For example, how strategic alignment is linked at the business unit level to the corporate or other functional levels is clearly needed. This also includes the notion of linking other domains of the organization (e.g., manufacturing) to the IT domain, creating, in a sense, a three-dimensional model of alignment. These more intricate and complex models may help capture the alignment "realities" of different industries or firms.

4. TAKING AN INTERNATIONAL VIEW

One of the key issues with respect to both concept development and testing of strategic alignment is the cross-national implications of the model. For example, do different cultures place different emphases on the various aspects of the strategic alignment model? The implications of the findings of these studies would be critical for the management and development of international joint ventures, strategic alliances, and management of the multinational enterprise. Prescriptive intervention would also need to have knowledge of these differences if such intervention is to have optimal results.

5. STUDIES THAT OCCUPY TWO OR MORE CELLS

The overall development of the strategic alignment concept would be greatly enhanced if studies were done that both developed and tested critical linkages and relationships. One of the weaknesses of the current literature is its fragmentation with respect to the tracking of a given idea across the multiple cells depicted in Figure A.1. How the various findings across the different types of study that have been done can be integrated to tell a "complete" story of the antecedents and outcomes of strategic alignment is missing from the literature. One way to remedy this void is to use prior studies as the groundwork for more comprehensive studies that thoroughly develop and test ideas associated with strategic alignment and related fields. Chapter 3 in this book could serve as such groundwork.

6. DEVELOPMENT OF A COMMON "ALIGNMENT" LANGUAGE

Perhaps one of the reasons for the fragmentation in the strategic alignment literature is the wide range of duplicative and contradictory terms and concepts that permeate the work. The terms "fit," "linkage," "integration," and even "alignment" are used interchangeably to refer to different aspects of the alignment concept (even across the chapters of this book). It is critical that researchers adopt a standard so that results and findings can be conveyed in such a way that they become cumulative.

Summary and Conclusions

The review of the strategic alignment research to date leads to the conclusion that there have been remarkable advances in the development of the concept but only minor inroads to the testing and validation of the model and its relationship to other organizational phenomena. Accordingly, the focus of research on strategic alignment needs to be placed on explanatory and predictive studies that test the relationships discussed in the earlier development and exploratory/anecdotal work. As with the development of theory in other fields, to support the assertions that strategic alignment makes a predictable difference in organizational effectiveness, we need to test those assertions across multiple organizations, multiple industries, and against other theoretical explanations.

The question becomes what direction this testing should take to capitalize on the existing work as well as to create new insights and expose opportunities for further development and testing. An overarching framework for directing strategic alignment research is offered in Figure A.3. The framework is intended to capture the focus of much of the existing work reviewed above and to be a vehicle for suggesting gaps in the existing literature.

The framework consists of four boxes—context, strategic alignment, action, and performance—that together represent the thrust of the extant strategic alignment research. The bulk of the work, as noted above, has been developmental, represented by the box labeled "strategic alignment." However, some work has attempted to link back into the organization to predict the nature of strategic alignment;[7] while other work, albeit quite limited, has attempted to link strategic alignment to the action and performance characteristics of the firm as it competes in the marketplace.[20]

As evidence accumulates on how these important ingredients in the management process impact, and are impacted by, strategic alignment, answers to the questions posed above can be formulated. Most importantly, evidence can be brought forward that answers the key question: Does alignment matter? Research can also be directed toward other critical areas, most notably the arrows that link the boxes in the framework (Fig. A.3).

For example, Venkatraman et al.[21] have developed a model of the align-

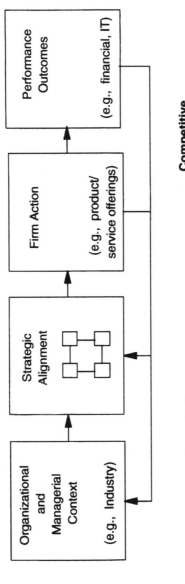

Figure A.3. Overarching Framework for Strategic Alignment Research

ment mechanisms that link strategic alignment to firm action; while Clark et al.[22] seek to uncover and test the nature of the mechanisms by which the changing organizational context affects the understanding of strategic alignment across the organization's membership. Ultimately, work that spans the framework over time (i.e., across multiple cycles, as depicted in Fig. A.3) and provides insight into the evolution of strategic alignment and its relationship to the organization and its competitive environment will be needed.

In many ways, the path of the research that has focused on strategic alignment has just begun. The opportunities for explaining and predicting organizational success/failure are being identified as we learn more about the nature of strategic alignment, its antecedents, and its consequences. By placing proper attention on the research that is needed and the methods by which that research is conducted, we extend our ability to assess strategic alignment and its impact on organizational outcomes. If we can test the assumptions that drive this critical relationship, strategic alignment promises to have an even stronger impact on the study of organizations as well as information systems.

Notes

1. J. C. Henderson, N. Venkatraman, "Strategic Alignment: A Model for Organizational Transformation through Information Technology Management," in *Transforming organizations*, T. Kochan, M. Useem, eds. (New York: Oxford University Press, 1992): 97–117.

2. P. G. W. Keen, *Shaping the Future: Business Design through Information Technology* (Boston: Harvard Business School Press, 1991); M. Scott Morton, *The Corporation of the 90's: Information Technology and Organizational Transformation* (New York: Oxford University Press, 1991).

3. M. Broadbent, P. Weill, "Improving Business and Information Strategy Alignment: Learning from the Banking Industry," *IBM Systems Journal*, 32: 1 (1993): 162–179.

4. J. N. Luftman, P. R. Lewis, S. H. Oldach, "Transforming the Enterprise: The Alignment of Business and Information Technology Strategies," *IBM Systems Journal*, 32: 1 (1993): 198–221.

5. N. Venkatraman, "IT-Induced Business Reconfiguration," in *The Corporation of the 90's: Information Technology and Organizational Transformation*, M. Scott Morton, ed. (New York: Oxford University Press, 1991): 122–158.

6. J. C. Henderson, J. B. Thomas, N. Venkatraman, "Making Sense of IT: Strategic Alignment and Organizational Context," Working Paper 3475-92 BPS,

(Boston: Sloan School of Management, Massachusetts Institute of Technology, 1992).

7. J. B. Thomas, R. DeWitt, "Linking Strategic Alignment to Firm Action and Performance," Working Paper (Pennsylvania State University, 1993).
Venkatraman, N. 1990. Performance implications of strategic coalignment: A methodological perspective. Journal of Management Studies, 27, 1, 19–41.

8. W. V. Stoughton, "Merging Two Hospitals," *Business Quarterly*, 55: 3 (1991): 84–88; D. H. Lander, "Strategic Alignment at Canada Post," *Business Quarterly*, 55: 3 (1991): 100–106.

9. C. C. Snow, J. B. Thomas, "Field Research Methods in Strategic Management: Contributions to Theory Building and Testing," *Journal of Management Studies* (1995).

10. J. C. Henderson, J. B. Thomas, "Aligning Business and Information Technology Domains: Strategic Planning in Hospitals," *Hospital and Health Services Administration*, 37: 1 (1992): 71–87.

11. J. Edwards, "Revitalization of the Canadian Public Service," *Business Quarterly*, 55: 3 (1991): 113–118.

12. W. C. Harker, "Alignment for Success in the 1990's," *Business Quarterly*, 55: 3 (1991): 107–112.

13. B. F. Mayoff, K. R. Caldwell, "Benchmarking Strategic Alignment of Information Technology," *Strategic Systems* (January 1993): 1–10.
B. H. Reich, I. Benbasat.

14. Y. E. Chan, S. L. Huff, "Investigating Information Systems Strategic Alignments," in *Proceedings of the International Conference on Information Systems*. (Vancouver, Canada, 12/93).

15. "Development of Measures to Investigate the Linkage between Business Information Technology Objectives," Working Paper 93-MIS-011 (Vancouver: University of British Columbia, 1993).

16. Y. E. Chan, "Business Strategy, Information Systems Strategy, and Strategic Fit: Measurement and Performance Impacts," Dissertation, (London: University of Western Ontario 1992).

17. J. Luftman, R. Papp, T. Brier, Information Week July 1995.

18. N. Venkatraman, J. E. Prescott, "Environment–Strategy Coalignment: An Empirical Test of Its Performance Implications," *Strategic Management Journal*, 11 (1990): 1–24.

19. A. Kaplan, *The Conduct of Inquiry* (San Francisco: Chandler, 1964).

20. For example, Thomas and DeWitt, "Linking Strategic Alignment," and Chan and Huff, "Investigating Information."

21. N. Venkatraman, J. C. Henderson, S. Oldach, "Continuous Strategic Alignment: Exploiting Information Technology Capabilities for Competitive Success," *European Management Journal*, 11: 2 (1993): 139–149.

22. S. Clark, J. B. Thomas, R. DeWitt, "Sensemaking and Sensegiving: The Mechanisms of Strategic Alignment Transformation," Working Paper (The Pennsylvania State University, 1993).

Appendix B

Glossary of Strategic Alignment Terminology

❖

JERRY N. LUFTMAN

Information Technology (IT)

The generally accepted term that encompasses the rapidly expanding range of equipment (e.g., computers, data storage devices, network and communications devices), applications (e.g., airline reservation systems, payroll, computer-aided design), services (e.g., help desk, application development, end-user computing), and people (e.g., programmers, analysts) used by organizations to deliver data, information, and knowledge.

Business Strategy

Business Scope   Decisions that determine where the enterprise will/ should compete. Often viewed as market segmentation, these choices define the types of product, niche, customer, and geography that determine the reach/range of the enterprise. They include the competitive forces (buyers, suppliers, substitutes, potential entrants).

Distinctive Competencies   Areas that determine how the enterprise will/ should compete in delivering its products and services. Why would a customer choose to buy or use the offerings from a particular company? These decisions determine those attributes of the strategy that create the capability of the enterprise to differentiate its products and services from the competition.

Examples of such choices include pricing strategy, the focus on quality, or the development of a superior marketing channel. Leveraging core competencies (competencies with substantial superiority over competition) plays a significant role in the derivation of strategies. Organizations should assess core competencies in light of their critical success factors (elements key to achieving the firms' strategies).

Business Governance Choices that focus on the issue of ownership. Will the enterprise enter a particular market as a single entity or via alliances, partnerships, or outsourcing? Governance choices today reflect a significant aspect of strategy by which a business may garner traditional advantages of scale through alliances rather than ownership. Other areas to consider include government regulations and how important decisions are prioritized.

Organizational Infrastructure and Processes

Administrative Structure The roles, responsibilities, and authority structures of the enterprise. Will the enterprise organize based on product offerings, geography, or functional departments? How many layers of management will be required and to what extent will decisions be decentralized? Should the structure be hierarchical, a matrix, teams, or some combination of these? These choices establish the structure within which the management and work processes will operate.

Processes The manner in which critical business activities will/should operate or flow. Essentially a value chain issue, these choices decide the extent to which work flows will be restructured, perhaps integrated, to improve effectiveness and efficiency. Emphasis should be placed on activities that create value for customers. Often, the improvement of processes relies on changes to IT. At other times the effective use of IT requires major redesign of central business processes. Business reengineering methods concentrate on adding value to strategic choices focusing on organizational infrastructure and process, especially regarding process.

Skills Choices concerning the people who will carry out the strategy. What experience, competencies, commitments, cultures, values, and norms do the professionals require to meet the strategy? Will the business strategy call for new skills? Do implied changes conflict with traditional values and norms of the enterprise? How are employees trained and motivated? The organizational infrastructural strategy must clearly define the human resource considerations for carrying out the work. Opportunities for outsourcing are also considered here.

IT Strategy

Technology Scope   Specific technologies and applications that are important to the organization (e.g., knowledge-based systems, electronic imaging, robotics, multimedia, etc.). These decisions position the technology necessary to be successful.

Systemic Competencies   Important capabilities and strengths of IT that will be critical to the creation or extension of business strategies (e.g., information, connectivity, accessibility, reliability, response). Leveraging the information that the firm has regarding its customers is an important consideration.

IT Governance   How to prioritize and select projects is the primary focus. The extent of ownership of technology (e.g., end-user executive, steering committee) or the possibility of technological alliances (e.g., partnership, outsourcing) or both are other important areas to assess. Financial considerations necessary for negotiating with systems integrators and software houses entailing make or buy decisions are also included here.

IT Infrastructure and Processes

IT Architecture   Choices, priorities, and policies that enable the integration of applications, data, software, networks, and hardware via a cohesive platform. This includes the integration of old and new technologies. Implementation of these choices is critical and time- and resource-consuming.

Processes   Design of major IT work functions and practices such as application development, systems management controls, or operations.

Skills   Experience, competencies, commitments, incentives, culture, values, and norms of the individuals working to deliver the IT products and services.

Strategic Fit

The vertical relationship of the strategic alignment model, strategic fit emphasizes the need to make choices that position the enterprise in an external marketplace. These choices decide how to best structure internal arrangements to execute this market positioning strategy. The choices that position the organization in a market are called strategy. Those choices that determine the internal structure of the organization are called infrastructure and processes. Performance is defined by the extent to which the choices defining the relationship of strategy and infrastructure are consistent. As business strategies change, the organizational processes must keep pace.

Functional Integration

The horizontal relationship of the strategic alignment model extends the strategic fit notion across functional organizations. As business strategies change, IT strategies and processes must also keep pace. It is in these situations that different functional relationships are defined. Unfortunately, the traditional view of IS strategy is too often narrowly defined as decisions concerning only applications, data, and hardware architectures.

This internal perspective does not address the need for management to understand how these architectural choices position the firm in a highly dynamic, evolving marketplace. Effective positioning of the firm in the technological market is critical to its ability to adapt and effectively leverage technology. Functional integration gives IT the opportunity to provide competitive advantage. The strategic alignment model can be expanded to include functions other than IT (e.g., marketing, manufacturing, finance). This implies extending the functional integration relationship across the enterprise. The strategic alignment model can also be expanded to assess IT with regards to specific functions within the enterprise (e.g., marketing, manufacturing, finance).

Strategic Perspectives

Each of the strategic alignment perspectives reflects an interplay among three quadrants (boxes). By creating perspectives that apply to three quadrants, one is always considering a relationship that involves both strategic fit and functional integration. Each perspective consists of three quadrants:

Domain anchor   Provides (drives, catalyzes, or enables) the change forces applied to the domain pivot. This quadrant is typically the strongest.

Domain pivot   Problem or opportunity being addressed. This quadrant is typically the weakest.

Impacted domain   Area affected by a change to the domain pivot.

Strategic Planning

The traditional view of strategic planning flows from the vision and mission of the company. If you can't imagine the future, you can't create it.

Vision is a brief inspirational statement expressing the chief executives' futuristic picture of the enterprise. It describes where the enterprise is going.

Mission presents a broad description of the purpose of the organization. It describes what business the enterprise is in and includes a description of what the organization does and why and when it does it.

Strategies describe the way in which the business allocates resources and takes action to achieve the vision and mission. They are a pattern of policies and plans of action that develop competitive advantage over a given period. Following the creation of strategies, *objectives* (general statement about the organizational direction) and *goals* (specific targets with time frames) are defined.

Strategic planning sets the direction for an enterprise so that it overcomes potential threats that stand in its way while it takes advantage of opportunities that present themselves. It plans the essentials for the effective and efficient conduct of the enterprise. The strategy provides a lasting set of values for customers that far surpasses that of the competitors. The methods used to create the strategic plan must include elements that are meaningful, understandable, and executable as they are communicated and carried out. The following subsections provide an overview of several methods available to transform the business.

IT Strategy and Planning Methods

IT strategy and planning are pivotal for an enterprise. These methods link the strategic directions of the business to the technologies that can best leverage those strategic directions. Business unit and operational strategies drive decisions that determine where and how the enterprise will compete.

Understanding an enterprise's approach to generating value can be translated to the appropriate application of IT. These decisions drive the IT strategy and planning to support the business. IT strategy and planning produce opportunities for the future use of technology in the enterprise.

Companies, before using these methods, should have developed a vision of where their business is headed. Companies should also have developed a set of key business strategies that will position their products and services in the markets in which they choose to compete. Last, companies should have decided the organizational structure and business processes that must be addressed to execute the business strategies effectively.

Using the business strategies, organizational structure, and understanding of key processes, the creation of an IT strategy will develop a set of IT initiatives that will provide the enterprise with a technological advantage in competing effectively and efficiently. The creation of an IT plan will define the actions necessary to bring the IT strategy to reality. It uses the aligned business and IT strategies to produce valued projects that encompass a full range of implementation activities. The methods focus on clearly defining what the organization can do to obtain competitive advantage, strategic advantage, business performance improvement, and growth opportunities.

Business Process Reengineering Methods

Business process reengineering provides a detailed approach to transforming an enterprise through total quality management and changes to business functions and activities. Business process reengineering includes continuous process improvement, process innovation, and breakthroughs for companies of all types and sizes. Application of the methods will result in a comprehensive course of action that defines what the organization can do to enable the business to achieve and sustain measurable benefits and advantages over competitors. Changes typically span across functional areas, divisions, and corporate boundaries.

Although corporations are developing strategies to respond to intensified competition, they are also undergoing pressure to improve business performance. Their responses frequently involve some combination of automation, streamlining/simplification, and continuous improvement. Unfortunately, these traditional approaches are not resulting in the continual innovations and breakthroughs that companies need to succeed, let alone survive. Breakthroughs represent reinvention changes that could not have been predicted in the past.

By integrating several known analysis methods and examining the interrelationships of the business strategy, IT investments, and business organization, maximum benefit can be derived and sustained from reengineering efforts. (Note: Many people suggest that you cannot reengineer a process that has not been previously engineered. For simplicity, the term "reengineering" refers to both.) Significant value is achieved by applying quality principles to areas of planned change and considering the perceived value from the perspective of the customer. The primary objective of these methods is to enhance the business through the rethinking of process to increase productivity and improve services.

The fundamental focus should be on delighting the customer. Benefits are obtained by improving quality and services and reducing cost and cycle time. Many of these benefits result from improvements in the processes that extend beyond the enterprise (e.g., vendors, suppliers, actual customers). Assessing complete processes and how they interact with all parts of the organization is key.

Business process reengineering uses IT strategy and planning methods to provide any required study of the company's IT investments. "Improving" old processes by simply applying IT ignores organizational infrastructure and processes and performance deficiencies. Administrative structure, processes, and skills that were created in a very different competitive environment should be evaluated for opportunities of redefinition before technology is applied. Such action implies going beyond merely enhancing existing processes. The emphasis is on transformation.

The competitive environment will continue to change dramatically. Companies must emphasize quality, customer satisfaction, speed, and cost avoidance to survive. To forge ahead and manage change, companies have no choice but to transform their businesses. Business process reengineering and total quality management provide methods to meet the challenges.

Functional Methods

The creation of systems architectures and deriving and implementing IT plans for application development, end-user workstations, networking, and IS management follow the development of an IT strategy or an IT plan. These methods ensure that detailed technical considerations are integrated into a comprehensive, cohesive design that will deliver the aligned IT strategy. The objective of these methods is to address the question of how to do it.

For example, rapid prototyping techniques improve business processes by capturing the business vision and quickly demonstrating the value of the application to the organization. Many of these prototypes evolve to executable business applications. The basic premise is to exploit the current IT infrastructure by unlocking the electronic data that exist today on disparate systems and data bases and presenting the data as information and knowledge required to make critical business decisions.

A second example is the assessment of IT processes such as the management of problems, changes, capacity, performance, availability, operations, and help desk. Recommendations and plans are documented to the IT organization, structure, processes, politics, standards, and technology to realize improvements in the effectiveness, efficiency, and adaptability of resources. Naturally, harmony between the previously described management methods and these functional methods is essential.

Index